SOCIAL CONTROL

SOCIAL CONTROL

Social Organization and
Disorganization in Process

PAUL H. LANDIS

The State College of Washington

Lippincott Sociology Texts—Floyd N. House, *Editor*

J. B. LIPPINCOTT COMPANY

CHICAGO   PHILADELPHIA   NEW YORK

PRINTED IN THE UNITED STATES OF AMERICA

To
BESSIE

PREFACE

Three major concepts have dawned during this century to change the foundations of social and psychological thought. One is the new concept of human nature for which the works of Ivan Pavlov, a neurologist, John Watson, a psychologist, and L. L. Bernard, a sociologist, are to be credited insofar as credit for any new idea can be given to individual workers. Pavlov's discovery of the conditioned response principle provided the foundation for a new and different approach to the study of human nature. Watson's experiments in child psychology gave a hint of the implications of this principle for the building of human nature. Bernard's assault on instinct, making use of the above principles, cleared the vista of many useless obstructions, and pointed the way to a more realistic interpretation of human nature as a social product.

Second among the revolutionary concepts is the idea of social interaction, the notion that reciprocal stimulation and relationships between individual and group, and between groups, permeate all of human life, that the individual is a part and product of the interactive social forces. For these ideas in America we are perhaps most indebted to John Dewey, philosopher, and C. H. Cooley, sociologist. The sociologists' debt to Cooley is the greater for he showed most fully the significance of interaction processes to individual personality and group welfare, conceiving of the group and the individual as part of one organic whole. W. I. Thomas and Florian Znaniecki showed the far-reaching importance of primary and secondary groups in the interaction process in their monumental treatise, *The Polish Peasant in Europe and America*. To the Chicago school of sociologists, fathered chiefly by E. L. Faris, Robert E. Park, and E. W. Burgess, usually is given the credit for the development and application of the interaction concept to the city.

To the cultural anthropologists belong the credit for the third dynamic concept—the so-called "culture concept." Their theory is that man is a product of his civilization, that the interaction processes are carried on within the bounds of this civilization, and that human nature is formed in the culture mold. Cultural anthropology as such dates from Edward B. Tylor, but certainly Sumner's *Folkways* paved the way for the reception of this approach by the sociologist.

This book attempts to bring to bear on the problem of social control these three dynamic concepts of contemporary social thought. As yet we are far from fully understanding the implications of these combined concepts to society and to personality. This writing has helped the author to clarify in his own mind certain problems and their implications. It is to be hoped that others may share this experience.

The term "social control" employed as a title has disadvantages, because it has been given diverse meanings. To many it immediately suggests force or coercion, which are often thought to be the principal means of control. But if one conceives of social control as a social process by which the individual is made group responsive, and by which social organization is built and maintained, it has broader significance. Thus conceived, it not only provides a basis for understanding the process of social organization, but for understanding the process of social disorganization as reflected in pathological conditions that result in the individual and in society when social control proves ineffective. The term "social control" as used here covers the series of social processes having to do with the building and maintenance of social order.

In a work of this character one draws ideas from many sources, and in the end wishes that time and circumstances made it possible to draw from even a greater number. In this sense the book is a synthesis of others' ideas, or perhaps of what the author thinks others' ideas are after he has sorted them over, reworked them, and made them a part of his own thought processes. These persons, when the source of the idea can be traced, are recognized in footnotes and bibliographies. Others contribute by direct suggestion and criticism. Professor John M. Foskett of the University of Idaho read and discussed with me all parts of the manuscript, shared at most points the views developed, and contributed valuable suggestions growing out of his background in the history of social thought. Others reading the manuscript in full and making helpful criticisms and suggestions were Dr.

Floyd N. House, General Editor of the Lippincott series, my colleagues, Dr. Carl F. Reuss and Richard Wakefield, and Rev. Charles P. Milne. A number of students of social control, and those giving courses in this field have read a detailed table of contents and passed on their criticisms. Among them are Professors Elon H. Moore, University of Oregon; Elton Guthrie, University of Washington; John P. Johansen, North Dakota Agricultural College; Joel V. Berreman, Stanford University; and Fred R. Yoder, The State College of Washington. But even when friends and colleagues have done their best to save one from rashness and error, a man must shoulder the responsibility for his own shortcomings.

PAUL H. LANDIS

CONTENTS

PART I. THE PROBLEM OF SOCIAL CONTROL

Chapter   Page

1. SOCIAL CONTROL DEFINED   7
   Points of View
   The Point of View of This Work: A Preliminary Statement
   The Field Delimited
   Social Control as a Deliberate Process of Regulation by Conscious Agents
       Giddings on sovereignty
       Ross on the foundations of social order
       Ross on super-social control
       Kimball Young on enforcing rules of the game
       Lumley on effective will transference
       Park and Burgess on interference with the social process
       Dowd on paternal control and social control
       Russell Gordon Smith on restricting control to conscious regulation
   Social Control as a Process of Regulation by Impersonal Forces
       Control through tradition
       Control as social definition of the individual's wishes
       Howard on domination of the individual by the group
       Bernard on keeping people orderly
       Hiller on regulation of the few in the interest of the many
   Conclusion

2. THE NATURE OF THE PROBLEM OF SOCIAL REGULATION. .   24
   The Dual Problem of Order and Authority
   The Dawn of Modern Views of the Problem of Maintaining Order
       The Greeks
       Hobbes

CONTENTS

Locke
Rousseau
Durkheim
Contemporary Views of the Problem of Control
Man Is Human Because of Control
Conclusion

3. THE ORIGINAL NATURE OF MAN AND THE REGULATIVE
   PROCESS   36
   Are the Roots of Orderliness in Original Nature?
   Incorrigible "Human Nature" Calls for Control
     Atavistic man
     Carnal man
     Freud's concept of the "libido"
     Anti-social instincts
     Some will be rebels
     Human nature contains a vicious streak
   Man's Native Equipment
   The Learning Process
   A Summary View of Original Nature
   Levels Upon Which Man May Be Controlled
   Conclusion

PART II. THE PERSONALITY FORMING PROCESSES AS THE BASIS OF SOCIAL ORGANIZATION

4. THE BUILDING OF HUMAN NATURE FOR THE SOCIAL ORDER .   53
   Views of Human Nature
   Social Consciousness
   Identification of Ourselves with the Group
   Socialized Man Always Aware of the Group
   Conscience the Voice of the Group Rather than an Inner
     Voice
   Social Expectancy
   The Habit of Conformity
   Conclusion

5. THE ROLE OF THE GROUP IN SOCIALIZATION   65
   The Priority of Group Patterns
   The Group Defines Life Situations
   Mental Concepts Are Limited by Social Definition

Chapter   Page

The Group Limits Individual Experience
The Child Absorbs the Life Patterns of His Group
The Deterministic Nature of Group Patterns
Groups Differ in Their Definitions
The Diversity of Definitions Within the Same Society
Man Develops as Many Social Selves as He Has Groups
Effect of the Biological Composition of the Group on
    the Process of Control
Conclusion

6. CULTURE AS A FACTOR IN SOCIALIZATION   79

Culture as a Phase of Group Experience
Continuity of Culture
Culture as a Mold for Personality
Culture as a Technique of Adjustment
Folkways
Mores
   The mores defined
   The mores are "right"
   The unconscious assimilation of the mores
The Authority of Custom
An Example of Control by Custom
Conclusion

7. THE GOAL OF LIFE AS A FACTOR IN CONTROL   95

Concepts of Drive
Goal not an Organic Drive
The Social Aspect of Values and Goals
Goals of Age Groups in Relation to Social Control
   Goals of childhood and youth
   Goals of middle age
   Goals of old age
Goals of the Different Sexes
Race and the Goal of Life
Goals of Social Classes and Problems of Social Control
Caste, a Device for Limiting Access to Values
Goals of Life Within the Vocation
The Goals of Life Among Professional Criminals
The Importance of a Unifying Goal
Religion as a Goal

Chapter   Page
          Family as a Goal
          Utilitarian and Materialistic Goals
          Youth Without Goals Open to Propaganda
          Models as a Source of Goals
          Conflicting Models and Personality Problems
          Personality Conflict Resulting from Divergent Goals
          Changing Social Values
          Conclusion

 8. GOALS OF AN AGE AS FACTORS IN SOCIAL GUIDANCE . . 116
          The Concept of Cultural Goals
          Roads to Status Marked by Culture Patterns
          Patterns of Culture Define the Goals of Life
          Integration of Cultural Goals and Personal Integration
          Mental Epidemics as Factors in Control
          Major Values of Our Time
               The competition-success pattern in our culture
               Competition and the open class system
               Progress, reform, improvement, and change
               Individualism, sacredness of personality
               Epicureanism
          Conclusion

 9. SOCIAL CONTROL AND THE PROBLEM OF INDIVIDUAL FREEDOM   134
          The Problem Stated
          Unity of the Individual with the Social Group
          Individual Differences and Conformity
          Individuation Hindered by Social Control
          The Relation of Self-Control to Social Control
          The Importance of Discipline to Personal Freedom
          Practical Implications of Contemporary Views of Indi-
               vidual vs. Social Responsibility
          Conclusion

PART III. SOCIAL CONTROL AND SOCIAL PROBLEMS
IN THE PRIMARY AND SECONDARY GROUP WORLDS

10. SOCIAL CONTROL AND SOCIAL PROBLEMS IN THE PRIMARY
          GROUP 151
          Control in a Closely Knit Communistic Colony
          The Nature of the Primary Group

Chapter   Page

The Kinship Group as an Example of Primary Group
    Control
Permanence of the Primary Group Permits Accommo-
    dation
Sentiment as a Factor in Primary Group Control
Reputation as an Aspect of Primary Group Control
Effectiveness of Control in the Primary Group
Gossip in the Primary Group
Opinion as a Whip in the Intimate Group
Homogeneity of Primary Group Patterns: Assets and
    Liabilities for Control
The Primary Group in a Dynamic Society
Personality Stress in the Shift from Primary Group Con-
    trols
Conclusion

11. SOCIAL CONTROL AND SOCIAL PROBLEMS IN THE SECONDARY
    GROUP   168
The Passing of the Neighborhood as a Unit of Control
Secondary Group Defined
The Transition to Secondary Group Social Organization
Impersonal Nature of the Secondary Group
Difficulties of Control in the Urban World
Bernard on Problems of Control in the Secondary (De-
    rivative) Group
Establishing Controls in the Secondary Group
Primary and Secondary Group Values: A Contrast
Personality Problems Growing out of Secondary Group
    Experience
Conclusion

12. THE LIABILITIES AND ASSETS OF AGENCIES OF MASS IMPRES-
    SION TO SOCIAL CONTROL IN A WORLD OF SECONDARY
    GROUPS   185
P. T. Barnum, Incorporated
The Dilemma in Mass Control
Conflicting Mass Stimuli
Our Inability to Evaluate Conflicting Mass Stimuli
Publicity as a Negative Instrument of Secondary Group
    Control

Chapter   Page
       Control by the press through suggestion
       Publicity as a Positive Instrument of Control in the Sec-
             ondary Group
       Propaganda an Instrument of Control in the Modern
             World
       Censorship as an Instrument of Selective Mass Impression
       Relative Effectiveness of Agencies of Mass Impression
       Conclusion

PART IV.   INSTITUTIONS AS AGENCIES OF SOCIAL
                           CONTROL

13. PROBLEMS OF THE AMERICAN FAMILY AS AN AGENCY OF
       SOCIAL CONTROL   209
       The Development of a Personality under the Controls of
             a Closely Knit Family Pattern: A Case Study
       The Important Place of the Family as an Agency of
             Control
       The Authority Pattern in Family Life
       Control by Latent Patterns in the Family
       Failure of the American Family as an Agency of Control
       Conflict of Family Patterns in a Culturally Marginal
             Generation
       The Breakdown of Control in the Immigrant Group with
             the Decay of the Large Family
       Conclusion

14. PROBLEMS OF THE CHRISTIAN CHURCH AS AN INFLUENCE IN
       SOCIAL CONTROL   236
       Supernaturalism as a Factor in Control: A Case Study
       The Christian Church as an Influence in Social Control
             in American Society
       Diversity of Control Patterns and the American Culture
             Setting
       Controls Employed by the Eternity-Centered Christian
             Church
             The appeal to authority
             The operation of other-worldliness as a control device
             The appeal to personal adjustment
             The appeal to duty

Chapter   Page

> Control by prophecy
> Everlasting life
> Conversion
> Evangelism
> The Christian model
> The Shift of Emphasis in Social Control in the Morality-
>   Centered Church
> Difficulties of Moral Definition Facing the Morality-
>   Centered Church
> The Social Appeal and Church Influence
> Religious Disillusionment as an Aspect of Diverse Insti-
>   tutional Forms in an Open Class Society
> Christian Influences as Cultural Compulsives
> Conclusion

15. FORMAL EDUCATION AS A SOCIALIZING AGENCY   256

> Educational Aims as Goals of Social Control
> Biological Plasticity Extends Human Modifiability
> Control of Biological Factors by Education
>   Control of the romantic impulse through education
> The School as an Agency for Socialization in Contem-
>   porary Society
> Education and the State
> Education for Political Indoctrination
>   Fascist education
>   Education in Germany
>   Political education in Russia
> Formal Education as Selective Participation in Social
>   Experience
> Universal Education as an American Social Value
> Conclusion

16. ECONOMIC FORCES PROMOTING SOCIAL ORDER AND DISORDER   273

> The Discipline and Destiny of the Job
> The Significance of Work to Social Control
> Unemployment and Personal Frustration
> Pecuniary Valuations as Forces in Control
>   Veblen
>   Ross
>   Cooley

Chapter   Page

The Power of Pecuniary Valuation in a Non-Pecuniary
    Realm
Possibilities of Constructive Social Control Through the
    Pecuniary System
Control as Practiced by Business
The Folklore of Capitalism
Conclusion

17. GOVERNMENT AND LAW AS REGULATIVE AGENCIES . . . 288
Authoritative Aspects of Government and Law
Ideals and Authority
Increasing Importance of Government and Law in the
    Field of Social Control
Weakness of Law as a Control Device in Contemporary
    Society
The Authority of Stateways Compared to that of Folkways
Control by the Extra-Legal Invisible Government
The Political Party and the Invisible Government
Control Techniques of the Political Party
    Myth making
    Enemies of straw
    The appeal to achievement
    The appeal to tradition
    Manner of address
    The appeal to universality
    The patronage pattern
Conclusion

18. SCIENCE AND TECHNOLOGY AS AGENCIES OF SOCIAL CONTROL   309
Tested Knowledge and Behavior
Technology as a Factor in Contact, Diffusion, and
    Change
The Effect of Mechanical Invention on Non-Mechanical
    Spheres of Activity
Effects of Inventions on Institutional Controls
Technicways in Contemporary Society
Cultural Lag and Problems of Control
Technology and the Life Philosophy of Progress
The Place of Social Science in an Age of Technology
Conclusion

PART V. MEANS OF SOCIAL CONTROL

Chapter   Page

19. MEANS OF SOCIAL CONTROL 331
    General Classification of Means of Social Control
    Physical Force and Human Symbol Methods
    Formal and Informal Controls
    Conscious and Unconscious Control
    Rewards and Punishments
    Education and Socialization and Sanctions
    Paternal Control and Social Control
    Devices Establishing Order and Those Maintaining It
    Special Control Devices Employed in Building Social
        Order
        Ceremony, the original form of regulation
        Ritual as a means of habituating the individual to group
            practices and attitudes
        Codes as a means of standardizing group practices
        Tradition as a blueprint
        Control through building superstitious fears
        The dictates of fashion
    Special Control Devices Employed in Maintaining Social
        Order
        A comparison of non-resistance and force as means of
            social control
        The penalties for violating taboos
        Superstition as a means of maintaining group patterns
        Laughter as a means of maintaining group standards
        Ridicule as a device for abolishing war, crime, and mis-
            doings
        Public opinion as a pervading force
        Law
    Conclusion

20. SOCIAL CONTROL AND BEHAVIOR PROBLEMS AMONG CON-
    TEMPORARY YOUTH 362
    The Controls in the Child's World
    The Transition from Childhood Controls to Adolescence
    Adolescence as a Sociological Fact
    The Transfer of Youth to the World of Adult Controls
    Controls among Contemporary College Youth: A Col-
        lection of Case Studies

Chapter   Page

The Dominance of Family Patterns
    "It's not religion but family responsibility that keeps
        me right"
    "Mother rules me"
    The planned life
    Family standards
    Projection
    "A sense of obligation to my family"
The Realization of Group Expectancy
    "I respect others' opinions of me"
    " 'Be conventional' is my motto"
    "It's expected of me"
    Public Opinion

21. SOCIAL CONTROL AND BEHAVIOR PROBLEMS AMONG CON-
    TEMPORARY YOUTH (Continued) 377

Institutionalized Patterns
    "The day of judgment and regard for my present
        status"
    "I have been taught what is 'proper' "
    "My habits have been formed by social institutions"
    Law and custom
    "What keeps me from doing what I wish"
Emotional-Temperamental Qualities
    "True to form usually but at times I am a rebel"
    "I fear the consequences of behavior"
    "The meek inherit the earth"
    "I am the retiring type"
    "I protect my emotional complexes"
Models
    The influence of example
    Example and precept
The Code of Youth
    "Once my family, but now my friends and my purse
        control me"
    "My ideas of conduct"
Conclusion

PART VI. THE BREAKDOWN OF SOCIAL CONTROL AS A FACTOR IN SOCIAL PROBLEMS

Chapter *Page*

22. THE RELATION OF SOCIAL CONTROL TO PERSONALITY DIS-
ORGANIZATION 403

    Personality Development under Dual Systems of Control:
       A Case Study
    Personal Disorganization and the System of Social
       Control
    Social Control and Special Personality Problems
       Suicide and the breakdown of social control
       Personal degeneration and the breakdown of tradition
       Personality disintegration and the cultural structure
       The hobo, a man with freedom but without purpose
    Personality in an Uncertain World
    Change and Personal Demoralization
    Mobility and Personal Disorganization
    Mental Disease and the System of Social Control
    The Marginal Man and Social Control
    Personality Disorganization Growing out of the Inability
       to Adjust Organic Drives to Social Restrictions
    Limited Group Participation in a Complex Social System
    Conclusion

23. THE BREAKDOWN OF CONTROL AS A FACTOR IN SOCIAL PA-
THOLOGY. 426

    Delinquency and Crime in Relation to Social Control
    Suicide and Social Control
    Poverty and Social Control
    Problems of Reacculturation
    The Breakdown of Control and Social Decay among
       Primitive Peoples
    Examples of the Temporary Breakdown of Social Control
       Breakdown of control in a crisis
       Breakdown of control on the frontier
    Culture Lag as a Defect in Social Control
    Insecurity and Individualization as Related to Pathology
    Locating Responsibility for Social Pathology
    Conclusion

Chapter   Page
24. SOCIAL REVOLT 442
    Revolt as a Normal Social Process
    Revolt and Individualization
    Nonconformity as a Phase of Revolt
    Youth Revolts More Often than Age
    Historical Examples of Individual Revolt
    Literature of Protest
    The Process of Breaking Social Controls as a Phase of
        Mental Experience
    On the Organic-Psychological Necessity for Revolt
    Individual Differences and Revolt
    The Established Channels for Revolt in American Life
    Where Does Revolt End?
    The "Debunking Process" as an Aspect of Revolt
    Violent Revolt and the Complete Breakdown of Control
    A Glimpse at a World without Social Control
    The Aftermath of Revolution Is a New Social Order
    The Process of Re-establishing Controls after Revolution
    Conclusion

25. THE PROBLEM OF CONTROL IN OUR DYNAMIC SOCIETY: A
        CONCLUDING SUMMARY 465
    Personality Building in a Dynamic Society
    Heterogeneity vs. Homogeneity of Patterns as Related to
        Individualism and Authority
    Individualism, Its Price and Benefits
    Possibilities of a Functional Individualism in a Changing
        World
    Personal Objectives vs. Realizations in Our Time
    The Quest for Goals in a World without Authority
    Culture Consciousness and the Problem of Authority
    Change and Definitions
    Sins of Omission of Sociologists
    Social Science as a Guide to Order in a Dynamic Age
    Conclusion

SOCIAL CONTROL

INTRODUCTION

Fears of a divinity which shapes human ends through predestination have disappeared with the slow decay of the other-worldly-centered culture of the Middle Ages. The days are passing when a simple, instinctive, natural order can be accepted as the foundation of social discipline, as in the heyday of instinct psychology. An equally fatalistic concept of determinism by the domination of geographical and biological forces is being discarded, as the early enthusiasm for natural science as a cure-all is tempered by more mature judgment. We are beginning to have a live realization of the power of social and cultural forces to shape conduct. At least in part we now appreciate the deterministic influence of social and cultural environments in shaping personality, and so it is in these realms primarily that we need to seek the foundations of orderly behavior.

This book is an attempt to answer five questions concerning the process of social control: (1) Who or what is to be controlled? (2) By whom? (3) For what purpose? (4) By what means? (5) With what results in contemporary society?

The answers cannot be as briefly stated as the questions, if indeed they can be found, but the essence of such answers as are given can be condensed sufficiently to give the reader a perspective of the point of view. The first three questions are answered in Part I in substance as follows: The *individual* is to be controlled by *society*, chiefly for *society*, although it is assumed that regulation also works for the welfare of the individual. Most attention is given to the fourth question: By what means is control realized? The answer is found in the educative process broadly conceived, through which personality is formed in the social environment, and made to fit the system of social organization in vogue. This process is largely natural in the sense that it is for the most part fairly spontaneous and informal, even unplanned, and to a considerable extent unconscious. This personality forming process is the theme of Part II.

Part III shows the comparative effectiveness of the personality

3

building process in the *milieu* of interaction of two contrasting types of groups in contemporary society, the primary and secondary groups, and traces many problems of our society to the shift in emphasis of contemporary life from the primary to the secondary group.

The more formal and conscious institutional structures in society which assume the responsibility for control in relation to specialized social aims are considered as agencies of control in Part IV. While these institutions often are no more rational than the less formal environment covered in Part II, they are more conscious and more purposeful in their functions. Society realizes certain specific ends in control through these institutions, and at the same time the institutions embody much of the less formal experience of the race, and so function in the informal sphere as well. If institutions fail as agencies of control, pathological conditions arise, and greater burdens for control are imposed upon other institutions if social maladjustments are to be ameliorated.

Special means and devices of control are often isolated by the student from the general scheme of integrated patterns that characterize a society, and discussed separately. While there is some danger of presenting a false picture by such procedure, it has precedent, and also has an advantage. One has a chance to scrutinize these isolated devices and learn something as to their effectiveness as tools of social control, and to study the individual's response to them. Part V deals with this topic.

The final section, as well as certain parts throughout the entire work, shows that our society does not control with complete success, and describes the effects of the failure of the system of control on society and the individual. Some questions are raised as to the successes and failures of social control in our dynamic order, and we grope for some satisfactory answer for the failures reflected in our major social problems. Here we think out loud about the underlying causes of our social problems, rather than state satisfactory solutions. Our generation will not find all the solutions to the numerous problems that have arisen due to the failure of social control, but it is time we began to seek them more seriously.

PART I

THE PROBLEM OF SOCIAL CONTROL

CHAPTER 1

SOCIAL CONTROL DEFINED

POINTS OF VIEW

Social control, conceived very broadly, encompasses almost the entire field of sociological thought. All applied sociology is aimed directly at the problem of controlling some particular phase of society, the correction of some evil, or the redirection of social energy toward some more ideal goal. Conceived in a narrower sense, social control can be applied only to those voluntary purposeful activities of man, which when directed immediately would regulate some particular phase of human behavior.

The first concept is too broad to be meaningful; the second is too narrow to be useful. Between these two extremes there is much territory to be explored. The particular territory will depend to a considerable extent upon any writer's definition of the term "social control."

THE POINT OF VIEW OF THIS WORK: A PRELIMINARY STATEMENT

Social control is conceived in this book as being concerned primarily with an understanding of (1) how society makes its members susceptive to its regulative system, and (2) how it makes them conform to it. The basic problem is one not only of how social order is maintained, but of how society itself is maintained and perpetuated. The explanation as here conceived lies chiefly in the field of social psychology. The emphasis is on the way in which the individual is made to fit into the soc scheme rather than on the way in which the group, through development of public opinion, establishes the abstract of control. It will be obvious to students of society th two approaches are in many respects very similar. It of placing the emphasis. The emphasis is here plac social influences operate on the individual to control him rather than upon an analysis of society's regulative scheme as such.

The Field Delimited

The study excludes for the most part what may be better termed group control; that is, that extensive realm in relationships which is concerned with the way in which one large group regulates another large group in the social sphere. Therefore, we deal very little with the whole system of class control, class struggle, racial accommodations, and so forth. This field is, in itself, so large that any adequate treatment of it would require a volume as large or larger than this one. Also, even though the author is interested in understanding the effect of social control upon the individual, little attention is given to suggestion, "group mind," so-called, or crowd phenomena generally. Much literature already has been developed in the field of social psychology dealing particularly with suggestion and its effect on crowd phenomena. While the principle of suggestion is involved in most social control, it finds only an incidental place in this book.

Social control as used here does not embrace control of man and society over nature, or geographical forces. Therefore, it does not even cover all activities in which man is the active agent. Man's regulation of nature is most certainly control, but we prefer not to include it in a study of social control.

What is ordinarily termed self-control is not discussed at great length as such. By self-control we ordinarily mean control arising from within because of habit, conscience, or idea-emotional restraints of various sorts, as contrasted with pressures arising from the social group external to the individual. Actually, much of what we consider self-control has its origin in the group, so that there is much overlapping of so-called self-control and social control.

Social Control as a Deliberate Process of Regulation by Conscious Agents

A great number of authors who have dealt with the subject of social control have limited their definition to those influences by which society consciously attempts to regulate the activities of its members. Such are the definitions which follow.

Giddings on sovereignty. Professor Giddings' concept [1] of social control is one of sovereignty through which obedience is obtained. Obedience is required for the attainment of desirable social relationships and is usually realized through some form of governmental organization. The legal regulation of the individual is supplemented by the development of social pressures of two sorts: (1) consciously exerted disciplinary measures and restraints, which he labels primary pressure, and (2) the group influence acting upon members to hinder variation from type, which he labels secondary pressure. These pressures constitute what he calls "social self-control."

Society then is a collective unit acting under self-direction, imposing restraints upon itself and controlling its own processes. In early society this control is largely unconscious, through customs and taboos, but later it becomes conscious, bringing to bear legal pressures through the state. He concludes:

. . . Control is the work of controllers. In any organization there is a division of labor. Differing individuals perform different tasks. There is also, necessarily, a direction of activities and a more or less successful correlation of specialized efforts. This implies co-ordination. Some individuals must functionally stand in a higher rank than others. Some individuals must functionally stand in subordination to others. Social control, in like manner, is a phenomenon of interacting superiorities and inferiorities. Some men influence and command; other men are influenced, and they obey.[2]

Ross on the foundations of social order. Edward A. Ross, the author of the first book entitled "Social Control," wrote the entire work without giving a clear-cut definition of the term. He says he is dealing with that field of social psychology which has to do with social ascendancy. The subtitle of the book perhaps explains more fully what he had in mind—"A Study of the Foundations of the Social Order." The book, having been written in 1902 when instinct theories were still used as a tool in interpreting human nature, is couched in different terms than he would use today. The interpretation is in harmony with the

---

[1] Franklin H. Giddings, *Studies in the Theory of Human Society*, pp. 200 ff.
[2] Franklin H. Giddings, "Social Control in a Democracy," *Proceedings of the Twelfth Annual Meeting of the American Sociological Society*, 1918, vol. 12, p. 202. By permission of the American Sociological Society.

general conception of that time, that of explaining human activities in terms of both inborn patterns and patterns acquired from the environment. Consequently he conceives of a natural order which is induced by inborn mechanisms—sympathy, sociability, sense of justice, and resentment—and then elaborates on the artificially developed order which grows out of the pressure of social control.

In his discussion Ross assumes that social control has to do with social ascendancy. Social ascendancy is of two types—the unconscious, unintended domination of society over the individual, and the purposeful domination of society over the individual. He confines social control to this purposeful domination of society over the individual.[3]

Ross on super-social control. Writing later, Ross coined the term "super-social control."[4] With this term he covers activities of scheming groups which come to dominate society itself. He cites as an example the "deliberate molding of German education, ideals, and public opinion" during a period of years preceding the World War by a group headed by the Kaiser—a group which had determined to use the German people to fulfill their designs for conquest and aggression.

Kimball Young on enforcing rules of the game. Kimball Young likens society to a game in which individuals are members of various teams. Each team has to do with the various functions of living which come to be represented by the larger institutions. In order to play the game effectively, man must have rules. For the social game, consequently, in primitive as well as in modern societies, men have developed these rules which may be used to govern the course of effective group participation. So there develop laws protecting property, regulating health conditions, governing the relations between the sexes, and providing group codes. He writes this definition for social control:

. . . We shall define *social control* as the use of coercion, force, restraint, suggestion, or persuasion of one group over another, or of a group over its members or of persons over others to enforce the prescribed rules of the game. These rules may be set down by the members themselves, as in a professional code of ethics, or they

[3] E. A. Ross, *Social Control*, preface.
[4] E. A. Ross, *Principles of Sociology*, first revision, chap. 40.

may be those laid down by a larger, more inclusive group for the regulation of another smaller group . . .[5]

Lumley on effective will transference. Lumley, in outlining the field of social control, makes the assumption that "regulations arise out of the attempt to maintain order" so as to avoid "general social chaos." After indicating that no satisfactory definition of social control ever has been formulated, he supposes that in order to have social control there must be a program of action, and an adequate system of communication, and "free and impressable individuals or groups" who are ready to respond.

Social control has usually meant that kind of life-pattern which a government, through its officers, imposes upon the citizen. But we have seen that social control means vastly more than that. We might speak of it as the practice of putting forth directive stimuli or wish-patterns, their accurate transmission to, and adoption by, others whether voluntarily or involuntarily. In short, it is effective will transference. . . .[6]

He states that "Ideally, social control would be in the hands and the interests of the inclusive group whatever it is; practically, however, it is in the hands of, and often in the interests of, some few members who have usurped power and know how to use it." [7]

Park and Burgess on interference with the social process.

. . . What we ordinarily mean by social control is the arbitrary intervention of some individual—official, functionary, or leader—in the social process. A policeman arrests a criminal, an attorney sways the jury with his eloquence, the judge passes sentence; these are the familiar formal acts in which social control manifests itself. What makes the control exercised in this way social, in the strict sense of that term, is the fact that these acts are supported by custom, law, and public opinion.[8]

---

[5] Kimball Young, *An Introductory Sociology*, p. 520. By permission of the American Book Company.
[6] Frederick E. Lumley, *Means of Social Control*, p. 13. Used by permission of D. Appleton-Century Company, Publishers, New York, N. Y.
[7] *Ibid.*, pp. 13–14.
[8] R. E. Park and E. W. Burgess, *Introduction to the Science of Sociology*, p. 789. By permission of the University of Chicago Press.

Dowd on paternal control and social control. Dowd also uses control in the telic sense, meaning by it "guidance," or "direction," as "to control an engine by a lever." [9] The terms paternal and social control as he defines them imply an active agent consciously aiming at preconceived ends. However, he allows for instruments of control which are not necessarily conscious, such as folkways, but then concludes: "The sole source, or controlling agency, in any society consists of one or more individuals who, on account of some kind of prestige, are able to bring people together for some common purpose, and to induce or compel them to conform to the group interest." [10]

He uses the term "paternal control" for systems under which the sole source of authority for each organization is some one person or small group. Social control refers to that condition in society which results when organization has become social, and control has diffused among great numbers; in other words, he uses social control to refer to democratic control.[11]

Russell Gordon Smith on restricting control to conscious regulation. Perhaps the most elaborate critical discussion of the general theory of social control and its significance is that by Russell Gordon Smith, which appears in the introduction to his vivacious and stimulating work, *Fugitive Papers.*

He concludes that the term social control, if it is to mean anything scientific and precise, must be confined to that realm of relationships which has to do with the rational, purposeful control of social phenomena.

We thus understand by social control the attainment of ends through collectively conscious adaptation of means to those ends. We mean something of what Ward means by "telesis," though we prefer not to bury our meaning in polysyllabic Greek derivates. The use we here make of the term "social control" may be distinguished from other usage by the adjective "rational."

It is needless to say that the number of organizations in modern society which exercise rational social control is almost unlimited. That their variety is just as great will also be apparent upon a moment's reflection. We may have every nuance of form and func-

---

[9] Jerome Dowd, *Control in Human Societies,* p. 6.
[10] *Ibid.,* p. 11. Used by permission of D. Appleton-Century Company, publishers, New York, N. Y.
[11] *Ibid.,* chap. 2.

tion, from the gang of East-Side thugs who by certain second-story tricks make a big haul from a savings bank, to the up-to-date church that ameliorates the conditions in a poverty-stricken and crime-stained community. Government commissions, labor unions, philanthropic societies, censorship committees, the church, the press, and the state itself might all come under the category of organizations exercising rational social control. It is evident, then, that our effort to limit the application of the term "social control" amounts quantitatively to little more than a bisection of infinity. But in restricting the term to the conscious adaptation of means to end we have perhaps made a qualitative limitation that will be of service to clear thinking. Perhaps, too, our attempt to be precise, in a field where precision is so rare, is a precedent not entirely useless.[12]

The common assumption of all these definitions is that social control deals with the regulation by society of its members. This seems valid. But all of these writers make a second assumption which is questionable, that social control should deal with the conscious, purposeful regulation by society of its members, primarily. They assume that a conscious, purposeful agent of control must maintain order. In spite of Smith's good logic, and that of several of the other authors quoted, it seems that such a concept of social control eliminates a large field of social influences by which the group regulates the behavior of its members.

The whole body of thought that has been developed in recent years by anthropologists and social psychologists is an interpretation of human nature and personality in terms of patterns existing in the group, many of which operate without the individual's being conscious of them and without any conscious active agent at the helm. The most deep-seated and important influences in the development of the socialized personality, and in the regulation of human institutions, come from the nonrational, unconscious, all-pervasive influences that mold the individual without his knowledge. They are a part of the general culture and become incorporated there without any conscious attempt on the part of any particular group, or even of a society, to develop or foster them.

The great weakness of our urban-industrial culture grows out of

[12] Reprinted from Smith: *Fugitive Papers*, by permission of Columbia University Press.

the fact that we have attempted to depend largely on rational, formal control devices chiefly in the realm of law, delegated to law enforcement agents. This form of control proves to be generally superficial and ineffective as compared to these more pervasive influences which have characterized primary groups throughout history.

It is true that in given situations conscious control is highly important, and that in special instances designated individuals and authorities may be very conspicuous in the field of control. Every human being, broadly speaking, has something to do with the regulation of others. Actually, however, in any society there are certain groups, individuals, and authorities who exercise most of the power of regulation. Ross has suggested that the source of social power varies with social changes, or with differing societies.[13] In primitive society it may be the elders; in a society in upheaval it will be the soldier; in societies particularly concerned with a future life, the priesthood. In paternal states, the state may become the source of social power. In most societies, the wealthy, the learned, and the elite are focal points from which social control emanates. He says further that the tenor of the social order will reflect the source from which social power emanates.

But in a more comprehensive sense there is no "who's who" in the realm of control except in specific situations. The very question, "Who exercises social control?", is somewhat misleading, for it is likely to betray a misunderstanding of the nature of social processes. In the final analysis one can never point out *the* one who controls or *the group* which controls. There is no such person or group, even in a dictatorship.

Much more important than the question of who exercises social control is the question of what forces exercise social control. Social control, as conceived in this work, must include not only the work of the individuals or groups who deliberately act to regulate the behavior of others, but also those impersonal and abstract social and cultural influences which permeate the personality of each individual, and act as impelling, although often unconscious forces, in the forming of his behavior. These influences may best be described as the general cultural *milieu* of the time, or the ethos

---

[13] E. A. Ross, *Social Control*, pp. 78–85. Also see his *Principles of Sociology*, first revision, pp. 402–403.

of the cultural age, which determines the general pattern of living at a given time. It includes also those subtler influences of group ethics and culture standards which emanate from the smaller groups, classes, and clans which make up any particular society; those family traits constituting the family heritage, which will persist in the development of the child's personality without any conscious part being played by those who influence. These things in the life of any individual, or in the experience of any society are far more important than the influence of any individual or group of individuals who may be in a position of authority, prestige, or leadership.

Of course, individuals, groups, and particular authorities, or leaders have their functions to perform. They set the subtle social and cultural forces in motion; they are the source of human energy and group activities, and thus, in the final analysis, any single pattern which pervades the social order, originates in the interacting social group. But, beneath all external manifestations of personal authority, is there not a body of custom and tradition that gives the leaders their authority? Is there not this deeper stratum of influence at work? Let us begin the answer with an illustration.

SOCIAL CONTROL AS A PROCESS OF REGULATION BY IMPERSONAL FORCES

Control through tradition.

In the Arunta tribe of Australia, as among many primitive peoples, ultimate authority seems to reside in the traditions as these are interpreted by the elders who deliberate on tribal affairs. They discuss the traditions, are not always in agreement as to their interpretation, and probably sometimes modify them. Since ultimate authority hovers about tradition and this select assembly, only he who plays a role in it can deflect the current of tribal affairs. In Southeast Australia more importance attaches to the totem group, which frequently acts as a unit in affairs of importance, one group resisting the encroachments of another. Here ultimate authority appears to inhere not so much in the elders as in the totem group, but the latter must follow tradition. Among the Toda no specific group of men interprets and perpetuates the traditions. Tribal authority radiates from one of the two endogamous groups, the Tartharol or the

Teivaliol, and originates in one of the component clans of these endogamous units. The formal outlines of Chilkat social structure are similar to those of the Toda, the tribe being divided into two exogamous units composed of smaller groups. In the Chilkat, however, the constituent groups within the dichotomous unit comprise a hierarchy, the headman of the highest totem group being, by virtue of his office, head of the entire exogamous division, while the head of one of the two exogamous divisions, or phratries, is *ipso facto* tribal chief. In both tribes the chief must follow tradition and custom, though, at least among the Toda, tradition has sometimes been successfully challenged by a headman.

In Dahomey and in Ashantee the central figure is the king. Subordinate chiefs preside over definite territory, and under the latter are chiefs of lesser importance. In typical feudal fashion authority centers in the king, not theoretically merely as in European vestiges, but in the reality of unquestioning obedience, even to his most extravagant demands. There seems to be no limit to the authority of Dahomey and Ashantee kings and none to the unwavering obedience of their subjects.

Though the New Zealand chief had considerable authority, and his person was *tabu*, his power was limited by a not infrequent assertion of group will. Ordinarily great chiefs wielded almost unlimited power over subjects, but in important matters their actions were regulated by advice from a council and they deferred to public opinion. In this primitive democracy honor could be won by men of humble descent if they possessed ability and courage. Tradition was potent, though some were able to set it aside temporarily. A man who was daring, courageous, and had military genius, though descended from slaves, might become a leader and a war chief. This rarely occurred, however, and toward such a leader the Maori did not entertain the respect which they paid to men of noble birth. Their attitude toward a successful upstart was comparable with that of the European aristocracy toward Napoleon. The lineage of a war chief might be of the nobility, but captivity tainted his name and made him a slave and chattel, with reduced social personality; subsequent honors mitigated but did not remove the stigma. But if limitations involving qualifications of birth beyond the individual's control were placed upon men of merit, there was also insistence upon the possession of personal qualities in addition to royal lineage. Under rare circumstances the priestly power of a first-born prince might be lost, but more probably his temporal power would be challenged and revoked. As a rule he was supposed to receive at birth a spiritual appointment from heaven, but leadership of the people in peace or in war, and especially in war, must be confirmed by the popular opinion of tribesmen. The chief must be brave, intelligent, and generous. No coward, fool, or niggardly fellow might lead the Maori warriors. If, in consequence of a glaring physical or intellectual defect, a man was incapable of being leader and commander, by the unanimous consent of the tribe he was set aside for another, usually an uncle or a brother. The selection of a successor was made in silence, as though by a sympathetic appreciation on the part of the notables that a certain man was their choice. Since discussion of the qualifications of the chief was a breach of etiquette, they made the selection by an apparently silent understanding. The chosen man became the war chief, the director of the council, and exercised the royal privilege of veto. The warriors would not accept as leader one who was a chief merely in name. When descent was interrupted by death of the proper heir, theoretically the succession reverted to the grandfather on the paternal side. If he was old and unable to act as leader a meeting was held in the council house for the purpose of choosing a successor. In silence the brothers of the proper heir stood up, one after another, and when the right man arose a low cough, the sign of approval, ran through the assembly.— Thus among the Maori ultimate authority seems to hover with uncertainty between tradition, personal merit, and popular approval or public opinion. The requirements for the chieftainship are fundamentally traditional and social; and virtues of a powerful leader are those required by the tribe, which has effective means of enforcing its will through a group of influential men. In the simpler Algonkian tribes there is little formal organization, though where chieftainship is recognized, fitness for office is a prerequisite. In Iroquois society a further distinction is made between fitness to conduct tribal affairs in time of peace and ability to lead the warriors. Among the Eskimo, authority hovers with uncertainty now about this individual, now about that one. A daring adventurer may awe the community and cow his enemies into subservience, but the halo of authority is as evanescent as a wandering will-o'-the-wisp. At any time the dominated community may turn the scales and suppress the upstart with heavy hand and severe penalty. Burchardt describes similar conditions among the Berbers. Upon the slightest provocation a man

may kill many people with his own hands and overawe the community—until he himself is killed. Such authority cannot long
maintain itself unless it has the support of tradition and the sanction of popular approval. Given these buttresses, almost anything
is possible.[14]

In this analysis Wallis has revealed the very significant fact that
back of designated rulers and appointed sovereigns who pose as
the embodiment of authority, there are impersonal forces which
actually give the ruler his authority. The immediate reply is,
"But he is describing primitive societies." Yet is the situation
any different in modern society? Actually, is there not a body of
influence which is more powerful in regulating the affairs of men
in our society than the conscious agents whom we usually associate with authority? Do we not here see working in primitive
society that which works less obviously in all societies? Underlying law, authority, priests, intelligentsia, military attachés, and
rulers, is the great body of tradition, mores, and custom, which
controls even the controllers. Certainly leaders play a part and
may have considerable influence in deciding which traditions shall
dominate, but they do not make the traditions and could not control without them.

A great many recent works have recognized that there is authority more significant than that of rulers. The monumental
studies of Thomas and Znaniecki dealing with the Polish peasant
in Europe and America reveal clearly that the attitudes of the
individual and the values about which his personality is built are
the real regulating forces in his experience. His attachments to
group life keep him oriented and orderly in his personal conduct.

The following definitions which recognize impersonal forces
in social control reflect the influence of recent developments in
social psychology and anthropology.

Control as social definition of the individual's wishes. Dawson
and Gettys feel that social control does not necessarily involve
purposeful regulation on the part of any group, but that the mere
fact that human beings live together assumes the regulation of
conduct.[15] In homogeneous groups controls are of an informal

---

[14] Wilson D. Wallis, *Culture and Progress,* pp. 187–189. By permission of
the McGraw-Hill Book Company.
[15] Carl A. Dawson and Warren E. Gettys, *An Introduction to Sociology,* revised edition, p. 613, The Ronald Press Company, New York, 1935.

nature, whereas in the larger groups of a heterogeneous society they tend to be more formal. They define social control as "the social definition of the wishes of the individual and their incorporation in the common attitudes and objectives of the group."

Howard on domination of the individual by the group.

Now, what is social control? . . . The "constraint of the one by the many"; the "dominance of the individual will by the group-will"; the "ascendancy of the social consciousness over the personal consciousness"—these and similar phrases convey a practical meaning quite well understood. They signify a control, if perfect, which has behind it the whole weight of the group or society, whether the society be a club, a trade-union, a nation, or an alliance of nations. They imply an authority which at its best rests on the free and intelligent choice of all the psychically interacting personalities which constitute the society. It refers to a power broader, deeper, more complex, than political power. It means a unity of strength whose source becomes higher and purer as humanism advances. But under present conditions social control is never perfect. . . . There are many grades in the quality of social control, some lower and some higher, according to the source of authority or to the kind of instruments employed. . . .[16]

Bernard on keeping people orderly.

Bernard says: "Anything, stimulus or environmental process, which helps keep people behaving with some degree of regularity and calculability with reference to one another may be called a social control."[17] He then distinguishes a "social control" from "social controls," saying,

Those characteristics which cause people to act in groups, which modify the behavior of individuals in groups, are social controls. These things are attitudes, but back of the attitudes lie other factors, such as the individual's biological inheritance and the various

---

[16] George E. Howard, "Ideals as a Factor in the Future Control of International Society," *Proceedings of the Twelfth Annual Meeting of the American Sociological Society*, 1918, vol. 12, p. 2. By permission of the American Sociological Society.

[17] Davis, Barnes and Others, *An Introduction to Sociology*, p. 467, selection by L. L. Bernard. By permission of D. C. Heath and Company.

phases of the environment . . . which account for the development of the attitudes in individuals.[18]

Hiller on regulation of the few in the interest of the many.

In order that the group may function successfully and maintain cooperative efficiency, it must preserve a measure of regularity and predictability of behavior, and it must direct the self-seeking activities of its members so that the rights of all will be preserved. The very existence of social standards implies conformity, but obedience is never automatic and complete. Accordingly, the group attempts to suppress those acts which are at variance with the prevailing norms and to encourage those which facilitate internal harmony and collective welfare. The chief means by which this is accomplished are the attitude- and personality-forming factors. But in addition to supplying and inculcating standards, the group, either through its officials or through the common support of the mores, actively encourages some forms of conduct and discourages or suppresses others.

This regulation of the few in the interest of the many constitutes social control. . . .[19]

CONCLUSION

There seems to be general agreement that the member of a society is the subject of control. The disagreement seems to be in deciding whether or not the term social control is to be used to refer to those regulative processes which are informal and unconscious, such as custom, tradition, ceremony, mores, and so forth, or whether one should consider social control as embodying only those voluntary, formalized, fairly well-institutionalized overt devices which are often prominent in societies, or whether one should include both types of influences in his analysis.

In this work both types of control are accepted. According to the point of view here developed, in society as it has existed in the past and as it exists at the present time, these latent, unconscious, or semiconscious elements in the environment are the prime elements in social control. Rational, planned control aimed at obtaining designated ends by a conscious means has been at a premium in human society. It has been so scarce that no society

---

[18] *Ibid.* By permission of D. C. Heath and Company.
[19] E. T. Hiller, *Principles of Sociology*, p. 601. Reprinted by permission of Harper and Brothers.

could have depended upon it. To control by voluntary and purposeful methods assumes knowledge and understanding of man's social life. Such knowledge has not been available in the past and only a rudimentary knowledge has been acquired in our own day of social science investigation. Man cannot be expected to control by rational methods that which he does not fully understand.

While it is true that in modern society external and observable controls of various sorts consciously developed and put into exercise by the group protrude themselves at every turn of the road, it is equally true that beneath all of this superstructure there is a much more important, and much more pervasive system of regulation, which operates in the emotional-psychological realm. It is these latent factors that for the most part form personality. In the forming of personality the group lays the foundation for social order.

These latent factors have without doubt been the more important in all societies, past and present. In simple societies, there is a relative absence of the more formal controls which exist in the modern world. But even in the modern world "men act from motives they do not comprehend to fulfill aims they are but dimly conscious of." [20] So this analysis takes into account not only the conscious deliberate attempts of society to regulate its members, but also those subtle, unconscious, latent, underlying factors which operate in group situations. For this reason, it holds that social control embraces not only such agencies as law, authority, punishment, codes, and creeds, but also mores, customs, traditions, the subtle influence of group expectancy, and other such factors.

Social control is concerned fundamentally with problems of orderliness in the human world, how it is obtained, how it is maintained. One reaches different conclusions as he approaches this phenomenon from different angles. One who is thinking of society as being regulated primarily by conscious external forces must necessarily find a considerable part of his explanation in terms of law, discipline, sovereignty, and external restraint. One who approaches the problem more from the standpoint of subtle factors influencing human behavior must necessarily find his

---

[20] Park and Burgess, *Introduction to the Science of Sociology*, p. 30.

explanations in terms of instinct, ceremonies, customs, and similar factors which operate in a rather unconscious manner.

Interpretations of how it is achieved are bound to fluctuate
from time to time, as new conceptions appear in the field of
sociology and social psychology. A rapid survey of the problem
of control as it has occupied the minds of social philosophers during the past few centuries will help explain how contemporary
views have developed. The next chapter is devoted to this survey.

SELECTED REFERENCES

Davis, Barnes, and Others, *An Introduction to Sociology* (selection
by L. L. Bernard), pp. 467–479. D. C. Heath and Company, New
York, 1931.

Dowd, Jerome, *Control in Human Societies*, chaps. 1 and 2.
D. Appleton-Century Company, New York, 1936.

Finney, Ross L., and Zeleny, Leslie D., *An Introduction to Educational Sociology*, pp. 232 ff. D. C. Heath and Company, New
York, 1934.

Giddings, Franklin H., "Social Control in a Democracy," *Proceedings of the Twelfth Annual Meeting of the American Sociological
Society*, vol. 12, pp. 202 ff. 1918.

Giddings, Franklin H., *Studies in the Theory of Human Society*,
pp. 200–202. The Macmillan Company, New York, 1922.

Gillette, J. M., and Reinhardt, J. M., *Current Social Problems*, chap.
25. American Book Company, New York, 1933.

Hiller, E. T., *Principles of Sociology*, chap. 38. Harper and Brothers,
New York, 1933.

Howard, George Elliott, "Ideals as a Factor in the Future Control
of International Society," *Proceedings of the Twelfth Annual
Meeting of the American Sociological Society*, vol. 12, pp. 2 ff.
1918.

Knight, Frank H., "The Newer Economics and the Control of Economic Activity," *Journal of Political Economy*, vol. 40, pp. 433–
476. August, 1932.

Lumley, Frederick Elmore, *Means of Social Control*, chap. 1.
D. Appleton-Century Company, New York, 1925.

Park, R. E., and Burgess, E. W., *Introduction to the Science of
Sociology*, chap. 12. University of Chicago Press, Chicago, 1924.

Ross, Edward Alsworth, *Principles of Sociology*, first revision, chap.
40. D. Appleton-Century Company, New York, 1930.

Ross, Edward Alsworth, *Social Control*, preface and part 1. The Macmillan Company, New York, 1929.

Smith, Russell Gordon, *Fugitive Papers*, pp. 61–83. Columbia University Press, New York, 1930.

Spencer, Herbert, *Principles of Sociology*, vol. 2, part 4. D. Appleton-Century Company, New York, 1879.

Wallis, Wilson D., *Culture and Progress*, pp. 187 ff. McGraw-Hill Book Company, New York, 1930.

Young, Kimball, *An Introductory Sociology*, chap. 26. American Book Company, New York, 1934.

Young, Kimball, *Source Book for Sociology*, chap. 26. American Book Company, New York, 1935.

CHAPTER 2

THE NATURE OF THE PROBLEM OF SOCIAL REGULATION

THE DUAL PROBLEM OF ORDER AND AUTHORITY

The problems of order and of the authority by which it may be maintained are perpetual ones and have been the concern of almost every phase of human thought dealing with conduct—philosophy, ethics, religion, law, sociology. These problems have been handled according to the points of view prevailing during particular periods of time, but the conception of them is never a static one. The dual and inseparable problems of order and of authority must necessarily be dynamic, in that they are based on concepts of the nature of the universe and the nature of man. These underlying concepts change, and as they change, the problem of maintaining authority and establishing order takes on new aspects.

One need not go far into the Middle Ages to view an epoch during which the world was held to be under the careful scrutiny of Deity, each event ruled by Him, even to the minute affairs of individual conduct. The universe teemed with supernatural powers for these, our forebears, as for many primitives throughout the centuries. True, our early European ancestors had rationalized more than many peoples have. Part of this supernatural power found expression in earthly kingdoms. Kings were God's appointed representatives in government, and as such ruled by divine right. In spiritual matters priests were the infallible representatives of God. Law in both spiritual and temporal realms was absolute and final. The universe was full of certainty. Man might rebel, sin, and be condemned here and damned hereafter, but he knew well what course to take to avoid both penalties. Human nature in this epoch had two ultimate potentialities—sainthood on the one hand, and sin, degradation, and satanic domination on the other—and the outcome depended

24

upon the choice of man, who was endowed with free will by the Creator. The world and man were ruled by two powerful forces that had been in combat since the fall in Eden; their conflict was to continue until the end of time. Both forces were building a kingdom on earth with men as subjects. Every man chose to align himself with God or with Satan. The righteous obeyed God's law, both as expressed in the spiritual kingdom by priests and in the earthly kingdom by monarchs, as long as the two systems of authority did not conflict, and during the Middle Ages the two were closely allied. The problem of controlling the sinners, and of redeeming the social order from chaos was a part of the greater problem of controlling evil. Heavy penalties, imposed by rulers with absolute power and tinged with the sting of social revenge, were dealt to those who broke the laws of the earthly kingdom; the penalty for breaking the laws of the spiritual kingdom was eternal torture in burning brimstone where unsatiated thirst and a remorseful conscience haunted one forever. One made his peace with God on earth or was forever damned.

Gradually a new concept of the nature of the universe and of man developed in the West, and with it came a new approach to the problem of control. This new concept revealed a natural world controlled by natural law, and a human nature also subject to natural law. The old concept did not immediately pass from the field of human affairs; nor has it yet fully disappeared. Men still project divine law into the social scene but with a new emphasis. God is no longer a terrible Jehovah but a benign Father who helps man attain man's deepest wants, whatever these may be; not despotism but a give-and-take relationship is seen to exist. Natural law is not to be bowed to if any way around it can be discovered, and in an amazing number of cases ways are found for overcoming what was once assumed to be implacable law.

Now man is seen as an aggressive, courageous creature, coming to terms with both God and nature and at long last, with the dawn of social science, beginning to come to terms with himself. Perhaps the other steps were at first necessary, but now that he has found a fairly satisfactory answer to the other problems he seeks to understand his new and independent self, and to know the limits of freedom and responsibility of a social creature.

The new concept of natural law and of man as a part of nature was a product of centuries, and its full implications are not yet fully understood. A brief review of the dawn of the concept in our immediate past will make clear some of the problems it has created in the field of social control, for the new concept of the nature of the universe and of man initiated a long struggle with the dual problem of order and authority which is the essence of the problem of social control, and the underlying cause for many forms of social pathology. The great social thinkers who laid the foundation for the modern period came to grips with this fundamental issue.

THE DAWN OF MODERN VIEWS OF THE PROBLEM OF MAINTAINING ORDER

The Greeks. The Renaissance in Western European thought had its roots in Greek thought, and it is among Greek thinkers that one finds man first struggling with the problem of social order and social authority along modern lines.

Plato and Aristotle, conceiving of the universe as natural and of man as a natural creature, lived during the early days of the decline of Greek culture. In the social and political disorganization of their time they saw the passing of the old authority based on Greek mythology, and with it the decline of social order. They recognized the need for a new basis for order, for a new influence about which social cohesion could be built. The problem of social order and how it might be maintained was a major one. Plato propagated his answer in *The Republic* and *The Laws*, in which he tried to show how the state came into being as an outgrowth of human nature. Both he and Aristotle identified the state with society, and conceived of the state as being the prior authority over all institutions and over the individual, and of justice as being the essence of social morality. Aristotle in his *Politics* says:

The proof that the state is a creation of nature and prior to the individual is that the individual, when isolated, is not self-sufficing; and therefore he is like a part in relation to the whole. But he who is unable to live in society, or who has no need because he is sufficient for himself, must be either a beast or a god: he is no part of a state. A social instinct is implanted in all men by nature, and yet he who first founded the state was the greatest of benefactors. For man, when perfected, is the best of animals, but, when separated from law and justice, he is the worst of all; since armed injustice is the more dangerous, and he is equipped at birth with the arms of intelligence and with moral qualities which he may use for the worst ends. Wherefore, if he have not virtue, he is the most unholy and the most savage of animals, and the most full of lust and gluttony. But justice is the bond of men in states, and the administration of justice, which is the determination of what is just, is the principle of order in political society.[1]

Early social theorists of the modern period, struggling with the same problem of how order is maintained in human society, were faced with a problem similar to that which Plato and Aristotle faced—the decline of the supernatural order in the spiritual realm and of the feudal structure in the temporal realm. About them on every hand was evidence of social decay. The old order was passing, and in its place was rapidly developing the urban-industrial-commercial order. Under the impetus of these changes social philosophers began to seek a new source of authority, a new reason for regulated human conduct. It is natural that they turned to the answers of the Greek philosophers.

Hobbes, having lost faith in the authority of the church, set out to seek authority, and found it in human nature. The struggles of Hobbes, Locke, and Rousseau with the dual problem of order and authority have been excellently summarized by John M. Foskett:

Hobbes.

He pictured man as he must have existed in the state of nature when there were no controls and hence no order and security. In this original condition there was a "war of every man against every man." The problem then was, how could social order be achieved out of this original chaos? By means of introspection it is revealed that original man was endowed by nature with certain passions and with reason. Natural selfishness led each man to seek his own welfare and thus brought him into conflict with others. However, reason dictated to him how he might better secure his individual ends and so he came to recognize a third party who should act as a judge. "And reason suggesteth convenient articles of peace, upon

---

[1] *Aristotle's Politics*, translated by Benjamin Jowett, pp. 29, 30. By permission of The Clarendon Press, Oxford.

which men may be drawn to agreement." Disregarding the political implications of this account of the origin of government, the social contract theory is primarily an explanation of social order, how it came into existence and how it is maintained.[2]

Locke.

With John Locke (1632–1704), as with Hobbes, the problem of sovereignty was essentially a problem of the true source of social order. Not only did this problem exist in literature but the actual circumstances of the time made it of foremost concern. Sixteen years of age at the time of the Revolution of 1648, Locke could not help but be impressed with the disturbed state of affairs. Indeed, he later wrote: "I no sooner perceived myself in the world than I found myself in a storm." The events following 1648 served to emphasize the problem of attaining and maintaining some sort of a stable and secure society. The theory of social order as propounded by Hobbes was not satisfactory in the light of the turn of events, and the English psychologist sought a new authority for social and political conduct. Where Hobbes attempted to justify an absolute monarchy, Locke found it necessary to support a constitutional form of government. He was anxious to protect the interests of the middle class of traders and landowners against the powers of a king and his court. Thus his enthusiasm for the alien house of Hanover with its foreign-speaking kings which left affairs in the hands of an aristocratic group. In his view of the original condition of man, Locke differed from Hobbes, author of *Leviathan*, in that he regarded it as a pre-political rather than a pre-social state. He could not conceive of a time in which men did not live in peace and happiness with their fellows, in which there was not some kind of community, some sort of regularity in human relationships. Thus Locke's analysis of social order went one step beyond that of Hobbes in that he recognized a source of order other than that of political authority. Indeed, in this respect he really anticipated later developments in sociology concerning social interaction and social products in the form of customs, mores, and institutions. What Locke attempted to show was that men, being what they are, and living together with common interests, would come to govern their conduct for each other's benefit. Political organization arises in the course

---

[2] Quoted by permission of the author, John M. Foskett, from the manuscript of a work in preparation on "Emile Durkheim and the Problem of Order."

of time only because of inconveniences experienced in the state of nature.

As indicated above, the social contract theory is essentially an effort to account for social order. The various versions of this theory represent varying points of view as to the nature of man and how he must have lived prior to society.[3]

Rousseau.

Jean Jacques Rousseau (1712–1778) departed from his predecessors to insist that all authority rested in the people and could not be alienated to a sovereign. This principle was arrived at by means of deduction from what was to be considered the original condition of man. In the state of nature man was neither good nor bad, for these qualities are a product of society. Life was "simple, uniform and solitary," and each man, living according to instinct, found his every want satisfied. In the course of time, however, conditions changed and man was led to associate with his fellows in order to preserve his own welfare. But what was to be the nature of an association that would give man security and yet not destroy his natural liberty? "The problem is to find a form of association which will defend and protect with the whole common force the person and goods of each associate, and in which each, while uniting himself with all, may still obey himself alone, and remain as free as before." The answer is the social contract. "Finally, each man, in giving himself to all, gives himself to nobody; and as there is no associate over whom he does not acquire the same right as he yields others over himself, he gains an equivalent for everything he loses, and an increase of force for the preservation of what he has." As a result of this association there comes into existence a "general will" which, once formed, takes on a moral quality and requires conformity by all. In brief, social order is achieved through the formation of a general consensus or, as Rousseau would put it, a tacit contract in which each individual is bound to obey the will of the majority. It is of some significance that Rousseau saw the sources of social order or social control resident within society itself.[4]

Durkheim. Foskett continues to show that Durkheim also tried to combat social disorganization, and as a tool to this end

---

[3] *Ibid.*
[4] *Ibid.*

attempted to establish a science of morals on a positivistic basis. Being interested in the conditions of social order, harmony, and solidarity, he conceived of morals as the ties which held society together, and not metaphysical criteria of right and wrong.

Thus understood the problem as envisaged by Durkheim is fundamentally the same as that which concerned Hobbes, Locke and Rousseau, Saint-Simon, Comte, and Spencer. In each case there is the original concern over a present state of affairs characterized by conflict, turmoil, and insecurity. Established values and forms of conduct appear to be in danger. Whether it be due to war, economic and political changes, or shifting concepts of the universe, the picture is the same—social anarchy. Although the initial difficulty is one of disorder, it is at the same time to be observed that human beings are capable of, and, in a measure, do succeed in living together harmoniously. All is not chaos, for in every society there is a body of established and accepted ways of acting giving rise to orderly relationships between individuals. Wherever people live together in groups, large or small, there arise rules of behavior to which people conform. There grow up in the course of time social bonds uniting men with each other and making for cooperation. Because this is an ideal to be attained, reflection then turns from the initial difficulty to social order. How is it to be accounted for? What are the factors making for this result? What are the ties producing unity and cohesion? If this were known we would have a body of knowledge with which to consciously and purposely bring about further order. This age-old problem, of particular importance in the modern period, became the core of positive social philosophy.[5]

Contemporary Views of the Problem of Control

This era of thought paved the way for both natural and social science. A universe permeated by natural law is one in which orderly sequences may be sought and future repetitions predicted. Man, it was later conceived, is a part of nature. He, too, then must be subject to natural laws. Psychological and social sciences have grown apace, and with each change in their concept of the nature of man, new approaches to the problem of control have been offered.

Owing to mistaken application of the Darwinian theory of

---

[5] *Ibid.*

organic evolution, early psychological thought placed man in the immediate sequence of animal life, and built human mental science on animal instinct. The problem of control grew out of the nature of man's instincts, some of which were social and some antisocial. The conflict of instincts was different in one respect from the old conflict between good and evil. Instincts were inborn, the product of hereditary law. In no sense were they supernatural.

It was at this stage of thought that Ross wrote the pioneer treatise in social control in which he dealt with the problem of social order, viewing it in terms of social instincts which made for a natural order, but holding also that the sublimation of antisocial instincts through social pressure greatly improved upon this natural order. But social and psychological thought broke with the interpretations of human nature as instinctive more than ten years ago. In fact, the break had been in process much longer, and is now fairly complete. New concepts of human nature call for a new interpretation of social control.

MAN IS HUMAN BECAUSE OF CONTROL

The traditional emphasis on social control as insurance against group disintegration is but half the story. Social control is equally essential to the individual. Not only is society maintained by social control, but individuals survive only under the system of regulation which society affords. Man's nature becomes human only because of the disciplinary influences of social regulation. It is the product of social control. To use the dramatic imagery of Ross, it is no longer held "that normal human beings are born with a set of commandments etched upon the soul." [6] They have to be placed there by a social group. The human being, born as he is without definite fixed patterns of life, must depend upon the social group for these patterns. This is a generally recognized conclusion upon which all modern educational theories are based. In fact, it is the generally accepted premise of modern psychology, social psychology, sociology, and cultural anthropology. The individual develops a system of behavior only by being placed in a relatively orderly systematic social environment. He achieves personality integration only to the extent that he absorbs the patterns

---

[6] E. A. Ross, *Social Control*, part 1.

of an orderly system. He feels secure only insofar as he develops those personality patterns which fit the larger patterns of the social group. Thrown outside of this orbit of action, he becomes a misfit, a lost soul.

Thus, social control becomes important, not simply as a safety device for the social order, not simply as an insurance to the permanence of society, but as a means of preserving the well-being of each individual constituent in that society. It is not only that society must have well-disciplined individuals in order to survive; the individual himself, in order to develop a meaningful set of relationships in life, must live within a social order which is sufficiently systematic and permanent in its regulative system to permit him to develop patterns of life that will make him a part of the social whole. Some people cannot survive frontier conditions, where there are few regulations to protect a man from his own vices.[7] Sorokin's picture of a society in the grip of revolutionary violence is dramatic evidence of the individual's failure to discipline himself when the system of social discipline to which he is accustomed has temporarily disintegrated.[8]

To state this point in a slightly different manner, social control does stabilize the social order, but control is no more important to a stabilized social order than it is to the development of an integrated socially-effective personality. It is not just that society must harness the individual and whip him into line; it is as fundamentally a matter of the individual's being so oriented to the social system that he finds for himself a meaningful set of relationships.

Control not only makes society a functioning unit; it makes the person an organized entity. It not only assures a society of permanence, but it also insures the individual's mental well-being. A stabile system of social control finds its counterpart in the stabilized personality, or conversely, societies with disintegrated patterns of control are societies in which the individual finds stress and strain, and in which his personality may become so disorganized that insanity, suicide, or demoralization results.

---

[7] The author had this point driven home to him in studying the early history of mining settlements. See his *Three Iron Mining Towns*, Edwards Brothers, Inc., Ann Arbor, 1938, parts 2 and 3.

[8] P. A. Sorokin, *The Sociology of Revolution*, J. B. Lippincott Company, Chicago, 1925. See the quotation from this work which appears on pp. 457 ff.

This does not mean that we are to assume that individual initiative plays no part in social life. It has a rightful place, perhaps not the high place that some have given it, but certainly an important place.

Conclusion

We arrive at this conclusion: Contemporary points of view as to the problem of social control as they involve the problem of order and authority are a product of modern times and of modern philosophies. During the Middle Ages the problem of control was relegated largely to the realm of the supernatural. Authority was vested in Deity alone. Kings ruled by divine right as God's representatives on earth. The social order was permeated by the Divine Law. Concepts of an absolute right and wrong, good and bad, were universally recognized. Satan as the instigator of evil, as the cause of misbehavior, was no less a real character in human affairs than was God, the instigator of good, the One who gave man inner strength to live righteously.

With the decline in influence of the theory of divine right of kings, and the rise of Democratic ideals, political theorists had to turn to another source for authority. Hobbes, Locke, and Rousseau, at the outset of the modern period, rationalized the source of authority in a natural order resident in the social group. Authority rested in society, and society through the social contract, which represented the collective will of the group, appointed representatives from its numbers to represent it in exercising authority.[9]

Numerous events that ushered in the modern period—political revolutions leading to democratic government, the Reformation leading to Protestantism, the Renaissance in literature, the growth of science and of skepticism, the decline of the church as an institution dominating thought, and the growth of the school—have led man to seek an interpretation for order in man himself, or in his institutions.

To no small extent, the problem of why man behaves as an orderly civilized being, has concerned sociology since its origin. From fairly fixed concepts of control through natural forces inherent in the group or in the nature of man—"group mind" and

---

[9] See J. P. Lichtenberger, *Development of Social Theory*, chap. 8; also, F. N. House, *The Range of Social Theory*, pp. 477–478.

"instinct" theories—the quest for an explanation of social orderliness has turned to man's experience.

The overthrow of instinct theories, the last stronghold of
naturalistic theories, has made it necessary to seek a new source of
authority to explain behavior in the human group. Concepts
in the field of cultural anthropology, which place authority in
the realm of tradition, replaced the older notions of authority
more completely than any single discovery. These, supplemented
by the discovery of the conditioned response principle, and the
elaboration of contemporary theories of learning, make it possible to explain human orderliness in terms of man's experience
in the group. These developments, combined with an understanding of the processes of social interaction by which the individual partakes of group life, have laid the foundation for the
contemporary approach to the problem of social control.

Increasingly the sociologists of recent years have come to see
that man maintains an orderly system of life not because of inborn
patterns, or of external authority consciously imposed, or not
necessarily because of the conscious sense of being restricted, but
because of the normal effect of social experience upon personality.
The individual lives in society not with a consciousness that he is
being beaten into subjection by some visible or invisible authority. Instead he has a live consciousness of the presence of
others in the world he inhabits, he is alert to the teachings that
social experience brings, and he almost inevitably develops a sense
of responsibility to others because of certain lessons that experience teaches.

Order, then, finds its roots not in some universal law of nature,
not in the establishment of recognized external authority, but in
the social experience of the individual. Society is orderly because
men learn to live so; it remains orderly until some great revolutionary movement in the social system disturbs habit patterns of
individuals. When such a time comes, there is no evidence of
there being any eternal law of order. The order exists only in the
habits of the individual and in the customs of the social system.
When the social system is thrown out of gear, a new one somewhat in line with established habits must arise. We are finally
beginning to understand that social control is not only for society,
but also for the individual. The individual is able to live socially
and to function completely only as he is trained to fit a social

order. Personal development and personality organization are the products of social control, just as surely as is an orderly society. Since social order is built on the nature of man, we need to examine briefly man's native endowments which might provide a reason for or a means to social control, and an explanation for its frequent failure. Human nature is the theme of the next chapter.

SELECTED REFERENCES

Cooley, Charles H., *Human Nature and the Social Order*, chap. 12. Charles Scribner's Sons, New York, 1922.

Cooley, Charles H., *Social Process*, chap. 14. Charles Scribner's Sons, New York, 1918.

Dowd, Jerome, *Control in Human Societies*. D. Appleton-Century Company, New York, 1936.

Harvard Tercentenary Publications, *Authority and the Individual*. Harvard University Press, Cambridge, 1937.

Hiller, E. T., *Principles of Sociology*, chap. 38. Harper and Brothers, New York, 1933.

House, F. N., *The Range of Social Theory*, chap. 32. Henry Holt and Company, New York, 1929.

Jowett, Benjamin, *Aristotle's Politics*, a translation. Clarendon Press, Oxford, 1908.

Lichtenberger, J. P., *Development of Social Theory*, chap. 8. D. Appleton-Century Company, New York, 1925.

Lumley, Frederick Elmore, *Means of Social Control*, pp. 9–12. D. Appleton-Century Company, New York, 1925.

MacIver, Robert, *Society*, chap. 20. Farrar and Rinehart, Inc., New York, 1937.

Park, Robert E., and Burgess, Ernest W., *Introduction to the Science of Sociology*, pp. 41–43, 848–849. University of Chicago Press, Chicago, 1924.

Plato, *The Republic*, translated by Paul Shorey. G. P. Putnam's Sons, New York, 1930.

Ross, Edward Alsworth, *Social Control*, part 1. The Macmillan Company, New York, 1929.

Stein, Ludwig, "The Sociology of Authority," *Publications of the American Sociological Society*, vol. 18, pp. 116–120. 1923.

CHAPTER 3

THE ORIGINAL NATURE OF MAN AND THE REGULATIVE PROCESS

ARE THE ROOTS OF ORDERLINESS IN ORIGINAL NATURE?

In nature there are devices, largely automatic, by which plants and animals are controlled. Tropisms govern the action of plants in response to environmental influences. The sunflower turns its face toward the morning sun, follows its course throughout the day, and at nightfall faces westward. This tropic response is automatically regulated so that, granted a uniform environment, uniform behavior results throughout the species. Widespread development of instincts in animals explains the largely automatic and orderly action patterns which they possess. The geese in their annual migration form a V in the heavens and fly southward with instinctive regularity. Salmon, after having been hatched near the headwaters of an inland stream, swim toward the ocean. Four years later they return up the winding water course, there to lay their eggs and die, having completed the life cycle of their species. The so-called social insects—bees and ants—live in orderly communities. From the outset, without instructions from the parent or from the social group, the young bee fits into the organized social colony. Each bee knows how to form a relatively perfect hexagonal cell. Nature has provided for a division of labor in making drones, queens, and workers. No human colony was ever as fully, as completely, as harmoniously organized as a hive of bees. Nature has provided for orderliness in the whole animal kingdom by endowing her creatures with elaborate patterns in their nervous structure which function when the environment offers the stimuli. These patterns, called instinct, are a part of the animals' hereditary equipment. Some animals are gregarious, because in the germ plasm is buried a social pattern which prepares the individual to live as a member of the herd. Other instinctive mechanisms adapt the animal ideally for orderly behavior in his geographical world. So far as we know, these patterns are largely mechanistic and beyond the volitional control of the organism.

Students of human society a generation ago, reasoning largely by analogy, attributed to man the same mechanical patterns of behavior that are widely observed throughout the animal kingdom. They noted that man does things in an orderly manner, and immediately concluded that he must necessarily be regulated by the same inborn mechanisms. There seemed to be much evidence for such a point of view, especially when one was looking for it. Did not all children acquire possessions (acquisitive instinct)? Were they not all pugnacious in disposition (pugnacious instinct)? Did they not, like all the higher animals, mate when they reached maturity (mating instinct)? Did not mothers and fathers love their children? Then there must be maternal and paternal instincts. Since man everywhere has religion, he must possess a religious instinct. Such conceptions were elaborated to the point of absurdity.

Gradually these theories broke down in the light of the experiments in child psychology of John B. Watson, and the criticism of L. L. Bernard and others. Soon man was stripped of instincts, and in place of these was given simple emotions, reflexes, appetites, and physical sensations.

At a much earlier date, students of human nature had arrived at the conclusion that the human mind is without innate ideas. John Locke, the philosopher, in the latter part of the seventeenth century advanced his famous *tabula rasa* theory that the mind is a blank tablet, and the child enters the world without ideas.

One cannot then attribute human orderliness to ideas written upon the mind prenatally, such as certain views of conscience presuppose, or to any hereditary mechanism, such as instinct doctrines take for granted.

INCORRIGIBLE "HUMAN NATURE" CALLS FOR CONTROL

In the past, many different views of original nature have been assumed. Here we are interested in traits of original nature which have been thought to make control necessary, and which have been made the basis for explaining variations from social norms, such as are expressed in delinquency, immoral behavior, and crime.

Atavistic man. Famous in the field of criminological thought is the theory of Lombroso,[1] that approximately one-third of all criminals are so atavistic in nature that they cannot be made to conform to the regulative system of modern society. They might have fitted into a more primitive social order, but are hopeless in the complexities of modern society. This being the case, they find themselves running counter to the social system, and are treated by contemporary society as criminals. This third of the criminal population is antisocial because of inherent potentialities. There is no hope that they can ever be made to conform, and therefore society must employ disciplinary measures with them.

Carnal man. Some Christian theologians have explained misconduct by an evil bent in human nature which they place at the root of evil. People veer from the right way because an element in their nature—labeled by the Apostle Paul, "the carnal man," and by Methodism, "the old man of sin" or the "Adamic nature," (as contrasted with the "new man" that came after rebirth through conversion) is appealed to by the force of evil. The individual without the help of grace is unable to conform. Satan or his temptations usually have been used as a scapegoat. Because man has these evil propensities, Satan can tempt him to sin and make him do the things that violate the standards of the religious group. Control comes through reforming original nature.

Freud's concept of the "libido." Freud's interpretation of human behavior [2] assumes that the human race embodies sex urges that are much more fundamental and powerful than any social regulations. Even though these drives may be submerged by social regulation, they work to the surface in various ways, developing into perversions in personality, and sometimes causing serious eruptions in the form of insanity or psychopathic behavior. Unity of personality tends to be destroyed by the perpetual conflict between inborn tendencies and the system of social control developed by society.

Antisocial instincts. All of these theories and many others of more recent origin assume that there are certain forces within

---

[1] Cesare Lombroso, *Crime: Its Causes and Remedies,* translated by Henry P. Horton.

[2] For a statement of Freud's theory see his *General Introduction to Psycho-Analysis,* translated by G. Stanley Hall.

man himself that call for regulation. There are many explanations of human behavior based on instinct, akin to the theories already discussed, and until quite recently they had the sanction of what was supposed to be a scientific psychology. These theories presupposed the existence of such antisocial drives as the pugnacious instinct which led the individual into violent conflict with his neighbor, the aggressive instinct that made him seek to dominate, the instinct of greed that made him inherently selfish. These theories have been outmoded, as have those assuming that man is endowed by nature with an inner sense of "oughtness," sympathy, justice, or righteousness, which guarantees order within the human group.

Some will be rebels. More modern in point of view is the theory of Ross,[3] that in any society, whether mining camp or frontier town, there are individuals who are unwilling to abide by the ordinary restraints that the better elements find necessary, and so carry on a reign of terror until social force is applied to bring them into line. We have, therefore, the development first of the vigilante and later of a civil government and organized regulated institutions.

Lumley puts the problem similarly:

Within any society, some persons are always too dull to imitate successfully or to see the importance of imitating; some are too sick to imitate or to see the desirability of it; some are brought up in such impoverished environments that they never are confronted with good patterns or have much positive teaching; some definitely and positively repudiate the prevailing standard patterns because insane or infatuated with a vision; some are taught specific anti-social, nonconformance ways.[4]

Human nature contains a vicious streak. Sorokin viewed the carnage of the Russian Revolution, and concluded that the picture of man as a "good little boy" conceived by the eighteenth century and the modern rationalists was wrongly drawn. He says:

Before us we have not only a sensible being, but the elemental man, who is not only peace-loving, altruistic, compassionate, but also full of rancor, cruelty, bestiality; not only consciously clear-sighted,

---

[3] E. A. Ross, *Social Control*, pp. 51 ff.

[4] Frederick E. Lumley, *Means of Social Control*, p. 9. Used by permission of D. Appleton-Century Company, Publishers, New York, N. Y.

but often blind; not only gentle and creative, but wild and destructive. Of course certain features claimed for man by the rationalists have not been wanting, but they have been overshadowed by quite opposite qualities.

. . . To sum up: Man is the bearer not only of peaceful, gentle, virtuous and social impulses, but also of their opposites. On the other hand the Russian school of the objective method of analyzing the behavior of man and animals and the behaviorists have given still greater predominance to inborn or unconditioned reflexes, showing how completely conditioned or acquired forms of behavior depend on them . . .

"The real man is restless, aggressive, and aspiring." He is the bearer of various inborn reflexes. His instincts force him to desire not only peace, but warfare; not only self-sacrifice, but murder; not only justice, but the satisfaction of his necessities, though at the cost of his fellowmen; not only work, but idleness. They spur him to independence, at the same time, make him seek subjection to, or, upon occasion, domination over others; they teach him not only to love, but to hate others; the list of instincts includes such tendencies as pugnacity, gregariousness, ownership, rivalry, self-assertion, love of adventure, of leadership, of migration, of domination, of self-expression, etc. I do not even allude to such wants as man's desire for food, clothes, sexual satisfaction, etc. To sum up: The quantity and quality of man's impulses and reflexes render him, singularly, like a bomb full of different kinds of forces and tendencies capable of bursting and presenting us with a picture of wild disorder. To use Pascal's words: "Man is like an angel with a devil hidden beneath." [5]

MAN'S NATIVE EQUIPMENT

Man does, none the less, have a native equipment which makes him susceptible to social regulations. One can say this without being accused of accepting outmoded theories. Man has by birth the psychological equipment for learning, but he is born with a less organized nervous structure than almost any other creature.

Whatever man may have in the way of inborn patterns that would help explain his actions, is rudimentary, at most reflexes,

[5] P. A. Sorokin, The Sociology of Revolution, pp. 17–22. By permission of J. B. Lippincott Company, Chicago.

appetites, emotions, and physical sensations, which must be harnessed, socialized, and channelized by the social group.[6] Whatever he acquires in the way of emotional development, habit formation, moral insight, and mental integration must come through environment acting upon these basic patterns and developing and molding them into a personality.

Because the human being has the capacity to develop, there is almost no limit to the patterns which he may acquire. The significant fact from the standpoint of social control is that this plasticity of the human organism places upon the social group both the responsibility for building and the opportunity to build within the organism the patterns, attitudes, emotional sets, and ideational systems which will determine its later conduct.

This does not mean that the organism is a puppet of the environment. Rather it is a dynamic force. It has energy from within. The individual organism limits the number of possible activities and impressions. The emotions, habits, and sensations of the organism act as selective influences in relation to the stimuli presented from without. The organism has the power of integrating, organizing and developing into a meaningful constellation, experiences that are registered from without.[7] And yet, man is not an oriented, fully equipped creature of social experience at birth.

Man is social because he is suggestible,[8] and because of that fact we may assume that he is controllable, being readily susceptible to the idea, emotion, and action patterns of his fellow beings. It is not a matter of consciousness of kind, herd instinct, or mass mind, as was once supposed. The human being soon learns that suggestibility has utility in living, that doing as others do and following the suggestions of others brings satisfactions.

The same is true of imitation, which, though no longer considered an instinct, nevertheless becomes a definite pattern in human behavior, developed through experience. Imitation and

---

[6] Floyd H. Allport, in *Social Psychology*, chap. 3, classified the more important of the inborn patterns and drives as "prepotent reflexes." The six prepotent reflexes are: (1) starting and withdrawing (2) rejecting (3) struggling (4) hunger reactions (5) sensitive zone reactions (6) sex reactions.

[7] See Wolfgang Köhler's *Gestalt Psychology*; also, George W. Hartman's *Gestalt Psychology*.

[8] B. Sidis, *The Psychology of Suggestion*, pp. 310–312, D. Appleton-Century Company, New York, 1898.

suggestibility provide, therefore, the mechanisms for social regimentation through habit formation.

So, in discussing the native equipment of man and its relationship to the problem of social control, we see that, though man is not equipped by original nature with the patterns necessary for an orderly life in society, yet he is provided with the type of equipment which makes it possible for him to acquire experientially, through certain psychological mechanisms, a great variety of life patterns and habits of living.

He has certain basic reflexes, emotions, and sensations which make it possible for conditioning to begin. At first, pain and pleasure determine the direction of this conditioning process. As the child acquires language symbols and develops the power of observation, he forms habits of imitation, becomes susceptible to suggestion, and, through the combined forces of learning and acting, develops permanent attitudes, mental sets, and patterns. In fact, he becomes completely accustomed to expecting certain things of the group and having the group expect certain things of him. Such factors form the underlying basis of social control, as far as social control relates to the organic-psychic mechanisms of the individual. To add to the significance of these experiences is the fact that the human being has a long infancy and a delicate nervous system with which to acquire the patterns of the culture mass.

Because of his constant association with other people, upon whom he must depend for even the elementary patterns, the human being becomes social, learning to seek approval of others, learning to compare his own activities with those of others, coming to acquire standards and to get meanings from behavior in terms of the responses which his actions produce in members of his social world.

Man is born with the capacity to acquire and to build culture, whatever the culture of his tribe and his culture area may be. Language, skills, religious and moral systems—all these and many more patterns [9] can be absorbed. In any culture, most of the devices of control reside in these patterns.[10]

---

[9] Clark Wissler, in *Man and Culture*, chap. 5, discusses the universal culture pattern which includes culture complexes found in all cultures.

[10] Wissler describes man as a culture-building creature, culture patterns being expressions of his capacities and interests; *ibid.*, chap. 12.

The culture-building and transmitting power of man is a distinctly human trait, and grows chiefly out of the fact that man has the necessary original capacity for symbolic behavior. His nearest rival in communication is the ape, but the ape can transmit emotions only to his fellows. He has sound symbols for expressing his feelings, but none for describing external objects.[11] Man can describe objects by words, and even transmit to his fellows through word symbols a knowledge of complicated action patterns and social processes.

THE LEARNING PROCESS

Since man begins life with equipment rather than patterns, how is his personality formed in such a manner that he is made capable of living an orderly, regulated life such as society presupposes? Briefly, through a learning process.

The nature of this learning process is far from being fully understood, in spite of years of study by psychologists, educators, and sociologists.[12] That it is much more extensive in man than in other creatures is definitely known, and that it is a much more important process than early psychologists who approached the subject from an instinctive standpoint realized, is now generally accepted. It is presupposed in this discussion that learning is the basis of the society's power to control the individual.

The one discovery which, more than any other, shifted the interpretation of man's behavior from an instinctive-organic to a learning-environmental foundation was that of the conditioned response principle by Pavlov in his series of famous experiments. The experiment in which he placed a glass tube in the throat of a dog and watched the flow of saliva, first when meat was presented, then when meat was presented simultaneously with the ringing of bell, and finally when a conditioned response had been established upon the ringing of the bell alone, is too well known to make extensive discussion necessary here.[13]

The conditioned response principle, that is, the association of a biologically inadequate stimulus with a biologically adequate

---

[11] Wolfgang Köhler's study of apes shows clearly that the one chief distinguishing ability of the human being is that of developing and using symbols describing experience. See *The Mentality of Apes.*

[12] Richard La Piere and Paul Farnsworth, *Social Psychology,* pp. 44 ff.

[13] Ivan P. Pavlov's *Lectures on Conditioned Reflexes,* translated by W. H. Gantt and G. Volborth, presents his most important discoveries.

stimulus, to obtain the original response, has come to be looked upon as the basic element in the learning process. In its rudimentary stages it consists entirely in the association of new stimuli with the original responses, thus increasing the number of environmental influences which can set off the response. The extensive development of conditioning leads to the formation of habits which are quite as mechanistic as instincts, and operate in much the same manner. They are a little more modifiable than instincts, but once formed in the nervous system, are almost as rigid and permanent. At the same time an internal or efferent modification is going on within the organism, due to the selection and fixation of successful random movements establishing emotional and thought patterns.[14]

Through learning, the human personality is built to accord with the desires of society. Learning makes it possible for the plastic organism to grow in a great number of directions, permitting the establishment of skills, habits, attitudes, and values by influences from without.

Educators have studied the learning process and understand enough of its nature to point out teaching techniques by which individuals learn most readily. This entire subject is one which need not concern us here, the significant point being that human personality is shaped through learning, however this learning process may be carried out in any particular society, or whatever the fundamental principles that may be employed. Teaching and learning are presupposed in any system of social control.

The learning process begins in earliest childhood. Much of the child's conditioning experience occurs in the family, where the patterns of the social group are imbedded in his nervous system and so become automatic. As his experience widens in contact with other groups—the play group, the neighborhood, and later the community and the larger society—he acquires the complex behavior of the social world and in so doing he develops habit patterns to fit those of the group around him, so that he may function in an orderly manner in the group.

The responsibility for shaping each child's personality in such a manner that he will be a fit subject for group life is thus placed upon society. Herein is the secret of the group's power of con-

---

[14] For an excellent discussion of the neuro-psychic aspect of learning see Floyd H. Allport, *Social Psychology*, chap. 3.

trol over the individual, and at the same time an explanation of the individual's capacity to conform.

Every human being is molded in the pattern of a given society. Take him outside of this society and he is bewildered. The regulative devices of a strange society have no meaning for him, and not knowing them, he does not comprehend either what to expect of others or what others expect of him.

A SUMMARY VIEW OF ORIGINAL NATURE

Here then we have the individual as he is understood today— a thinking creature without innate ideas, a religious creature without conscience, an essentially social creature by capacity, but without social patterns, an animal without animal instincts, a beast in certain appetites, passions, and organic drives which must be sublimated by social training, a creature with abilities so extensive that he needs direction above all other creatures, but one with fewer organic patterns for routine behavior than any other of them. What is his guide? Where are the patterns by which he is regulated? Patterns must exist, because within any society man builds an orderly system of life, so orderly in fact that many still explain it by instinct, as in the case of birds and beasts.

Man has a guide, the guide of racial experience, not instinct; habit, not innate ideas; experimental truth, not absolute knowledge; trial and error, not revelation. This is the meaning which contemporary sociology, anthropology, and psychology give to social control.

Man learns to be orderly. He is potentially a habit-forming creature. He is potentially religious and can develop conscientious scruples and deep religious convictions that mean more than life to him. He is potentially social. He may come to hold the opinions of others as though they were of his own creation, and to value the life of another above his own. He is potentially wise, because he can absorb an almost infinite number of environmental impressions. He has a taste for truth but only one guide to it—experience. He likes revelation, the revelation of tested knowledge—science, and of Deity about equally well, but in our age he is developing some preference for that of science. He is capable of living an orderly life, but his one guide to this orderly life is experience.

What is experience? Certainly it includes more than the individual's own limited range of action. It can be broadened to include the whole experience of the race. Experience is conserved in the culture of a society and passed on to the individual. Society through the medium of its culture has stored up experience for ages of time. The social group has developed considerable skill in seeing that each new member is properly initiated and kept in line.

Man has a long memory. He does not soon forget the lessons learned. The memory of the race is longer still—as long as the race itself. Social life has continuity beyond the life of the individual, even though society consists only of individuals. Society is a never-ending stream of experience. Its culture has been long in the making and is still in process.

The individual, being the creature that he is, and possessing the potentialities that he does, fits into this endless stream of life, conforms to it, whether in this society or that, and becomes a part, and perhaps even adds a bit to the race's heritage. The process by which the individual becomes a part of this orderly scheme of life is the essence of the means by which social control is realized in society.

LEVELS UPON WHICH MAN MAY BE CONTROLLED

Human beings are capable of being appealed to on three levels. First but least important is the organic level, where control devices take the form of pleasure and pain. Control on this level is sometimes used in the early conditioning of the child, and out of this process of conditioning grow the first behavior patterns of the human being. The resultant behavior is not far different from the tropic response of plants or the instinctive response of animals, being quite automatic and reflexive.

Second, as the personality develops, control tends to shift from the very elementary organic level to the social level where suggestion, imitation, inhibition, and other forces play an increasing part. The group shapes the child's personality patterns in line with its interests for him.

Finally, and very important in the control of human beings, is the cultural or superorganic level, which consists of cultural phenomena, the folkways, mores, technicways, and the numerous symbolic-inventional patterns. The culture of any particular time is the mold in which personality is cast. In it are the regulative devices, the accepted patterns, the directive and restrictive pressures under which the personality is formed. The following chapters will carry forward the analysis of social control in terms of social and cultural influences.

Conclusion

Unlike other creatures, man is born without definite patterns to provide for an orderly life. His organic equipment for control at birth is potential rather than actual. He is a creature with almost no fixed organic patterns beyond simple rudimentary ones in the form of appetites, emotions, and reflexes, but with almost unlimited capacity for being molded. This being the case, one must seek an explanation for human orderliness chiefly in experience rather than in original nature. He is born with capacities for social experience and for acquiring culture, but without the established patterns for functioning effectively in society. Through the learning process he begins early to acquire the necessary habit patterns for social living.

A modern approach to the nature of man as it relates to the need for social control is not so much concerned with how society can develop restraints to curb carnal man effectively, suppress the atavistic type, harness the Freudian urge, balk the antisocial instinct, or control the rebellious temperament, but is concerned with the problem of building personality from raw and unformed material through a system of social discipline and guidance, effective enough to make man fit for society and society fit for man.

That control has operated in all societies is evidence of its necessity. Neither in nature nor in society is there such a thing as order without control. Nature provides mechanistic controls among lower creatures, but human society requires effort to maintain order. It must be maintained. It cannot be taken for granted. Those who take orderliness for granted in human society fail to appreciate both the nature of man and the nature of the social order. Society is strictly a man-made affair, and not necessarily a part of the law of nature. It is artificial and is maintained only by the constant surveillance of a system of social control.

Part II traces the socializing process through which the individual is educated to become an orderly, regulated individual.

It is the personality-forming process through which original nature is passed that produces an orderly conforming social creature, or the opposite, a rebellious, degenerate, or pathological one.

SELECTED REFERENCES

Allport, Floyd H., *Social Psychology*, chap. 3. Houghton Mifflin Company, Boston, 1924.

Anderson, John E., "The Genesis of Social Reactions in the Young Child," *The Unconscious; A Symposium*, pp. 69–90. F. S. Crofts and Company, New York, 1928.

Bernard, L. L., *Instinct*. Henry Holt and Company, New York, 1924.

Bernard, L. L., *Introduction to Social Psychology*. Henry Holt and Company, New York, 1926.

Brown, Lawrence Guy, *Social Psychology*. McGraw-Hill Book Company, New York, 1934.

Burnham, William H., "The Significance of the Conditioned Reflex in Mental Hygiene," *Mental Hygiene*, pp. 687 ff. October, 1921.

Crile, George W., *A Mechanistic View of War and Peace*, pp. 99–101. The Macmillan Company, New York, 1915.

Cooley, Charles H., "Heredity and Instinct in Human Life," *Survey*, vol. 49, pp. 454–456. January 1, 1923.

Cooley, Charles H., *Human Nature and the Social Order*, introduction. Charles Scribner's Sons, New York, 1922.

Faris, Ellsworth, "The Nature of Human Nature," *American Journal of Sociology*, vol. 32, pp. 15–29. 1926.

Freud, Sigmund, *General Introduction to Psycho-Analysis*, translated by G. Stanley Hall. Boni and Liveright, New York, 1920.

Hartmann, George W., *Gestalt Psychology*. The Ronald Press Company, New York, 1935.

House, F. N., *The Range of Social Theory*, chap. 10. Henry Holt and Company, New York, 1929.

Köhler, Wolfgang, *Gestalt Psychology*. Horace Liveright, Inc., New York, 1929.

Köhler, Wolfgang, *The Mentality of Apes*. Harcourt, Brace and Company, New York, 1925.

Landis, Paul H., *Three Iron Mining Towns: A Study in Cultural Change*, chaps. 7 and 8. Edwards Brothers, Ann Arbor, 1938.

La Piere, Richard, and Farnsworth, Paul, *Social Psychology*, chaps. 1 and 2. McGraw-Hill Book Company, New York, 1936.

Lombroso, Cesare, *Crime: Its Causes and Remedies*, translated by Henry P. Horton. Little, Brown and Company, Boston, 1911.

Ogburn, W. F., *Social Change*, part 1, section 2. The Viking Press, Inc., New York, 1923.

Park, Robert E., "Human Nature, Attitudes, and the Mores," *Social Attitudes*, Kimball Young, editor, pp. 22–24. Henry Holt and Company, New York, 1931.

Pavlov, Ivan P., *Lectures on Conditioned Reflexes*, translated by W. H. Gantt and G. Volborth. International Publishers, New York, 1928.

Sorokin, Pitirim A., *The Sociology of Revolution*, chap. 2. J. B. Lippincott Company, Chicago, 1925.

Williams, J. M., *Principles of Social Psychology*. Alfred A. Knopf, Inc., New York, 1922.

Winston, Sanford, *Culture and Human Behavior*, chaps. 2 and 11. The Ronald Press Company, New York, 1933.

Wissler, Clark, *Man and Culture*, part 3. Thomas Y. Crowell Company, New York, 1923.

Young, Kimball, *Social Psychology*. F. S. Crofts and Company, New York, 1930.

PART II

THE PERSONALITY FORMING PROCESSES AS THE BASIS OF SOCIAL ORGANIZATION

CHAPTER 4

THE BUILDING OF HUMAN NATURE

VIEWS OF HUMAN NATURE

Having concluded that the original nature of man is far from adequate in providing a basis for an orderly social life, how then can one explain human nature as found in the adult?

The conditioned response, the most elementary of the learned patterns which take shape in human nature, has already been discussed, but there still remains to be considered the range of stimuli which determines what conditioned responses the individual will acquire. These stimuli are to be found primarily in the group world of common social and cultural backgrounds.

If uniformity of stimuli in the environment, and uniformity of original nature were granted, human beings could be fitted into similar molds as far as their attitudes and behavior patterns were concerned. But no two environments are ever exactly the same, no two individuals are ever born with identical original natures, so human natures are infinitely variable. By human nature we mean the inborn nature of man as socialized by experience.

Cooley defined human nature as consisting of those sentiments and impulses which are considered superior to those of the lower animals, sentiments belonging peculiarly to mankind at large and not to any particular period in history or to any particular race of people.[1] He seemed to have in mind primarily sympathy with the "innumerable sentiments into which sympathy enters," such as feelings of social right and wrong, love, ambition, vanity, resentment, and hero worship.

Somewhat more specific is the concept of La Piere and Farnsworth, who think of human nature as "predictable behavior traits consisting in the common modes of behavior of a group," those

---

[1] Charles H. Cooley, *Social Organization*, p. 28.

"likenesses in behavior which are so consistent and persistent that they are to be taken for granted." [2]

In this chapter we are interested in showing how completely human nature consists in partaking of the common patterns of one's social group.

That the process of acquiring human nature is largely unconscious makes it none the less significant. Ordinarily we acquire and use culture patterns with little knowledge of their origin or of their importance to us. We find ourselves equipped for the journey through life without knowing how it came about. [3]

Charles H. Cooley holds that a person can hardly conceive of himself as being apart from some social group, or conversely, that one can hardly think of the group without thinking of his identification with it. [4] He dwells at considerable length on the fact that the individual and society are part of one complex social whole. When we stress personality we emphasize the individual aspect of the group, but when we stress the whole unit we accentuate the social aspect. In most conscious reflection we think of ourselves in relation to other persons, or of other persons in their mutual relationships. Self and society are "twin-born." We know the one as well as we know the other, and any notion of "a separate and independent ego is an illusion."

SOCIAL CONSCIOUSNESS

Sometime early in life the child awakens to a realization that he is a part of the group. Bernard puts this stage of consciousness last in order of development, after various stages of self-consciousness have appeared. [5]

Cooley suggests that social consciousness and self-consciousness are in reality a part of the same thing. [6] He even carried this concept of the identification of society with the individual to a further extreme, [7] in stating that our minds are never entirely dis-

[2] Richard La Piere and Paul Farnsworth, Social Psychology, p. 198.

[3] F. Stuart Chapin, Contemporary American Institutions, p. 47, Harper and Brothers, New York, 1935.

[4] Charles H. Cooley, op. cit., p. 5.

[5] See Davis, Barnes, and Others, An Introduction to Sociology, pp. 468–475, selection by L. L. Bernard.

[6] There is no necessary contradiction here. Bernard is tracing the origin of various stages of consciousness in the child. Cooley is analyzing the psychological experience of the developed personality.

[7] Charles H. Cooley, op. cit., p. 5.

tinct from the minds of other persons, but include all persons of whom we think, all of society which we manipulate in our thoughts. "Self and other do not exist as mutually exclusive social facts." [8]

IDENTIFICATION OF OURSELVES WITH THE GROUP

If one analyzes carefully his own psychological experience, he is made conscious of the above principles. He thinks of himself in terms of the attitudes of others. This point is well attested to by the fact that almost any magazine carries considerable advertising which appeals to one's consciousness of the effect of his own actions upon others. He is asked to buy certain soaps to avoid B. O. and thus retain favorable relations with others. It is suggested that the woman maintain the slender vertical line and avoid the thick shadow in order that she may be popular, have lovers, and succeed in winning favor; that the man buy this garment or that in order to appear prosperous and be accepted by the smart social class; that one take this correspondence course or that in order to improve his speaking, develop his personality, increase his charm, and win influence over others. Many are the people who are advised to take the simple and easy soap-and-water route to beauty. We have it on good authority that South American women today boast of being fat because it is generally recognized that to be plump and rotund increases one's possibilities for marriage. For centuries the Chinese women bound their feet in order to meet the standards of beauty of their time.

There is much in our attitudes that suggests that people are motivated to a great extent by what this or that group thinks of them. And there is reason to believe that men have always responded so to their fellows. If it were not so, fashions, fads, and crazes would be impossible.

As people come in contact with each other more frequently in the modern world, and make numerous superficial contacts in which first appearances count, these factors are becoming increasingly important in social relationships. Consequently, people tend to be regulated more and more by fads, some of which reach epidemic proportions because they attract the following of the masses.

---

[8] Charles H. Cooley, *Human Nature and the Social Order*, p. 126.

Socialized Man Always Aware of the Group

Sometimes in our current tendency to deride man's gullibility for fads we are inclined to underestimate the fundamental importance of group influence. Actually, man always has one eye cocked on the group of spectators about him. The Apostle Paul probed deeply when, thinking of Abraham, Isaac, Jacob, Moses, and all the patriarchs of faith who had gone before, said, "Wherefore seeing we also are compassed about with so great a crowd of witnesses . . ." [9] The limits of a man's consciousness of his group are set only by the limits of his understanding of the past history of the race and of his present contacts with human beings, for one who knows history has all of the prestige of the past bearing down upon him, and one who knows many people is faced with the responsibility of measuring up, to some extent at least, to their expectations. No man ever fully escapes this consciousness as long as he maintains his human nature. The more prominent a figure he becomes, the more fully is he conscious of the multitude of witnesses.

In countries where ancestor worship prevails, consciousness of the surveillance of the ancestral group is a constant source of control. Death-bed promises even in our culture may control a living person for life. Tradition and custom, most of which is a detritus of those who once composed the social group but who are now dead, keeps a close watch on society. In some cases the dead hand of the past may be the beacon light, pointing out the safe way ahead; in others it may point toward the dark labyrinths of a dismal past.

Conscience the Voice of the Group rather than an Inner Voice

In the past men have had much to say about conscience. Actually, conscience, that inner goad with which man is endowed, on closer analysis proves to be the voice of the social group rather than some mysterious voice originating in the secret recesses of the soul. One can develop a sort of conscience even in a dog. Having been taught to do a thing in a certain way, he soon learns through scolding or punishment that to do otherwise is wrong, and eventually he reaches the point where he will cower, put his

---

[9] Hebrews 12:1.

tail between his legs, or perhaps lie down and whine, when he has violated the regulation established by his master. This is no less conscience than that which man possesses, although man is born with a long memory and capacity for sympathy, suggestibility, social feeling, and reflection, all of which make possible the more complete development of the conscience.

If there were no social taboos there would be no consciences. Conscience begins in the child when he is first confronted with prohibitions. Teaching him that he must not commit certain actions sets up for him a standard of behavior. When he violates the standard, the realization that he is the object of group disapproval leaves him with a sense of guilt.

What we ordinarily think of as the pangs of conscience are feelings of remorse that come as a result of a realization of having betrayed some person or group, who retaliate by looking upon us with disfavor. In this sense conscience becomes a powerful factor in social control, and is essentially social in that it operates in connection with social groups and social values. The extent to which it actually proves socially effective depends upon the standards that the individual has developed.

In the human being it is possible to develop powers of perception of good and bad to a remarkable degree. In fact, it is possible to develop within the individual a conscience that will fit any group of which he becomes a member. He may have as many consciences as there are groups whose codes he accepts.

An interesting historical example is that of Apostle Paul, who after his conversion testified, "I have lived in all good conscience until this day." [10] That was in "all good" Jewish conscience which led him to enter homes of the Christians "hailing men and women committing them to prison." [11] After becoming a Christian he turned about-face and directed all of his energy to forwarding Christianity. In the light of this new conscience he became the most dynamic figure in the history of the early church.[12] He had accepted the standard of a new social group.

The difficulties of developing and maintaining a good conscience today have multiplied because most people live at various times in groups with diverse standards. This is especially

[10] Acts 23:1.
[11] Acts 8.
[12] Acts 22; 26:9, 10; I Timothy 1:13.

true in urban society, where the child frequently alternates between the family, the gang, the school, and other groups in the community beyond the family setting. In such a situation the child frequently develops no rigid conscience, or, if he acquires one, it will probably be that of the group which means the most to him. It is not amazing then, that in areas characterized by delinquency and crime, where the gangster has the highest status in the community, the child often emulates the criminal group and frequently takes over the conscience of the delinquent. It is simply an indication that this group means more to him and that he has accepted its evaluation of life and experience at face value. In so doing he develops a hatred for the larger group, an animosity for the ordinary codes, and acquires the traits of a gangster. What he considers bad is what the gang considers bad, and their codes consider bad such things as squealing on a mate, being yellow, and failing to live up to the gang standards of heroism, courage, and loyalty. Those who would understand the nature of any type of crime or delinquent behavior must understand the nature of these patterns which pervade certain social classes and community areas and become incorporated in human nature as it develops in such areas.

One of the clearest analyses of this basic factor in the crime patterns of American life has been made by Tannenbaum. The paragraph which follows clearly enunciates his philosophy:

. . . The criminal differs from the rest of his fellows only in the sense that he has learned to respond to the stimuli of a very small and specialized group; but that group must exist or the criminal could not exist. In that respect he is like the mass of men, living a certain kind of life with the kind of companions that make that life possible.[13]

Tannenbaum has also suggested that the dramatization in police courts of a youth's first crime gives him a new conception of himself, "a new looking-glass-self picture" of himself, if you will. Because of the attention he receives he may develop an altogether exaggerated notion of the importance of his new role and of the status accompanying it.

What happens in the case of the delinquent and criminal

---

[13] Frank W. Tannenbaum, *Crime and the Community*, Boston, 1938, p. 22. By permission of Ginn and Company.

happens in the case of all individuals. They absorb the standards and patterns, and consequently develop the conscience, of the particular group or groups which make up their social world. That they have the power to choose between these patterns one need not deny. Within limits they can select. What they select probably will depend on what interests them most, and what interests them most probably will depend upon a number of factors, not the smallest of which will be the degree of pleasure and satisfaction received from group relationships. If the family brings the child the most pleasure and satisfaction, he absorbs the patterns of the family; if the gang, then the patterns of the gang; if the school group or the church group, then it is their standards he chooses. In a world of conflicting patterns, human nature becomes complex, and conscience becomes perverse. One cannot be susceptible to all patterns; he cannot respond fully to the standards of different groups that are at variance with one another.

Thus, even human consciences are made, not born, and the processes involved in their formation are the same, whether in the making of a priest or of a gambler. Both types represent human nature, but the moulding process has been brought about by different sets of group influences.

Social Expectancy

Few except those who try to analyze experience and delve beneath the surface, recognize that underlying much behavior is the desire to measure up to the expectation of members of the social group or groups with which one is in contact at a given time. All of us have had the experience of having been observed when we thought we were alone. When it dawns on us that we are in the presence of others we immediately check back over our previous conduct, to see whether it has been socially acceptable. This is evidence that we expect ourselves to act differently in the group than in isolation. The factor of social expectancy in motivation is a powerful influence in shaping the activities of every person. Consider, for instance, the scientist. He is willing to endure years of labor in comparative seclusion from the world, denying himself the ordinary rewards that come from leisurely living, so that finally he may produce a work which will meet the expectations of his colleagues. Once he has established himself, he knows what they expect of him and governs himself accordingly so as not to fall below their standards.

In a lesser way each of us is deeply concerned with the effect of our behavior on certain groups. We try to measure up to what these groups expect of us, or perhaps we try to exceed their expectations and in this way increase our status.

Cooley incorporated this factor of social expectation into his concept of a "looking-glass self," the "looking-glass self" being the picture of ourselves that is reflected from the social groups with which we mingle.[14] Our estimate of our own ability, status, and rating is formed from the image reflected by our social groups. We have no other way of knowing ourselves. Self-respect is, in the final analysis, the respect we win from our group or groups. Success, likewise, is other people's evaluation of us. We accept their values, and because all of us are primarily interested in at least one group's evaluation of us, we tend to center our attention and energy on the role or roles that this particular group expects us to play.

Denison has expressed Cooley's concept in a very interesting manner, stating that characters of widely divergent types are produced in miraculous fashion by giving men different concepts of themselves.[15] He cites the example of two men, one of whom has been taught to think of himself as a Roman nobleman, the other to regard himself as a slave. The one may consider it his duty to put the other to death if he disobeys orders; the other develops a view of life which makes it wrong for him to rebel, even against brutality. He comes to accept the idea that he is a chattel, a piece of property of the nobleman.

One might make a similar analogy of the condition which existed in the South before the Civil War. Slave and master came to hold different ideas of themselves because of the system of relationships which had become established by custom and was accepted as the tradition of the culture. One sees this prin-. ciple in operation in many situations in contemporary society, although less so than in a society where caste principles are in operation, and where great gulfs are fixed between the social classes.

The point is that any individual comes to get a "looking-glass-

[14] Charles H. Cooley, Human Nature and the Social Order, pp. 184–185.
[15] J. H. Denison, The Enlargement of Personality, pp. 45, 46.

self" picture of himself in terms of his life experience. He learns to accept the group's evaluation of himself and to act accordingly. These reflected pictures of his personality penetrate into the very essence of his life, so that in order to maintain the particular view of himself to which he has been accustomed he may even resort to extreme measures.

Only recently has the ethnologist described the play of opinion in primitive society. Everywhere in savagery it is potent. The Eskimo can not withstand the ridicule of his fellows. No more can the manly Plains Indian, who can face without flinching the arrows of the enemy but not the ridicule of fellow-tribesmen. Among the Comanche, "public opinion, the sentiment of the camp, elevates those specially distinguished in war to the highest position of power." Among the Winnebago, the only restrictive measures which the chief or the community could adopt were disapproval, jeers, and temporary loss of social standing and prestige, but these were usually sufficient to hold the recalcitrant in check. So it is among primitive peoples in Africa, Australia, and the islands of the Pacific. Public insult will drive a Trobriand Islander to suicide, for neither man nor woman can stand accusation in the hearing of the entire community. Public opinion, by insults or ostracism, drives a guilty individual to suicide. Malinowski cites a case in which a girl, insulted in public, put on festive dress and ornamentation, wailed from the top of a palm tree, and jumped to her death. An almost identical case of suicide by a lad is cited by the same author.[16]

During the stock market crash in 1929, many prominent men committed suicide rather than face the mortification involved in having their groups know of their failures. They visualized in advance the snubs of former friends, the loss of the respect of those who had looked upon them as successful men, and who had emulated them as their superiors.

Williams describes the strenuous effort of individuals to save their social face.[17] He suggests that this is the key to modern behavior, that men are constantly struggling to attain feelings of worth according to their own evaluations of worth. They can sense worth only as other people recognize it in them.

[16] W. D. Wallis, An Introduction to Sociology, p. 192. By permission of F. S. Crofts and Company.
[17] Whiting Williams, Mainsprings of Men, pp. 146, 147.

Therefore, the desire to "count," to avoid the abyss of being disregarded, presses upon their minds. In order to have a realization that we are important, we must actually see ourselves in the eyes of some few or many who respond favorably to us. The mainsprings of men lie in these two forces: (1) the desire to be recognized as worthwhile, and (2) the satisfaction of encouraging approvals and opposing disapprovals of others who share our experience.

The Habit of Conformity

The ape and the human infant make more sounds than the human adult.[18] The human adult has long been subject to restraint. Conformity to social patterns requires that many sounds his vocal apparatus is capable of making never be uttered. The young child early learns to eliminate those sounds not approved by others. He learns to modulate the tone of his voice, to control it so that it is pleasing to others and so that it conforms to their ideas of proper sound. The type of sounds used differ from society to society, but within a given one conformity is the rule. Anthropologists report that members of a primitive tribe rolled on the ground in fits of laughter when they heard one of our most solemn pieces of music played on the phonograph.

What is true of the use of the voice is true of much of social action. Throughout the entire gamut of our social experience we are limited in our action by habits of conformity. The young animal soon learns that nonconformity is painful, that certain types of behavior will bring down wrath upon his head or place him in disgrace, that conventional dress must be worn to fit the occasion, that some mannerisms are sanctioned, others condemned. In this way the nonconforming child eventually becomes the conforming adult, interested in seeing that his behavior is similar to that of the group around him.

Fortunately, though, social control is not effective enough to assure the full conformity of each individual to every accepted social pattern. If it were, there would be no revolt, no change, no progress. Every now and then individuals galling under the yoke of conformity rebel, overthrow the existing social regula-

---

[18] Wolfgang Köhler, *The Mentality of Apes*. Thus, whatever capacities man may have by original nature for being a nonconforming animal, he tends to lose in the socializing processes by which human nature is made.

tions, and blaze new trails. Human nature, primarily because it is learned and not organic, is capable of existing under a great diversity of group patterns, and of being modeled to fit changing patterns of control.

CONCLUSION

From original nature, that nature with which man is born and which provides him with capacities for development and regulation, human nature is constructed. The social group for ages has been at the building of a regulative structure. From a social-psychological viewpoint, original nature becomes human nature only after group consciousness has developed. In fact, human nature consists first of all in social realization. When the child reaches the point where he is conscious of the group as a separate entity, and when he becomes responsive to it, he is then socialized, he is human, he has acquired human nature. The process of becoming human begins early and probably never ceases.

Important traits of human nature that have a bearing on social control are social consciousness, identification of the self with the group, constant awareness of the group, conscience, social expectancy, and the habit of conformity.

SELECTED REFERENCES

Allport, Floyd H., *Social Psychology*. Houghton Mifflin Company, Boston, 1924.

Bellamy, Edward, *Equality*. D. Appleton-Century Company, New York, 1897.

Bernard, L. L., *Instinct*. Henry Holt and Company, New York, 1924.

Bernard, L. L., *Introduction to Social Psychology*. Henry Holt and Company, New York, 1926.

Bogardus, E. S., *Fundamentals of Social Psychology*, second edition. D. Appleton-Century Company, New York, 1931.

Brown, Lawrence Guy, *Social Psychology*. McGraw-Hill Book Company, New York, 1934.

Cooley, Charles H., *Human Nature and the Social Order*, chaps. 2 and 10. Charles Scribner's Sons, New York, 1922.

Cooley, Charles H., "Social Consciousness," *American Journal of Sociology*, vol. 12, pp. 675–687. March, 1907.

Cooley, Charles H., *Social Organization*, chaps. 1 and 2. Charles Scribner's Sons, New York, 1909.

Cooley, Charles H., "The Roots of Social Knowledge," *American Journal of Sociology*, vol. 32, pp. 59–79. July, 1926.

Davis, Barnes, and Others, *An Introduction to Sociology*, (selection by L. L. Bernard), pp. 468–475. D. C. Heath and Company, New York, 1931.

Denison, J. H., *The Enlargement of Personality*, chap. 3. Charles Scribner's Sons, New York, 1930.

Faris, Ellsworth, "The Nature of Human Nature," *American Journal of Sociology*, vol. 32, pp. 15–29. 1926.

Finney, Ross L., "The Unconscious Social Mind," *Journal of Applied Sociology*, pp. 357–359, 361. March–April, 1926.

Ginzburg, Benjamin, "Hypocrisy as a Pathological Symptom," *International Journal of Ethics*, vol. 32, pp. 164 ff. January, 1922.

Heill, Clark L., *Hypnosis and Suggestion*. D. Appleton-Century Company, New York, 1933.

Köhler, Wolfgang, *The Mentality of Apes*. Harcourt, Brace and Company, New York, 1925.

La Piere, Richard, and Farnsworth, Paul, *Social Psychology*, chap. 3 and part 2. McGraw-Hill Book Company, New York, 1936.

Lippmann, Walter, *Public Opinion*. The Macmillan Company, New York, 1932.

Ogburn, W. F., *Social Change*, part 1, section 3–5. The Viking Press, Inc., New York, 1923.

Ross, Edward Alsworth, *Principles of Sociology*, first revision, chaps. 7, 38, and 54. D. Appleton-Century Company, New York, 1930.

Tarde, Gabriel, *The Laws of Imitation*, translated by Elsie Clews Parsons. Henry Holt and Company, New York, 1903.

Williams, J. M., *Principles of Social Psychology*. Alfred A. Knopf Inc., New York, 1922.

Williams, Whiting, *Mainsprings of Men*, pp. 125, 146–147. Charles Scribner's Sons, New York, 1925.

Wissler, Clark, *Man and Culture*, part 3. Thomas Y. Crowell Company, New York, 1923.

Young, Kimball, *Social Psychology*. F. S. Crofts and Company, New York, 1930.

CHAPTER 5

THE ROLE OF THE GROUP IN SOCIALIZATION

THE PRIORITY OF GROUP PATTERNS

In social experience, society precedes the individual by millenniums. As we have seen, the human being when born is one of the most helpless creatures, but he is a highly flexible, variable, and plastic organism. Because human experience is conserved for all generations, society is filled with patterns which the individual must absorb. The attitudes and habits of one generation become the traditions and customs of the next, and though there is not the uniformity of instinct found among animals, there is the efficiency of group-wide practices which are the product of generations of experience.

Every child faces this imposing world of social groups with a fixed pattern of life. The infant is placed in these groups and must learn to adopt their manners. Because of this fundamental fact, the social group has within it the power to build attitudes and habits which in themselves will constitute the entire basis for his social behavior throughout his lifetime. Russell Gordon Smith has dramatically stated:

. . . beyond your flesh and blood are ten million years of biological evolution, ten million years of adaptations, survivals, and selections, ten million years during which the germinal bases of your essential self have been slowly and inexorably fashioned. And beyond your mind—that baffling complex of sensations, perceptions, emotions, feelings—that mysterious unity of wishing, aiming, purposing, resisting, striving, competing, which some psychologists still vaguely name the ego, is an incredibly vast and complicated and ancient social heritage from which practically the entire content of your mind has been unconsciously derived.

. . . Nine-tenths of all you do or say or think or feel from the time you get up in the morning until the time you go to bed at night is done and said and thought and felt, not in independent self-expression, but in uncritical, unconscious conformity with rules, regulations, group habits, standards, codes, styles, and sanctions that were in existence long before you were born. You wear clothes of a certain cut not because your individuality impels you to, but because that cut is in style. You take off your hat to a lady of your acquaintance, not because your ego demands it, but because the social code prescribes it . . . You praise this man and denounce that one; you like this man and dislike that one; you accept this article of religious faith and reject that—and, if you think about these evaluations and preferences, you will be forced to the conclusion that practically all your standards and criteria have been socially created.[1]

The Group Defines Life Situations

W. I. Thomas, in a penetrating analysis, shows very clearly the utility and the significance of the fact that the group defines for the individual those situations which he most commonly meets. The child, being born into a group which has already worked out definitions for these situations, finds himself accepting the definitions as they are presented to him by the family and the community. Thomas says:

One of the most important powers gained during the evolution of animal life is the ability to make decisions from within instead of having them imposed from without. Very low forms of life do not make decisions, as we understand this term, but are pushed and pulled by chemical substances, heat, light, etc., much as iron filings are attracted or repelled by a magnet. They do tend to behave properly in given conditions—a group of small crustaceans will flee as in a panic if a bit of strychnia is placed in the basin containing them, and will rush toward a drop of beef juice like hogs crowding around swill—but they do this as an expression of organic affinity for the one substance and repugnance for the other, and not as an expression of choice or "free will." There are, so to speak, rules of behavior but these represent a sort of fortunate mechanistic adjustment of the organism to typically recurring situations, and the organism cannot change the rule.

On the other hand, the higher animals, and above all man, have

---

[1] Reprinted from Smith: *Fugitive Papers*, by permission of Columbia University Press.

the power of refusing to obey a stimulation which they followed at an earlier time. Response to the earlier stimulation may have had painful consequences and so the rule or habit in this situation is changed. We call this ability the power of inhibition, and it is dependent on the fact that the nervous system carries memories or records of past experiences. At this point the determination of action no longer comes exclusively from outside sources but is located within the organism itself.

Preliminary to any self-determined act of behavior there is always a stage of examination and deliberation which we may call the definition of the situation. And actually not only concrete acts are dependent on the definition of the situation, but gradually a whole life-policy and the personality of the individual himself follow from a series of such definitions.

But the child is always born into a group of people among whom all the general types of situation which may arise have already been defined and corresponding rules of conduct developed, and where he has not the slightest chance of making his definitions and following his wishes without interference. Men have always lived together in groups. Whether mankind has a true herd instinct or whether groups are held together because this has worked out to advantage is of no importance. Certainly the wishes in general are such that they can be satisfied only in a society. But we have only to refer to the criminal code to appreciate the variety of ways in which the wishes of the individual may conflict with the wishes of society. And the criminal code takes no account of the many unsanctioned expressions of the wishes which society attempts to regulate by persuasion and gossip.[2]

MENTAL CONCEPTS ARE LIMITED BY SOCIAL DEFINITION

In the development of mental concepts the group always plays a major part, for a person, after he acquires language, defines class objects chiefly in terms of what the group conceives them to be rather than in terms of his own sense impressions. This is natural because any individual's sensory experience is far more limited than that of the group. He therefore comes to define beauty in terms of the patterns of his time, and music in terms of the particular definitions that his own social group uses. Thick lips

---

[2] W. I. Thomas, The Unadjusted Girl, pp. 41–44. By permission of Little, Brown and Company.

may be considered graceful in one tribe, slender ankles in another. The rhythm of the tom-tom may define the highest type of aesthetic appreciation in one group, pipe organ music in another.

The social significance of mental concepts to social behavior is recognized by Walter Lippmann [3] who says: "For the most part, we do not first see, and then define, we define first and then see." Mental sets, or stereotypes, tend to limit what may enter our mind in the way of sense impressions, for we filter them, accepting only the patterns of our social group, thus narrowing our mental perspective. Having been told about the world before we have experience with it, we develop preconceptions which make us unaware of all except the selected portions of the panorama of life which pass before our vision. Those things which we have been taught to see by our social group are interpreted by us in terms of our existing mental sets. Lippmann takes the position that these stereotypes are a decided asset in that they tend to simplify our world by helping us to find unified meaning in our own personality and giving us a philosophy of life that will provide some degree of certainty and uniformity. By helping us exclude the new and the distasteful they enable us to absorb quickly that which already coincides with our mental patterns.

The significance of this analysis from the standpoint of control is that the group plays the deciding role in the development of our mental sets by confining our mental horizon.

The Group Limits Individual Experience

With a somewhat different emphasis, but embodying the same general idea, Frederick Teggart elaborates on the effect of the group in limiting sense impressions:

. . . if we consider the processes manifested in the fixity and persistence of idea-systems and ways of doing things, no one can be at a loss to discern the influence upon himself of the community in which he has grown up. From the beginning of life each one of us has been subjected to a discipline by those surrounding us which has determined and defined the avenues open to us for self-assertion or individual purposive activity. Again, each one of us is conscious of explicit restrictions in mental activity due to the particular selection of information and ideas which has been imparted to him at

---

[3] Walter Lippmann, *Public Opinion*, pp. 81–91.

the outset of his career; the mental equipment which each one receives represents only a limited selection from the whole body of knowledge at the command of the group, and yet this selection, which under any other circumstances whatever would have been different, has been, and must remain, a dominant factor in our lives.[4]

The social group, by virtue of its priority of experience, shields us from certain impressions and exposes us to others, thus very effectively restricting our experience. We become familiar with the accepted attitudes, ideas, standards, and patterns.

No man can comprehend the world in its entirety, so our social group takes care that we see it through its vision. As Ruth Benedict has so adequately expressed it in her analysis of the power of custom in primitive and modern societies, "No man ever looks at the world with pristine eyes." [5] Rather, he sees it through the spectacles of his group members, for their vested interests make it of vital concern to them that the infant view this world from their perspective. Gangster society desires its youth to be reared properly according to the underworld code, which means that they learn to outwit those who represent a different code. In a monastery, vision is focused on those ideals designed to produce a generation of the holy.

THE CHILD ABSORBS THE LIFE PATTERNS OF HIS GROUP [6]

A child born and raised among the Hottentots will acquire the habits, the attitudes, the morals of the Hottentots. If a boy is brought up among head hunters, he will likewise become a head hunter. If he is born and bred in the United States, he will take on the characteristics and peculiarities that distinguish the American. Of course, there is a greater variety of customs and other educational influences among the people of the United States than among the Hottentots or head hunters, but that does not change the principle involved. Furthermore, it does not make much difference whether the child is of the same stock as the people among whom he is raised or not, he will become one of them just the same. There

---

[4] Frederick Teggart, *The Processes of History*, pp. 153–154. By permission of the Yale University Press.

[5] Ruth Benedict, "The Science of Custom," *Century Magazine*, April, 1929, pp. 641–649.

[6] From Hermann Hilmer, "The Outlook for Civilization," *The Pedagogical Seminary*, September, 1924, pp. 247, 248. By permission of the Journal Press.

may be differences in racial endowments, although we are not so sure now about the once generally assumed inborn superiority of certain races. But even if such superiority exists, it would merely mean that the child of a superior race, if brought up among inferior people, say, the Hottentots, might develop into a more efficient Hottentot, a kind of super-Hottentot perhaps, but he would still be a Hottentot.

If now we should make a list of all the beliefs, habits, morals, and institutions of which we have a record as existing and having existed, we will find that at one time or another almost any conceivable practice has been tolerated and even glorified and also been condemned and suppressed. This bewildering diversity of morals and institutions admits of but one explanation, namely, that the decisive factors in molding our conduct are not unchangeable attributes of human nature, but habits acquired under the influence of environment.

"Nothing's improper somewhere," says Forbes, writing in *Collier's*.[7] Propriety is a matter of geography. Perhaps stating it more accurately, propriety is a matter of group boundaries, each society possessing its own standards of decorum.

THE DETERMINISTIC NATURE OF GROUP PATTERNS

There is determinism in the patterns which the group develops in the personality of its members, a determinism as fatalistic as heredity itself, and also as useful. As Edward Sapir expresses it,

. . . many things that an individual does and thinks and feels may be looked upon not merely from the standpoint of the forms of behavior that are proper to himself as a biological organism but from the standpoint of a generalized mode of conduct that is imputed to society rather than to the individual, though the personal genesis of conduct is of precisely the same nature, whether we choose to call the conduct individual or social. It is impossible to say what an individual is doing unless we have tacitly accepted the essentially arbitrary modes of interpretation that social tradition is constantly suggesting to us from the very moment of our birth . . .

No matter where we turn in the field of social behavior, men and women do what they do, and cannot help but do, not merely be-

---

[7] Rosita Forbes, "Nothing's Improper Somewhere," *Collier's*, vol. 78, September 18, 1926, pp. 22 ff.

cause they are built thus and so, or possess such and such differences of personality, or must needs adapt to their immediate environment in such and such a way in order to survive at all, but very largely because they have found it easiest and aesthetically most satisfactory to pattern their conduct in accordance with more or less clearly organized forms of behavior which no one is individually responsible for, which are not clearly grasped in their true nature, and which one might almost say are as self-evidently imputed to the nature of things . . .[8]

GROUPS DIFFER IN THEIR DEFINITIONS

Societies may differ widely in the definitions of right and wrong which they accept. In our time it is generally recognized, at least in many of the educated circles, that morality must be defined in relative terms. One who has studied history carefully or who is familiar with the comparative literature of anthropology, is driven to the conclusion that what one group considers a crime, another group may consider a virtue. The definition of sin varies with both the geographical and social boundaries.

Such a view is consistent with the general position already developed respecting the nature of man and his mental processes. If man is born without knowledge, as John Locke enunciated, the next logical conclusion is that whatever he gets in the way of rules to guide him through life must come from the social group of his time and place. Consistent with this theory then is the statement of Locke that:

. . . Virtue and vice are names pretended and supposed everywhere to stand for actions in their own nature right and wrong: and as far as they really are so applied, they so far are coincident with the divine law above mentioned. But yet, whatever is pretended, this is visible, that these names, virtue and vice, in the particular instances of their application, through the several nations and societies of men in the world, are constantly attributed only to such actions as in each country and society are in reputation or discredit. Nor is it to be thought strange, that men everywhere should give the name of virtue to those actions, which amongst them are judged praiseworthy;

---

[8] Edward Sapir, "The Unconscious Patterning of Behavior in Society," *The Unconscious; A Symposium*, pp. 118, 119, 141. By permission of F. S. Crofts and Company.

and call that vice, which they account blamable: since otherwise they would condemn themselves, if they should think anything right, to which they allowed not commendation, anything wrong, which they let pass without blame. Thus the measure of what is everywhere called and esteemed virtue and vice is this approbation or dislike, praise or blame, which, by a secret and tacit consent, establishes itself in the several societies, tribes, and clubs of men in the world: whereby several actions come to find credit or disgrace amongst them, according to the judgment, maxims, or fashion of that place. For, though men uniting into politic societies, have resigned up to the public the disposing of all their force, so that they cannot employ it against any fellow-citizens any further than the law of the country directs: yet they retain still the power of thinking well or ill, approving or disapproving of the actions of those whom they live amongst, and converse with: and by this approbation and dislike they establish amongst themselves what they will call virtue and vice.

That this is the common measure of virtue and vice, will appear to any one who considers, that, though that passes for vice in one country which is counted a virtue, or at least not vice, in another, yet everywhere virtue and praise, vice and blame, go together. Virtue is everywhere, that which is thought praiseworthy; and nothing else but that which has the allowance of public esteem is called virtue. Virtue and praise are so united, that they are called often by the same name. . . .

If any one shall imagine that I have forgot my own notion of a law, when I make the law, whereby men judge of virtue and vice, to be nothing else but the consent of private men, who have not authority enough to make a law: especially wanting that which is so necessary and essential to a law, a power to enforce it: I think I may say, that he who imagines commendation and disgrace not to be strong motives to men to accommodate themselves to the opinions and rules of those with whom they converse, seems little skilled in the nature or history of mankind: the greatest part whereof we shall find to govern themselves chiefly, if not solely, by this *law of fashion*; and so they do that which keeps them in reputation with their company, little regard the laws of God, or the magistrate. The penalties that attend the breach of God's laws some, nay perhaps most men, seldom seriously reflect on: and amongst those that do, many, whilst they break the law, entertain thoughts of future reconciliation, and making their peace for such breaches. And as to the punishments due from the laws of the commonwealth, they frequently flatter themselves with the hopes of impunity. But no man escapes the punishment of their censure and dislike, who offends against the fashion and opinion of the company he keeps, and would recommend himself to. Nor is there one of ten thousand, who is stiff and insensible enough, to bear up under the constant dislike and condemnation of his own club. He must be of a strange and unusual constitution, who can content himself to live in constant disgrace and disrepute with his own particular society. Solitude many men have sought, and been reconciled to: but nobody that has the least thought or sense of a man about him, can live in society under the constant dislike and ill opinion of his familiars, and those he converses with. This is a burden too heavy for human sufferance: and he must be made up of irreconcilable contradictions, who can take pleasure in company, and yet be insensible of contempt and disgrace from his companions.[9]

This analysis, made more than one hundred and fifty years ago, seems quite modern and quite sociological in its interpretation, for it indicates very clearly that vice and virtue are matters of group definition. It also suggests the difficulties one must inevitably face if he dares run counter to his group's definitions of vice and virtue.

The Diversity of Definitions Within the Same Society

The analysis so far would seem to indicate that life patterns must necessarily be automatic, uniform, and universal within any group. In the broadest sense of the term this is true, but within any large society there are numerous groups, all of which embody the more general codes of the society, which also have certain varying codes of their own. And there are within any tribe or nation divergent groups that may be in conflict with the patterns of society at large. This certainly is true of groups that we consider vicious, delinquent, or criminal.

So, what may have seemed thus far to be a rather simple social picture is actually a rather complicated one, consisting of wheels within wheels, divisions and subdivisions, little social units, or-

---

[9] John Locke, An Essay Concerning Human Understanding, pp. 476–480. By permission of the Clarendon Press, Oxford.

ganizations, little societies, crowds, groups, cliques, and clans, all coming within the larger social entity, and all tending to diverge from the general pattern. This being true, every class has its ethics, every profession has its codes, every family has its life patterns which differ somewhat from those of the larger group. And if one wants to go further, every individual, because he does have the power to select from the patterns presented by his social groups, is able in his own personality to make a unique configuration of patterns, which prevent his being merely an automaton of a group, making him instead a distinct personality capable not only of being controlled, but also of controlling himself to some degree. Though he usually chooses to control himself in harmony with the patterns of those groups which mean most to him, he frequently may vary from these patterns, and even revolt.

MAN DEVELOPS AS MANY SOCIAL SELVES AS HE HAS GROUPS

The significance of man's numerous group attachments in the growth of this complex pattern of group control is evident in William James's notion of the effect of "club-opinion" upon the numerous social selves which each of us has developed.[10]

He advanced the thesis that man has as many social selves as there are individuals who recognize him, and that to wound any one of them is to injure the person himself, so conscious of these images is he. Actually these social selves tend to become classified according to distinct social groups, and those social selves which originate in the social groups about whose opinions the individual cares most are the ones which mean most to him. In his experience with various groups he tends to play up to them, to manifest a different self in each group. The youth may be passive and demure among parents and teachers but may swear and swagger in the gang. The parent likewise may be a different person to his children than he is to his employer or his friends. Frequently there is such a contrast in the social selves that one is afraid to let the people of one group know how he acts in another.

One of the most interesting and peculiar social selves that James describes is the one in the mind of the person who is in love. If this social self fails to get recognition, the individual

---

[10] William James, *The Principles of Psychology*, pp. 294–296.

is likely to fall into the deepest state of dejection. When it gets recognition "contentment passes all bounds."

According to his view, fame, honor, dishonor, good, and bad are simply names for social selves. Honor is really man's image as seen by his social set. Frequently notions of honor may compel one to perform deeds of great heroism such as those which a captain undertakes in the case of the sinking of his ship, or a doctor or a priest in an epidemic where he dares not give way to fear regardless of the cost of staying by his duty. Thus he shows that "club opinion" is one of the strongest forces in life.

EFFECT OF THE BIOLOGICAL COMPOSITION OF THE GROUP ON THE PROCESS OF CONTROL

The social composition of groups, especially the age and sex composition, has much to do with creating the dominating currents of influence within the social group, and consequently with the operation of the system of social control. Traditionally, frontier areas with a dominant male sex composition are characterized by a careless attitude toward life, a rugged hardiness which disregards comforts and refinements for the sake of profit, survival, or simply for the sake of being a man's man in a community where such behavior brings approbation.

Many studies could be cited that attest to this fact. The author's study, *Three Iron Mining Towns*, demonstrates that during the frontier period in the settlement of the Mesabi Iron Range in northern Minnesota from 1892 to 1900, the culture took on characteristics that reflected the dominant male sex ratio. Many of the usual community controls were lacking. Accident rates were excessive, and suicides were numerous because there were few controls to protect a man from his own vices. Prostitution was rife and was sanctioned by the community mores. In fact, until well past 1900, no control devices were developed in the community to regulate the activities of the prostitute or even the location of houses of prostitution. The harlot and the saloon-keeper both enjoyed a high social status, a fact which shows very definitely the absence of even the ordinary regulative devices, such as public condemnation. Gambling dens were a part of the accepted order of things; only when county or state officials swooped down for a raid was anything done about their regulation. Drunken brawls were numerous; onlookers surveyed them quite casually. Special occasions, such as election day, inevitably found a high percentage of the population reeling down the streets in an intoxicated condition. To a considerable extent, we may explain these low community standards in terms of the dominant male sex ratio and the almost complete absence of respectable women.

This evidence proves that a system of control very definitely may be affected by the social composition of the group. Likewise, age composition may determine the control devices which will operate in a community. The popularity of the Townsend plan and the extreme political pressure exercised in its favor in the West Coast states is largely a result of the abnormally high proportion of old people residing in these states.[11] In the nation the aged will constitute a pressure group of increasing importance during the next thirty years, one with which politicians will have to reckon. In communities where there are children, social regulations are much more numerous, much more prominent, and much more effectively enforced than in areas without children. Consider, for instance, the relative number of controls in the Hobohemia of the average city as compared to the number in the suburban residential district where families dwell.[12]

The importance of age as a factor in social control is to a large extent dependent on what the society, through its super-structure of customs and traditions, makes of age. Among some primitive peoples, for instance, social regulations center about the adolescent rites which mark the child's formal entrance into adulthood. These ceremonies initiate him into the system of control and responsibility that accompany maturity in his society; other societies make little of adolescence, having no elaborate initiation ceremonies.[13] Some societies venerate age; others kill those who are no longer productive.

---

[11] Paul H. Landis, "Selected Population Problems in the Western States in Relation to Agricultural Adjustment," *Proceedings of the Western Farm Economics Association, Ninth Annual Meeting, 1936*, shows that the three Pacific States have a higher proportion of people over 65 years of age than any other region of the United States.

[12] See Harvey W. Zorbaugh, *The Gold Coast and the Slum*, University of Chicago Press, 1929. It is true that in the slums there is little control of children, but factors other than age composition, such as immigrant maladjustment and community disorganization arising from mobility, bring this about.

[13] Margaret Mead's, *Coming of Age in Samoa*, gives an interesting account of the meaning of adolescence in Samoan culture.

Conclusion

That man lacks the necessary organic equipment from which a satisfactory social order can spontaneously arise was indicated by the materials in Chapter 3. That man is highly susceptible to influences of the social group has now been shown. In the hands of society, therefore, is placed the responsibility for seeing that the young organism is taken under disciplinary custody. We have seen that the individual, because of the ever-present surveillance of a social environment, its patterns invented by human beings themselves, becomes so completely tuned to the life of the group that he thinks chiefly in terms of group opinion. Numerous group pressures bear down on him, most of them trying to force him into a groove acceptable to society. In every culture there is a system of "ways" and "manners" which are approved and which "well-formed minds" learn to relish.[14]

It cannot be assumed that all individuals conform to these established "ways" and "manners." Every society has its outcasts, its degenerates, its rebels, its problem cases. No system of socialization is ever one hundred per cent effective.

SELECTED REFERENCES

Benedict, Ruth, "The Science of Custom," *Century Magazine*, vol. 117, pp. 641–649. April, 1929.

Brown, Lawrence Guy, *Social Psychology*. McGraw-Hill Book Company, New York, 1934.

Cooley, Charles H., *Social Organization*, chaps. 3 and 4. Charles Scribner's Sons, New York, 1909.

Forbes, Rosita, "Nothing's Improper Somewhere," *Colliers*, vol. 78, pp. 22 ff. September 18, 1926.

Finney, Ross L., "The Unconscious Social Mind," *Journal of Applied Sociology*, pp. 357–359, 361. March-April, 1926.

Ginzburg, Benjamin, "Hypocrisy as a Pathological Symptom," *International Journal of Ethics*, vol. 32, pp. 164 ff. January, 1922.

Hilmer, Hermann, "The Outlook for Civilization," *The Pedagogical Seminary*, pp. 247 ff. September, 1924.

James, William, *The Principles of Psychology*, pp. 294–296. Henry Holt and Company, New York, 1890.

---

[14] A. J. Nock, "Study in Manners," *American Mercury*, May, 1925, vol. 5, p. 82.

House, F. N., *The Range of Social Theory*, chap. 13. Henry Holt and Company, New York, 1929.

Landis, Paul H., *Three Iron Mining Towns: A Study in Cultural Change*, chap. 3. Edwards Brothers, Ann Arbor, 1938.

La Piere, Richard, and Farnsworth, Paul, *Social Psychology*, part 5. McGraw-Hill Book Company, New York, 1936.

Lippmann, Walter, *Public Opinion*. The Macmillan Company, New York, 1932.

Locke, John, *An Essay Concerning Human Understanding*, pp. 476–480. The Clarendon Press, Oxford, 1894.

MacIver, R. M., *Society*, chap. 3. Farrar and Rinehart, Inc., New York, 1937.

Mead, Margaret, *Coming of Age in Samoa*. William Morrow and Company, New York, 1928.

Nock, A. J., "Study in Manners," *American Mercury*, vol. 5, pp. 82 ff. May, 1925.

Ross, Edward Alsworth, *Social Control*, chap. 24. The Macmillan Company, New York, 1929.

Sapir, Edward, "The Unconscious Patterning of Behavior in Society," *The Unconscious; A Symposium*, pp. 91–142. F. S. Crofts and Company, New York, 1928.

Smith, Russell Gordon, *Fugitive Papers*, pp. 23 ff. Columbia University Press, New York, 1930.

Tannenbaum, Frank, *Crime and the Community*, part 1. Ginn and Company, Boston, 1938.

Teggart, Frederick J., *The Processes of History*, pp. 153–154. Yale University Press, New Haven, 1918.

Thomas, William I., *The Unadjusted Girl*. Little, Brown and Company, Boston, 1923.

CHAPTER 6

CULTURE AS A FACTOR IN SOCIALIZATION

Most of a society's experience crystallizes in its culture. The conventional behavior, if it long persists, becomes the customary behavior. Precedent, if long honored, becomes tradition. Approved behavior, if long sanctioned, finds a place in the mores, which are always well supported by rationalizations of group welfare. Those behavior patterns foreboding ill to the group become taboos—the mores of prohibition. Habits, widely practiced, become folkways which have continuity beyond the life span of the individual. So it is that those patterns of group behavior assumed to have utility are preserved, and come to form the bulwark of man's nonmaterial culture. Every group has its heritage of nonmaterial culture, a mold in which the unsuspecting human organism is cast.

CULTURE AS A PHASE OF GROUP EXPERIENCE

The term culture as used in the anthropological sense is synonymous with civilization, which consists of all traits made or modified by man. Culture may be classified into material culture, which consists essentially in man's tools in the broadest sense of the term, and nonmaterial culture, man's customs, which in the broad use of the term include all of the subjective patterns that are passed on as a part of the experience heritage of the race. The experience of man in the group is so completely interwoven with the culture of the group that it is almost impossible at certain points to distinguish the social from the cultural.[1]

---

[1] Controls growing out of the culture have been named cultural controls by Sanford Winston. See Culture and Human Behavior, pp. 198 ff. There is perhaps good reason for separating this realm of control from the social, but no attempt is made to distinguish rigidly between the two in this work. The writer has attempted a distinction between social and cultural change in another work, Three Iron Mining Towns, Chap. 16, also, in "Social Change and Social Interaction as Factors in Culture Change," The American Journal of Sociology, vol. 41, pp. 52–58, July, 1935.

In one sense culture is a by-product of group experience. It is what remains from man's inventiveness to be passed on to modify the behavior of future generations. It consists of tested experience which, because it has proven useful to the social group, is conserved for succeeding generations. Thus, etiquette on the nonmaterial side is conceived of as a pattern of propriety in the realm of eating. It consists of those mannerisms in refinement which come to be considered good form. On the material side, machines, because they have proven to be useful, are conserved in the culture, improved, and transmitted from generation to generation.

Man is so much a culture-building creature that group life functions almost entirely according to the established patterns. It is true that there is a level of natural behavior for man, but seldom, even on a strictly biological level, does behavior escape the modifications of cultural forms or cultural tools.

Material culture consists of man-made objects accumulated through the centuries, and within any society, constitutes the tools and conveniences by which the people live. This culture, by virtue of its very existence, tends to form the habits of the people and to shape conduct. In fact, this material structure provides the framework for the society's activities. The mores, customs, traditions, moral philosophies, and general codes of conduct tend to conform to the necessities of the material order. If the material structure is extremely complex it demands a great number of human adjustments, and requires fairly rigid control devices in order to keep the social traffic moving in an orderly manner. On the other hand, if the material structure is very simple, men move about freely without much direction. Codes are few. Restrictions are limited. In our society there is almost an infinite amount of law, ritual, custom, and symbolism built about the economic structure, which is one expression of our material culture. In simple societies the nonmaterial culture growing out of the economic structure is very limited, as is the material structure. The same would apply to government, religion, or whatever institutions the particular society has developed.

Culture, as the extensive literature on cultural anthropology shows, accounts for most of the organized behavior of man. To paraphrase Malinowski, culture is a large-scale molding-matrix, a gigantic conditioning apparatus, which in each generation produces a type of individual, and which in each generation is in turn being reshaped by its carriers.[2]

CONTINUITY OF CULTURE

Culture is of profound significance in social control because it gives continuity to human experience. It is a heritage rich with the learning of all peoples who are in the line of historical antecedents that preceded the given culture. Because man has the power to accumulate and store culture in memory and in writing, and because he has the power to transmit experience through the training of his offspring, experience has continuity. In fact, its lineage is as eternal as the lineage of the germ plasm itself. Culture differs in the respect that it is more variable than the germ plasm, but most important material inventions and most human customs, like the germ plasm, are rooted deeply in the past. Culture has so much continuity that some anthropologists hold that a cultural object, once invented, never dies. It always finds some method of transmission. This statement may be a little extreme, but many seemingly unimportant culture traits have been traced by cultural anthropologists to a remote past, indicating that at least the tendency of culture is to be continuous.

These facts have tremendous significance to the individual and to the group. The group has its patterns of life encased in the culture. The individual grows up in the cultural mold. He, as a member of society, after having absorbed the elements of his group's culture, and having become habituated to the manner of life it outlines, hands it down to his offspring. Because culture has continuity, human experience too has continuity—as much continuity as instinct provides in the animal kingdom, but based on an entirely different principle—a principle which permits greater variation, greater individuation, and which at the same time provides for sufficient mechanization to make life orderly.

CULTURE AS A MOLD FOR PERSONALITY

Man is civilized by culture. Civilization is in one sense a huge, artificial, man-made system of control. It is civilization that

---

[2] B. Malinowski, "Culture as a Determiner of Behavior," *Scientific Monthly*, November, 1936, pp. 440–449.

makes man human. It is civilization that does for man what nature has done in a more automatic but simple way for animals, making him an orderly, regulated, purposeful creature.

On the subjective side, personality becomes deeply woven into the cultural structure, so much so that in a real sense culture is but a projection of one's personality, or, stated from the reverse angle, the nonmaterial culture resides in the subjective attitudes, emotions, and ideals of the individual. One can understand the individual and the meaning of life to him only as he understands this identification of the individual with his culture patterns, and that problems of behavior, normal and abnormal, are a reflection of the interaction of the individual with this cultural structure. In fact, personality derives its meaning and integration from the culture.

CULTURE AS A TECHNIQUE OF ADJUSTMENT

Most creatures make rather automatic adjustments to the environment, having been prepared to do so by hereditary equipment. No man is enabled to make adjustments by native endowment.[3] Yet man makes more adjustments to the environment than any other creature. For the most part these adjustments are not individual, but rather are they racial adjustments which have been tried out through ages of experience, and recorded in the culture of man.

Man is a self-domesticating creature, his domestication having been accomplished through his culture. The "group definitions," to use Thomas' terminology, become a part of the permanent cultural structure of society. These definitions are man's method of adjustment to the social group. Similarly, on the material side man begins with tools, and eventually achieves the invention of machines, all of which are but techniques of adjustment.

A certain amount of individual adjustment is inescapable but much of the shock has been absorbed in that the race has provided the tools for adjustment through experience. The significance of this fact is vividly described by Kroeber,[4] who contrasts

---

[3] Refer again to Chapter 3.

[4] A. L. Kroeber, "The Super-Organic," Reprint, Sociological Press, Hanover, 1917; also "The Possibility of a Social Psychology," American Journal of Sociology, 1913, vol. 23, pp. 633 ff.

the adjustment of a bird and of man to the air. Birds obtained wings only by biological change, which according to accepted theories was through a process of organic change spanning centuries of time. Man, in order to take to the air, depended not upon biological change, but upon inventiveness, upon accumulating sufficient experience in the realm of mechanical invention to put together enough existing culture traits to compose a flying machine which would carry him into the air. Both adjustments accomplished the same end—the one by means of nature, the other by the artificial means of human invention. Probably man will never achieve the bird's perfection of flying, but yet he does have one advantage: he can vary the pattern of flying in a way no bird ever can. Man can keep on improving his techniques, and can readapt himself to different conditions because of his inventiveness. He has proven to be the most adaptable creature now living, inhabiting almost every temperature, altitude, and climatic zone. Why? Certainly not because he is particularly adaptable organically. He is not. But man, through inventiveness, can ease the shock of any problem of adaptation.

It is in the realm of culture that a large part of man's regulative machinery is developed and stored. It is through the cultural heritage that the patterns of life are established, in it that the disciplinary procedures, notions of authority, of the good life, of the socially proper come to reside. In a true sense it is the culture of a people that determines the system of social control which is effective with them. Even though the cultural heritage of every people is different, no people is without one.

The social habits of the individual perish with his death, but the habits of living which have become group-wide in practice never die. Sex taboos among human beings are as ancient as the experience of the race. True, being a product of human inventiveness, they vary with different groups, but all have them. No race of people will ever exist without them; and conversely no animal will ever possess them. A similar situation applies to every phase of human behavior. Control devices become imbedded in the cultural structure, and man, being a product of the culture, weaves his own experience out of the cultural strands, and when the weaving process is complete the red and beastly streaks of original nature have all but disappeared.

It is not our purpose here to discuss in detail various aspects of our own culture as it operates in social control. The remaining part of this chapter, by way of illustration, indicates how folkways and mores, the fairly constant subjective patterns of a society, operate in controlling the individual. We also show how custom comes to have authority among a people, illustrated by the experience of the Chinese, among whom certain customs have great antiquity and established sanctity. In later chapters other aspects of the cultural structure appear. In fact, when one discusses human institutions he is of necessity discussing some of the great cultural structures of contemporary society. The controlling aspects of some of our basic institutions are discussed in Part IV. In that section we also deal with science and technology and suggest the extent to which modern technological devices in our material culture are reflected in behavior patterns of the individual and consequently are influential in shaping conduct.

FOLKWAYS

Sumner first centered the attention of social scientists upon the importance of folkways in human experience. In his extensive work entitled *Folkways* he defined folkways as being those methods of behavior which have grown out of man's trial and error adjustments. The first problems of man were the obtaining of food, and protection. Through trial and error, he devised successful ways for supplying these basic needs of life. Such common ways of behavior indispensable to obtaining the fundamental necessities of life are the folkways.

The folkways provide a limitless number of signposts throughout society, guiding the individual of the given culture area to the accepted, practical, successful way of doing things. It is the folkways which dictate that a man tip his hat when he meets a lady, that he take off his hat in her presence, that when walking with her, he take the outside path. It is the folkways which provide the pattern for preparing the meal, for catching fish, for planting grain, and for growing crops.

The essentials of this world of patterns, infinitely complex, are mastered by us during our childhood, so that by the time we reach maturity our habit systems conform perfectly to the folkways. As long as we live in the same cultural environment these habits serve us very well for the routine phases of existence. They work so automatically that we are not conscious of them until we shift to another community, where an entirely different system of folkways may be in use. In this new environment our old set of habits suddenly becomes of no value, and we awaken to the fact that unconsciously our behavior has been regulated by numerous controls.

In the modern world applied science has replaced the more crude forms of trial and error adjustment. Our extensive system of machine technology has tended to replace many folkways with technicways.[5] The latter are discussed at length in another chapter.

Mores

The mores defined. Certain folkways, Sumner pointed out, take on peculiar significance, becoming identified with group welfare through a process of rationalization.[6] Folkways, as we have seen, are trial and error methods that have been worked out for making adjustments to life. But a tribe may come to feel that certain of these techniques of adjustment are imperative to group welfare, and that if they are violated the interests of the tribe will be jeopardized. When a folkway reaches such a state of development it becomes a part of the mores, or in other words, a part of the life philosophy of welfare of the tribe. At this stage it is no longer an individual matter whether the folkway be followed; the practice is made compulsory. Or in the case of negative mores, the taboos, avoidance of a practice is made compulsory. The mores in general are the essence of all that is considered moral in a society. There is a great body of custom which we identify, and which all peoples identify with group welfare. Monogamy in our society is not a matter of individual inclination, but is associated with the moral welfare of the group, that is, it is in the mores. Any violation is a challenge to the foundations of domestic order. Numerous such folkways come to embody the idea of group welfare, and as mores become compulsory.

---

[5] Howard W. Odum, "Notes on Technicways in Contemporary Society," *American Sociological Review*, vol. 2, pp. 236–246. Parts of this article are reproduced in Chapter 18.

[6] W. G. Sumner, *Folkways*, pp. 59–60.

The mores are "right."

At every turn we find new evidence that the mores can make anything right. What they do is that they cover a usage in dress, language, behavior, manners, etc., with the mantle of current custom, and give it regulation and limits within which it becomes unquestionable. The limit is generally a limit of toleration. Literature, pictures, exhibitions, celebrations, and festivals are controlled by some undefined, and probably undefinable, standard of decency and propriety, which sets a limit of toleration on the appeals to fun, sensuality, and various prejudices. In regard to all social customs, the mores sanction them by defining them and giving them form. Such regulated customs are etiquette. The regulation by the mores always gives order and form, and thus surrounds life with limits within which we may and beyond which we may not pursue our interests (e.g., property and marriage). Horseplay and practical jokes have been tolerated, at various times and places, at weddings. They require good-natured toleration, but soon run to excess and may become unendurable. The mores set the limits or define the disapproval. The wedding journey was invented to escape the "jokes." The rice and old shoes will soon be tabooed. The mores fluctuate in their prescriptions. If the limits are too narrow, there is an overflow into vice and abuse, as was proved by seventeenth-century puritanism in England. If the limit is too remote, there is no discipline, and the regulation fails of its purpose. Then a corruption of manners ensues. In the cases now to be given we shall see the power of the mores to give validity to various customs. The cases are all such that we may see in them sanction and currency given to things which seem to us contrary to simple and self-evident rules of right; that is, they are contrary to the views now inculcated in us by our own mores as axiomatic and beyond the need of proof.[7]

The unconscious assimilation of the mores.

The mores come down to us from the past. Each individual is born into them as he is born into the atmosphere, and he does not reflect on them, or criticize them any more than a baby analyzes the atmosphere before he begins to breathe it. Each one is subjected to the influence of the mores, and formed by them, before he is capable of reasoning about them.

---

[7] W. G. Sumner, *op. cit.*, pp. 521, 522. By permission of Ginn and Company.

. . . We learn the mores as unconsciously as we learn to walk and eat and breathe. The masses never learn how we walk, and eat, and breathe, and they never know any reason why the mores are what they are. The justification of them is that when we wake to consciousness of life we find them facts which already hold us in the bonds of tradition, custom, and habit. The mores contain embodied in them notions, doctrines, and maxims, but they are facts. They are in the present tense. They have nothing to do with what ought to be, will be, may be, or once was, if it is not now.

A society is never conscious of its mores until it comes in contact with some other society which has different mores, or until, in higher civilization, it gets information by literature. The latter operation, however, affects only the literary classes, not the masses, and society never consciously sets about the task of making mores. In the early stages, mores are elastic and plastic; later they become rigid and fixed. They seem to grow up, gain strength, become corrupt, decline, and die, as if they were organisms. The phases seem to follow each other by an inherent necessity, and as if independent of the reason and will of the men affected, but the changes are always produced by a strain towards better adjustment of the mores to conditions and interests of the society, or of the controlling elements in it. A society does not record its mores in its annals, because they are to it unnoticed and unconscious. When we try to learn the mores of any age or people we have to seek our information in incidental references, allusions, observations of travelers, etc. Generally works of fiction, drama, etc., give us more information about the mores than historical records. It is very difficult to construct from the Old Testament a description of the mores of the Jews before the captivity. It is also very difficult to make a complete and accurate picture of the mores of the English colonies in North America in the seventeenth century. The mores are not recorded for the same reason that meals, going to bed, sunrise, etc., are not recorded, unless the regular course of things is broken.[8]

The Authority of Custom

Few of us realize the importance of custom as a factor in social control. Because it is so commonplace in our experience, we are unconscious of its influence. It envelops us so completely that

---

[8] W. G. Sumner, *op. cit.*, pp. 76–79. By permission of Ginn and Company.

we become a part of it. Ruth Benedict expressed the idea exactly when she said:

. . . No man ever looks at the world with pristine eyes. He sees it edited by a definite set of customs and institutions and ways of thinking. Even in his philosophical probings he cannot go behind these stereotypes; his very concepts of the true and the false will still have reference to the structure of his particular traditional customs . . .

. . . In any study of behavior it is these cultural patternings (customs) that turn out to be compulsive, not any original instincts with which we are born equipped. Even the basic emotions of fear and love and rage by the time they have been shaped over the different cultural lasts are well-nigh unrecognizable. Is there a jealousy of the mate innate in our sexual organization? Perhaps, but it will not dictate behavior except according to a cultural permit. Over a large part of the world, the woman is aggrieved if her husband does not take other wives—it may be to aid her in the duties of the household, or to relieve her of child-bearing, or to make plain her husband's social importance. And in other parts of the world, the male's virtues of generosity and of dignity are chiefly summed up in his practice of sharing his wife, and his calm acceptance of her desertion. Is there a maternal instinct? It will always be operative according to the conventions of the group. If there is great emphasis upon rank, women may voluntarily kill their children to raise their own status, as among the Natchez, or the Polynesian Tonga. If there is a pattern of seemingly meaningless adoption, most families will place their infants in other households, sometimes assigning them before birth. And how often have different apologists tried to give reasons for infanticide, when all the reasons they list are just as operative outside as within the region where this cultural compulsion rests upon the women.

Man evolves always elaborate traditional ways of doing things, great superstructures of the most varying design, and without very striking correlations with the underpinnings on which they must each and all eventually rest. It is only in a fundamental and non-spectacular sense that these superstructures are conditioned by their foundation in man's original endowment. And it is the superstructure in which man lives, not the foundation. The compulsion of folkways in a well-knit culture is just as strong as the compulsion of a style in architecture, Gothic, or Renaissance, or Egyptian. It fashions as it will the instincts of the people who live within it, re- making them in conformity with its own requirements. So it is that the cultural patterns are themselves creative; they take the raw ma- terial of experience and mold it into fifty different shapes among fifty different peoples. The traditional patterns of behavior set the mold and human nature flows into it.

It follows that man's established folkways are also his morals. Judgments of right and wrong and of the glory of God grow up within the field of group behavior and attach themselves to those traits that have become automatic in the group. Interference with automatic behavior is always unpleasant, and it is rationalized as evil. No people have any truly empirical ethics; they uphold what they find themselves practising . . .[9]

We in America, perhaps more than other peoples, have been unaware of the tremendous power of custom in the making of our nation's history. Because we tend to hold custom in dis- respect, we deceive ourselves into thinking that we are never bound by it. Our lack of contact with other cultures has made us provincial. We make our own way, with little regard for the steps which our ancestors trod. The fact is, our past has become so customary, so much a part of our basic patterns, that we are oblivious to its existence.

The primitive says frankly that he does a thing because his ancestors did it. We do many things for a similar reason, but instead of admitting the fact, we rationalize, asserting that our actions are governed by moral or scientific or religious motives.

An Example of Control by Custom [10]

Not only do Americans fail to grasp the Chinese form of social control, but Japan shows by her frequent criticisms of China how far she is from understanding her next-door neighbor. Japan's chief argument in favor of her advance into Asia is that, since China is such a disorganized group, she needs somebody or some group to take her in hand. Like the West, Japan fails to see, below the sur-

---

[9] Ruth Benedict, "The Science of Custom," *The Century Magazine*, April, 1929, pp. 641, 647, 648. By permission of the author.
[10] Josephine E. Budd, "Don't Worry About China," *North American Review*, September, 1932, vol. 234, pp. 238, 249, 250, 251. By permission of the publishers.

face of Chinese life, the power of China's social control as accomplished largely through her guild organizations. Far from being the least organized country, China is the most highly organized.

For thousands of years everybody and everything in China has been organized into some form of guild. Ricksha men have their hongs; every family has its tong; even thieves and beggars have their guilds. Out of these guild organizations a power has developed to mobilize psychological attitudes for political, social and economic ends in ways which are intangible to the West, but none the less mighty.

Millions of guilds in China protect the finances of the common people belonging to them. Each one has its own method of insurance and its own peculiar way of taking care of the economic life of its members. To make more understandable the way this elaborate system works for the nation as a whole, let us take two illustrations: first, how the average ricksha hong operates to protect its members financially; secondly, how this invisible power of the guilds helps the Chinese financier to borrow money without the necessity of any of the outward ceremonies and guarantees that we use in the West.

Ten ricksha men get together and create a capitalization fund. Each man puts in a dollar. Lots are then drawn to decide who shall use the money the first month, the second, and so on. The man who has the money keeps all he makes over and above the borrowed sum and returns the borrowed amount to the next one to use. And so it goes. At the end of the tenth month the money is redistributed.

A Swedish gentleman who thought he understood the Chinese was talking to one of the managers of a branch of a large banking corporation when a Mr. Chen entered. The banker greeted him, and asked if there was anything he could do for him.

"Yes," said the Chinese, "I should like to borrow $25,000."

"We will be glad to see that you have it, Mr. Chen." Beckoning to one of the runners, the banker said, "Tell the cashier to place to the account of Mr. Chen $25,000." He then pulled a small book from his pocket, made a note of the transaction, and turned to the Chinese to ask if there was anything else he could do for him.

The Chinese thanked him, said, "No," and went out.

"But that man gave you no written record nor signed any receipt for money received," the Swede stammered. . . .

"It is quite unnecessary," answered the banker. "He is a member not only of his trade guild, but also of both his provincial and family guilds. His whole community, as well as all the members of his trade and his family, stand back of his word. If anything should happen to him, they all would assume his financial responsibilities. So many thousands of people stand back of his word that as long as any of them live they would feel responsible for his debts. There are no such things as loose, floating individuals in China. It is a case of one for all and all for one, where blood counts far more than ink."

It is true that in many cases today these methods are not always pursued by the Chinese, especially in port cities where frequent contact with the West has forced them to change. However, while an increasing number of exceptions to this old system do exist all over China, the individual responsibility assumed by the guilds has built up a type of ethics that is worthy of our serious consideration.

The Chinese use this type of social control not only in relation to their financial life, but also in all other situations where the West would ordinarily call in the police or some form of organized law. For instance, if something outrageous happens in a Chinese home, the five nearest neighbors may be held responsible, dependent on their proximity to the one who has committed the crime. The Chinese reason that, if neighbors were what they ought to be and had set the example they ought to have set, the wrong deed would never have been committed. It is the negligence of neighbors that has provided the occasion for such wrong to develop. In old times the magistrate himself was often punished on the theory that if he had been a good magistrate the evil would never have occurred. What use, therefore, can the Chinese possibly have for Western forms of external control in cases where such social pressure works so effectively?

In the town of Yu Yin, Dr. Albert E. André, a scholar of the Chinese language, early one morning entered a small store and put his watch into the hands of one of the servants of the store to see that it was repaired. The servant agreed to attend to it, but, busy at the time, laid the watch on a small table in front of a window. When the servant turned around to get it, it was gone. Dr. André sent word immediately to the subordinate magistrate of that district. The magistrate sent back word, "Do you think that I am God that I should know where such a small thing as a watch could be found in a city of a hundred thousand people?"

"Ask him," replied Dr. André, "what he takes me to be, an igno-ramus that knows nothing? Ask him if he wants me to come down and run his office and teach him how to govern the Chinese people according to Chinese ways of doing things and Chinese customs?"

The servant of the magistrate blushed, but carried the message as given. Immediately the magistrate set to work. First, he called all the "fencers" of that town together. Now there were in that town eight wards and each ward had a fence—which is a sort of pawn-shop for stolen goods. The magistrate questioned the fencers, threatening them with dire punishment—hanging all of them by their thumbs—unless the article were delivered within three hours' time. Each man denied that he had had anything to do with the theft, yet every one of them knew that the fencer for the district in which the watch was stolen was the only one who could possibly have bought the watch, since each fencer is very jealous of his area and would kill the man who attempted to usurp his business. Also, the one who had bought the watch knew that if all were punished for his guilt he would be ruined by a form of social ostracism far worse than death.

The magistrate insisted on his threat of punishment; the fencers persisted in declaring themselves guiltless. After a time a runner came into the room to announce that the watch had been found. Chinese social pressure brought the needed results and accomplished, in a few hours, what might have taken days of futile searching in the West.

Conclusion

The group-wide practices, beliefs, and values of man become crystallized in culture. The web of nonmaterial culture pat-terns provides the way of life within the area over which the culture extends. Culture molds the personality into the desired shape.

The folkways, mores, and customs of a culture are reproduced each generation in the habits, values, and life philosophies of the individual. These ways are the sanctioned ways, the group's patterns of approved conduct. Material culture, often requir-ing that life be fitted to it, plays an important part in forming the nonmaterial patterns and thus shaping conduct.

Through the storing up of experience in culture, and through cultural transmission, experience gains continuity. The past comes to regulate the present; the present comes to regulate the future. Man becomes a time-bound creature, his past helping him to solve present adjustment problems and providing the techniques and codes for so doing. Culture makes for order in social life in that the techniques of adjustment are transmitted with mechanical regularity, not the absolute regularity of instinct, but the regularity of acquired habit. Culture thus provides a "large-scale molding-matrix, a gigantic conditioning apparatus," in which individuals are made to order for society.

SELECTED REFERENCES

Benedict, Ruth, "Configurations of Culture in North America," *American Anthropologist*, vol. 34, pp. 1–27. 1932.

Benedict, Ruth, "The Science of Custom," *The Century Magazine*, pp. 641–649. April, 1929.

Budd, Josephine E., "Don't Worry About China," *North American Review*, vol. 234, pp. 238–251. September, 1932.

Chapin, F. S., *Cultural Change*. D. Appleton-Century Company, 1928.

Davis, Barnes, and Others, *Introduction to Sociology* (selection by M. M. Willey), pp. 495–586. D. C. Heath and Company, New York, 1931.

Davis, Barnes, and Others, *Readings in Sociology* (selection by M. M. Willey), pp. 607–713. D. C. Heath and Company, New York, 1927.

Hobhouse, Leonard Trelawney, *Morals in Evolution*, parts 1 and 2. Henry Holt and Company, New York, 1906.

House, F. N., *The Range of Social Theory*, chap. 12. Henry Holt and Company, New York, 1929.

Keller, A. G., *Man's Rough Road*, pp. 35–37, 250–254. Frederick A. Stokes Company, New York, and Yale University Press, New Haven, 1932.

Kroeber, A. L., "The Possibility of a Social Psychology," *American Journal of Sociology*, vol. 23, pp. 633 ff. 1913.

Landis, Paul H., *Three Iron Mining Towns: A Study in Cultural Change*. Edwards Brothers, Ann Arbor, 1938.

Lowie, Robert H., *Culture and Ethnology*. Harcourt, Brace, and Company, New York, 1929.

Malinowski, B., "Culture as a Determiner of Behavior," *Scientific Monthly*, pp. 440–449. November, 1936.

Malinowski, B., *Myth in Primitive Society*. W. W. Norton and Company, New York, 1926.

Ogburn, W. F., *Social Change*. The Viking Press, Inc., New York, 1922.

Park, Robert E., "Human Nature, Attitudes, and the Mores," *Social Attitudes*, Kimball Young, editor, pp. 36 ff. Henry Holt and Company, New York, 1931.

Plant, James S., *Personality and the Cultural Pattern*. The Commonwealth Fund, New York, 1937.

Sapir, Edward, "Culture Genuine and Spurious," *American Journal of Sociology*, vol. 29, pp. 401–429. 1924.

Sorokin, Pitirim A., *Social and Cultural Dynamics*, vol. 3, chap. 15. American Book Company, New York, 1937.

Sumner, William Graham, *Folkways*. Ginn and Company, Boston, 1906.

Wallas, Graham, *Our Social Heritage*. Yale University Press, New Haven, 1921.

Westermarck, Edward Alexander, *The Origin and Development of Moral Ideals*. The Macmillan Company, New York, 1906.

Willey, M. M., and Herskovits, M. J., "The Cultural Approach to Sociology," *American Journal of Sociology*, vol. 29, pp. 188–189. 1923.

Winston, Sanford, *Culture and Human Behavior*. The Ronald Press Company, New York, 1933.

Wissler, Clark, *Man and Culture*, part 3. Thomas Y. Crowell Company, New York, 1923.

Zorbaugh, Harvey W., *The Gold Coast and the Slum*. University of Chicago Press, Chicago, 1929.

CHAPTER 7

THE GOAL OF LIFE AS A FACTOR IN CONTROL

CONCEPTS OF DRIVE

Much has been said in the past about innate drives which give the organism a centralness of purpose, a unity of action. On the biological level phrases often uttered are "self-preservation is the first law of life," and man lives "to reproduce the race," thereby fulfilling his normal "life cycle." Freud found in the libido the dominant urge of life, the compelling organic purpose in social adjustment. W. I. Thomas, with a sociological outlook, named four desires—the desire for new experience, the desire for recognition, the desire for response, and the desire for security—as motivating the individual with reference to the environment. Theologians of the old school saw in natural man the "carnal nature" which gave him a "bent to sinning." Adler conceived of the individual as being dominated by the masculine urge which could be appeased only by the recognition of the group. These are but a few of the many concepts of innate forces supposedly operating to give the organism a central, forward-looking drive.

Whatever goal one recognizes, and whatever drives one incorporates within man, at least it must be admitted that human motivation is a powerful factor in determining courses of action. From a sociological perspective one is inclined to take the position that innate drives, if such there be, are always supplemented by external experience. In fact, known organic drives, even the most potent of them, are conditioned by the social environment, as, for example, the sex impulse, hunger, or the desire for "self-preservation."

Socially conditioned drives may take precedence even over these bodily urges. Many a person, caught in a combination of circumstances which threaten to rob him of his status in the group, readily commits suicide rather than face social humilia-

95

tion. This means that for the time being at least the individual considers certain social values and goals of more worth than life.

The sex drive is a very powerful force in the lives of members of the human race, as in the lives of all creatures. Man lives to perpetuate the race, but society has found it necessary for the welfare of the group to limit his sex activities, and even to deny sexual expression completely to some individuals and groups. Sex may be given numerous meanings, according to the interpretation of the general culture pattern, or according to the existing social taboos of the society. Originally an animal drive, it has been embellished by custom and tradition until today it finds its highest expression in romantic love and in the family.

That the human being craves response and recognition, and that he strives to gain a feeling of superiority, is very true, especially in certain cultures, but instead of being a part of the masculine urge, these desires have originated in, or at least have been greatly encouraged by, the social group, which from early childhood teaches the individual to think in terms of his status in the group, to evaluate himself in terms of group appraisal. The only possible conclusion, then, is that man's so-called organic drives take on social meaning from the environment.

Goal Not an Organic Drive

In developing the concept of "goal," we have in mind something other than physical drives, important though they may be. But of this much the writer feels confident—none of these organic factors, however forceful they may be, are as important to personality and to social control as the socially conditioned goals and purposes upon which the individual focuses most of his energies in order that he may attain some degree of happiness or success. Even that first law of organic life, "self-preservation," as has been suggested, means nothing to the man who, having fixed his interests on some social goal and failed, takes recourse in suicide.

This concept of goal as a centralizing force in personality is not in any sense original, nor can one credit it to any one source. Thomas' and Znaniecki's definition of value is near to it.[1] By a

---

[1] W. I. Thomas and Florian Znaniecki, The Polish Peasant in Europe and America, vol. I, second edition, pp. 21–22. By permission of Chapman and Grimes, publishers.

social value they meant "any datum having empirical content accessible to the members of some social group and a meaning with regard to which it is or may be an object of activity." By attitude they meant "a process of individual consciousness which determines real or possible activity of the individual in the social world. . . . The attitude is thus the individual counterpart of the social value; activity, in whatever form, is the bond between them."

The person's attitude is his own mental counterpart to this value or, as they stated it, the attitude is the individual counterpart to the social value and the social value is the externalization of the attitude. Activity is the bond between attitudes and values. A person's values may be very unsound from the standpoint of objective behavior but they none the less may be effective factors in controlling his actions.

The concept of goal proposed here goes a step further and assumes that certain values have more meaning to the individual than others, and that for many persons some one or some few values may acquire so much significance as points of orientation that they become the dominating influence in their whole personality organization.[2] The Presbyterian catechism, for instance, assigns one supreme value as the object of all man's social effort and thus defines the one ultimate goal in life, "To glorify God and enjoy Him forever."

From a psychological standpoint, what has usually been called "will" probably consists primarily in the capacity to center attention on one or at most a few values that appear to be of most importance, and to strive toward the attainment of these values with unswerving purpose. There is social power in such behavior, whether it is labeled by the term "will-power" or by some other.

Character, when defined as the strength of man's energy output, probably relates very closely to this concept of will, for the amount of energy expended is determined to a considerable degree by the extent of personality organization. A strong cen-

---

[2] Thomas undoubtedly had something like this in mind when he said: "Viewed, then, as a configuration, a personality would be a background of attitudes and values common to everybody, upon which certain attitudes and values, or constellations of attitudes and values, assume a prominent or perhaps a dominant position," "The Configurations of Personality" in *The Unconscious, A Symposium*, pp. 143 ff.

tralized attack on the environment is possible only insofar as the personality is organized about a definite goal.[3]

At this point Adler's "individual psychology" has considerable meaning. In its underlying philosophy it does not differ greatly from the viewpoint expressed above. Adler, in developing his notions of the "life urge," "masculine urge," "inferiority complex," and "compensation" is thinking at least to some extent of personality as being centered in social achievement. His emphasis on "organ inferiority" gives his interpretation a more biological tinge than the sociologist would find necessary. However, there is much in Adler's theory to indicate that in any highly competitive culture the feelings of social inadequacy and, conversely, of social adequacy, which grow out of experience and social comparisons, very frequently determine the goal of life for the person.

But after all no writer is obliged to reconcile his viewpoint with every existing theory. Rather he must state it, defend it, and let others judge whether it illuminates or merely further confuses understanding. The goal of life as conceived here is a social value, not a biological fact. It is acquired by experience, if acquired at all. It implies the centering of one's energies about some value or values defined in the society of which he is a member. As the concept becomes clearer in the analysis which follows, its importance to social control will become more obvious.

The Social Aspect of Values and Goals

Within any society and in the bounds of any culture area a few major values stand out, providing a focus for the orientation of activities of members of that society and participants in that culture. This point, which will be further elaborated in the next chapter, must be assumed here. Within the general scheme of values of the culture area there are many variations, depending on the nature of the individual and the group. Differences in goals, in our society at least, can be explained in the main in terms of differences in age, sex, and race composition, social classes, and vocational alignments.

In highly advanced societies, where groups vary markedly in

---

[3] June Etta Downey, The Will-Temperament and Its Testing, chap. 4, World Book Company, New York, 1923.

their patterns and philosophies, an individual has many opportunities to select goals. Those who live in a relatively undifferentiated social order, and whose experiences are necessarily confined, have relatively few values from which to choose.

The current emphasis placed on individual differences, and the interest in personality which has been aroused are no less a reflection of this increased opportunity to choose to do what one pleases than a phase of our democratic philosophy. As we multiply the opportunity for selecting goals of life, we multiply the opportunity for personal satisfaction in that life, and the chances for the individual to adapt himself socially. At the same time, of course, we create problems in social adjustment because some individuals inevitably come under the influence of groups whose goals are not compatible with their own personal interests and talents. Others choose goals of life which prove to be uncongenial. We also greatly increase possibilities for choosing goals that are not in harmony with social purposes. It even appears that the social structure may become so complex that many do not even know what the major social values are. It is at this point that social orders begin to disintegrate for want of effective social control.

GOALS OF AGE GROUPS IN RELATION TO SOCIAL CONTROL [4]

. . . It will appear that in connection with stages of physical and mental and emotional maturation the personality will be weighted differently with the different attitudes and values, and questions will always arise with reference to constitutional traits as against habit formation:

Goals of childhood and youth. The values which a society holds before childhood and youth are of great significance in disciplinary problems. In America, it has come to be assumed that childhood is an age for play. But even in his play the child can be motivated in such a way that worthwhile attitudes and interests will be instilled. Later, in adolescence, his participation in organized athletics and constructive types of work with proper motivation can serve to develop him into a more social-

---

[4] W. I. Thomas, "The Configurations of Personality," The Unconscious; A Symposium, p. 144. By permission of F. S. Crofts and Company.

ized individual. The modern tendency to make the existence of the child and youth as happy and carefree as is humanly possible has involved a lengthening of the duration of infancy. The serious work-a-day world of yesterday has been transformed for the young one into a world of fascinating activities, aimed at developing his social nature and broadening his knowledge of culture. In some communities his education includes vocational training, so that the transition from school work to a job is a comparatively easy one to make.

Many disciplinary problems can be solved by holding before the youthful age group values that appeal most to their physical, psychic, and social makeup. Many a community has found that a well-kept playground is more effective as an instrument of control than a police force; that a boy's club is the best antidote for the delinquent gang; that normal social outlets in line with the goals of childhood are the best insurance against youthful disorder.

Goals of middle age. In our culture, middle age has been considered the time of work (middle age here is used to mean 25 to 60 approximately) and it has been assumed that the man who has steady employment and is in the prime of his life very likely will constitute no great problem to society. We have even developed laws against vagrancy, which in many cities may mean little more than being a person without a job. When a crime is committed suspicion immediately fastens upon the vagrant. It seems a logical conclusion that one who lives without work must engage in crime.

As the working day has been shortened, and the working year reduced in seasonal occupations and those that are irregular for other reasons, and as an increasing number face unemployment, and others work at occupations which in themselves are unsatisfying, the problem of providing supplementary values multiplies. New forms of recreation, hobbies, clubs, and one and a thousand things have been sponsored in our culture, in an effort to furnish people with sufficient life goals. Much of the impetus that has been given to the purposeful use of leisure time has been considered necessary to preserve the social order. Undoubtedly such a course, to the extent that it proves fruitful, is an influential force in maintaining social discipline over great masses of middle-aged people.

Pioneer society faced no such problem, there being work for all. "Man is born to hustle," stated a boxhead carried in every issue of a newspaper in a frontier settlement less than 50 years ago.[5] On the frontier, man has no alternative, for if he does not hustle he may perish. In such a community the goal of life becomes survival, and following in its train, the conquest of nature for food and shelter, for land and a home. Pioneers need few of the more artificial and perhaps spurious values set before them which an age of leisure makes necessary.[6]

Goals of old age. One of the most tragic figures in our civilization is, with rare exception, the person who has reached the age when he must retire from an active life. Life is coming to a close; the major goals which gave it meaning have been realized, or if they have not, the old person must face the inevitable—that they will likely never be attained. For him, unfortunately, our culture has defined no well-recognized goals. A few years ago the aged obtained much satisfaction from the consolations heaven offered when toils and sorrows would be ended. This earthly existence was just a "dressing room" in which to prepare for the life hereafter. Like Job, they could endure the neglect of ungrateful children, the sting of poverty, the loss of friends, and the loss of status, for these were but tests of their fitness to respond when the Lord would call them home. But today, if we are to believe Lippmann's *A Preface to Morals*, and other signs of the times, in our overly-urbanized, supersophisticated world the thought of heaven offers slight consolation to world-weary souls.

Some societies have killed the aged when they reached the period of dependency. Others, notably that of China, have instituted the system of ancestor worship, loading their elders with luxury, giving them the best of everything that life affords, and worshipping them after death. In such a social scheme old age might well be termed the "glorious age."

Old age offers comparatively few problems in social control, because life's energies are waning and habits are fixed. Old people seldom experiment with new ventures outside their group definitions.

In the future of our culture, however, the old age group is

---

[5] Hibbing, Minnesota, in 1893.
[6] Landis, Paul H., *Three Iron Mining Towns*, chaps. 7 and 8.

likely to become politically significant. While they may always be a minority group, depending upon where the line is drawn between work and retirement, the proportion of those over 65 years of age in the nation's population is increasing, and will probably more than double by 1980.[7] As has been previously indicated, on the West Coast, where those over 65 years constitute a larger per cent of the population than in the nation as a whole,[8] they have made themselves felt through the Townsend movement, a depression phenomenon which may be a forecast of things to come. As the vigor of life is preserved beyond retirement years, old people will increase their political demands, perhaps insisting on a share of the luxuries of middle age at the expense of the younger working groups. Pensions and annuities may have to be increased to the point where they become a heavy burden to the rest of society.

GOALS OF THE DIFFERENT SEXES

Most societies set up different values of life for men and for women, and for this reason primarily the behavior of the sexes is dissimilar. Sex distinctions can usually be traced to the ideals of the group rather than to biological factors. Even our society, which boasts so much of equality of the sexes, differentiates.

It is true that many women find happiness in a career, but such is not considered the natural or normal thing. The role that a member of the female sex plays does much to determine the extent to which she constitutes a problem in control. If she is the buyer, advertising caters to her sense of values; if she does the reading, books that idealize feminine values are published. On the other hand, in a man's world most regulative devices are constructed in harmony with masculine values.

RACE AND THE GOAL OF LIFE

Goal is not a biological factor; it is definitely a social one. What, then, does it have to do with race? Precisely this. Wher-

---

[7] See Thompson and Whelpton's estimates for the nation and for the various states in *Estimates of Future Population by States*, National Resources Board, Washington, D. C., 1934; or Warren S. Thompson, *Population Problems*, second edition, chap. 15, McGraw-Hill Book Company, New York, 1935.

[8] Landis, Paul H., "Selected Population Problems of the Western States in Relation to Agricultural Adjustment," *Proceedings of the Western Farm Economics Association*, 1936, pp. 27–41.

ever two racial groups meet in the same society, conflict relations usually ensue. In the resolution of this conflict, definitions frequently develop which assign an inferior status to the weaker of the races. Through a process of accommodation the groups eventually become complacent in their relations with one another. The goals of the inferior race are greatly restricted; caste lines are drawn and then perpetuated from generation to generation, sometimes for centuries.

The caste system, defining as it does the exact position of each group in the social scale, becomes rigid and inflexible. Individuals are ranked in the scheme in order of social merit. The upper casteman enjoys certain privileges and prerogatives which govern his relations with members of other classes. To his own caste he owes definite obligations. Likewise, the lower casteman has his station fully defined for him and knows what conduct is expected of him by members within his own caste and also by upper castemen.

Such systems greatly simplify social control because, since possible goals for the different social strata are always well defined, each individual becomes accommodated to his particular role in society, a role delimited by tradition.

GOALS OF SOCIAL CLASSES AND PROBLEMS OF SOCIAL CONTROL

Social classes represent different degrees of social status and even in an open class society, class lines become factors in social control. Control is much more difficult of accomplishment in an open class system, however, where every member of a lower class regards himself as a potential candidate for a higher status, and so strives for upper class values, imitating the dress, mannerisms, and airs of the aristocrats. As a consequence of the tendency for the class below to challenge the superiority of the class above, the upper classes must maintain a ceaseless vigilance in keeping their values distinctly their own, or their prestige and authority may be undermined. Privileged classes in an open class system such as our own are usually based upon wealth, which carries with it authority, influence, power, and in general a high social status. These are values which set men apart as superior, even in a democratic society. But throughout history the priestly group has often been a privileged class, ascribing to itself values in the spiritual realm inaccessible to the mind of the layman.

The Mosaic Law, for instance, created a priestly class which had charge of the sacred exercises of the tabernacle. They alone could bear it in the journeyings of the Jews. They alone could handle its sacred vessels. Others who came near were to be stoned.[9]

Protestantism has greatly reduced the prestige of priestly classes in the Western World, for it has held out to the layman all the values that once were available only to the priest. The individual, through his own initiative, without the help of priests or prophets, is given access to sacred values, to form of them a goal of life. Even the Bible, once incomprehensible to the masses because of the Latin and Greek text, is today written in the vernacular so that all can read it. It is interesting to note that John Wycliff (c. 1320–1384), who first translated the New Testament into English, was burned at the stake by leaders of the church for his heresy. The sacred had been profaned by making it common property. Thus we see that even priests may be guilty of the desire to keep for themselves the tangible values that raise their lives above the common herd.

Caste, a Device for Limiting Access to Values

It is in the maintenance of status and role that caste systems arise. In any competitive society, and most societies are to some extent competitive, a person, unless he is born at the top, achieves high status only after a long struggle, although to some extent ingenuity and lucky circumstances may also be important factors. Acquiring the values that bring high status is so arduous a process that those individuals who have achieved them immediately make plans for passing them on to their children. As a consequence, in most societies of the world, those groups which have attained a favorable status find ways of seeing that it is transferred to their offspring, thus assuring them the pleasures that come with social favor. This process of stratification which consists in the fencing off of values, making them accessible as goals to only selected groups, is operative in all societies. Where it succeeds, a few persons, through historical accident, or work, or merit, come to occupy the dominant positions of social control. As the society with the passing of time becomes more rigid, frequently individ-

---

[9] Numbers 1: 49–54.

uals inherit high social status who would never have been capable of earning it and who, except for the traditions of blood, ancestry, and custom, could not long maintain their position of authority and honor. When such a condition exists revolution, or some less violent form of revolt may be the eventual outcome, as it has been in the history of Western Europe at times when foolish, ignorant, or intolerant monarchs inherited thrones.

New societies like our own, which was born of revolution, and nurtured on the frontier, may avoid extreme stratification for a long time. On the other hand, even in America there are evidences of vested interests trying to ensure those interests for their descendants. It is a generally recognized fact that no group in control likes to yield that control to another group. Capitalists and priests alike aim to see that the interests of their class are protected, even at the expense of every other group in the society.

In the United States the law has been designed to hinder hereditary privilege; legally, there are no aristocrats, no titles of nobility; and legally there is no landed gentry. Yet, we have our own home-spun methods of making gods of men. Money comes first, but pioneer or "Mayflower" ancestry adds distinction. Being a colonel is important in some localities. The professions also exact a certain degree of respect; perhaps we might say that the possession of a good education is second only to wealth.[10] Nevertheless, we have tried theoretically to keep all values as potential goals for all classes of men, and as modern societies go, we have realized this aim fairly well.

Dominant races, like dominant classes, devise numerous techniques for seeing that the status of the superior race is maintained, and that of the inferior race recognized by both races. Thus, stratified societies develop, and become effective forces in regulating the behavior of racial groups with reference to each other. Discriminatory patterns come to be accepted. The Jew, having been given a certain status by most peoples of the Western world, has had limited access to the values of the peoples with whom he has lived. Perhaps this fact as much as his religious philosophy, has kept him distinctive. His defense reactions have grown out of his recognition of the fact that he is a man forever doomed to play a peculiar role in another man's culture.

[10] K. F. Gerould, "Our Class Distinctions," *The Yale Review*, December, 1931, p. 251.

GOALS OF LIFE WITHIN THE VOCATION

In a specialized society like our own, where there is a broad range of vocational choices, each occupational group tends to develop certain values which to some extent control its activities. In fact, each vocation offers a slightly different road to status, and sets at the pinnacle of the climb a different reward. In the realm of politics, such values as spoils, patronage, acquaintanceship, or knowing the right people come to have great meaning. In the scientific field, the satisfaction of knowing that one has the confidence of critical scholars, the glow that comes with seeing oneself cited as an authority, the gratifying experience of being in demand by business-minded institutional administrators who know the type of talent that is most scarce—these rewards are motivations much stronger than money. In the medical field, to be recognized as a competent specialist, to be sought by people from great distances, are marks to be achieved.

Frequently the values within the vocation clash with one another, a condition which at the present time exists most often in the field of women's vocations. Conflicting values necessarily mean conflicting motivation with resultant personality problems for the individual, who does not know whether to follow the dictates of one system of control or those of another. In the stenographic field, for instance, there is a constant struggle in many circles, perhaps more in cartoons and in general philosophy than in actual reality, between woman's desire to maintain a high professional status, to be efficient and to hold her job entirely on the basis of ability, and her age-long desire to be loved, to appear interesting and attractive to men. In applying for a job with a male employer, the girl wavers between two courses of action. Shall she use her appearance and the charms of her sex to gain her ends, or shall she make the application entirely on the basis of merit and skill? We do not mean to imply, however, that this conflict of vocational values is caused solely by the incompatibility of women's values. Men are equally responsible, in that they have difficulty in accepting women on a strictly professional basis. Such a system of dual values makes it very difficult to develop codes of ethics and standards of professional quality. Regardless of how high the professional code, the majority of working women keep their eyes trained on two

different objects. They are interested in the job, yes, but also
in marriage, and because of the peculiar biological function they
play in reproduction, there is no way of evading the fact that
marriage always interferes with the job. It may always, therefore, be difficult to establish work codes which the majority of
women will take seriously as life-long goals.

THE GOALS OF LIFE AMONG PROFESSIONAL CRIMINALS

Criminals and delinquents are people who are trying to attain
values similar to those of people in general; but they are doing it
by means which are not approved by society at large. The
criminal wants status, he wants wealth, he wants thrills, but at
the same time he wants security. Because of low birth, bad
habits, or poor training, or perhaps because of having fallen in
with the wrong group, he starts out on a course in which he
attempts to achieve these values by means that isolate him from
normal society. Once having become identified with the criminal
population he begins to imitate the professional criminals, who
for the most part have adopted goals of life entirely outside of
the code of the larger group. Having absorbed their point of
view, and their mores and patterns, he naturally seeks to achieve
his goals by methods of which this smaller group approves, thus
gaining their recognition.

THE IMPORTANCE OF A UNIFYING GOAL

The centering of personality on a definite goal in life, and the
pursuit of that goal, is probably the most significant single factor
in both self-control and in social control, provided the goals are
in harmony with the culture pattern of one's time, and with the
larger purposes of the social group. On the other hand, people
whose life goals are directly counter to the social group, but
yet are well established, create the greatest problem of social
control. In this classification belong the lifetime recidivists.
Among them are the professional criminals, delinquents, and
problem cases. The nature of their goals menaces society.

Another large group which obstructs society is that composed
of individuals definitely lacking in any life goal. They live a
vague, aimless sort of life in which the consciousness of society's
ends for them never penetrates. In this group are a large number
of social inadequates, confirmed paupers, delinquents, who could

hardly be dignified with the status of professional criminal, down-and-outers who, recognizing that they have reached the bottom, still become quite fully accommodated to a life without status.

RELIGION AS A GOAL

In the past, religion probably did more than any other one force in the social order to unify the life processes of great masses of people. Many churchmen could say, like the Apostle Paul, "But this one thing I do, forgetting everything which is past and stretching forward to what lies in front of me, with my eyes fixed on the goal, I push on to secure the prize of God's heavenward call in Christ Jesus." [11] Righteousness, holiness, eternal life, loyalty to the commands of the Word of God, faithfulness to the precepts of the Church, loyalty to the Church as an institution, even unto death—these values have loomed large since the origin of Christianity in determining the goal of life for the great majority of people in the Western World. In other creeds, and in many non-Christian societies the same type of values have also held sway, though differing in details.

With the recent waning of religious influence, goals of life for many have been shattered. A generation of youth has grown up with no inkling of the values which religion may provide, values meant to be incorporated into one final, all-inclusive life purpose. Many today do not acknowledge the Bible as the Word of God, and many more confess that they are not exactly sure what is right and what is wrong. "Sin," as some of our conservative preachers express it, has been so often "whitewashed in the pulpit" that there are few sinners left. Many modern youth have no conception of sin, but there was a time when it was a vivid reality, when his Satanic Majesty was to be reckoned with as the instigator of sin. He supplied the scapegoat for the sins one couldn't help. Good and bad were thus given a concreteness which few could ignore. Religion was the only road to the good life because man needed the Power of God in his life in order to live uprightly.

FAMILY AS A GOAL

There are many goals aside from religion, about which life purposes can be centered, though perhaps none are as effective

[11] Philippians, Weymouth Version, 3:13, 14.

or as all-inclusive. Most women in the past found in the family situation goals that completely absorbed their personalities. The rearing of their children, the conducting of a successful family life, the fruition of their hopes in realizing their own ambitions in their children and their grandchildren—these factors have provided a comprehensive goal of life which has been a dominant factor in controlling the mother's behavior, in developing her self-control, and in helping her to master her own self in relation to her time.

UTILITARIAN AND MATERIALISTIC GOALS

Wealth has often been made the goal of life; many people direct their entire activity toward its accumulation. For some people wealth is an end in itself; for some, an index of success; and for others, a road to status. Not only the wealthy have centered their lives about these values; in our society with its materialistic emphasis, thousands of the relatively poor have striven diligently toward utilitarian or materialistic goals.

YOUTH WITHOUT GOALS OPEN TO PROPAGANDA

The rise of the modern totalitarian state with its fanatical insistence on complete loyalty, even to the extent of absorbing the entire life of the individual, has flourished in part because modern man has lacked a creed bigger than his ego. Especially has this been true in Western European countries since the World War. Confidence in the old prewar traditions was blasted. The young generation was reared without the motivation of any great social purpose. In Russia, Communism answered the crying need of the masses for a new gospel, a great faith that would demand a man's all. Similarly, Mussolini and Hitler have offered to the youth of their nations a purpose, a goal in life far above the individual, big enough to engross him completely, difficult enough to challenge his energies, heroic enough to demand loyalty, righteous enough to captivate patriotism and emotional fervor; a goal social enough to bring forth a whole-hearted devotion that would not stop at any sacrifice.

In its implications perhaps the most catastrophic problem that can face any society is to have a generation of youth without goals. Masses of men who have no great purpose as a center for personality development are easy prospects for every messiah, craze, or fanatical movement that appears.

Center a man's personality in a great religious faith, in a great political movement, in a great social ideal, even in a great war, and his behavior will be guided largely in the light of that ideal. The problem of social control with respect to him is largely solved, provided that the ideal is reconcilable with the purposes of the society in which he lives.

MODELS AS SOURCE OF GOALS

To no small extent one obtains his goals in life from models, that is, from persons whose achievements serve as examples. These models exert great influence on the personality development of children and youth, as well as of adults whose goals they help to objectify. The young child finds his model primarily in his parents, though other idols may come to hold great sway. For one group of boys Al Capone in his day was the pattern; for many others Buck Jones was the acme of perfection. Less famous characters in the home, school, or playground environment, if they possess qualities which the child finds admirable, may also be made the objects of his worship. Youth finds exemplars in teachers, famous athletes, movie stars, and the other adult heroes that may happen to cross its path. Even the scientist has a model in the man or men whose accomplishments he wishes to parallel or even exceed. John Dewey has provided the pattern for many aspiring educators and philosophers, and Karl Pearson for many statisticians.

Leadership of the more vital sort consists, in part at least, in having acquired sufficient prestige and status to be recognized as a model by a group of followers who accept the leader's tenets in their entirety. Frequently the leader becomes a sort of mythical figure, the symbol of great values, the tangible representative of life goals. In such a case he commands great authority, not merely as an ideal man, but as a source of life principles and social doctrine.

The priestly group has always enjoyed unusual prestige, and through their prestige, unusual power and authority over the masses. The high esteem in which it is held has come largely through identification of its interests, work, and ideas with Deity. Few are the clergymen who speak their own message;

rather, they speak the message of the Infallible One, so their voice must be heard. Because of their ability to interpret for mankind the will of the gods, they themselves are accepted as unusually sacred, as unusually wise, and consequently they enjoy prestige little less than that of the gods whom they serve. This "instrument-of-God" technique frequently has the effect of lifting the leader to an unusual pinnacle of prestige among his disciples. Father Divine, the Negro charlatan of New York City, is actually the earthly manifestation of God, in the eyes of his followers.[12]

No less effective is the message of demagogues, dictators, war lords, and revolutionary leaders, all of whom speak the fervent message of a great cause, or breathe forth the authority of great principles. They stand for all that makes life worth while. The more their programs reach epidemic proportions, the more the masses lose themselves in the spirit of these symbolic models.

Outstanding success in one sphere frequently so enhances the prestige of a man that his leadership is immediately valued in numerous other fields, even in those in which he is sure to be a miserable failure. Two great generals were made presidents of our nation. General Washington succeeded in political leadership as he had in military leadership, but the great General Grant was a notable misfit in the presidential chair. When Lindbergh accomplished the daring feat of crossing the Atlantic by airplane, his opinion was immediately sought in almost all conceivable phases of life. The numerous companies who hounded him for statements were not interested in the opinion of the man, but rather they wanted to buy for their organizations the chance to bask in the reflected glory of this man who had suddenly become a national idol. They hoped by obtaining his services or advice, or permission to use his name, to gain for their products something of the prestige and respect which the public had given so freely to Lindbergh. Life insurance companies, similarly motivated, frequently furnish great football stars with unusually lucrative opportunities. Pictures of glamorous ladies of the stage and screen adorn soap, cigarette, shoe, and clothing advertisements. Child box office attractions are reproduced in miniature in the form of dolls. Even fictitious characters that have become

---

[12] For an account of Father Divine's activities see St. Clair McKelway and A. F. Liebling, "Who Is This King of Glory?", Reader's Digest, September, 1936, pp. 79–84.

famous in literature, pictures, or on radio programs, are sought and dearly paid for by manufacturers. Mickey Mouse, Popeye the Sailor Man, Amos and Andy, Snow White, and Dopey the dwarf—the list is interminable.

All this is a recognition that prestige commands dollar value in our modern world of competitive economic enterprise. The leader who achieves it has no trouble in selling it for high prices to various concerns. The fact that many will imitate his behavior makes him an ideal model for use in commercial exploitation. Thus, there are few fields in which testimonials are not solicited.

The fact that people who know so little about a product are allowed to use their prestige for exploiting the public is suggestive of the extent to which one with a great name can get by with deception. Perhaps it is also indicative of a lack of public control over exploitive commercial leadership.

CONFLICTING MODELS AND PERSONALITY PROBLEMS

One of the difficult problems of personality development as it relates to social control in the modern world lies in the fact that models are very numerous and diverse in character. They pass before us in a rapidly shifting panorama, some adorned with glitter and tinsel that appeals to the sensuous, others somber under a heavy burden of duty, some promising pleasure to the full, others success, some wealth plus status, others status without wealth, others rewarding with adventure. No man is versatile enough to copy very many of these models and yet maintain a sense of unity within himself. Consistency, predictability, and certainty of behavior are necessary to efficient social control. Dr. Jekylls and Mr. Hydes are far too numerous in our society. They have tried to incorporate in their personality the opposing values represented by different models, and end up with something of a dual personality.

PERSONALITY CONFLICT RESULTING FROM DIVERGENT GOALS

Many individuals are constantly torn by personality conflict because they try to embody within themselves two or more inconsistent goals of life, both of which can never be realized. Invariably a certain amount of schizophrenic development results. In our culture, where numerous organizations and numerous groups bait the individual with an imposing array of values, it is inevitable that many people who have not yet fixed their purposes and goals will be rent between one or more values and will thus be left in a state of mental torment. Such people are almost as much to be pitied as those who have no goal at all.

CHANGING SOCIAL VALUES

How may the goals and values of life be changed? Usually values are changed by the gradual process of diffusion of the mores through social change, a process unconscious and unplanned. However, it often is possible in specific realms to effect radical changes in the values of life in a short length of time. One of the interesting attempts at changing the value of death in our culture is that made by Hubert Eaton, who initiated the building of Forest Lawn Memorial-Park at Glendale, California. "The Builder's Creed" reads:

I BELIEVE in a happy Eternal Life.

I believe those of us left behind should be glad in the certain belief that those gone before have entered into that happier Life.

I believe, most of all, in a Christ that smiles and loves you and me.

I therefore know the cemeteries of today are wrong because they depict an end, not a beginning. They have consequently become unsightly stoneyards full of inartistic symbols and depressing customs; places that do nothing for humanity save a practical act and that not well.

I therefore prayerfully resolve on this New Year's Day, 1917, that I shall endeavor to build Forest Lawn as different, as unlike other cemeteries as sunshine is unlike darkness, as Eternal Life is unlike Death. I shall try to build at Forest Lawn a great park, devoid of misshapen monuments and other customary signs of earthly Death, but filled with towering trees, sweeping lawns, splashing fountains, singing birds, beautiful statuary, cheerful flowers, noble memorial architecture with interiors full of light and color, and redolent of the world's best history and romances.

I believe these things educate and uplift a community.

Forest Lawn shall become a place where lovers new and old shall love to stroll and watch the sunset's glow, planning for the future or reminiscing of the past; a place where artists study and sketch; where school teachers bring happy children to see the things they read of in books; where little churches invite, triumphant in the knowledge that from their pulpits only words of Love can be spoken; where memori-alization of loved ones in sculptured marble and pictorial glass shall be encouraged but controlled by acknowledged artists; a place where the sorrowing will be soothed and strengthened because it will be God's garden. A place that shall be protected by an immense Perpetual Care Fund, the principal of which can never be expended—only the income therefrom used to care for and perpetuate this Garden of Memory.

This is the Builder's Dream; this is the Builder's Creed.[13]

The fact that more than seven thousand weddings have been performed in the two little churches in this cemetery indicates that Mr. Eaton has already brought about a considerable change in attitudes toward death.

CONCLUSION

This chapter is based on the assumption that certain values defined by society come to be motivating forces in the life of the individual, to the extent that they become the goals at which his efforts are directed. As such, they become powerful factors in influencing individual conduct. Most social values are limited to certain individuals and one must order his life within the realm of these selected values; in fact, he must choose his goals from those lying within the limits of the values open to him. The biological facts of age, sex, or of race may set boundaries to the values within reach of the individual. More important still are those artificial barriers by which the group confines access to values to certain ages, classes, sexes, or races.

Some societies, by an elaborate system of stratification, establish permanent boundaries limiting access to values. Such are described as caste societies. Others are very liberal in providing an open way to every man to struggle for the values which the culture emulates. Such a society is our own, which holds out to every individual numerous values from which he may choose a goal. Among the commonly accepted goals of our society are religion, wealth, and family. Because of the very laxity of our social system, which permits so many choices, some individuals

---

[13] Used by permission of the Forest Lawn Memorial-Park Association, Inc. The Builder's Creed is copyrighted and cannot be used without permission. For a description of the cemetery see B. Barton's, "Cemetery without Gloom," Reader's Digest, August 1937, pp. 73–76.

are unable to make a choice of goals. In such a situation a constant threat exists that leaders may arise to offer men a great motive for life, as they have done in several countries of the world now under the control of dictators.

Also growing out of the lack of established values is the problem of many individuals at times being torn between numerous alternatives, not knowing which ends in life to seek. This is the personal aspect of change in our culture, which frequently redefines the goals of life, and keeps many individuals in a state of mental turmoil in their effort to select from among conflicting values.

SELECTED REFERENCES

Allport, Gordon, "Attitudes," *A Handbook of Social Psychology*, Carl Murchison, editor. Clark University Press, Worcester, 1935.

Downey, June Etta, *The Will-Temperament and its Testing*. World Book Company, New York, 1923.

Groves, Ernest R., "Socializing Human Nature," *The Child, The Clinic and the Court*, pp. 192–193. The New Republic, Inc., New York, 1925.

Holland, Gerold, "The Social Register," *American Mercury*, pp. 179–184. June, 1932.

Landis, Paul H., *Three Iron Mining Towns: A Study in Cultural Change*, chaps. 7 and 8. Edwards Brothers, Ann Arbor, 1938.

Lippmann, Walter, *A Preface to Morals*. The Macmillan Company, New York, 1929.

Tannenbaum, Frank, *Crime and the Community*, chap. 7. Ginn and Company, Boston, 1938.

Thomas, W. I., "The Configurations of Personality," *The Unconscious; A Symposium*, chap. 6. F. S. Crofts and Company, New York, 1928.

Thomas, William I., and Znaniecki, Florian, *The Polish Peasant in Europe and America*, vol. 1, pp. 1–86. Chapman and Grimes, Boston, 1918.

Van Loon, H. W., "To Have or To Be," *School and Society*, vol. 36, pp. 6–8. July 2, 1932.

Williams, James, *Our Rural Heritage*. Alfred A. Knopf, Inc., New York, 1925.

CHAPTER 8

GOALS OF AN AGE AS FACTORS IN SOCIAL GUIDANCE

THE CONCEPT OF CULTURAL GOALS

Many students of culture have been of the opinion that cultures tend to move with definite integration in a certain direction. F. C. Bartlett, in discussing the borrowing of cultural traits,[1] has emphasized the proclivity of the group to shape the new trait in harmony with the "trend of development" of the culture. Malinowski, in his emphasis on functionalism, and his belief that one can understand a people only by knowing the meaning of their culture to them,[2] assumes that the peculiar manner of integration of a culture pattern gives it special meaning known only by those living in the culture. Willey and Herskovits have developed the view that each culture has a distinctiveness of pattern because a peculiar significance is attached to complexes within the culture.[3]

Ruth Benedict has stressed the peculiar "patterns of culture" that characterize various civilizations, showing that each culture has its *dominant drive*, its *supreme ideal*.[4] The Romans drove toward political empire, the Greeks toward the ideal of symmetry and balance; the Egyptians strove to prepare for life after death, the French for clarity and reverence for form, the English for emotional reserve, "character," and self-control. She says that the culture may have one or more such dominant ideals, some dealing with external achievements, others with the "management of personality and emotions."[5]

---

[1] F. C. Bartlett, *Psychology and Primitive Culture*, chap. 5.
[2] See for instance his *Myth in Primitive Society*.
[3] M. M. Willey and M. J. Herskovits, "The Cultural Approach to Sociology," *American Journal of Sociology*, 1923, vol. 29, pp. 188–199.
[4] Ruth Benedict, *Patterns of Culture*.
[5] Ruth Benedict, "Configurations of Culture in North America," *American Anthropologist*, 1932, vol. 34, pp. 1–27.

116

James S. Plant in his *Personality and the Cultural Pattern*, in describing cultures, has used the terms "God-centered," "family-centered," "state-centered," "profit-centered," and "individual-centered" cultures and has suggested that all cultures tend to be centered around one such major goal.

Margaret Mead says that each culture has developed its values; each new generation is shaped to the "dominant trend" of that culture.[6]

V. F. Calverton has used the term "cultural compulsives" to describe the tendency of trends of influence within the culture to shape the thought of those living within it.[7] With similar emphasis Vjalmar Stefansson, in his lectures on the "friendly Arctic," commented on the fact that at Harvard the professors in the Medical School were teaching that it was impossible for a man to live on a diet of meat alone while the professors in the department of anthropology were teaching that several thousands of people in the world lived exclusively on meat.[8] The medical men were reflecting concepts of our culture. Stefansson had viewed intimately a different culture.

Sumner, in his *Folkways*,[9] spoke of the national ethos or national character. By the ethos he meant the "totality of characteristic traits by which the group is individualized and differentiated from others."

Though methods of expression vary markedly, observation of cultures indicates that dominant currents of influence tend to pervade them, that certain values in them come to predominate. It can be assumed that these prevailing patterns have much to do with the regulation of behavior. W. H. R. Rivers implies this in describing the unfortunate effects on primitives of the influence of Western civilization.[10] Their major culture patterns may become so disrupted that the natives lose interest in living; a process of decay of character and degeneration of racial quality

---

[6] Margaret Mead, *Sex and Temperament in Three Primitive Societies*.

[7] V. F. Calverton, *The Making of Man, An Outline of Anthropology*, Introduction.

[8] This conflict led to Stefansson's experiments with a meat diet later, under laboratory observation at Harvard. See his series in *Harper's Magazine*, November, 1935, and January, 1936, "Adventures in Diets," vol. 171, pp. 668–675; vol. 172, pp. 46–54, 178–189.

[9] See p. 36.

[10] W. H. R. Rivers, *Essays on the Depopulation of Melanesia*, pp. xviii–116.

sets in, so that in a short time both their civilization and their race become extinct.

Ruth Benedict tells of an old Indian chief who had "straddled" the Indian's and the white man's cultures.[11] He remarked, "God gave to every people a cup, a cup of clay, and from this cup they drank their life," and then he lamented, "Our cup is broken now. It has passed away." This sage had seen the passing of the fabric of his people's values, the disruption of the patterns of their culture. Is it any wonder that he sorrowed? The old set of goals and values had meant life to him and to his people.

Knight, writing in a somewhat ironical vein, observes,

The point is that the "principles" by which a society or a group lives in tolerable harmony are essentially religious . . . not merely is it immoral to oppose it, but to ask what it is, is morally identical with denial and attack.

To inquire into the ultimates behind accepted group values is obscene and sacrilegious; objective inquiry is an attempt to uncover the nakedness of man, his soul as well as his body, his deeds, his culture, and his very gods . . . Individuals have to have clear, clean-cut distinctions, like right and wrong; and groups have to have agreement and like-mindedness to survive. Social tolerance of alien innovations is a symptom of decadence."[12]

The more prominent individual goals within any culture are the products of cultural goals, compulsives, or patterns, as one chooses to describe them. Of course, many goals originate in the values of the smaller primary groups living within the general cultural milieu, but seldom do they vary greatly from the stamp of the general culture pattern.

ROADS TO STATUS MARKED BY CULTURE PATTERNS

The problem of social status is an instance. As discussed in the preceding chapter, status is accorded one with reference to the kind of role he plays in a given group. As he approaches the goals which the group holds desirable he raises his status; the farther he falls short the lower is his rank. But the paths to status in any group are fairly well marked by the culture pattern.

---

[11] Ruth Benedict, op. cit., chap. 2.
[12] Frank K. Knight, "The Newer Economics and the Control of Economic Activity," Journal of Political Economy, August, 1932, vol. 40, pp. 433–476.

These roads vary with the culture. Among some tribes of American Indians the man who achieved the highest status was the man who gave away the most wealth. In our society he seems to be the man who can acquire the most wealth, although there have been philanthropists who, having built up great riches, find a road to recognition in redistribution of a part of it among charitable organizations.

In China the first question asked a stranger is, "How many years have you?" or, "What is your glorious age?" because in that culture age and status are almost synonymous. The person of advanced age takes great pride in his years; he is an object of respect and veneration among all his fellows. In our society "How old are you?" may be considered as almost an insult, especially if directed toward a woman past thirty.

A Hebrew proverb declared: "The hoary hair is a crown of glory, if it be found in the way of righteousness." [13]   But in our culture the henna shade has been preferred to the hoary crown. We seek youth with a vigor rivaling that of Ponce de León who sought the famed Fountain of Youth. Our vast numbers of beauty parlors, with their startling array of face creams, treatments for wrinkles, inventions for face lifting, and other aids to youthful appearance, indicate the supreme value which our culture places on youth.

The old man in China who can afford one, buys his coffin years before death, and in his declining years takes great comfort in sleeping in it each night. In our culture we avoid the undertaker and make no previous preparations. As long as life lasts we shun all thoughts of dying, but when death approaches, we want to be buried luxuriously. We compete even more ostentatiously in death than in life, so that elaborate funeral services even for the poor have become a necessary part of American life.

God asked Father Abraham to look heavenward to count the stars; to look on the ocean beach and number the sands of the seashore.[14] Then he thrilled Abraham with the promise of a goal that was supreme in early Hebrew culture, that his seed should be as numberless as these. "Multiply and replenish the earth" expressed a cultural value very meaningful at one time.[15]   The

---

[13] Proverbs 16:31.
[14] Genesis 15:5, 18, 17; 22:17; 32:12.
[15] Genesis 1:28; 9:1; 35:11.

average American of today would react quite differently to the prospect of numberless progeny, fearing what his neighbors might think. A large family no longer is a road to status.[16]

Detecting witches and burning them without mercy was a mark of divinity and sainthood not so many years ago in Christian culture. One could hardly climb to status by that route in our time. Pope Innocent VIII urged his people to rescue the Church from the power of Satan, that is, from the power of witches. Luther recommended that all witches be burned without compassion. Jonathan Edwards and Cotton Mather, religious leaders of the Puritan period in American culture, were men of unquestioned intellectual ability and penetrating insight; yet they denounced witchcraft by proclamations from the pulpit, and by written exhortations to the faithful.[17] Mather, a Doctor of Divinity, wrote a book entitled *The Wonders of the Invisible World*,[18] in which he gave an account of "the trials of several witches lately executed in New England." Today these narrations seem as though they originated with an ignorant, intolerant, backward people, instead of being penned by the leaders of an age, men who, like the masses that followed them, were dominated by a thought pattern entirely superstitious in nature and yet compulsive enough to cause the death of thousands of innocent women accused of practicing the black magic of witchcraft.

PATTERNS OF CULTURE DEFINE THE GOALS OF LIFE

Within the system of any people, if that system is properly integrated, goals of life are distinctly defined. The simpler the culture, the more clearly these goals stand out; the more complex the culture, the greater the diversity of goals, and the more difficult to lay one's finger on them. In a culture like our own, rich with elaborate institutions, socially sanctioned goals are legion.

Among the Indians of central North America, adulthood meant warfare; their rituals and ceremonies, their education for

---

[16] Willey and Rice studied the reactions of students at Dartmouth College to size of family a few years ago, and reported various unfavorable reactions to the large family, most students desiring very small families for themselves, two being the favored number of children. See "College Men and the Birth Rate," *Journal of Heredity*, 1926, vol. 17, pp. 11–12.

[17] B. Sidis, in *The Psychology of Suggestion*, D. Appleton-Century Company, New York, 1898, discusses the witchcraft mania at length.

[18] Published by John Russell Smith, London, 1862.

youth, their myths and magic, revolved about it. The pre-
eminent goal of life was honor, and honor came by way of self-
torture and prowess in deeds of savagery. Among the Australian
aborigines, the goal of the adult male was participation in the
activities of male secret societies, from which all women were
excluded under penalty of death.[19] Goals of societies, as numerous anthropological accounts demonstrate, are adequately marked
by the cultural pattern.

Benedict has shown that no people ever exploits very many of
the total possibilities of human nature or of culture.[20] Each era
concentrates on a few characteristics and makes much of them,
while at the same time other eras may disregard them almost
wholly. People living in an era consider the values of their time
human, worthy, and if you will, the end or goal of life. These
configurations within a culture define the meaning of life, and at
the same time have a compelling influence in shaping life in
harmony with this meaning. Worship may attend old age in one
culture; in another the aged may be slaughtered by their children
as a matter of duty.

The martyr pattern, which has no sanction as a goal in our
culture, has nevertheless been prominent enough historically in
Western civilization to exercise a controlling influence. Martyrs
are made by an age. In the early church it was easy to brave
persecution and even to die for the faith in the church, because
one was under pressure of a three-way social process. First, the
intense loyalty and belief in one's own group was intensified by
oppression. Second, an opportunity was thus provided for one
to testify to unbelievers that his belief meant more to him even
than life. Third, but by no means least, there was an undying
faith in the eternal rewards that the righteous Judge for whom
one died would give.

An isolated person does not perform the martyr act. No individual, with perhaps the exception of him who is most conscious of the realities of another world, ever would play the role
of martyr without spectators, nor would he play it except as his
group's culture defines conditions under which martyrdom is approved behavior, and under which it brings its reward.

---

[19] See Ruth Benedict, *Patterns of Culture*, Chapter 2.
[20] Ibid., p. 36. See also her "The Science of Custom," *Century Magazine*,
April, 1929, pp. 641–649.

Not far removed from this role is that of the daredevil hero in our culture who, having developed a certain picture of himself in the group, hardly dares vary from that picture for fear of losing status. His role, in some respects, is similar to that of the gangster who dares not quit for fear of being "taken for a ride." The daredevil who quits his role will be destroyed socially with equal force by those who have come to expect certain behavior of him. Thus, he will brave dangers and endure much hardship rather than permit destruction of his social status. In time he comes to demand of himself those things which onlookers expect of him.

Apparently the role of daredevil is accepted in our culture, just as was dying for the Christian faith in another age.

INTEGRATION OF CULTURAL GOALS AND PERSONAL INTEGRATION

Cultural values are not always integrated. The marginal culture which bridges two culture areas may include a strange mixture of different patterns. Any culture which is borrowing heavily from another is likely to lack established and integrated definitions. When two peoples with different cultural backgrounds meet, a great number of maladjustments in the culture patterns may result.[21] In cases where one culture far overshadows the other, the patterns of the weaker culture may disintegrate, as has been the case with the American Indian under the influence of white civilization. The old Indian culture was oriented on one line, and set before the individual one set of goals; the white man's culture is oriented in different directions, and sets forth many goals.

In our social organization, orientation, as has been suggested in the preceding chapter, is broken down into sectors by vocational and class lines. Many minor patterns of culture exist within the general cultural milieu. An individual who participates in several occupations, or associates with people on different levels of the social stratum may find himself struggling to attain goals that in themselves are incompatible. Others, failing to select any goals, find themselves without motivation. As a consequence, random activity in many directions characterizes

---

[21] Various possible adjustments when cultures meet are outlined by G. Pitt-Rivers in "The Effect on Native Races of Contact with European Civilization," Man, 1927, vol. 27, pp. 2–7.

their life organization, even in a culture which in its totality may possess an integration of patterns. In any complex social order the general patterns of the total culture are likely to be beyond the mental grasp of many individuals. Others lack the capacity to weld from the numerous minor patterns an organized set of goals.

MENTAL EPIDEMICS AS FACTORS IN CONTROL

In the field of mass behavior, mental epidemics have been influences in social control with reference to particular values that become exaggerated in the thought patterns of a time. These epidemics always center in a value which a particular age exalts in its culture. The great mental epidemics of the last several hundred years furnish examples. The Crusades were the product of a Christian culture that, lacking a tangible field for earthly conquest, created an issue in line with Christian values, that of rescuing a sacred object profaned by infidels. Similarly the Flagellants movement fitted the pattern of a self-humiliating ascetic Christian culture. Just as truly, the Mississippi bubble, the California gold rush, the Florida land boom, and the 1929 stock market craze reflected the predominant materialistic values of their age. Mental epidemics serve to raise prominent existing values to the point of mass action.

Mental epidemics as devices of control are temporary in effect, and their results often are of questionable value. They control perhaps too effectively, in prompting people to act with reference to cultural values which, becoming temporarily the single goal, throw the social system seriously out of adjustment.[22]

MAJOR VALUES OF OUR TIME

Werner Sombart, inquiring into the nature of American culture, draws an analogy between the American ethos and the values of a child.[23] He finds the characteristic essence of America in her emphasis on (1) bigness (we value mere size), (2) speed, (3)

---

[22] The psychological factors which sow the seeds of mental epidemics, and the pervasiveness of their influence, have been examined extensively in works in social psychology. Excellent analytical descriptions of most of the important epidemics in the Western world during the Christian epoch are to be found in articles summarized in Kimball Young's *Source Book for Social Psychology*, chap. 24.

[23] Werner Sombart, *The Quintessence of Capitalism*, chap. 12.

novelty (we are attracted by the new and sensational), and (4) power (we desire superiority over others).

That we stress these values, however, does not deny the existence of many others, perhaps equally vital in our lives. In fact, our cultural values are so numerous that it is practically impossible to isolate them all or even to select the most important ones. Those discussed below illustrate as well as any how cultural compulsives control a people.

The competition-success pattern in our culture. Chief among the patterns of the Western world has been that of success, a culmination of our Protestant-capitalistic philosophy.[24] Protestantism originated in Luther's idea that each individual was a free moral agent, able to seek out his own salvation, without direction of priest or institution, and it has continued to stress the importance of individual initiative and enterprise in working out one's own moral welfare.

Parallel with the development of this philosophy of religion has gone the development of a capitalistic philosophy based on the assumption that in the economic sphere every man is free to work out his own economic destiny, to take possession of the means of production, to appropriate natural resources, to acquire authority and prestige through the use of money, and to manipulate large blocks of the social-economic domain to his own personal advantage. Because of these prevailing patterns in our social world, the success pattern has developed as perhaps in no other culture, although in many cultures it tends to be dominant. The person who does the outstanding thing is recognized all over the world. But in societies where competitive values are not emulated, the success pattern is not so obvious as in the Western world.[25]

This pattern, because it is much objectified in our culture, becomes a driving force in the personality of the individual. Just as in the biological world self-preservation is considered the

[24] The relation of Protestantism to the growth of capitalism has been discussed at great length by Max Weber in *The Protestant Ethics and the Spirit of Capitalism*, translated by Talcott Parsons, Charles Scribner's Sons, New York, 1930, and by B. W. Towney, *Religion and the Rise of Capitalism*.

[25] Margaret Mead describes the Arapesh civilization as one in which there is little competition. See *Sex and Temperament in Three Primitive Societies*, Part 1; also, her *Cooperation and Competition Among Primitive People*, McGraw-Hill Book Company, New York, 1937.

first law of life, so we might say in the social world, as far as occidental culture is concerned, recognition becomes the first law of social behavior. This law has been described by sociologists and anthropologists in various terms. W. I. Thomas indicated that one of man's fundamental wishes is the desire for recognition. Adler said the basic drive of life lay in the masculine protest, that is, the desire to be recognized as a full man. Anyone who falls short of this recognition suffers from a feeling of inferiority and compensates by striving to acquire success in some field.

One might argue at great length as to whether this craving for recognition is an inborn drive, whether it grows out of organ inferiority as Adler has assumed, or whether it is something that the imagination of the child catches very early in life from his experience in a competitive social order. Our culture, and to some extent probably all cultures, lead people to indulge in comparisons. A man measures himself by the same yardstick which his fellows use. Different tribes employ different measures which are generally recognized by the particular group. People struggle to meet whichever standard is approved by their group. The sociologist and anthropologist on the whole tend to favor the view that experience lies back of the competitive urge, primarily because of the fact that in societies which do not emphasize competition and success, manifestations of this tendency do not seem to be so prominent.[26]

Much in our school system fosters the spirit of competition, with a consequent neglect of other, more important values. Most grading is based on the curve, which ranks each individual in relation to each other member of the class rather than by an absolute standard. Most of the games we play are competitive; the object of practically all athletic events is to win. Debates are usually conducted on a rivalry basis. Even little children boast to their parents of being the best reader in the class or of having received the best grade in spelling. Gold stars, or black marks, as the case might be, stimulate them to further effort. Dull indeed is the child who, by the time he is seven years of age, has not realized the practical value of proving one's superiority in the group. Even in his conversation *his* daddy is biggest.

---

[26] See Margaret Mead, *op. cit.*

In the economic sphere, there is, in spite of the few voices crying in the wilderness, almost universal adherence to the doctrine that competition is the life of trade. The customers of any small town store always bewail the high prices in terms of the lack of competition.

One outgrowth of the competition-success complex is an emphasis upon the spectacular which, as Sombart has suggested,[27] in the eyes of cultures with differing values undoubtedly approaches the childish or the naive. That we do exaggerate the importance of size is reflected in our predilection for big houses, long bridges, high dams, tall towers, and big cities. Bigness has merit in itself in our culture, considerations of quality seldom receiving attention. We make competitive situations out of many relationships, and the successful in each wins renown. In the pioneer days the great sinners were held in high repute, as witness certain famous gunmen and demimondes. The most prominent gangster becomes Public Enemy No. 1 today, the envy of many a youth or weak-kneed adult criminal. We create numerous competitive situations by artificial means. Tree-sitting contests, hog-calling contests, pie-eating contests, dance marathons—each opens a path to a chance at success. Such patterns become very commonplace. For instance, it is a moot point as to whether the scientist who strives to accomplish some noteworthy object is doing it for science or for the sake of success and resulting fame. Thus mixed condemnation and respect were tendered Admiral Byrd during his last trip to the Antarctic. Thus public opinion alternated between admiration and disdain during Amelia Earhart's last spectacular flight in the southern seas, which ended so disastrously.

It is inevitable that such questions will be raised in a society in which the success pattern is prominent. With rare exceptions, people crave success for the rewards it brings in the way of status. That there are scientists who are interested in the discovery of truth for its own sake and that they would perform equally well if there were no newspapers is believed only by a few credulous individuals. We naturally assume that the success pattern has much to do with the control of individual behavior. We need also to assume that it has much to do with the behavior

---

[27] Werner Sombart, op. cit.

of certain groups within our society. We can assume further that the success pattern has much to do in the modern world with interactions of nations in their relations toward one another.

No attempt will be made here to evaluate this pattern in our society. It has its advantages and disadvantages.[28] Our interest is merely to indicate that it is a basic pattern of life laid down in our culture, and that as such, it inevitably controls and becomes a motivating force in our activities. Theoretically in our open class society every door of opportunity is open to every man.

Competition and the open class system. Most values in any society reach only a limited number of people. Prizes are few. Social orders which permit little exercise of individualism usually confine their highest rewards to a favored few, designated by birth or by well-understood social custom. But in a society like our own which holds out some sort of booty to every man, regardless of birth or station, the only limitation being his ability to earn, a great deal of competition naturally results, and much honor is bestowed upon the one who outdistances his rivals. Even the most democratic of societies must limit the number of prizes. Wealth is not exhaustless. In caste societies it is concentrated in the hands of one class, which will never surrender it until a possible day when social revolution makes redistribution compulsory. In such a society authority is inherited. The crown rests upon a royal head, but royal heads are determined by royal germ plasm. In democratic societies which recognize no caste principles, wealth is for those who can acquire it. The weak succumb to the strong, until, through a process of merciless competition, the baron of wealth emerges victorious. But the movement may be also down; he may mismanage or otherwise lose his money, in which case he again becomes one of the common lot, and another rises to take his place. Democratic traditions place the possibility of some day becoming president within the grasp of every child. Through successful competition one man rises step by step to this highest honor, which represents supreme political success, but his son has no better chance of filling the same position than any other youth, except as he succeeds in competing with over twenty-five million others who are equally eligible.

---

[28] Ruth Benedict has shown some of its unfavorable effects in Kwakiutl society where rivalry is prominent. See *Patterns of Culture*, pp. 246–250.

In our traditional open class system the competition-success pattern can be observed in almost every phase of social experience. In school, in church, in bank and factory, "to the victor belong the spoils," the victor being the one who wins the game, or who beats the other person to the coveted position. From the standpoint of individual motivation this is perhaps the most compulsive pattern in our culture.

Progress, reform, improvement, and change. With the exception of times of crisis, when general pessimism may grip the nation, the American public, and to a lesser degree peoples everywhere in the western hemisphere, have assumed that better days lie ahead. We are conditioned to such views perhaps largely by our knowledge of material things, of which new fashions are produced almost annually. It is taken for granted that the new model will be an improvement over the old, and certainly in the field of mechanical devices at least, this faith is justified by repeated experience.

The idea in all probability has been stimulated also by the doctrine of evolution now popularized to the extent that great numbers of people believe in the operation of a law of universal improvement. Even those with a most superficial knowledge of biology assume that man ascended from the ape or some ape-like creature, and some even go further and hold that man began his existence as a one-celled creature, evolving only after millions of centuries to his present state. Such an achievement in nature in an upward direction is not to be gainsaid.

Far different is the modern perspective from that of the Middle Ages, when the Garden of Eden with its perfect and superlatively happy pair basking in divine approval was considered the point from which man started. Man's earthly life was viewed as one of toil, poverty, satanic domination, and moral darkness, cursed for sin. For the generation of that day there was hope, but not progress. Hope was for the world to come; there was no cure for this world. The race must suffer on until those faithful few who isolated themselves from worldliness and sin and possessed their souls in patience would be called home, finding rest and eternal redemption.

Even the emphasis of the Christian Church has shifted in the direction of progress. Little is heard today from the pulpit of "Adam's fall that cursed us all." More is heard of the regeneration of society through a social gospel and of ushering in a millennium here on earth.

To understand the average American's attitude toward life and the world about him, one needs to understand his belief in progress and human betterment. Advertisers who identify their products with progress elicit a hearty response. Politicians who identify their cause with progress uncover a sympathetic following. Preachers who propound a gospel of social progress find a multitude of disciples among the socially minded with whom such doctrines are taken for granted. Reformers who are striving toward the realization of social ideals are always able to rally support for their programs in the form of money and prayers. Then, too, many youths stand ready to consecrate themselves to any service that has as its goal the improvement of conditions.

Individualism, sacredness of personality. Our western Protestant, capitalistic, democratic culture began its emphasis on individualism during the revolutionary movements of the 18th and 19th centuries. Protestantism, which had its beginnings with the Reformation in Germany, stresses salvation through individual effort. "Work out your own salvation," has always been its motto. Capitalism, the most individualistic economic system ever conceived, has reached its fullest development in our society. In the political sphere, democratic governments are based on the theory that every individual has a right to cast a ballot, thus having a part in determining how he shall be ruled. In literature and art, the Renaissance of the same period ushered in a revival of Greek enterprise and initiative.

Notions of the importance of individual enterprise have brought with them a sense of personal worth such as few societies have ever attained. Each individual is offered a wide range of choice, and every group possesses more liberty than is common in most societies of the world. There is naturally less domination, less social stratification, less rigid control by fixed and permanent patterns. On the other hand there is more personality stress, more responsibility for choosing one's own way, and more danger of choosing the wrong path.

This characteristic of our culture must be kept in mind in any discussion of social control, whether analyzing the family, the political order, religion, or some other phase of society. The child in an individualistic regime has much latitude of choice.

He need not follow his father's footsteps, in religion, politics, or even vocation. He may select his own mate. Such liberties are seldom a part of family systems elsewhere.

This sturdy philosophy has been given a vicious thrust in recent years when numerous troubles have harassed the world. Certain nations of the West have sacrificed it to political messiahs with a message of national hope. In America it has been seriously challenged as an economic doctrine, some even charging it with breaking down our personal liberty guarantees. But as a cultural value individualism will in all likelihood continue to weather even more severe attacks in the future.

In spite of propaganda to the contrary, this philosophy is still a prominent compulsive in our culture. We still practice freedom of speech and press; we still worship gods of our own choosing; we still compete with few effective restrictions for control of economic goods. We still guarantee to every man "life, liberty, and the pursuit of happiness" within broad limits.[29]

Epicureanism. Closely allied to individualism is the notion of supreme happiness for the individual. Pleasure rather than duty tends to become the goal of life. Our school system speaks much of motivation, and of emphasizing the play interest instead of stressing discipline or work. Marriage has become an institution designed for the supreme happiness of two individuals with romance, not progeny, its function. Recreation patterns have taken on a nearly sensuous character. The church has fallen in line and now tries to rival other organizations in making man's life pleasant and beautiful.

Back of this epicurean trend are a number of other compulsives aside from individualism. A forced leisure has made essential the development of recreational institutions, which always stress the pleasure side of life. A marked shift has taken place, from concern over ultimate values of the hereafter, to a short time quest for the most this life can give, in the spirit of the epicurean motto, "eat, drink, and be merry, for tomorrow we die."

Conclusion

There develop within cultures idea systems which act as compulsives, directing the thinking of the masses and setting the

---

[29] For a further discussion of individualism as a value in our culture see David C. Coyle, et al., *The American Way*, pp. 11 ff., 153–170.

general patterns of their lives. In order to understand the guiding principles of a social order, and to see the underlying factors which tend to shape social behavior one needs to search into the nature of the culture values predominating in an age. The acts of every individual as well as of the social masses fall under the shadow of these values. In fact, in their broadest sense, they constitute the most general, yet the most pervasive, elements of social control, in that they permeate all groups and all classes. Their impact is so diffusive and so general that only the trained analyst recognizes them; they set the stage for more specific and specialized forms of control; they are the mass-motivating ideas of a society, having their origin in historical experience.

Every society is characterized by what anthropologists call ethos, national character, patterns, or compulsives, these patterns being the result of an overemphasis on certain complexes in the civilization. Every age and every locality has its own peculiar ethos which defines the chief goals of life, and defines them so completely that certain distinctive habit patterns develop. Thus an entire generation may sway to and fro in harmony with the dominant ethos. Every culture has an ethos usually quite permanent, stable, and enduring over a period of time, until transformed through some revolutionary force or through the gradual process of social evolution. It is at times when mental epidemics suddenly sweep over a particular culture area that one sees the extremes to which values of life as defined by a particular culture at a particular time can control the inhabitants of the culture area. But in every culture at all times, powerful forces are making for uniformity in behavior, unobtrusively but yet fairly completely controlling the attitudes, habit patterns, and philosophies of life of the people. In one age men become martyrs for the sake of Christianity, in another, the conquerors of wealth, of disease, or of a political faith. "Give me Christ or all is lost" is the cry of the martyr at the stake in one age; "liberty or death" the stern alternative in another.

SELECTED REFERENCES

Addams, J., "A Modern Devil Baby," *American Journal of Sociology;* vol. 20, pp. 117–118. 1914.

Bartlett, F. C., *Psychology and Primitive Culture*, chap. 5. The Macmillan Company, New York, 1923.

Benedict, Ruth, "Configurations of Culture in North America," *American Anthropologist,* vol. 34, pp. 1–27. 1932.

Benedict, Ruth, *Patterns of Culture,* chaps. 2 and 8, and p. 36. Houghton Mifflin Company, Boston, 1934.

Bossard, Joseph H. S., *Social Change and Social Problems,* revised edition, chaps. 5 and 6. Harper and Brothers, New York, 1938.

Calverton, V. F., *The Making of Man; An Outline of Anthropology,* introduction. The Modern Library, New York, 1931.

Cooley, Charles H., *Social Organization,* part 4 and chaps. 28 and 29. Charles Scribner's Sons, New York, 1909.

Cooley, Charles H., *Social Process,* chap. 13. Charles Scribner's Sons, New York, 1918.

Coyle, David C., and Others, *The American Way.* Harper and Brothers, New York, 1938.

Gandhi, M. K., "Untouchable," *Survey,* vol. 55, pp. 285 ff. December 1, 1925.

Hart, H., "As a Social Scientist Sees It," *Christian Century,* vol. 48, pp. 119 ff. January 21, 1931.

Kenyon, T., "Witches Still Live," *North American Review,* vol. 228, pp. 620 ff. November, 1929.

Kittredge, George Lyman, *Witchcraft in Old and New England.* Harvard University Press, Cambridge, 1929.

Kroeber, A. L., "The Possibility of a Social Psychology," *American Journal of Sociology,* vol. 23, pp. 633 ff. 1913.

Link, Henry C., *The Return to Religion.* The Macmillan Company, New York, 1937.

MacIver, R. M., *Society,* chap. 9. Farrar and Rinehart, New York, 1937.

Malinowski, B., *Myth in Primitive Society.* W. W. Norton and Company, New York, 1926.

Mead, Margaret, *Cooperation and Competition among Primitive People.* McGraw-Hill Book Company, New York, 1937.

Mead, Margaret, *Sex and Temperament in Three Primitive Societies.* William Morrow and Company, New York, 1935.

Plant, James S., *Personality and the Cultural Pattern,* chap. 9. The Commonwealth Fund, New York, 1937.

Platt, C., "Class Consciousness," *American Journal of Sociology,* vol. 30, pp. 558 ff. March, 1925.

Rivers, W. H. R., *Essays on the Depopulation of Melanesia,* pp. xviii–116. Cambridge University Press, Cambridge, 1927.

Sapir, Edward, "Culture Genuine and Spurious," *American Journal of Sociology*, vol. 29, pp. 401–429. 1924.

Seldes, G., "Fads and Fanaticisms," *Catholic World*, vol. 128, pp. 602 ff. February, 1929.

Sombart, Werner, *The Quintessence of Capitalism*, chap. 12. T. F. Unwin, Ltd., London, 1915.

Stefansson, Vjalmar, "Adventures in Diet," *Harper's Magazine*, vol. 171, pp. 668–675; vol. 172, pp. 46–54, 178–189. November, 1935, and January, 1936.

Sumner, W. G., *Folkways*. Ginn and Company, Boston, 1907.

Wallis, W. D., "Prejudices of Men," *American Journal of Sociology*, vol. 34, pp. 804 ff. March, 1929.

Willey, M. M., and Herskovits, M. J., "The Cultural Approach to Sociology," *American Journal of Sociology*, vol. 29, pp. 188–189. 1923.

Young, Kimball, *Source Book for Social Psychology*, chap. 24. F. S. Crofts and Company, New York, 1933.

CHAPTER 9

SOCIAL CONTROL AND THE PROBLEM OF INDIVIDUAL FREEDOM

THE PROBLEM STATED

One cannot survey the process by which human nature is built, by which man is socialized, educated, and made a conforming creature (call it what we will, it is one and the same process), as has been done in the past few chapters, without immediately being challenged with the question, "Are you not forgetting the individual? Have you not robbed him of his dignity, of his power of free-will and choice?" This problem is important and an answer to it is justified.

Certainly, one who views the individual as powerless in the grip of social forces may well be accused of having robbed personality of a factor which is essential to self-respect and ego-consciousness. Moreover, he has penalized society because he who makes the individual a mere automaton in a social process places all the responsibility for human conduct upon society and none whatever upon the individual.

Is there a place for individualism, even in a system of complete socialization? Does the human being have the power of choice? Is there something in his organic capacity that gives him the power to integrate experience and make it distinctly his own? Are there elements in personality that are unique? Interestingly enough, parallel with the development of the knowledge of the processes of socialization as we have come to understand them in our culture has come the development of a knowledge of individual differences. Not only has the effect of socialization on conduct begun to be realized, but much evidence has accumulated to the effect that every individual is a unique creature, so original in his makeup that there is no other person in the world like him, either in hereditary endowment, social experience, or personality. One cannot face the facts and still maintain that the individual is only a robot. He does have power to integrate experience, to create within himself a world of meaning from the environment. In other words, the individual integrates experience and develops a personality distinctly different from all others. For this reason every individual constitutes a peculiar problem in social control. Motives differ, the response of the individual to social authority differs, the success with which personality is integrated, granted similarity of experience, is different; in fact, one must recognize individualism even in the most regulated authoritative social order, even though it is less prominent there than elsewhere.

Where should one set the limits between individualism and authority, between personality expansion and group safety? This is a very fundamental problem in social control, one that all societies must face. Different answers have been given, depending on the cultural structure of the particular period of history.

But there is no such thing as a society which permits the fullest development of individualism, if we are thinking of an individualism of extreme eccentricity, because as such it can have no functional value in that society. Every individual, with the exception of the few Casper Hausers or fabled Romuluses and Remuses, is reared in a social group and partakes of the socializing patterns of that group's culture. Some societies, however, permit a much greater range of individual variation than others; some define practically all of the life situations for each member, while others define only those which are considered to be the most important, leaving the member free to choose within broad limits.

In Spartan society a rigid pattern of life for youth was fixed by the state. In our society the state makes the education of youth compulsory; otherwise, he is free to make many choices, to select the subjects in which he will enroll, the vocation for which he will prepare, and, to a certain degree, the length of time he will remain in school. In oriental society and, in fact, in most societies of the world, parents or matchmakers choose the mates for youth; in America, though we insist upon pair marriage, generally speaking we let each youth choose his own mate.

The frontier in the United States, with its need for self-reliance, for courage, and for personal adjustment to hardships, probably tended, first, to select an individualistic, aggressive, courageous type of migrant and then to exaggerate these traits. If this hypothesis is correct, Americans have come by their extreme individualism naturally.

The fact that our culture is one of the most individualistic ever conceived creates numerous problems in social control. The assumption that individualism is the proper way of life naturally affects our attitudes toward social control. In our society then, more than most others, but certainly to some extent in all societies, the individual faces the perpetual struggle between the desire to exercise his prerogatives and the imperious demand of the group for uniformity—the struggle between personal freedom and social discipline.

There is therefore, always a rivalry between the spontaneous definitions of the situation made by the member of an organized society, and the definitions which his society has provided for him. The individual tends to hedonistic selection of activity, pleasure first; and society to a utilitarian selection, safety first. Society wishes its member to be laborious, dependable, regular, sober, orderly, self-sacrificing; while the individual wishes less of this and more of new experience. And organized society seeks also to regulate the conflict and competition inevitable between its members in the pursuit of their wishes. The desire to have wealth, for example, or any other socially sanctioned wish, may not be accomplished at the expense of another member of the society—by murder, theft, lying, swindling, blackmail, etc.[1]

UNITY OF THE INDIVIDUAL WITH THE SOCIAL GROUP

The individual and the social order are parts of one system of life [2]—the personality has its counterpart in the culture, and the culture has its counterpart in the individual. This idea has been expressed frequently by sociologists, and is generally recognized as the correct interpretation of the relationship between society and the individual. As Bogardus states it, "Group control and personal initiative are two poles of social life. Both must be constant in their operation if society is to function smoothly." [3]

---

[1] W. I. Thomas, The Unadjusted Girl, pp. 42–43. By permission of Little, Brown and Company.

[2] For a statement of the organic oneness of society and the individual see Charles H. Cooley, Human Nature and the Social Order, chap. 1.

[3] E. S. Bogardus, Sociology, p. 306, The Macmillan Company, New York, 1934.

Ruth Benedict considers that society and the individual are not antagonistic, but that culture provides the raw material from which the individual makes his life.[4] In fact, one's opportunity for personal expansion hinges upon the culture heritage of his group. The relation of the whole social structure to the development of a person has been well stated by Hiller. The substance of his discussion follows:

This discussion attempts to analyze the way and the degree in which, if at all, the social and personal configurations coincide. The person, viewed in relation to a social structure, must be considered as internal to the given social system. By this we mean that what persons, as elements in a social organization, are and do, is, at least in various important ways, the counterpart of the system which they constitute; and, obversely, that their traits affect and set limits to the social system. The ego and the social are correlatives and the structure of each has an equivalent in the other.

Our introductory formula, that the ego and the social are correlatives, calls attention to the necessity for viewing the person in a social system as embodying the characteristics of the system he helps to constitute. If such a statement seems vague, this is not because it is lacking in support by ready observations but because it is contrary to our predilections for the dichotomous view of society and the individual. Under suitable circumstances maturation brings the given individual into essential identity with his society, which supplies both content and organization to the developing ego. The culture is objectified thought and the ego is an internalized phase, an active constitutive element, of the differentiated but integrated structure.

The individual so constituted is the person. He is united with others by virtue of sharing a common nature. He can speak because he incorporates societal facts (language, ideas) in himself. When he speaks he is behaving societally. Communication is an exchange by means of symbols and meanings which are internal to the interlocutors but which were essentially prior to them. They are particular forms of the social. They can converse because they are internal to objective mind. A similar social nature must be premised for the processes of reasoning and reflection. Internalization of culture is a

[4] Ruth Benedict, *Patterns of Culture*, pp. 251–253.

condition of the subject's growth; and from the first his unfolding mind has a social content. His personality thus embodies the modes of conduct that are prior to himself as he learns to act in ways constituting the given culture. Thereafter his thinking proceeds from the same premises and to the same conclusions as those channelled in his culture.

If, now, we regard the culture as having organization or integration, it follows that personality should also reflect a culturally derived organization. Further, if the social structure is, as we suppose, essentially cultural, it, too, should present an organization reflecting that of the given culture integration. We shall consider in turn the patterning due to (1) the form of culture integration and (2) the character of the social structure.

Each culture contains some dominant motif which serves as a selective norm and as a center with reference to which conduct is directed and which supplies a general definition of the situation—an interpretation or point of view and eventually a policy regarding behavior. While every norm, opinion, and innuendo may serve as such a point of reference, a dominant motif supplies a construction and a general scheme of relative values which persons organize as elements in their mental life. Although cultures are not equally integrated, they have distinctive hierarchies of values. For instance, they differ in their emphasis upon individual success, technologies, ceremonialism, monetary values, the importance of life and death, the present and the hereafter. Each also has lesser constellations of culture complexes which do not reflect the dominant motif to an equal extent. But there is a general tendency for the elements to harmonize and cohere in their meaning—a fact which Sumner called the "strain toward consistency." Insofar as the culture achieves such integration it patterns conduct in a like manner by encouraging some, and inhibiting other, acts.

If, as has been reiterated, these culture values are internal to the members of the given society, the personality structure is, in so far, comparable to the culture configuration. These personal equivalents of a dominant culture motif, which may be designated the *ethos personality pattern*, are illustrated by the variations, not only in such matter-of-fact items as fashions, tastes, and technologies, but also in the fundamental processes of perception, memory, and the conclusions drawn from evidence. Equally certain are the culture sources of social conduct, such as assertiveness, aggressiveness, competitiveness, egoism, cooperativeness, sympathy, revengefulness, stoicism, or other hierarchized values prevailing in different groups. These values and their relative priority or importance are given in a culture. They are reflected in the constituent persons as dominant motives and valid judgments, and supply the implicit or explicit presuppositions—in a word, the ethos. So much is this true that values which are demanded in one culture may be regarded as abnormal in another. Accordingly, human nature as we know it, is due to the culture integration which we know, whether implicitly or explicitly.

Such ethos type patterns are recognized by the observation concerning the variations in the personality of races. But the pattern is cultural, not biological, in origin, as is evidenced by the fact that different locality groups of a given race have unlike personality patterns; while different races constituting a natio-cultural society may have in common similar personality patterns.

The manner in which personality patterning occurs in the process of culture integration is suggested by the way the culture and the social organization facilitate memory and mediate preferences and choices. Thus, according to the experimental evidence supplied by F. C. Bartlett, people show reliable recall about those objects that stand high in the scale of the group values. Equally striking mental equivalents have been recorded as to the established relationship between persons and their recognition of similarities. Thus in culture groups in which certain persons stand in close relation to one another, physiognomic similarity is recognized as between father and sons but is not perceived as between brothers and still less between brothers and sisters, between whom social distance is prescribed. In general, perception and experience depend upon prior perception and mental organization; and these, like motivations, judgments, and reasonings, are fashioned by the patterning of ideas in the culture.

Thus on the one hand, the person is integrated by the culture structure; and on the other hand, the culture is integrated by the logico-meaningful responses of the person. Such an approach enables us to abandon unfruitful dichotomies and to dispense with the dissection of the mind into unreal psychological units. The culture elements, likewise, are seen as interrelated in a structural dependence.[5]

---

[5] E. T. Hiller, "The Social Structure in Relation to the Person," *Social Forces,* October, 1937, pp. 34, 36–38. Reprinted by permission.

Individual Differences and Conformity

The preceding materials, while they accurately state the socio-logical conception of the relationship between the individual and the group, give a somewhat oversimplified picture of the individual as he fits into the general scheme of social regulation. Not only is the individual a part of the social order, but he is also an organic unit with capabilities which make him a unique unit in the social mass. This fact has certain significant implications for personality development and for the problem of social control.

First of all, it is generally recognized that individuals vary greatly in their mental, emotional, and temperamental make-ups. Under the same system of control in a family or other group, one individual will react differently from another. To explain why this should be so requires a careful analysis of the mental and emotional traits of the individuals involved. It is not possible, therefore, for a system of social control to prove equally satisfactory to all members of the group, nor is it possible for all individuals to conform equally well to the established system. As Winston puts it, a system of social control can at best fit only the median of these complicated factors of heredity and environment.

. . . Of course in considering the behavior of *individuals*, the fact of variability must never be lost sight of. Within the same complex modern culture, no two individuals, with the possible exception of identical twins, are born with the same biological components. This fact must never be neglected in the consideration of individual behavior. Individual biological differences at birth exist in the quality of the nervous system as well as in possibilities of developmental usage of the various parts of the human organism. In addition, no two individuals, even in the same family, have quite the same *social* environment. As a result, the surrounding cultural controls have different degrees of potency. Human behavior is in generalized terms the product of hereditary and environmental factors working in combination with and through each other. The cultural controls can only reach the medium of these complicated factors. Hence there is the diversity of the reactions of individuals towards the cultural controls. In some cases, as in regard to the eating of human flesh, the cultural controls are almost one hundred per cent perfect. From this and other similar types of behavior there is a series of gradually less completely controlled reactions. Human behavior is inadequately explained without reference to the particular cultural controls involved, and no amount of knowledge of the physiological behavior of the human body can ever supply by itself the necessary explanation.

Typicality or atypicality in human behavior thus largely resolves itself into the degree of variability allowed by society and the remaining within or the overstepping of the boundary limits on the part of the individual. It matters not to society whether the individuals be saviours or criminals. The fundamental cultural consideration is that the generalized type of behavior required by the given society has not been fulfilled. Where the divergence is slight, the societal reaction is usually slight. Where the departure is a serious one, the reaction of society is likely to be severe, often involving social or biological destruction of the individual.[6]

In a further discussion of this topic, Winston points out that because some individuals differ from the norm, controls which may be satisfactory to the majority tend to be coercive to them.

. . . There are individuals whose behavior is indicative of the fact that the persuasive, educative devices have lacked complete effectiveness. Such asocial individuals are persons who behave in a manner sufficiently different in some important respect from their society so that there is a societal reaction against them in consequence.

When the behavior of persons is not in satisfactory adjustment with the existing folkways and mores, the control devices tend to work in a coercive manner. The reaction of society might be characterized as the more forcible control of the asocial individual, when persuasive educative devices fail to work in particular cases.[7]

Individuation Hindered by Social Control

In one sense of the word, all social control tends to interfere with the process of individuation and to reduce individual differences. The presence of uniform diffused patterns in the environment, the eternal persistence of these patterns, and the tendency of group members to look askance at any variation from them—these and other influences work against the expression of exotic tendencies, and help to cast the individual in the common mold. Standardization of personality inevitably results.

---

[6] Sanford Winston, *Culture and Human Behavior*, pp. 204, 205. By permission of The Ronald Press Company.

[7] *Ibid.*, pp. 200–202. By permission of The Ronald Press Company.

E. A. Ross, commenting on the virtues of individualism,[8] says that social commands would choke life, if it were not for the resistance of the rebel who defies orders, preferring to do as he pleases. Cooley, also, extolls the virtues of nonconformity,[9] saying that conformity tends to put society in a rut. Usually, he holds, the nonconformist is the first to point the way toward progress and reform.

THE RELATION OF SELF-CONTROL TO SOCIAL CONTROL

In connection with individuation the problem of self-control arises. The human mind has the power of organization and integration of experience and of self-determination within limits and, because of this fact, each individual is capable of developing a degree of self-control. This ability to control self helps the individual to shape his personality and direct his behavior in line with group patterns. Sometimes, though, self-control may lead to a revolt from group patterns. Ellwood has attempted to reconcile socialization and individualism under the concept social self-control.

A reconciliation of social control and the necessary freedom of the individual is found in the process of socialization. External forms of social control depend upon constraint of the individual, while socialization would place control within the individual. Socialization involves the achievement of self-control on the part of the individual, so that he consciously and voluntarily modifies his behavior and shapes his purposes to promote the welfare of the whole group. We might say, therefore, that the socialization of the individual, when achieved, results in *social self-control*. We have already seen that the highly socialized individual has a sense of responsibility to his group and, if his socialization is broad enough, to humanity as a whole. He is, therefore, dependable and helpful in social relations, mindful of the value of social usage, but also independent in thought, courageous, willing to experiment, but with full responsibility for the results. He is tolerant, his beliefs are subject to review and modification; he is open-minded, but insistent upon evidence, critical rather than fault finding, inventive and creative. Hence, in the process of individual socialization we have a method of social control which is

---

[8] E. A. Ross, *Social Control*, p. 84.
[9] See, for instance, his *Human Nature and the Social Order*, pp. 293–297.

suitable to the highest civilization. It creates personal character. In its highest forms it results in the moralization of the individual. It is hardly necessary to add that agencies of social control when properly developed proceed largely through undertaking the socialization of the individual." [10]

The Importance of Discipline to Personal Freedom

The drift in child training in our society is away from discipline and toward greater freedom of expression. Perhaps we have passed the zenith of this fashion, but the emphasis on freedom still predominates. As a result of our attempts to make all duty pleasant to the child, he tends to become epicurean in his taste. The implications of this philosophy to adult life have been best demonstrated by Margaret Mead in her study, *Growing Up in New Guinea*. In this culture few restrictions are placed on the child. His is a glorious existence, with the whole world centered in him. All youth regret the coming of maturity and the initiation rites which mark the assumption of adult status as symbols of a personal tragedy. The carefree Manus child naturally never learns to enjoy adulthood with its attendant responsibilities. Having never been conditioned to discipline and a sense of obligation, he finds life drab and unattractive.

Personalities that can fulfill their normal function in adult society and find satisfaction therein are products of a normal discipline. Satisfactory adulthood is in no small measure the result of having been required in childhood to do things that were not pleasant, simply because adults, who understood the role the child would eventually have to play, required him to develop habits which would fit an adult role.

Many social philosophers have discoursed on personal freedom, and most of those with a social point of view have been inclined to take the position that only in a controlled order can man be free. The seeming contradiction here is easily explained. In a world where men live in close proximity a human being can enjoy freedom only by observing laws by which the social traffic moves, making room for all to operate. Social control and individual freedom are not necessarily incompatible, in fact, such

---

[10] Charles A. Ellwood, *The Psychology of Human Society*, pp. 394, 395. Used by permission of D. Appleton-Century Company, Publishers, New York, N. Y.

limitation is equally as healthful for the individual as for the group.

Cooley stated the point well when he suggested that even though it is generally assumed that the ordinary person is self-sufficient in many respects and that he could exist in isolation, actually there is never such a thing as complete absence of restraints in the sense of social limitations.[11] He has stressed the important fact that there is no life apart from society, that personality can develop only under a system of social order, that there can be no freedom without some social restraint.

MacIver has stressed a very important point in this connection,[12] that social norms can never take care of the particulars of any situation, but must prescribe principles within the wider zone of conduct, leaving to individual judgment the working out of details.

PRACTICAL IMPLICATIONS OF CONTEMPORARY VIEWS OF INDIVIDUAL VS. SOCIAL RESPONSIBILITY

The close identification of the individual with the group, along the lines presented in the preceding part of this chapter, has been dynamic in changing public attitudes toward problems of individual discipline. Once delinquents were tortured to rid them of evil spirits. Then men believed that the delinquent was motivated by supernatural forces. Later when delinquency had come to be considered the outgrowth of evil traits in human nature, full responsibility fell upon the individual's head for his violations of social rules. But now that we identify the person with his group, we expect the group to share responsibility if he fails to live up to the social standards. Thus we have come to make an entirely new approach to the treatment of problems of delinquency and crime.

Increasingly the socially minded individuals, who have studied problems of human behavior, have been forced to recognize that man's guide is experience, that human behavior in the case of the individual and the tribe is the product of experience, and that the effectiveness with which self-control operates within the individual depends upon his own experience.[13] The implications

---

[11] Charles H. Cooley, *Human Nature and the Social Order*, p. 422.
[12] Robert MacIver, *Society*, pp. 383–388.
[13] Refer again to Chapter 2.

of this philosophy are seen in every phase of the modern humane treatment of socially inadequate groups. No longer do we condemn the poor for their poverty and assume that it is entirely a matter of personal responsibility and personal failure. The whole philosophy of the case method is to examine the individual's experience, and see what factors in that experience have contributed to his present state. Similarly, in dealing with juvenile delinquents and criminals, no longer do we pounce upon the individual with threats of violence and punishment. Modern treatment calls for an analysis of the individual's past experience, and for an explanation of the cause of crime in terms of that experience. Treatment is aimed at reform and it is now assumed that the proper method of reform consists in helping the individual to participate in the type of experience which will establish new habits, new attitudes, and new goals in life. So the older forms of prison discipline—torture, mutilation, solitary confinement—have given way to prisons which are training schools in self-control and industry, which furnish a social atmosphere with normal association, books, work, and play. Modern prison discipline assumes that the offender, through normal participation, may acquire a new type of experience which will help him to live the kind of life that society wants him to live when he leaves the institution.

Even the church has changed its approach in dealing with the sinner. Once all the blame was placed upon the sinner, the only recourse being to plead forgiveness and through a miraculous process of conversion be transformed into a new man. The modern church no longer charges the individual alone. It recognizes original nature as normal rather than as carnal. Religious life comes by participation in the institution which stands for the best that religion has yet developed. That institution is designed to help the individual share in the religious experience of the social group. He becomes religious by becoming a member, by assuming the responsibilities of the institution, by practicing the habits of life for which the institution stands.

So also in the school, the days of teaching to the tune of the hickory stick are past. The idea that the rebellious child must be beaten into submission has no part in modern educational philosophy. In the better equipped schools, a visiting teacher examines the problem child's experience background to learn the factors which may have caused the queer quirks in his personality. The origin is usually found to lie in a strange mixture of influences among which experiential factors loom large. Once the cause is revealed there is no reason for blaming the child. The problem of control becomes a social, not an individual, one.

These are but a few of the numerous illustrations that might be cited in showing the extent to which our new concept of social rather than individual responsibility in the realm of control has come to influence disciplinary institutions in the contemporary period.[14]

Conclusion

The maintaining of a proper balance between individual freedom and social control is of concern in any society. Too much discipline surpresses individuality and breeds revolt; too much freedom brings social chaos. Because of individual differences, no established system of regulation can be equally congenial to all. For some the best designed regulations will appear coercive. But anyone who denies all control is antisocial and has little if any place in society. Social control does hinder the growth of individualism, but since order and responsibility are necessary in any social scheme, the child should be prepared to share the burdens of a disciplined adult world.

In the shaping of personality, too much freedom foreshadows personal degeneration and cultural decline. Too much discipline, on the other hand, blights individualism, smothers initiative, makes for cultural stagnation, and breeds revolt.

Today, with an increasing realization that the individual is of necessity closely identified with the group, is part and parcel of it and its patterns even in a society permitting great freedom, we are ceasing to place full responsibility on the individual for failure to obey social controls. Rather we blame the failure on his past life and as a part of treatment we examine it and seek therein the reasons for his conduct. This examination has so often revealed the fact that the individual's experience has been warped somewhere along the line by social influences, that we are inclined to be tolerant toward him, and to force the social group to share in the responsibility for his misdeeds.

---

[14] A fuller discussion of some of these problems and their meaning to contemporary society is presented in Part VI.

SELECTED REFERENCES

Benedict, Ruth, *Patterns of Culture*, chap. 8. Houghton Mifflin Company, Boston, 1934.

Cavan, Ruth Shonle, *Suicide*. University of Chicago Press, Chicago, 1928.

Cooley, Charles H., *Human Nature and the Social Order*, chaps. 1–6. Charles Scribner's Sons, New York, 1922.

Cooley, Charles H., *Social Organization*, chap. 9. Charles Scribner's Sons, New York, 1909.

Cooley, Charles H., *Social Process*, chap. 14. Charles Scribner's Sons, New York, 1918.

Coyle, David C., and Others, *The American Way*, chap. 1. Harper and Brothers, New York, 1938.

Cross, F. C., and Castle, M. J., "Suicide," *Forum*, vol. 89, pp. 76–80. February, 1933.

Dublin, L. I., "To Be or Not To Be," *Harper's Magazine*, vol. 161, pp. 486–494. September, 1930.

Editorial, "Two Suicides Per Hour," *World Tomorrow*, vol. 15, pp. 318–319. October 5, 1932.

Ellwood, Charles A., *The Psychology of Human Society*, pp. 394–395. D. Appleton-Century Company, New York, 1931.

Hartmann, George W., *Gestalt Psychology*. The Ronald Press Company, New York, 1935.

Harvard Tercentenary Publications, *Authority and the Individual*. Harvard University Press, Cambridge, 1937.

Herrick, Judson C., "Self-Control and Social Control," *The Child, the Clinic and the Court*, pp. 171–176. The New Republic, Inc., New York, 1925.

Hiller, E. T., "The Social Structure in Relation to the Person," *Social Forces*, pp. 34–38. October, 1937.

Keller, A. G., *Brass Tacks*, chap. 9. Alfred A. Knopf, Inc., New York, 1938.

Keller, A. G., *Man's Rough Road*, chap. 25. Frederick A. Stokes Company, New York, and Yale University Press, New Haven, 1932.

Kempf, E. J., "Meaning of Suicide," *The New Republic*, vol. 50, pp. 324–327. May 11, 1927.

Köhler, Wolfgang, *Gestalt Psychology*. Horace Liveright, Inc., New York, 1929.

La Piere, Richard, and Farnsworth, Paul, *Social Psychology*, chap. 13. McGraw-Hill Book Company, New York, 1936.

Layman, Geoffrey, "An English View of Personal Rights," *Harper's Magazine*, pp. 763–773. November, 1929.

MacIver, Robert, *Society*, chaps. 3 and 20. Farrar and Rinehart, New York, 1937.

Mead, Margaret, *Growing Up in New Guinea*. William Morrow and Company, New York, 1930.

Richards, E. L., "Discipline and Adjustment," *Education*, vol. 54, pp. 403–409. March, 1934.

Ross, Edward Alsworth, *Principles of Sociology*, first revision, chap. 56. D. Appleton-Century Company, New York, 1930.

Russell, O. D., "Suicide in Japan," *American Mercury*, vol. 20, pp. 341–344. July, 1930.

Teggart, Frederick J., *The Processes of History*, pp. 154 ff., 107–111. Yale University Press, New Haven, 1918.

Thomas, William I., *The Unadjusted Girl*, pp. 43–50. Little, Brown and Company, Boston, 1923.

Tolson, C. A., "Youth and Crime," *Vital Speeches*, vol. 2, pp. 468–472. April 20, 1936.

White, William Allen, and Meyer, Walter E., *Conflicts in American Public Opinion*. American Library Association, Chicago, 1925.

Winston, Sanford, *Culture and Human Behavior*, pp. 200 ff. The Ronald Press Company, New York, 1933.

PART III

*SOCIAL CONTROL AND SOCIAL PROB-
LEMS IN THE PRIMARY AND SECOND-
ARY GROUP WORLDS*

SOCIAL CONTROL AND SOCIAL PROBLEMS
IN THE PRIMARY GROUP

CONTROL IN A CLOSELY KNIT COMMUNISTIC COLONY

The Amana Colony, a communistic group living in Iowa, had its origin in post-Reformation Germany. The community, consisting of approximately fifteen hundred persons living in seven villages, owns twenty-four thousand acres of farm land. At the time of the writing of the article below it had maintained its communistic form of organization but in 1932, due to economic conditions, it was reorganized as a capitalistic corporation, which no doubt has changed its form of culture somewhat, but not its essential primary group characteristics.

The following account describes the community as a unit of control, as it existed in 1929.

. . . As an institution for the training and control of children, it [the Amana family] is unique. In spite of the employment of both parents in community functions, their prestige and authority are unimpaired. The kindergarten, the school, the factory, and the farm, are organized to assist the parents in producing the kind of children the community wants as citizens. Informal methods of control, such as spontaneous gestures of disapproval, and gossip, are used by the whole community. The parent need only remind the child of this state of affairs and he will conform.

Said a mother to a boy who was carrying a ball-bat when the prohibition against playing ball was in force, "You had better not let them see you with that." The boy went into the house immediately and left the bat. Obedience and disobedience are not personal matters between parents and children. Both alike must answer to the community. All formal methods of control are in the hands of the elders. In case of a violation of the mores, the parents are held responsible jointly with the children, and suffer a reduction in religious status. If a young person leaves the community, the mother is compelled to go to church with the young girls for six months, while the father undergoes a similar punishment. This system of joint accountability to the community promotes a close, sympathetic relationship between parents and children, and exercises an added restraint upon the young people.

Thus said a girl, debating whether or not to have her hair bobbed two years ago, "I would not have my hair cut for anything, because the elders are going to have a big meeting, and the girls who have had their hair cut will be kept out of church along with their parents. My father is an elder. I would not want to do that to him." And later, "But it is no sin to have your hair cut." Neither parent nor child feels any vindictiveness toward the elders, however. The pressure of community opinion and the prestige of the spiritual leaders makes for acceptance. Somehow, the situation is inevitable and must be borne. Children, parents, and community are all a part of an inclusive group control.[1]

THE NATURE OF THE PRIMARY GROUP

Professor Cooley's concept of the primary group as one characterized by intimate, face-to-face association and cooperation is well known.[2] In advancing this idea he indicated that the primary group develops in its members their primary ideals, such as honor, honesty, love, justice, humility, and sympathy.

The chief primary groups are the family,[3] the play group, and the neighborhood, and are practically universal as a nursery of human nature. Undoubtedly it is in the primary group that those personality traits which mean most in the regulation of a person are inculcated.

Control in the Amana colony previously described is undoubtedly more rigid than in the average primary group, because every agency in the environment exerts its pressure to enforce the same controls as are found in the family. As Chaffee stated, "The kindergarten, the school, the factory and the farm are organized to assist the parents in producing the kind of children the community wants as citizens." But many primary groups, espe-

---

[1] Grace E. Chaffee, "Control in an Integrated Social Group," *Social Forces,* September, 1929, vol. 8, p. 94. Reprinted by permission.

[2] Charles H. Cooley, *Social Organization,* pp. 23 ff.

[3] The family as an agency of control is the topic of chap. 15.

cially those located in isolated rural areas, of themselves exercise a great deal of control over their members.

The Kinship Group as an Example of Primary Group Control

The kinship system of old China, with its great family, represents one of the most elaborately developed primary groups in the world, and one of the most efficient agencies of social control. There, all members of the family lived in the common locality, expanding until frequently an entire village came to be made up of relatives, all of whom were under the patriarch and all of whom yielded him their veneration. The system was further fortified by the development of ancestor worship which extended the dead hand of patriarchal authority over the living. In this close-knit group problems of crime, delinquency, and conduct in general were handled efficiently by the kinship group.

In many tribal societies among primitive peoples the rule of elders in the primary group has been a dominant influence in the regulation of conduct. Frequently within this family-tribal society elaborate customs come to control birth, marriage rites, death, and the economic processes.

In rural society generally, and most societies of the world have been rural, the sparsity of settlement makes for a close-knit family and neighborhood group. Throughout the experience of the race this family-neighborhood association has had most to do with the regulation of intra-family and intra-tribal behavior. Only modern urban-industrial society, with its high degree of mobility permits the rapid escape of the child from the authority of the kinship group. Only in the great anonymity of the modern city, where men live so close together that they must develop artificial barriers to intimacy in order to enjoy privacy, has the relatively complete breakdown of the neighborhood with its vigilance over the conduct of the individual occurred. The primary group has been in the past, and is today in most parts of the world, a group which exercises the function of social control more effectively and more universally than any other type of group.

Permanence of the Primary Group Permits Accommodation

Primary groups tend to be much more permanent than most social groups, the individuals living in them remaining there over a long period of time. In the family, for instance, the child usually spends at least eighteen years of his life, the most important years from the standpoint of educability. Similarly the play group and neighborhood are fairly permanent in the case of the child. A group which is relatively permanent is influential in controlling the individual primarily because impressions are repeated over a sufficient period of time so that they register deeply and provide a basis for the formation of habits, attitudes, and values. The primary group is characterized by intimate relations partly because of its permanence. Intimacy tends to make experience register deeply. Here is "a certain fusion of individualities into a common whole." [4] In a permanent group one knows what others think, and is concerned about their reaction to his personality and to his conduct. It is partly for this reason that the primary group becomes an efficient agency in the regulation of the individual.

The individual who is placed in any one environmental situation for a period of time develops a sense of smugness, of fitness to the commonplace world of his experience. This process of complete adaptation to a particular social situation is frequently referred to as *accommodation*. The primary group probably more than any other permits the accommodation of the individual in his manner of living. Frequently in the primary group there is a total lack of those cross currents of stimulation produced by conflicting social influences, so that the individual becomes almost too completely accommodated to his experience-world, not too well accommodated for purposes of control, but too well accommodated for purposes of individualization.

Sentiment as a Factor in Primary Group Control

The primary group is one of intimate face-to-face relationships. Experience is heightened by emotion; teaching is flavored with affection, or at times with wrath. Even the ordering and forbidding technique is not impersonal, but often quite emphatic and pointed. In such a situation the tentacles of the group take strong hold of the individual and bind him well.

Often the child is obedient because he has learned that disobedience will be taken personally, that the parent will feel hurt

---

[4] C. H. Cooley, *Social Organization*, p. 23.

as though it were an insult to him, and not just a violation of his precepts. Throughout the range of primary group contacts one learns to think of how one's conduct will make others feel, and in turn of how their reactions will make oneself feel. Sentiment and emotion are always present in the operation of control devices. This fact is often observed in the behavior of college students who still think of conduct in terms of the way their parents would feel, avoiding some experiences they would personally like because their parents would be deeply grieved by their disobedience.[5]

REPUTATION AS AN ASPECT OF PRIMARY GROUP CONTROL

Reputation for most individuals is confined to their primary group and consists essentially in the name one has established for himself, the status he has acquired because of having responded in a consistent manner to the influences of a permanent group of acquaintances. The individual, in establishing a reputation for himself in the primary group, sets a standard of social expectancy to which he feels obliged to conform. If he has acquired a reputation for honesty, justice, goodness, and generosity, he feels under obligation to keep his behavior consistent with these recognized patterns. Conversely, if he has established the reputation of being the community drone he, in Rip Van Winkle fashion, tends to play up to this pattern. Or if he has come to be known as the reprobate of the community he probably finds it easy to maintain his reputation and to exaggerate his proclivity along this line in order to satisfy the expectation of his group. One tends to play up to the picture he has seen of himself as reflected by the social group. This tendency is especially obvious in the case of the child who, having obtained the reputation of being the worst boy in the neighborhood, goes about with bare chest and projected chin, cursing whom he will and in general making himself the terror of the community. Such a boy frequently has been transformed by giving him a school policeman's uniform, or by other devices which serve to give him a new concept of himself through the eyes of the group.

Of course, the ordinary group with little insight into human nature, instead of using such devices to alter the boy's picture of

---

[5] The author has had occasion to notice this reaction frequently in the autobiographies of college freshmen written in introductory sociology classes.

himself, keeps on talking about "that little tough," thus intensifying the child's tendency to make the most of his reputation. Social workers, delinquency experts, and others working with children often find that the child who fails to develop sufficient reputation to attain any sense of importance turns to delinquency because through this technique he immediately challenges the attention of the community and becomes somebody of consequence. For most people, to be somebody is more gratifying than to be nobody, even though being somebody requires being a person of reproach. A bad reputation is more important in satisfying the ego than no reputation at all.

EFFECTIVENESS OF CONTROL IN THE PRIMARY GROUP

As the individual grows up in the primary group, he is increasingly made conscious that his conduct always is scrutinized by others. For this reason he habituates himself to thinking of his conduct in terms of the response it elicits from others, and, therefore, he becomes highly sensitive to group opinion. Fear of gossip, a desire for praise, and above all, the avoidance of censure come to motivate his every action. To him nothing is more painful than the lash of ridicule; nothing has a deeper sting than unfavorable group opinion. "What will the neighbors think?" always looms large in one's consciousness, for this brings with it humiliation and a loss of status.

The primary group upholds a system of rigid discipline. Since its standards are well established and well understood by every member of the group, behavior is predictable in terms of these standards. Anyone who falls short has committed an inexcusable sin and, like the character in The Scarlet Letter must therefore bear the mark of public disfavor. The red letter on the front of Hester Prynne's garment was sufficient unto itself, needing no comment, for everyone in the primary group understood its significance. The culprit could expect neither pardon nor mercy. She had violated a well-defined rule· of the group and so encountered only intolerance and lack of sympathy and forgiveness.

GOSSIP IN THE PRIMARY GROUP

Blumenthal, in his study, Small-Town Stuff, shows how people in a small community are wittingly or unwittingly affected by a fear of gossip. This is so much the case that they learn to analyze their actions in terms of how other people will regard them. A person's reputation is often greatly endangered by malicious or idle chatter. He, therefore, is usually reluctant to allow himself to be made the object of conversation. Whispers such as "don't breathe a word of this" are frequently uttered, and even in formal meetings someone may propose, "We had better watch our step or the whole town will be on our necks before we adjourn." Most small town inhabitants know they are being talked about, and can only hope that it is more favorable than unfavorable.

Kennethe Leslie describes a small community, which he calls Mytown, thus:

To the people of Mytown the loss of social status is the most powerful of all fears. The fear of being "talked about" is a conscious element in directing their actions. One often hears remarks like these: "What will people think," "We had better walk the straight and narrow line or the whole town will be down on us," or "Be very careful that this does not get out of this house or it will be all over town by dark." All Mytownites have a horror of being objects of gossip. Their station in life is never so obscure that they are not affected by the gossips who will "find them out" and "hound the life out of them."

No one in Mytown has a monopoly on gossip, but three or four individuals gossip so much that they are recognized as professionals— and take pride in that recognition. Two of them are Mr. and Mrs. "Fat" Cummings, who work together very effectively, he specializing in the happenings downtown and she in the gossip of the other areas. Occasionally, however, their technique fails to function properly. One day about four o'clock in the afternoon "Fat" went home to inform his wife that he had heard downtown that Mrs. John Rowe had had her baby girl, and also that Jim Roe had whipped his mules and they had run away from home. When "Fat" got home, he found that his wife had gone out for the afternoon. Fearing that she would come in before he got back, he wrote a note telling her of the happenings.

Mrs. "Fat" came home and, in the excitement of reading the note, she "got the information down wrong." (That was the excuse she gave for telling the story that she told.) She immediately rushed from the house to tell this story:

"Did you hear about poor Mrs. Rowe? Well, she had her baby. It was a precious little baby girl. Mr. Rowe was so mad because it was not a boy that he beat her up, and now he has left home. How in the world is poor Mrs. Rowe going to take care of herself, let alone the poor little baby?"

The next morning the whole town was buzzing over the conduct of Mr. Rowe, only to find out to their amazement that he was at home and a proud father of the little girl. Mrs. "Fat" went and apologized to the bewildered parents and assured them "it was said in all innocence."

But Mrs. "Fat" still talks.[6]

OPINION AS A WHIP IN THE INTIMATE GROUP [7]

Opinion could not influence men if they did not allow it to do so. Yet they do react to the opinions of others, and few things play so large a part in the lives of men living in social groups as do the opinions of their fellows. Indeed, in many cases one is more influenced by the opinions of others than by one's own. They constitute the portion of the individual's environment to which he reacts with most care and caution. The reaction of individuals to the opinions of others is evidence that these opinions have efficacy. Even when no opinion is given in words, there may be marked reaction to personal attitude, for vocal utterance is not the only means of expressing opinion.

> He speaketh not; and yet there lies
> A conversation in his eyes.

A facial or a bodily movement, a smile, a frown, a shake of the head, a pained expression, may reveal one's feeling and be more effective than uttered words. "Bodily gestures and facial expressions reflect hidden psychic activities so that men and women interpret each other's motives by sympathetic and antipathetic responses." Since in effect these attitudes constitute language, being current in the group and conveying meaning to those able to "read" them, they are expressions of opinions which influence conduct. There are prevalent views, standards, and judgments of value, of right and wrong, of expediency and inexpediency, which are accepted by most members of

---

[6] Kennethe Leslie, "Smaller Town Stuff," *Studies in Sociology,* 1936, vol. 1, pp. 25–26. By permission of the Southern Methodist University.
[7] From Wilson D. Wallis, *An Introduction to Sociology,* pp. 190–192. By permission of F. S. Crofts and Company, 1930.

the group. Such opinions are efficacious in influencing conduct, and in bringing it into conformity with the attitude of the group.

A common means, and usually an effective one, for making the recalcitrant individual conform with group opinion is ridicule. Few people can withstand ridicule, least of all when it is voiced by those whose opinions they value. Our conventional expressions, "enjoying the approbation of his fellows," and "withstanding the ridicule of the crowd," show the manner in which we typically react to these respective attitudes. Seldom do men "enjoy ridicule" or "withstand approbation."

Closely allied to ridicule as a social force is laughter. Few people enjoy being laughed at; some, in fact, are resentful if others do not laugh with them, for refusal to laugh at a man's pleasantries is a silent rebuff. Men wish others to agree with them not merely in their serious pursuits but in their lightness and humor as well. "He who laughs last laughs best," means that he who in the end has the best of the argument is in the most enviable position. Laughter is a jolly policeman, keeping social traffic moving in the approved channels, and is none the less efficient because jolly. It is one of the most effective forces making for social conformity and social solidarity. "More terrible than their rage is the peoples' laughter, and if it rends tyrants, with equal zest it pursues the saint and the wise man." Those who can laugh at the same thing have something in common; those who can not, little or nothing. A man's laughter is the measure of his genius, and laughter is sometimes a terrible weapon.

But opinion is not merely a restraining and a constraining force, which keeps people from flouting the customs, traditions, and standards of the group; it acts directly and positively in initiating action, impelling the individual to conform with group standards. Encouragement is one of the means by which the opinions of others influence an individual. We resort to it to good effect in order to improve the behavior of children; we use it commonly, if not always consciously and deliberately, in bringing the behavior of adults up to par and keeping it there.

The conditions of everyday life in savagery give greater force to opinion there than in civilization because all live a common life in which each knows the thoughts of his fellows and privacy is almost impossible. All think aloud. In civilization there is more individual isolation and a man may follow his ideas with greater freedom from intrusion. Even so, the individual seldom is free from the opinions of his fellows, for they jostle his thought in disturbing manner. If he is a weakling he solves the problem by giving up the conflict and accepting the voice of the people as the voice of God. "The contempt of one's class is often a stronger force than many a legal punishment."

HOMOGENEITY OF PRIMARY GROUP PATTERNS: ASSETS AND LIABILITIES FOR CONTROL

Throughout the primary group, social expectancy has an almost perfect environment in which to operate. Because there is a homogeneity of patterns in the realm of morals, attitudes, values, and goals induced by the common experience of a homogeneous cultural mold, every individual knows exactly what the group expects of every other member. For this reason there is no excuse for individual delinquency, in fact, no excuse for any variation from established norms. Everyone knows exactly what the reaction will be if he falls short of primary group standards. In such an environment magistrates have few problems of discipline. Law seldom protrudes itself into the regulative scene. Every individual has established a reputation; his case history is recorded in the memory of his fellow group members. In the more stable primary group areas the older generations have observed children grow to youth and manhood within the same community. They recall many anecdotes in connection with the character development of the child. They know his strength and weaknesses. In case of delinquency they know whom to suspect. If there be deeds of service to be performed they know who may be relied on to respond. They know the institutional connections of all of their members, their interests, and their ambitions. In such a group social control takes care of itself through the operation of spontaneous devices which develop in the community. Tradition, custom, standards, and the general community mores are effectively enforced by gossip and censure—with more success than laws, police, courts, and other institutions and agencies for punishment in the anonymous community of the secondary group world ever achieve.

The general homogeneity of patterns within the primary group community makes for effective control to the extent that every individual tends to be molded in the common form. This is an asset from the standpoint of orderly behavior, although there are primary groups in which patterns develop which are hardly conducive to the best interests of society at large. The homogeneous world, if the patterns are of a high order and represent the better values in the total culture, is an excellent nursery for human nature. Many primary group patterns are undesirable from the standpoint of the larger society, so that the very effectiveness of regulation tends to handicap the individual in his later adjustment. This is often true of the patterns of the rural community in contemporary society. The child is very thoroughly regulated, but according to codes which are outmoded in the urban-industrial society in which many migrating rural youths will eventually have to fit. Often ideas and techniques of adjustment in isolated communities lag far behind those of more progressive communities which are in closer contact with the stream of ideas which flows through the social group. Remote from diffusing influences, they develop a cultural inertia, a resistance to change and to progress which reflects in the personality of group members and tends to make them unfit for participation in the life of their time.

Generally speaking, primary groups effectively regulate their members so that juvenile delinquency, crime, suicide, and other pathological manifestations of behavior tend to be less prominent than in large secondary group associations. On the other hand, if the primary group takes a delinquent turn, or if a neighborhood develops characteristics of poverty, these patterns, as well as the more normal patterns, tend to fix themselves on the entire population of the group. So we have in our cities neighborhood gangs in which any individual would have a difficult time in resisting the delinquency pattern. So also there develop pathological rural communities. This one is characterized by excessive drunkenness, vice, and immorality, that one by poverty, another by inbreeding and the degeneration of biological stock. In any primary group, once a delinquency pattern has been initiated and accepted by leaders of the community, it rapidly tends to grip the entire community and only the most courageous soul dares to stand out against it.

The point is that the primary group controls with exceeding effectiveness, whether in the realm of normal conduct or in the realm of abnormal conduct. The boy's gang with high ideals masters its members fairly completely but no more effectively than the boy's gang with ideals entirely out of line with those of the society. So also, the family with desirable patterns of life as judged by the standards of the time is the most effective agency in existence for seeing that these standards are perpetuated in the next generation. But with equal force the family possessed of delinquent patterns can pass on these traits and make them live in the next generation.

An integrated primary group does not guarantee social progress. It only guarantees effective regulation, whether for progress or for degeneration depending on the patterns that characterize the homogeneous culture of the group. Because of this fact an individual in a secondary group society who feels himself independent of group restraints is frequently in a better position to choose the course in life he will take than the person in the primary group, who is practically condemned by the limitation of his experience to accept whatever patterns are presented. The secondary group by its very heterogeneity of patterns permits individualization by extending the range of possible experience.

THE PRIMARY GROUP IN A DYNAMIC SOCIETY [8]

In a static community the individual lives in a single set of mores. All of life is integrated in conformity to a common rule that finds expression in the church, the law, and the morals, manners, and prejudices of the community. In this sense the individual lives a life integrated with the community as a whole. The small stable community gives every member in it a share in shaping the character of all the others. Group judgment and group condemnation or criticism are universal phenomena which all share and in which all participate. The teacher, the minister, the shoemaker, the merchant, the banker, all share in the responsibility and all share in the pleasure or discomfiture that comes from good or bad behavior of any member in the community. A man's private and public character are cut from common cloth and shaped to a common model. The mere smallness of the community tends to make differences in moral standards unbearable, and conformity and uniformity almost inevitable. The space is too small to tolerate great diversity. The entire community is a face-to-face community; people live in public, in the eye

---

[8] Frank W. Tannenbaum, *Crime and the Community*, p. 29. By permission of Ginn and Company.

of their neighbors all the time, and the limits of tolerance are well known and firmly executed.

Against this background Tannenbaum projects the urban-industrial age of change with its mobility and confusion. The industrial revolution effected heavy inroads on all institutions, and even the family has suffered. Children become independent of parental control at an earlier age. Family members diffuse over wide areas, often living miles apart. The influences of common experience and mutual interest tend to be lost, and everywhere evidences of individualization become apparent. Even the village is in a transition stage; the customary controls of the primary group are being challenged, as outside contacts bring youth face to face with new and attractive patterns.

As Steiner depicts the situation for the small town,

In this emergence of the small town from its old isolation, nothing is more revealing than the efforts of the young people to escape from the thralldom of old traditions. The young people are naturally the storm center where the struggle between group practice and individual variation is being constantly waged. All local institutions and other means of control bring their influence to bear upon the rising generation, for unless the latter conform, the old continuity cannot be maintained. As long as access to the outside world remains difficult, the issue of this struggle is rarely in doubt. Here and there in the more benighted places, an exceptional individual may escape, but the rank and file of the young people fall ready victims to the social pressure to which they are subjected. It is true that today there is a decreasing number of communities sufficiently isolated to maintain absolute control.[9]

PERSONALITY STRESS IN THE SHIFT FROM PRIMARY GROUP CONTROLS [10]

. . . The face-to-face group (family-community) is a powerful habit-forming mechanism. The group has to provide a system of behavior for many persons at once, a code which applies to everybody and lasts longer than any individual or generation. Consequently the

---

[9] J. F. Steiner, "Village Mores in Transition," *Social Attitudes*, Kimball Young, editor, p. 168. By permission of Henry Holt and Company.

[10] From William I. Thomas, *The Unadjusted Girl*, pp. 70–72. By permission of Little, Brown and Company.

group has two interests in the individual—to suppress wishes and activities which are in conflict with the existing organization, or which seem the starting point of social disharmony, and to encourage wishes and actions which are required by the existing social system. And if the group performs this task successfully, as it does among savages, among Mohammedans, and as it did until recently among European peasants, no appreciable change in the moral code or in the state of culture is observable from generation to generation. In small and isolated communities there is little tendency to change or progress because the new experience of the individual is sacrificed for the sake of the security of the group.

But by a process, an evolution, connected with mechanical inventions, facilitated communication, the diffusion of print, the growth of cities, business organization, the capitalistic system, specialized occupations, scientific research, doctrines of freedom, the evolutionary view of life, etc., the family and community influences have been weakened and the world in general has been profoundly changed in content, ideals, and organization.

Young people leave home for larger opportunities, to seek new experience, and from necessity. Detachment from family and community, wandering, travel, "vagabondage" have assumed the character of normality. Relationships are casualized and specialized. Men meet professionally, as promoters of enterprises, not as members of families, communities, and churches. Girls leave home to work in factories, stores, offices, and studios. Even when families are not separated they leave home for their work.

Every new invention, every chance acquaintanceship, every new environment, has the possibility of redefining the situation and of introducing change, disorganization, or different type of organization into life of the individual or even of the whole world. Thus, the invention of the check led to forgery; the sulphur match to arson; at present the automobile is perhaps connected with more seductions than happen otherwise in cities altogether; an assassination precipitated the World War; motion pictures and the *Saturday Evening Post* have stabilized and unstabilized many existences, considered merely as opportunity for new types of career. The costly and luxurious articles of women's wear organize the lives of many girls (as designers, artists, and buyers) and disorganize the lives of many who crave these pretty things.

In the small and spatially isolated communities of the past, where the influences were strong and steady, the members became more or less habituated to and reconciled with a life of repressed wishes. The repression was demanded of all, the arrangement was equitable, and while certain new experiences were prohibited, and pleasure not countenanced as an end in itself, there remained satisfactions, not the least of which was the suppression of the wishes of others. On the other hand the modern world presents itself as a spectacle in which the observer is never sufficiently participating. The modern revolt and unrest are due to the contrast between the paucity of fulfillment of the wishes of the individual and the fullness, or apparent fullness, of life around him. All age levels have been affected by the feeling that much, too much, is being missed in life. This unrest is felt most by those who have heretofore been most excluded from general participation in life—the mature woman and the young girl. Sometimes it expresses itself in despair and depression, sometimes in breaking all bounds. Immigrants form a particular class in this respect. They sometimes repudiate the old system completely in their haste to get into the new. There are cases where the behavior of immigrants, expressing natural but random and unregulated impulses, has been called insane by our courts.

CONCLUSION

The intimate face-to-face group is without doubt the most effective unit of social control that exists. It is found universally and its informal devices are sufficient to regulate the ordinary human relationships, although as society becomes more complex, these devices must be supplemented by more formal ones. The primary group owes its efficiency to its uniformity of patterns, attitudes, and goals, which are indelibly stamped upon the individual growing up within it. Life is certain within this circle and possesses a consistency of meaning as long as one abides by the patterns, seeking favorable group opinion and avoiding the sting of gossip, ridicule, and disfavor.

The primary group is the nursery of human nature, and human nature can be made good or bad depending on the characteristics of this primary group. If the family, or neighborhood, or gang pattern is one of demoralization and vice, character in the child tends to be formed according to this pattern as readily as it is shaped by what we ordinarily consider the social virtues possessed by more normal primary groups. Because patterns tend to be uniform throughout the primary group, primary groups may be much more fatalistic in their influence over the child than secondary groups, for they offer little opportunity to choose alternatives.

In our time, except in the isolated rural community, few children grow up under the influence of any one primary group. Many of them experience a diversity of stimuli and learn many opposing codes. Since modern man must learn to regulate his conduct to conform to the impersonal secondary group relations of adult life, it is perhaps well that most children experience these various group standards. Those who do not, and who later shift to the secondary group, have a much more difficult time in making satisfactory adjustments. Finding themselves in a world where the old controls do not operate, they are forced to seek a new basis for being "good." The secondary group's definition of the "good" life may vary radically from that of the primary group. When such is the case, life-long habits and well-established attitudes have to be abandoned, or mental conflict will ensue. The unfortunate individual who experiences only one pattern of life frequently is unable to make the necessary adjustments in the sudden shift from the primary to the secondary group, and as a consequence finds himself maladjusted. Much of our so-called degeneration is simply evidence of the fact that the person, torn between two codes, has given up trying to reconcile them and has deserted them both.

This analysis turns us immediately toward a consideration of the problem of control in the secondary group world which has become very prominent in our time. In this group we will find that primary group influences are neutralized to a considerable extent.

SELECTED REFERENCES

Blumenthal, Albert, *Small-Town Stuff.* University of Chicago Press, Chicago, 1932.

Chaffee, Grace E., "Control in an Integrated Social Group," *Social Forces,* vol. 8, pp. 94 ff. September, 1929.

Cooley, Charles H., *Social Organization,* chaps. 3 and 4. Charles Scribner's Sons, New York, 1909.

Hiller, E. T., *Principles of Sociology,* chap. 35. Harper and Brothers, New York, 1933.

House, F. N., *The Range of Social Theory*, chap. 11. Henry Holt and Company, New York, 1929.

Leslie, Kennethe, "Smaller Town Stuff," *Studies in Sociology*, vol. 1, pp. 25–26. 1936.

Lewis, Sinclair, *Main Street*. Harcourt, Brace and Company, New York, 1931.

Shaw, Clifford R., and Others, *Delinquency Areas*. University of Chicago Press, Chicago, 1929.

Steiner, J. F., "Village Mores in Transition," *Social Attitudes*, Kimball Young, editor. Henry Holt and Company, New York, 1931.

Stern, Bernhard J., editor, *The Family Past and Present*, pp. 141–144, 287–314. D. Appleton-Century Company, New York, 1938.

Sumner, William Graham, *Folkways*. Ginn and Company, Boston, 1907.

Thomas, W. I., and Znaniecki, Florian, *The Polish Peasant in Europe and America*, vol. 1; vol. 2; vol. 5, chap. 2. Chapman and Grimes, Boston, 1918, 1919 and 1920 respectively.

Thomas, William I., *The Unadjusted Girl*. Little, Brown and Company, Boston, 1923.

Thrasher, Frederic M., *The Gang*. University of Chicago Press, Chicago, 1927.

Young, Pauline V., "Social Problems in the Education of the Immigrant Child," *American Sociological Review*, vol. 1, pp. 419–429. June, 1936.

CHAPTER 11

SOCIAL CONTROL AND SOCIAL PROBLEMS IN THE SECONDARY GROUP

THE PASSING OF THE NEIGHBORHOOD AS A UNIT OF CONTROL [1]

. . . A high authority has called Chicago "an aggregation of separate self-centered units with no common purpose." "Chicago," it has been said, "doesn't know why it exists; it has no soul." To quite an extent this is true of all American cities and of all of American society.

If we had been members of a small New England community 150 years ago we would have been living in a community where religion, neighborliness, and public-mindedness had a working alliance. In this community the farmer, the lawyer, the doctor, merchant, baker, banker, and candlestick-maker would have been carrying on various useful functions in simple, neighborly ways. The farmer refrained from selling too many bad eggs because he expected to see in church the next Sunday the person who bought the eggs. The shoemaker was held back from making a bad pair of shoes because he expected to see on the street the person who was wearing those shoes. Public and social control grew rather naturally out of relationships of this kind. The social imagination by which a man puts himself in the other man's place was easily evoked by the face-to-face contacts of such a community.

But something happened in American life. The miller left this simple New England community; you will find him in the milling district of Minneapolis. The butcher can now be found running a packing plant in Chicago. The wagon-maker will be found in South Bend, Indiana. The banker is on Wall street, and the seamstress is in a garment workers' factory. The farmer who left this community and went south became a cotton farmer; if he went to California he became a fruit farmer; and if he went to Iowa he became a corn and

---

[1] From Arthur E. Holt, "Our Common Perversion," *The Christian Century*, June 26, 1935, vol 52, p. 850. Reprinted by permission.

hog farmer. Now all these people are engaged in rendering a service to people whom they never expect to see. All the old neighborly control and social imagination which came out of neighborliness has now gone. Men are interested in the success of their business, judged solely on the basis of whether it could show a profit or a loss at the end of the year. A new standard of success has the right of way. The best business was that which made the most money. As Mr. Insull recently said, his business was to make money.

Secondary Group Defined

Holt in this discussion is contrasting life in the primary group with that in what has come to be called the *secondary group*. As has been indicated, Cooley first developed the primary group concept and elaborated on its significance in the building of personality. Later writers have developed the concept of secondary group which includes all groups aside from primary groups. All of these other groups are characterized by more superficial, transitory contacts. They tend to be more competitive in nature and to submerge the interest of each individual as a human being in the specialized functioning of the group. It is this general loose meaning of the term which we imply in the discussion of this chapter. Of course, there are classifications of groups based on different approaches which are valid, such as, for example, crowds, mobs, and publics, but for present purposes we are not interested in these.

Bernard uses the term "derivative group" instead of secondary group, implying apparently that all other groups are derived from primary types of association. We are interested here in focusing attention on secondary, impersonal, derivative groups, call them what we will, as they operate as influences in social control.

The Transition to Secondary Group Social Organization

Man has traveled a far distance from the simplicity of primitive life to life in the modern metropolis. In primitive society groups were usually small and intimate in nature, and provided only one definition of "The Right." Individuals were thoroughly impressed with this pattern, and as they seldom were exposed to the patterns of other groups the problem of choice never arose to plague them. The society of yesterday, as we have seen, was mainly of this simple kind.

In an industrialized world, groups become large, culture becomes complex, and standards multiply. In our own country, we have had, in addition to the factor of industrialization, the complicating feature of a heterogeneous population. Regardless of the kinds of behavior in which an individual indulges, he almost certainly will be able to find approbation of it from some other person or group. Indeed, a person living in an intricate society belongs to many groups, several of which may differ considerably in their conception of the moral and the good, and consequently opinion tends to be much more tolerant than in simpler societies. Thus, an individual is permitted a great range of behavior.

For this reason, established control in the secondary group operates less rigidly than in the primary group, and those agencies influential in primary groups—the home, the neighborhood, and the play group—may become less efficient in secondary group control than the more impersonal agencies, such as the press, the radio, the moving picture, and other instruments which transmit rather superficial but nevertheless very fascinating patterns.

Most people have lived in familiar surroundings. They have known only one environment, and that permitted very little variation. Today, in the Western world, there are many social environments. The father, because of business contacts, may belong to a different social circle than his son, mother, or daughter. Recreation in separate fields, according to each one's tastes and habits may draw family members farther apart. Not only is each personality torn between numerous alternatives growing out of group associations, but each is caught in a swirl of social change in the secondary group—change which tends to undermine old foundations. New inventions bring new situations; old codes become obsolete; new adjustments become necessary. The contacts of each individual in the modern world are numerous and diverse, and though many are superficial and fleeting, they nevertheless require regulation.

Systems of social control in the past have been built on a more slowly moving order, and one which tended to be more homogeneous. In a world as changing and as heterogeneous in group structure as today's, it is extremely difficult to maintain the poise necessary to consistent living, and to define a broad and objective morality.

Impersonal Nature of the Secondary Group

The secondary group is one of impersonal contacts where people are little concerned with the conduct of others as long as the others keep out of their way. The control devices of the primary group—gossip, public opinion, and social expectancy—largely disappear. The individual cares less what others think of him and formulates few definite opinions regarding the actions of others. Because of the impersonality of contacts, individuals usually take little interest in what others do. Seldom do they censure or condemn.

In the absence of primary group control devices, the secondary group attempts to control by laws. These laws regulate many phases of behavior, but tend to be very superficial in their effect. They find no place in the individual's attitudes, nor are they dominant in his consciousness as are standards of the primary group. When he is aware of the vigilance of his social group he is likely to be careful of his actions. As a general rule it can be stated that the more cosmopolitan the group and the more cosmopolitan its standards, the greater will be the laxity of control.

Difficulties of Control in the Urban World [2]

The great city is a world of impersonal secondary group contacts. In it are many behavior patterns and many standards. It is a world of contrast between the weak and the strong, the poor and the rich. Millionaires and those in poverty live only a few blocks apart. Hoboes and captains of industry tread the same streets. Towering skyscrapers cast their shadows on the hovels in the tenements. The palatial lake-front dwellings have at their back doors the Ghettos, Chinatowns, and Little Sicilies. The great department stores meet the needs of one class, pawnshops and second-hand stores those of another. The palatial theaters are only a few minutes' walk from the crude burlesques of Hobohemia. First-class hotels meet the needs of one group; the flophouses those of another. The peal of bells in steepled churches calls certain classes to worship; the gospel songs on the street corner call others to the downtown missions.

In this world of many manners of life, behavior patterns are

---

[2] Adapted from Paul H., and Judson T. Landis, *Social Living, Principles and Problems in Introductory Sociology*, pp. 480–484. Ginn and Company, 1938.

equally diverse. It is little wonder that traditions break down, and that mores tend to be disregarded. There are none of the controls here of that intimate world of primary relationships where neighbor knows neighbor, accepts the same standards and is susceptible to the same regulative devices.

In the great city one's actions are not subject to the scrutiny of those whose opinions mean much. In the urban community there is freedom. The control devices so effective in the open country and in the small town become ineffective. Divorce, desertion, crime, vice, insanity, and suicide find more fertile soil in this world of mottled patterns.

It is true that the great city has developed much more efficient protective machinery designed for control than rural areas. The city has more policemen, more detectives, more regulations, more laws, more crime commissions, more vice crusades; but in spite of all this protective machinery, it is difficult to regulate multitudes of people who live in a relatively anonymous world.

BERNARD ON PROBLEMS OF CONTROL IN THE SECONDARY (DERIVATIVE) GROUP

In depth of insight into the problem of control in the secondary group world Bernard's analysis is unsurpassed.[3] (Bernard uses the term derivative group instead of secondary group, but with the same meaning.) The work is so much a classic that the gist of it is reproduced here.

He shows that, with the increased complexity of modern society due to the growth of inventions and spread of industrialization, the problem of the modern world has come to be that of social control rather than of subsistence, as in primitive communities. Problems in social control have originated out of the following: (1) the insufficiency of the primary attitudes for the control of modern, complex social life; (2) the present, common practice of manipulating the primary attitudes for the defeat of the better derivative social ideas; and (3) the necessity of finding an improved means of generating and universalizing the higher types of derivative social ideals.

Elaborating these points, he shows that folk literature and folk

---

[3] L. L. Bernard, "The Conflict Between Primary Group Attitudes and Derivative Group Ideals in Modern Society," The American Journal of Sociology, March, 1936, pp. 611–623.

religion are the chief agencies of social control, though frequently the use of force is necessary. These three main types of control are operative in society today, but are a product of the primary direct contact group relationships, and function most effectively there.

He concludes that it will not be possible to meet the problems of social control in modern society by the improvement of these devices of the primary group. In fact, these very devices may come to be exploited. The tendency in the field of religion, for instance, is to evaluate relationships in terms of primary group attitudes rather than to extend its interpretation to the world of impersonal derivative experience.

Or, in another of his examples in the field of civic relationships, he says,

Religion, in order to serve the present needs of mankind, must discover and teach the most complex derivative and constructive social idealism and not confine itself merely to a limited personal idealism. As yet religion has met this demand very poorly, with surprising inadequacy. Perhaps it will do better in the future.

Now some quarter of a century ago each of ten business men in one of the largest cities of the United States contributed $10,000 to constitute a corruption fund of $100,000 with which to purchase the election of a certain man to the United States Senate. They accomplished their purpose, but in doing so they aroused so much popular resentment that an investigation of this election was forced upon the Senate and the person thus corruptly elected was denied a seat in that highest of our legislative bodies. In order to prevent this final action from being taken, which ultimately ruined the public career of this man, every possible effort was made by him and his supporters to counteract the testimony of the witnesses.

One of these efforts will be mentioned because it illustrates so well how the primary group virtues are frequently employed to offset or corrupt the civic virtues. This senator's priest was called as a character witness and he testified that the person being tried for corruption was of his certain knowledge a model husband and father, the implication being that he could not therefore be a bad citizen. One need not deny the statement of the priest that this man was a model husband and father. He may also have been an acceptable and even a model communicant of the church of which he was a member. But the evidence presented before the Senate investigating committee showed conclusively that he was very bad citizen. From all of these facts together one may draw two conclusions, as follows: (1) It seems to be quite obvious that being a model husband and father (that is, perfection in primary group relationships) is not the same thing as being a good citizen (perfection in derivative group relationships); and (2) that if such a man could nevertheless be an acceptable communicant of his religion, this fact seems to be proof positive of the further contention that such a religion has not evolved morally *pari passu* and in keeping with the ethical demands of our complex derivative civilization; it has failed to meet the moral demands of society made upon it for ethical guidance and control; it still lives and teaches on the basis of a primitive tradition and philosophy which is not in keeping with the higher ethical values and idealism necessary for our age. And this is true of any religion which would dare to shelter and defend any man guilty of such serious civic and moral dereliction as was this man, regardless of the name of the religion.

There was also good evidence that this man was a good neighbor in the primary attitudinal sense of this term. He visited the sick and paid their doctors' bills and bore the expenses of funerals for the deceased. He sent fuel to those who had not wherewith to heat their habitations; he bought food for the hungry; he paid the rent for the unemployed in his congressional district; and he whispered in the ear of the judge and secured the dismissal of charges of criminal behavior against his political supporters. All this he did willingly, even gladly, and apparently with a genuine feeling of sympathy for the unfortunate. Many American politicians and bosses are similarly kind-hearted and neighborly. But for each dollar that he contributed to the relief of the poor by such direct neighborly services, he took three or five out of the public treasury by devious and civically questionable measures. Being a good neighbor did not make him a good citizen. Yet, the masses of his political supporters—the men he had aided personally while he robbed them publicly—were strong partisans of his and condemned his removal from public life.[4]

Establishing Controls in the Secondary Group

What can be done to transfer the controls of the primary group world to the world of secondary group relation, or if this cannot

---

[4] *Ibid.* By permission of the University of Chicago Press.

be done, to build new control devices effective for the modern world? This question is more easily asked than answered. What we have done increasingly is to resort to law on the formal side and to propaganda and publicity of various sorts on the informal side. New laws are constantly being placed on the statute books; restrictions and regulations in ever larger numbers are being imposed in response to modern conditions.

At the same time, a thousand voices are raised by press and radio, attempting, with soft persuasion or strident demands to coerce the people into turning this way or that, according to the wishes of those in charge of the channels of publicity, or of those who buy their services.

Can primary group controls be made to work in secondary group relations? Mowrer has suggested in his study of the family [5] that the task of the modern case worker is to restore primary group control in place of the socially inadequate control of the city. Social work, as he views it, is a form of organized gossip which attempts to define the situation for the individual. The social worker attempts to make the relatives of a dependent feel their responsibility for his welfare; whereas in the rural community, the gossip of neighbors performs the function. The social worker exerts pressure on the employer in an attempt to reduce the number of jobless. In the rural community, public opinion often tends to hold the employer in check so that he will not exploit or carelessly dismiss a worker. The social worker also assists in the formulation of community attitudes with reference to the conduct of individuals, groups, or communities, regulating the standards of families, neighbors, school authorities. The process of unorganized gossip has the effect of bringing the divergent individual into line.

The social worker tries to establish community norms where none exist. In an urban area, many psychopathic, mentally deficient, and neurotic cases often would remain anonymous were it not for the efforts of the social worker, whereas in the rural community, neighborhood gossip would soon expose them as such.

William G. Mather, Jr. has shown how the newspaper through its human interest story may succeed to some extent in transposing gossip, a primary group control, to the urban world of secondary groups. He says:

---

[5] Ernest R. Mowrer, *Family Disorganization*, pp. 275 ff.

. . . The social world has for long generations been a world of small, primary, intimate, face-to-face groups, with each man knowing each detail of his neighbor's life, and being so known by him. Mankind is as yet a stranger to the modern urban life with its casual, secondary, one-purpose contacts. And as a stranger, it is not possible for him to become lonely—lonely for the old intimacy and publicity of his and his neighbor's lives, back in Grubb's Corners?

The human interest article of the newspaper gives something of that intimacy. In the reading of it, we become neighbors, to a certain degree, of those famous and infamous ones who have hitherto been but names and faces to us. By it we peek into their closets and count their suits and dresses, as we used to lift the corner of the sitting-room curtain to peek at the neighbors' Easter array; we overhear their quarrels, just as we used to listen to Jed Simpkins argue with his wife; we gaze at the slain gun-Moll, as we peered through the doorway of the undertaker's at the luckless tramp whom the constable shot rifling the clothing store safe. It satisfies our insatiable desire to peek and pry, and to be peeked and pried at.

For we each of us have a desire to know thoroughly and to be known thoroughly. That is one of the reasons for marriage; by it we have an interchange of the little intimate hopes and fears and thoughts and habits, become important to someone, and acquire someone who is important to us. The newspaper human interest story may be just such another mechanism for the satisfaction of that human desire for intimate response.

Certain it is that many of them, written by the principals themselves, have little reticence. They are obviously a means of relief to the tellers, particularly the most bragging ones. Generally their publication is followed by a flood of letters to the writers or the written-about, letters which praise or condemn, offer advice or matrimony, tell personal troubles in return, or ask for gifts. The first individual has bared something of his secret to the public, and the public, in turn, seeks to share its own and complete the cycle of intimate expression and response.

It may well be that the newspaper, in its role of neighborhood gossip, thus renders a distinct service to its readers. Of course, we do not all like it—consciously. Some of us have come to hate gossip in any form—openly. But it is hard to stop reading a real human interest story, just as it is hard to hush a gossip when she bears delightfully shocking news. We know it is evil, yet we feel its pull. And perhaps the more sophisticated of us do wrong to condemn too loftily that which may be an essential part of the social life of our fellows.

After all, something like the human interest story may be an absolute necessity to our modern urban world. There has never been an enduring civilization built upon secondary relationships in the world. The neighborhood, with its strong social controls, may be a necessity if the human animal is to be properly trained and disciplined into safe society. But we cannot go back to the real neighborhood and still keep our urban civilization. The "psychic neighborhood" which this strange kind of writing creates may be as far from Grubb's Corners as we dare to go.

The more we are fascinated by, and yet repulsed by, the human interest story, the more valuable it will become as a means of social control. For in the old neighborhood where humanity was reared some of us conformed to the conventions only because we knew full well that if we did not, Susie Pry would spread the tale of our misdeeds far and wide. And the threat of having the cut of one's undershirt discussed in a neat little box in the Evening News may be having the same salutary effect today! [6]

In concluding his discussion of the difficulty of employing primary group controls to the secondary group, Bernard decides that the solution is not to be found in extending primary group controls to the secondary group, but in the development of new ideals of general social welfare that will fit the secondary group world:

. . . Those who have recognized the inadequacy of personal or primary attitudes, developed in the adjustment process at work in primary and primitive groups to meet the needs of social adjustment in modern derivative group relations, have usually mistaken the necessary method of creating derivative group or social and civic ideals. Professor Cooley himself suffered from his insufficiency of analysis. Such persons, still under the dominance of the old primary attitudes and unable to break through the bonds of a literature, and art, and a religion formed essentially in the matrix of primitive group life and perpetuating the limitations as well as the virtues of these primitive modes of adjustment, have generally believed that it would be sufficient to extend and to universalize throughout society . . . the primary and primitive group attitudes.

---

[6] William G. Mather, Jr., "A Use for Human Interest Stories," *The North American Review*, December, 1934, pp. 544–545. Reprinted by permission.

Thus Cooley speaks of the extension of sympathy from the family and local groups to international and world-wide relationships, so as to include all races and peoples in the brotherhood of man. But, unfortunately, even the sympathy and affection of the family do not protect its members against exploitation by wider derivative group relations. For example, modern industry destroys the family in fully industrialized countries because it reshapes personal relationships and attitudes to fit the conveniences of mass production and an individualized wage-labor system, and thus neglects the personal relationship needs of the weaker historical institution, the family. In a similar manner, the modern derivative political organization, the industrial state, destroys the old neighborly and local affective relationships that went along with the ancient neighborhood and independent self-governing community. Instead, all the world comes more and more to be made of a single pattern. The masses here and everywhere are protesting against the same capitalistic system; and the same pattern of war, made not for the welfare but for the exploitation of peoples, is universal.

It is not possible to solve the problem of the generation and diffusion of a new social and civic idealism, adequate to control modern social relationships in the interest of all the people, merely by expanding primary group sympathies to cover all classes, races, and nations. That was the slogan of the old democracy which arose in the eighteenth century as a protest against class distinctions and exploitation. It no doubt had a recognizable and an indispensable value. But the old democracy has not proved to be adequate for the modern derivative world. Its idealism did not free itself from the motive of exploitation, but merely from the ideal of the exploitation of the lower classes by the upper classes. The democratic ideal which served as the rallying slogan of the nineteenth century was still exploitation—the exploitation of the rich by the poor, of nature by man, of science for the sake of personal gratification.

The new social ideal that must be erected in the place of this old democratic ideal of majority exploitation (which in the eighteenth and nineteenth centuries of our era replaced the still older social ideal of minority exploitation) is that of the general social welfare. It must become the aim and purpose of mankind to forget the magical belief that something can be created out of nothing and a miracle of social providence be performed by means of a mere arrangement of words and phrases into a constitution. Instead, it must become the intelligent and persistent ideal to determine by concrete scientific sociological analysis what are the conditions of social welfare and to put these into practice regardless of the personal incidence of any of these scientifically determined conditions. Concretely, this means to substitute the ideal of public welfare for that of private profit in our economic relations; social justice for the old ideal of piece-meal, traditionally determined legal justice; a new social democracy for the old political democracy; equality of opportunity and responsibility for equality of consumption and enjoyment; universal scientific education for the propaganda of traditionalism; a condition in which the state becomes the advocate and administrative protector of all the people instead of certain classes and interests; the cooperation of peoples, races, and nations instead of their mutual exploitation; and a thousand and one other constituent social ideals.

Such ideals can never be objectified and particularized merely by the extension of sympathy, as necessary and as indispensable as sympathy is for their proper realization. The work of formulation of these derivative social ideals must necessarily come before that of their realization in social practice. The formulation is a work of very concrete and specific and detailed and laborious analysis of both present social conditions and of future social needs. It is not so much a work of inspiration as of hard labor in analysis and constructive logical, educational, and legislative synthesis. When once these social ideals, as yet scarcely recognized in our present society, have been formulated by this meticulous and laborious method, then we may call upon the expanded primary personal sympathies to help put them into effect. The preliminary work in the creation of a new social idealism adequate to care for those adjustments made necessary by our expanded and derivative civilization belongs to the hard-working scientific sociologist. The final task of their realization in the life of humanity is partly the work of the calm administrator and partly that of the benevolent enthusiast. But it is, first of all, necessary for us to realize that there is a field for derivative social idealism, the modern complement of the primitive affective attitudes, which persistently demands our attention as sociologists.[7]

We have here surveyed three possible approaches to the development of more effective social control in the secondary group. The first two suggest techniques for increasing group pressures

---

[7] L. L. Bernard, op. cit. By permission of the University of Chicago Press.

over the individual in the secondary group, the last suggests new
controls by motivating the individual in the secondary group
through social ideals adapted to the secondary group world, ideals
which define general social welfare and which do not make all
groups subservient to the welfare of the more powerful groups.

At this stage in our thinking on problems of control in the
secondary group, any approach which holds the least promise
should be attempted. In the end it seems likely that the most
effective technique will be that suggested by Bernard—new ideals
for the secondary group world. It seems doubtful that effective
control can be realized until new ideals are born. The difficulties
of creating these new ideals may be suggested by a contrast in
certain values of primary and secondary groups.

PRIMARY AND SECONDARY GROUP VALUES: A CONTRAST

In contemporary American society one sees the most sharp
contrast in values and life goals by comparing the isolated rural
group, which is the most characteristically primary, with the
urbane group of the great metropolis, where the environment is
most secondary. We shall make the comparison in terms of
three major life goals.

Rural primary groups are interested in land, work, and family.
These are not all their values, but probably for the majority constitute the major goals of life. The acquisition of land in our
society has motivated rural peoples of our nation from the time
of its founding. It remains today a major interest. The desire
for land has been so intense that land has always tended to be
priced at a higher level than returns could ever justify. About
this goal centered thrift, enterprise, security, status, drive, and
ambition. Among urban sophisticated classes a desire for property seems to have practically disappeared, and with it security,
thrift, and many other homely virtues of a rural primary group
society. The new goal that is being erected in urban society
seems to be that of conspicuous consumption, that is, spending
lavishly and on those goods which will assist one in putting on
"front." This difference in economic goals is dynamic with
implications to social control. To take but one example, W. F.
Ogburn in his study of changing functions of the family [8] has

[8] W. F. Ogburn, writing in Recent Social Trends in the United States, pp.
664–679, McGraw-Hill Book Company, 1933.

shown that the decline of economic functions has been an important factor in the loosening of the marriage bond, and consequently, in increasing the divorce rate. In this study he produces abundant evidence to show the extent to which economic functions have disappeared from the urban home.

The basic rural goal *work* is being supplanted in urban society by the goal *recreation*. The Puritan-pioneer supreme emphasis on work as a virtue and on leisure and idleness as a curse still persists to a considerable degree in American rural society. In the rural primary group one gains status by such acts as being the first one in the field in the morning, raising the best crop, and putting on the biggest load of hay. Life is built about strenuous toil. Many values center there. The new urban value which seems to be developing is to reduce work to the minimum and to get the most return from the least work. Rather than interest, community respect, and status centering in work, they center in recreation. The amount of time one can spend at the theater, in the country club, or on the vacation, and the class of entertainment he can afford, bring status.

The family has always been, and is today, a major value of rural primary group society. Most rural people expect to marry, and those who marry expect to have children. Marriage is ordinarily looked upon as a permanent contract in our rural society. The family has been considered a practical socio-economic institution, but in our urban-industrial society the romantic pattern of marriage and the family has developed. The family has become an institution for happiness, not progeny. Marriage is a venture in romantic felicity, not a social sanction for a life-long blending of flesh with flesh. The implication of this new goal for the family to problems of control are too obvious to need elaboration here.[9]

True, the above contrasts in three major life goals of rural as compared to urban society deal with extremes. But they are both extremes which can be found in our culture. As urban patterns tend more fully to dominate our society, we tend to move from the rural primary group extreme toward the urban, sophisticated ideal. The most effective control devices of our society are adapted to the old rural ideals. The new control de-

---

[9] The selection reproduced on pp. 258 ff. of this book gives certain implications of this new philosophy.

vices that will be effective in secondary group society will have to take into account the ideals of the new society.

PERSONALITY PROBLEMS GROWING OUT OF SECONDARY GROUP EXPERIENCE

One of the interesting personality problems in contemporary society arising from primary-secondary group relationships is the mental conflict which results from a lack of similarity between primary group ideals and secondary group realities.

Almost every individual has his personality shaped and fortified for living in some particular primary group or groups. Habits, life philosophies, and general standards of values are deeply ingrained through primary group experience. As the individual faces the realities of readjustment to the secondary group, he may find that some of the old patterns are so much dead wood in the larger setting. Thus he sometimes is compelled to cast aside old regulations and to accept new standards. This is a dangerous transition stage, and one which for some persons culminates in complete demoralization, because once they begin casting away old standards they may find it difficult to know when to cease. In the end they may find themselves without sufficient moral and social stability to become an acceptable member of any normal group.

One frequently observes this process among college youth who leave the home setting, where life patterns have been well established and enforced by primary group influences, for the impersonal secondary group relationships of a large college campus. The old restraints are lacking. The youth experiences a new sense of liberty. He meets companions with standards quite different from those of his home community. Under this pressure the youth may forsake most of the life patterns which he once took for granted. Some individuals go so far in throwing off restraints that they soon become misfits, even in the secondary group.

The process of maladjustment growing out of the transition from the primary to the secondary group also operates extensively in the migration of the rural youth to the urban community where he suddenly finds himself free of old codes. He necessarily faces the process of readjustment and re-evaluation of the environment and his place in it. This is one phase of the process which Carpenter has described as "culture shock", which the migrating individual experiences in arriving in a new area.[10]

CONCLUSION

The modern world gives an increasingly important place to secondary groups, so their part in the system of social control is naturally of great moment. It is generally agreed that primary controls, while still very effective, are less adequate in modern society than in primitive society, and in the urban society of today than in the rural society of yesterday. Control is one of the major problems that our modern generation must solve, it being comparable, Bernard says, to the problem of subsistence in primitive societies. Numerous and diverse patterns of behavior characterize the social environment; countless suggestions emanate from sources seen and unseen; many groups play a siren's song to entice the wayfarers of the secondary group environment, some of whom have no compass, off their course. The problem exists; where is the remedy?

In this sphere, as in so many other fields of social relationships, there is no magic solution at hand. Cures for social ills are always in the making, and here as elsewhere we must put numerous expedients to the trial and error test. Laws have been multiplied on the formal side, and devices of mass suggestion have increased on the informal side, but problems of control still distress the urban-industrialized world.

Can we extend primary group controls over the anonymous world of the metropolis, or over the expanse of a modern nation, or over international relations? Will social work, the modern press, or some other tool make man conscious of the surveillance of the group, as gossip makes him conscious of it in the primary group? Although certain agencies might help to make the answers to these questions positive, Bernard, on the whole, is probably right in assuming that new definitions of the "moral," the "right," the "social," and the "human" will have to be made.

A few concepts of morality fitted to the secondary group have already been developed. Certain articles of social legislation, the growth of secondary group charity, the humanized attitudes toward juvenile delinquency and crime, which place upon the com-

---

[10] Niles Carpenter, *The Sociology of City Life*, pp. 271 ff., Longmans, Green and Company, New York, 1931.

munity its rightful share of the responsibility—these and many similar gestures of our times suggest that a new type of thinking in terms of general "social welfare" may have reached at least the embryonic stage of development.

SELECTED REFERENCES

Beach, W. G., *Social Aims in a Changing World*, chap. 1. Stanford University Press, Stanford University, 1932.

Bernard, L. L., "The Conflict Between Primary Group Attitudes and Derivative Group Ideals in Modern Society," *American Journal of Sociology*, vol. 41, pp. 611–623. March, 1936.

Bossard, Joseph H. S., *Social Change and Social Problems*, revised edition, chaps. 5 and 6. Harper and Brothers, New York, 1938.

Cooley, Charles H., *Social Organization*, chap. 5. Charles Scribner's Sons, New York, 1925.

Dowd, Jerome, *Control in Human Societies*, chap. 28. D. Appleton-Century Company, New York, 1936.

Holt, Arthur E., "Our Common Perversion," *Christian Century*, vol. 52, pp. 850–852. June 26, 1935.

Mather, William G. Jr., "A Use for Human Interest Stories," *The North American Review*, pp. 544–545. December, 1934.

Mowrer, Ernest R., *Family Disorganization*, pp. 275 ff. University of Chicago Press, Chicago, 1927.

Plant, James S., *Personality and the Cultural Pattern*, chap. 8. The Commonwealth Fund, New York, 1937.

Thomas, W. I., and Znaniecki, Florian, *The Polish Peasant in Europe and America*, vol. 5, part 1, chap. 3. Chapman and Grimes, Boston, 1920.

Wallas, Graham, *The Great Society*. The Macmillan Company, New York, 1920.

Winston, Sanford, *Culture and Human Behavior*, pp. 202–205. The Ronald Press Company, New York, 1933.

CHAPTER 12

THE LIABILITIES AND ASSETS OF AGENCIES OF MASS IMPRESSION TO SOCIAL CONTROL IN A WORLD OF SECONDARY GROUPS

P. T. BARNUM, INCORPORATED

In the field of exploitive mass leadership, P. T. Barnum of circus fame has no peer.[1] He called himself the "Prince of Humbugs" and no one challenged the appropriateness of the title. Working on the assumption that "a sucker is born every minute" he learned to play on human motives to get men to do what he desired.

To advertise his museum in New York, he employed a very novel idea, but one based on a sound knowledge of psychological motives. After having a man place each of four bricks at a designated location on the city streets, he had him spend the remainder of the day walking in impressive silence from brick to brick, exchanging the one on the walk for the one in his hand. At the end of each hour he presented a ticket at the museum entrance, walked through the building, and out the back door to continue walking with his brick. Soon great crowds were following him and buying tickets to the museum, hoping to discover there the secret of his mission. After a few days the congestion in the streets became so serious that the police had to interfere. For weeks afterward the press played up Barnum's bricks.

As another advertising scheme, he placed an elephant on his farm in the charge of a keeper dressed in brightly colored Oriental costume. Every time a passenger train passed, the occupants were treated to the sight of this elephant cultivating a six-acre tract. Soon newspapers throughout the nation and even in continental Europe were carrying news stories featuring Barnum, proprietor of a New York museum and the first man ever to use the elephant as an agricultural animal.

---

[1] For a fascinating account of Barnum's activities see M. R. Werner's, *Barnum.*

Barnum presupposed that the way of the world was "to promise everything for next to nothing" and he followed this creed
wholeheartedly. In fact, he followed it so well that soon his personality was a common topic of conversation and his numerous
ventures, aimed not only to "please" but also to "astonish" kept
it so. To obtain the patronage of the righteous he labeled his
exhibit "Barnum's Great Moral Show," giving free passes to min-
isters of the gospel.

His activities in many respects are comparable to what we see
in current propaganda and advertising. His build-up to a mythical figure of public importance is typical of all leaders of great
masses of people.

The Dilemma in Mass Control

Society, as has been pointed out (Part II), must build within
its members a susceptibility to those regulative principles which
form the foundation of social order. It must enforce order,
largely by making the individual receptive to the opinions, attitudes, and suggestions of his group. Any socialized individual is
responsive to suggestions and social pressures that arise from the
social environment.[2]

Since members of any effective society respond to social pressure, they are open to exploitation at the hands of ruthless interests with purposes that are primarily selfish rather than social.
In the primary group, with its unity of opinions and cultural patterns, such abuses on a large scale are not possible, even if the
desire were present. Close public scrutiny and the censorship of
primary group opinion soon discourage any would-be exploiter.
However, in the modern world with its great diversity of standards and its tools of diffusion made effective through the development of modern means of communication, unscrupulous interests and individuals fostering selfish purposes by the use of propaganda, advertising, and even news itself, sway the masses to a
degree that would be impossible under other conditions. Not
all of the interests using these means of diffusion are exploitive.
Many of them are. Individuals who can afford to use these
modern instruments are usually those who have axes to grind—
politicians, profit seekers, or groups with selfish or predatory mo-

---

[2] B. Sidis has stated that man "is social because he is suggestible." The
Psychology of Suggestion, pp. 310–312, D. Appleton-Century Company, 1898.

tives. These devices have proven an invaluable aid in the hands of governments, powerful industries, and other manipulators of the means of communication in securing the desired behavior.

Secondary groups must have access to these means of diffusion if large political and social units are to function. These agencies of mass impression have enabled us to conceive of a world society and to carry on many relationships on a nearly worldwide scale. Because we live in an age of rapid dissemination of information, news, and propaganda, social changes tend to permeate all of society, indeed, to sweep over nations almost instantaneously. A new discovery, a new tragedy, the results of an election, any major drama, even in a remote corner of the world, circles the globe in the space of a few minutes or hours. Because of this fact, new inventions and new ideas affect the whole social order and usher in changes of far-reaching import to our whole system of social organization and social philosophy.

CONFLICTING MASS STIMULI

As a result of these changes, which are a necessary part of societies such as the modern world has developed, we are subject to more and more conflicting stimuli which, though they may help us to make decisions, in most cases keep us constantly struggling between a choice of this value and that value, this luxury and that luxury, this goal and that goal. We are beset on every hand by agencies that are definitely trying to make up our minds for us by slipping their own ideas into the news, magazines, books, and cartoons, or by trying to flaunt before us their advertisement, sometimes coating it with humor, sometimes with art, frequently with sex. We are enticed to lay aside the old and adopt the new, to seek pleasure, to be modern, to avoid the undesirable in appearance. Everywhere there are those who would shape our minds to suit their purposes—businessmen, political groups, people of eminence or prestige who have notions to sell us about life, health, or happiness, and those who, balked by the social order, want to solve the world's troubles with their particular brand of utopia.

Large utility and industrial enterprises employ press agents, publicity men, public relations experts, all of whom try to prejudice the public in favor of their particular organization or product. Political parties, in addition to their spokesmen who try to sway the public with their fervent pulpit oratory, maintain highly paid pressmen who constantly fill the newspaper columns with information or cartoons designed to impress the public with the importance of their party, and the questionable character of the opposition party. The movie-goer or radio-listener frequently wonders who is paying the bill when he sees or hears something that is obviously tinged by propaganda. Constant harangue in the newspapers for a large navy may be news or editorial conviction, but more likely it is neither. In the background may lurk the endowment of a munitions or steel company, a circumstance revealed in some of our government inquiries of a few years ago. The public has a legitimate right to know, in such instances, the identity of the interested parties, but in a secondary group society it seldom knows. It is an easy matter for vested interests to start paper wars with Mexico, China, or Japan in order to boost their sales. It is an easy matter to start a crime wave in the newspapers, and undoubtedly they have been started in that way with some ulterior motive in view—if for nothing else, to sell more newspapers.

Our Inability to Evaluate Conflicting Mass Stimuli

In the "great society" with its numerous distracting stimuli the individual becomes incapable of evaluating the relative merits of the many issues with which he is faced. Not only is the average citizen often grossly ignorant on vital affairs, but even the man of political authority, no matter how conscientious he may be, is many times compelled to vote on bills without adequate information. On the one hand he is bombarded by the pleas of the lobbyists, friends, and constituents, fighting for the issue because of selfish interests. On the other he is coerced by the propagandists, lobbyists, and citizens who feel that the bill would be detrimental to public welfare. Very frequently, if not in the majority of cases, he votes in relative ignorance of the social implications of the measure. It could hardly be otherwise when one considers the number of issues that are presented in the average state legislature, or in a session of Congress. If this is true of the supposed expert, whose business it is to know, how much more true it must be of the average citizen who probably depends for all of his information on one newspaper, which frequently is committed to an editorial policy favoring one faction.

Little wonder that the social seas are recurrently set in turmoil by waves of fashion, hurricanes of mob action, war hysterias, and epidemics of gang attack. Today the "red herring" of communism is drawn across the trail, tomorrow the dark shirt of fascism.

These issues and numerous others tend to become weighted with emotional symbols that call forth a violent response from the masses, and behind it all stand the leaders who, by manipulation of clever propaganda, work their will upon the masses.

In the case of European countries, straw men in the enemy's camp—Jews, Ethiopia, eugenics, race myths—almost anything will suffice to focus mass attention, provided a man with a bold chin and a messianic voice stands before the microphone and speaks to the multitudes with the fervor of one inspired by a divine call.

PUBLICITY AS A NEGATIVE INSTRUMENT OF SECONDARY GROUP CONTROL

The press and radio, through the selection and presentation of sensational news are sometimes considered influences in the increasing incidence of crime. That publicity is a powerful factor in suggestion in this field is borne out in the waves that sweep the country, paper crime waves stimulated by widely publicized details of criminal misdeeds, suicide waves that apparently originate with the notoriety attending famous suicides. There are undoubtedly crimes that have been perpetrated at the suggestion of the movie. Crime on the front page may have done much to stimulate criminal activities, both in its effect upon the egotistical criminal who gloats to see his name in print, and on the impression of universality that it gives many highly suggestive individuals who, like sheep, are always willing to go with the crowd.

The following selections from an editorial present the situation.

Control by the press through suggestion.

For a long time thoughtful portions of the community have been disturbed by the way in which sensational treatment of crime and sex news in the press has contributed to the increase of those same evils. Two weeks ago the *Saturday Evening Post* published a cartoon showing a gang chief, surrounded by his hoodlums, gloating over newspaper accounts of the gang's activities. But more than six years ago *The Christian Century*, in an editorial open letter to the newspaper proprietors of Chicago, tried to point out the social damage being done by overemphasizing of such news. "Day after day, whether consciously or not," that letter declared, "the press seems to be operating on the basis of competition in penetrating to the lowest depths of our city's life in order that the dregs from thence might be flaunted." And an appeal was made for an experiment in a different sort of journalism, in which crime, bestiality, and the sordid aspects of life should be not left out of account but "played down," while the constructive activities of the city should be "played up."

No direct answer was given to this open letter. Such newspaper-makers as discussed it in any form tended, with few exceptions, to justify newspaper practice on two grounds. They contended, in the first place, that crime and sex constituted sensational news; that sensational news is the thing that the public wants; that the newspaper must supply what the public wants, or go out of business. Or if they were not ready to defend their course on quite such a crassly materialistic basis as that, the newspaper-makers declared that the printing of such news, revolting as it might appear, really performed a therapeutic function in the body politic. Unless the dreadful facts were fully known, how could the community understand the enormity of the conditions with which it must deal? Scandal-mongering and crime-reporting were in this fashion elevated to the distinction of important social services.

It is probable that few thoughtful citizens were taken in by such casuistry. But these defenses of newspaper practice in respect to a wide range of news have become almost standard in the journalistic profession itself, and have been accepted as conclusive by far too many journalists. It has been the easier for these journalists to salve their disturbed consciences by falling back on this fallacious reasoning because there never has been, up to the present, an objective standard of newspaper practice in another field by which to make comparisons. Such a standard has now, however, been given. By the test which it supplies, the practice of the press in sensationalizing its reports of crime and sex is proved to be totally without the social justification which has been claimed for it.

Fittingly enough, it has been the city of Chicago which has thus tested the pretensions of the newspaper. On Saturday, June 6, serious financial trouble developed in at least one, and perhaps more than one, of the city's largest banks. Hundreds of the city's bankers were in feverish conference all that night, all day Sunday, and early on Monday morning it was announced that four of the city's largest banks had been merged into two. The terms announced made it clear that one of these mergers had been simply the taking over of the deposits of one bank by another, and that not even this measure of "rescue" would have been achieved had not a separate guarantee fund of more than $12,000,000 been raised to protect the bank accepting the transferred deposits.

In the train of this upheaval in banking circles in the city's loop district, disaster fell upon smaller banks in residential sections. On Monday, when the loop mergers went into effect, six outlying banks closed their doors. On Tuesday, twelve more failed to open. On Wednesday, six more collapsed. On Thursday, two more went to the wall. Confidence in the financial structure of the city was, naturally, badly shaken; in the south and west side residential districts something closely approximating a panic spread.

Here was news, and about as sensational as occurs. The mergers in the loop represented, as every well-informed citizen knew, the practical wiping out of one of the city's oldest and supposedly strongest banks, and the combination of two others to secure needed resources for a period of peril. Under ordinary circumstances, the failure of a single bank will be given large newspaper headlines; here were 26 bank failures within four days! The city was filled with wild rumors; a recital of the actual facts in the order of their sensational (and panic-creating) value might easily have precipitated a social catastrophe of the first order. What happened? The newspapers unanimously treated the matter in such a way as to minimize the fact of the financial crisis and to magnify such elements of stability and order as the situation contained!

Take, for example, the journalistic course followed by the conservative *Daily News*, an evening newspaper. On the Monday on which the story "broke," it began its account of what had happened with this sentence: "Increased power and prestige for Chicago as a financial center are resulting from two big bank mergers announced today." Only in the seventh column on page 4, under the smallest sized headline used in the paper, was there to be found: "Several banks closed in path of big merger." On the next day the closing of twelve banks was again shoved into the inside of the paper, while the main story declared: "The general feeling in financial circles, the

comment of business leaders, bankers and others today indicated that
the bank consolidations will result in increased prestige for Chicago
as a financial center." This news policy was maintained without
deviation throughout the critical period. . . .

The *Tribune* was equally instructive. Its Monday story, under an
8-column banner headline, read: "Big Loop Banks in 2 Mergers."
But only by inference, by "between-the-lines" writing, was the serious
nature of the situation which had confronted these banks so much
as hinted. On the next day the story began: "The greatest banking
consolidations in Chicago's financial history . . . were received with
surprising calm yesterday." Further on: "The statements of Chicago's financiers . . . appeared to have allayed all uneasiness . . .
There seemed to be a feeling that the events of Sunday had 'cleared
the atmosphere' and that the mergers had resulted in increased power
and prestige for Chicago as a financial center. Chicagoans appeared
to take pride" in what had happened.

But perhaps most informing of all was the course followed by Mr.
Hearst's *Herald-Examiner*. On Monday it had the usual banner,
"Two Big Loop Bank Mergers," but not a line to indicate the sensational features of the situation. On Tuesday its first page headline
read, "Mergers Fortify City Banks," and only in column five on page
two could the reader discover that there had been six bank failures
on the previous day. On Wednesday there was nothing about the
Chicago banking situation on the first page at all, but a general story
headed, "Chicago Leads in Revival of U. S. Trade." On page 13,
under the headline, "Business Nearly Normal as Banks Complete
Merger," there was a story which had tucked away in it this gem:
"While serenity prevailed downtown, unsettlement [sic!] cropped
out in the outlying districts, and 13 minor banks were forced to sus-
pend after abnormal withdrawals." By Thursday the *Herald-
Examiner* had the story in a single column on page 23, but a subhead
did mention the fact that six more banks had failed the day before!

Now, these examples of newspaper practice are not detailed in
order to take exception to them. It is possible to argue that, in view
of the general public knowledge of the seriousness of the situation,
this obvious "playing down" of its sensational elements might produce the very opposite of the effect sought. But, all things considered, the newspapers were probably justified and wise in pursuing
the course which they did. This course, however, stands in glaring
contrast with the course which they have pursued when dealing with,

let us say, the activities of Mr. Alphonse Capone, or with the tragic outcome of a high school drinking party.

Why this difference of journalistic practice? The answer is plain. During the critical events of last week, the newspapers of Chicago felt a genuine responsibility to the welfare of the city's financial community. More than that, they felt themselves a part of that community; their fate tied up with its fate. If it crashed, they crashed. So they went to unprecedented lengths to play up every possible hopeful and constructive element in the financial situation, and to play down every discouraging and sensational feature.

In contrast, the newspaper simply does not hold the same sense of responsibility to or implication in the moral community. The newspaper may give lip service to morality, both public and private, but it is really an amoral institution. It conceives itself as standing on the sidelines, merely reporting in objective fashion such breaches in the moral fabric of society as it observes. In reality, it has been seeking to build circulation at the expense of moral breakdown. To be sure, such breakdown can go to the point where it actually does threaten the real interests of the newspaper, in which case there comes an immediate change in newspaper policy. In Chicago, for instance, it is instructive to contrast newspaper reporting of gang operations in 1925 with such reporting at present—or since the effect of Chicago's gang-ridden reputation began to be felt by the city's business. But these forces operate only slowly and over a long period. Generally speaking, the newspaper reaction to a moral disaster is to play its sensational aspects up for all they are worth, and let the community take care of its own future interests—if it can.

Perhaps it should be said that in writing these words *The Christian Century* has no intention of singling the Chicago newspapers out for especial reprobation. The newspapers in other cities would have done what the Chicago papers did during the financial crisis, just as most of them have done the same things about crime and sex. It only happens that this demonstration has taken place in Chicago; its revelations apply to every big city newspaper that is still "playing up" sensational news on the ground that it is what the public wants and is for the ultimate good of the public.

That old plea can stand no longer. It has been swept out of court by the newspapers themselves; swept out of court in this Chicago experience. For the newspapers themselves, by the course they have pursued when financial ruin stalked the streets of their city, have admitted that an event may be news, but that it may not be for the public good to have it sensationalized. On the basis of that admission, now made, the public has a right to demand of the entire newspaper profession a raising of the average standards of social responsibility.[3]

PUBLICITY AS A POSITIVE INSTRUMENT OF CONTROL IN THE SECONDARY GROUP

Much is written concerning the bad effects of publicity in our modern world of secondary group relations. But this is not an unmixed evil. There is much to be said for publicity as an effective and constructive social control device.

Crime waves, even though they may at times exist only on paper, may have a decided value from the standpoint of social control in driving the public to concerted action against crime and against the codes which are the fundamental causes of crime. There is little doubt but that the creation of many of our crime commissions and perhaps even the creation of the Federal Department of Justice have been provoked by the widespread attention which has been focused on gangsters and racketeers through the medium of the American press and newsreel.

Some even suggest that crime news has another value[4] in that it offers an outlet for the primitive, sadistic impulses dormant in the breasts of overcivilized, overcontrolled modern men. By providing this vicarious outlet for these drives, crime news saves many from participating in antisocial behavior, whereas such suggestion as leads people to crime leads only those of the suggestible type who are so weak-willed that they are not worth saving anyway. Whether this is true or not is debatable but, at least, that crime news does frequently whip public opinion into action is evident.

Fear of publicity has kept many a person in the straight and narrow path, whether in public office or in private life. Certain industrial groups and other interests have feared public investigation more than any other one weapon. This is primarily because the results will be heralded by press and radio to people through-

---

[3] Editorial, "The Newspaper and Social Responsibility," *The Christian Century,* June 24, 1931, vol. 48, pp. 830–832. Reprinted by permission.

[4] E. A. Dewey, "Crime and the Press," *Commonweal,* December 30, 1931, Vol. 15, p. 231.

out the nation. The Senate investigation is a powerful tool of Congress in making known to the public the antisocial activities of certain types of industrial organizations. The publicity given to the munitions inquiries, for instance, has made the nation conscious of the role ammunition-makers have played in the past in the development of war scares and in the perpetuation of war.

The following extracts from various sources illustrate the point more fully. The first is by Associate Justice Black, written while he was a member of the United States Senate. After describing a Senate investigation he summarized their importance to the public welfare and concludes:

... Most valuable of all, this power of the probe is one of the most powerful weapons in the hands of the people to restrain the activities of powerful groups who can defy every other power.

Public investigation committees, formed from the people themselves or from their public representatives, exist always in countries where the people rule. They have always been opposed by groups that seek or have special privileges. The spokesmen of these greedy groups never rest in their opposition to exposure and publicity. That is because special privilege thrives in secrecy and darkness and is destroyed by the rays of pitiless publicity.[5]

Curtis H. Clay, though condemning front page display of general crime news, has the following to say regarding the value of publicity in curbing corruption in public office:

The question recently was put up to us: "What would you do if confronted with a situation wherein the people were being defrauded by corrupt officials?"

The gist of our answer was that no one can deny that publicity does have an important effect in ending such a condition. The press has brought many a treasury looter to justice. Page-one display of a campaign against such crime could not be put in the general category of crime news. A public official who violates his oath should get what he deserves, including *pitiless* publicity. But the newspaper should be honest and not use its power for political expediency; its own objective must be above reproach. To campaign against crime does not require playing up crime itself. Stories demanding protection of the public against crooked officeholders, hoodlums, racketeers,

---

[5] Hugo L. Black, "Inside a Senate Investigation," *Harper's Magazine*, February, 1936, p. 286. Reprinted by permission of Harper and Brothers.

etc., are not news; they are crusade articles; and there is a vast difference between them and the news accounts relating to what crimes
have been committed, by whom, and how.[6]

The lengths to which vested interests go in an attempt to color
the news and thus gain publicity favorable to their interests is
discussed by Mr. Flynn in these words:

I have been glancing through some recent investigation records in
newspapers. And I have been interested to see standing out so
clearly all over these reports faint finger-prints of the public-relations
counsel. It brings to mind a fact of which not only readers but newspaper editors ought to be keenly aware. News editors are usually
hard-boiled persons. And there is nothing they resent so dearly as
the attempt to fool them with subtle poisoning of the news that flows
over their desks. They very justly feel that they should have the
right to do it themselves.

There is a whole new technique that has been developed in investigations. Its aim is to divert attention from the essential facts of
the investigation, to steal the spotlight away in the first few days of
the public hearings when public attention is fixed on the performance
and when an impression may be made that will remain throughout
the hearing.

Hence, persons of importance and power who are about to be
investigated by a Senate Committee employ a public-relations man
and sometimes a battery of subordinates to plan the exhibition during
those first days. It is amazing what a good publicity man who knows
his way around can do, how by a slight touch he can apparently completely change the news.

For instance, I recall last summer when Senator Wheeler was getting rather busily after O. P. Van Sweringen. Wheeler had sub-
poenaed Van Sweringen to appear at his office. Van Sweringen came
to Washington but did not go to Wheeler's office. The Montana
Senator was pretty hot under the collar about this. He felt the
Cleveland railroad promoter was trying to dodge him. He had Van
Sweringen's lawyers on the carpet. He talked straight from the
shoulder to them. Van Sweringen was trying to avoid going on the
witness stand. And after a good deal of argument and many confer-
ences with Van Sweringen's lawyers, Wheeler finally agreed to accept

---

[6] Curtis H. Clay, "Take Crime News Off the Front Page?", *The Rotarian*,
February, 1937, p. 60. By permission of Rotary International.

in writing from Van Sweringen the information he was after. Van Sweringen, under the authority of the subpoena, finally went to Wheeler's office and made the necessary agreement.

The following day, however, a two-column picture appeared in the newspapers of Washington and perhaps other cities. It showed O. P. Van Sweringen and his counsel, chatting in great good humor, with broad smiles, and it bore the caption: "O. P. Van Sweringen and his counsel called at the Capitol yesterday to confer with Senator Wheeler." What had actually happened was thus completely hidden behind that adroitly posed and captioned picture. This is merely one sample of the way the newspaper contact man, hanging on the fringe of the hearing, manages to give the story a helpful twist on its way to the city room.

Entertaining the reporters in Washington who cover the hearings is another important device. One of the big banking firms that appeared before Mr. Pecora had a pretty tough time of it. At the conclusion of the hearings, the bankers, who ordinarily look with contempt on newsmen, threw an elaborate party in their extensive hotel suite for all the reporters. The liquor, even champagne, flowed like water. All fraternized and put their arms about one another. It was a good investment, for one well-known writer tossed off a piece the next day giving the banking firm a complete bill of health and that piece was run on the financial pages of numerous papers throughout the country.

Another important device is to steal the show the first day. When the great banker or railroad man is called to the stand he asks permission, since he is under attack, to read a statement. In the past this has always been granted. But it has turned out to be costly. The statement is nowadays prepared in collaboration with lawyers and publicity men and is designed to develop some point which will make a good headline story. The investigator who lets an investigated magnate read an opening statement is falling an easy prey to what is now a very obvious stratagem.

Another device is to forestall the committee. When the investigation is about to begin, the investigated baron knows what he is in for and what is going to be brought out. If it comes out as a result of questioning it will look black against him. So he hands out a statement to the press before the hearing in which he tells the story himself. Thus the revelation comes from him instead of the committee. In making the statement he, of course, takes all the sting out of it and puts the pleasantest interpretation on it. He completely defeats its harmful character by being the first to make it known.

Meanwhile the work of seeing that the story is favorably told in the papers goes on behind the scenes. Editors at home do not, of course, know what is happening in Washington and they accept what they get with faith. They ought to have this new game, I think, called to their attention.[7]

Chicago policemen no doubt will be much more careful in their handling of strikes since the widely publicized Memorial Day riots of 1937, during which much violence occurred, resulting in the death of several people. The Senate Committee on Civil Liberties, which investigated the affair, publicly condemned the policemen for shooting pickets without just provocation. This committee revealed further that a local Chicago committee which also investigated the strike had whitewashed the activities of the officers involved. This publicity brought no immediate punishment to the policemen involved or to the responsible officials, but it is extremely doubtful whether Chicago would want another such bill of accusation to appear throughout the press of the nation.

PROPAGANDA AN INSTRUMENT OF CONTROL IN THE MODERN WORLD [8]

. . . It [propaganda] refers solely to the control of opinion by significant symbols, or, to speak more concretely and less accurately, by stories, rumors, reports, pictures, and other forms of social communication. Propaganda is concerned with the management of opinions and attitudes by the direct manipulation of social suggestion rather than by altering other conditions in the environment or in the organism.

Propaganda is a concession to the rationality of the modern world. A literate world, a reading world, a schooled world, prefers to thrive on argument and news. It is sophisticated to the extent of using print; and he that takes to print shall live or perish by the Press. All the apparatus of diffused erudition popularizes the symbols and forms

---

[7] John T. Flynn, "Other People's Money," *The New Republic*, November 18, 1936, p. 74. By permission of the New Republic, and of the author.

[8] From Harold D. Lasswell, *Propaganda Technique in the World War*, pp. 9, 221, 222. By permission of the author.

of pseudo-rational appeal; the wolf of propaganda does not hesitate to masquerade in the sheepskin. All the voluble men of the day— writers, reporters, editors, preachers, lecturers, teachers, politicians— are drawn into the service of propaganda to amplify a master voice. All is conducted with the decorum and the trappery of intelligence, for this is a rational epoch, and demands its raw meat cooked and garnished by adroit and skillful chefs.

Propaganda is a concession to the willfulness of the age. The bonds of personal loyalty and affection which bound a man to his chief have long since dissolved. Monarchy and class privilege have gone the way of all flesh, and the idolatry of the individual passes for the official religion of democracy. It is an atomized world, in which individual whims have wider play than ever before, and it requires more strenuous exertions to co-ordinate and unify than formerly. The new antidote to willfulness is propaganda. If the mass will be free of chains of iron, it must accept its chains of silver. If it will not love, honor and obey, it must not expect to escape seduction.

Propaganda is a reflex to the immensity, the rationality and willfulness of the modern world. It is the new dynamic of society, for power is subdivided and diffused, and more can be won by illusion than by coercion. It has all the prestige of the new and provokes all the animosity of the baffled. To illuminate the mechanisms of propaganda is to reveal the secret springs of social action, and to expose to the most searching criticism our prevailing dogmas of sovereignty, of democracy, of honesty, and of the sanctity of individual opinion. The study of propaganda will bring into the open much that is obscure, until, indeed, it may no longer be possible for an Anatole France to observe with truth that "Democracy (and, indeed, all society) is run by an unseen engineer."

Censorship as an Instrument of Selective Mass Impression

Much has been written on propaganda since the World War, when the masses first were made conscious of its influence and character as a control device. Today much is being written about censorship, which has limited the messages that are transmitted over the instruments of mass impression. Stalin, Hitler, and Mussolini indulge in political censorship on an extensive scale to protect their interests and forward their cause. In a less rigid manner, the press is selective in its presentation of news that might reflect unfavorably on its advertisers. Politicians are always careful to censor their remarks on any topic which might cause offense to their supporters. Censorship of the movies has been discussed extensively and practiced to some extent. As a device for limiting mass impression to those suggestions which the propagandist wishes to convey, censorship is an important influence in social control.

RELATIVE EFFECTIVENESS OF AGENCIES OF MASS IMPRESSION

There is little question but that the press has been, and perhaps still is, the chief channel through which propaganda, news, and advertising circulate. That the newspaper is sharing its influence with the radio was very convincingly demonstrated in the last election, when between 60 and 75 per cent of the newspapers were against the reelection of Roosevelt,[9] and yet the silver-tongued voice of this orator of the New Deal, carried over the air waves, won for the Democrats an overwhelming majority vote. This was not entirely a matter of the relative influence of the radio and the newspaper, but certainly it was some indication, especially when one considers that previous to the last election many anti-New Deal employers caused to be placed in envelopes and given to their employees terse notices suggesting that their interests lay with the opposition rather than with the party in power. The attacks of newspapers on many of the legislative measures of the New Deal, and the subtle thrusts of cartoons, however, seem to have been relatively impotent in determining the outcome of the campaign. Certainly the influence of the editorial page has declined; many other more subtle, more suggestive, and more universal means of impression are usurping its former position. That the paper still has influence on the party in power no one could deny. The relative freedom of the press in this country as compared to foreign countries, and the free expression of opinion in our society, are reflected to a considerable extent in our institutions of government, which must of necessity always have one ear to the ground to catch the slightest murmur of the voice of the people.

The radio, also, as long as it is available for all to use, and as long as dissenters may make themselves heard, is an instrument

[9] Special section on "The Press and the Public," New Republic, March, 1937, p. 179.

of a free people; but in many modern nations the radio has become instead the tool of a dictator, or of the political party in
power. As such it is a more powerful weapon for control than
in nations where differences of opinion are aired, but is usually
less responsive to popular sentiment.

The importance of the radio as an instrument of mass impression is strikingly presented by Kolodin. Selections from his
article follow:

When Franklin D. Roosevelt leaned over to the microphone on
that historic March fifth of 1933 and said "My friends," for the first
time on the air from the White House, he was inditing more than a
few remarks, important as they were at the time, on the Banking
Crisis. He was setting a precedent in the dissemination of propaganda by radio which has multiplied and diversified itself in a thousand ways since. Who could have foreseen in that sanctimonious
beginning the recent etherial dog-fight among the Messrs. Long,
Johnson, and Father Coughlin? It used to be said that a statesman
was a politician with a job; now it might be said that a statesman is a
demagogue with a microphone and a network.

To realize the vast potentialities of propaganda on the air one need
merely consider the most recent figures on the distribution of radios
in American homes. As a result of a survey embracing over 120,000
field interviews, a table in Radio Retailing (March, 1935) set the
number at 21,455,799—or, more graphically, established the fact that
69.4 per cent of all the homes in the forty-eight states are now radio-
equipped. Accepting NBC's own estimate of 3.1 persons per family,
this gives a potential audience of 66,512,977 to radio—or the power
to reach simultaneously well over half of the entire populace. This
marks by far the largest number of sets in use, the most considerable
potential audience yet at the disposal of radio, and, together with the
vastly increased use of its facilities for propaganda purposes, totals to
a situation the like of which has never perplexed our citizens before.
Demagoguery has ever flourished in what our forefathers were wont
to call "hard times" (thus imputing a measure of spirit-assuaging
sacrificial forbearance to a purely man-made economic situation); but
a Populist or Free Silver man or Single Taxer of forty years ago who
found an audience of a few thousand awaiting his words considered
himself blessed indeed; today's demagogue is scarcely a member of
the guild in good standing if he cannot persuade himself that a good

majority of those 21,455,799 sets are tuned to his wave length at the
appropriate hour . . .

Propaganda on a large scale via the air in America must be regarded
as an offshoot of the deepest period of the depression. Prior to 1932,
the easiest way for a broadcasting station to insure itself a fruitless
half-hour was to schedule a talk on national or international policy,
taxation or misrepresentation, civic reform or legislative corruption.

. . . But in February of this year, 6.4 per cent of all programs on the
networks of the National Broadcasting Company were officially described as "dealing with the social sciences" (as near to an admission
of shaping public opinion as the company permits itself). Or, in
more easily visualized terms, 17.2 per cent of all nonmusical programs.

It was the Bank Holiday, the talk of a Gold Standard, Inflation,
and Currency Depreciation to which this interest may be attributed.
For they aroused in the public mind a vast if superficial curiosity.
Every clerk, homeward bound on the subway or streetcar, could ac-
quaint himself with the profundities of economic policy, from his
newspaper, and shortly establish himself as an expert in any field that
suited his fancy. Thereafter, reading became too much trouble; the
radio offered itself to him as a device permitting him to be pupil and
critic simultaneously, without even the trouble of reading. With the
concurrent usage of the gadget for state purposes, as a favor of the
commercial networks, by the President of the United States (thus
placing an official seal upon its authority), the establishment of radio
as a prime organ of propaganda was but a sequential happening in an
illogical chain of events.

Quite the most illogical of these happenings was the elevation of
a priest of the Catholic Church to a position of counselor on every
conceivable subject to 30,000,000 Americans. The loudest noises of
Father Coughlin have unquestionably been those released in the
political and economic arena; but he is as proud of the fact that
during some weeks as many as 200 divorces have been averted by the
replies he sends to the frantic pleas of his harassed listeners as he is
of the 200,000 telegrams to the Senate incited by his address in opposition to the World Court (on January 27) or the 100,000 messages supporting the Patman Bill after his broadcast urging that
course (on May 5). In the one role he may be conceived to be
functioning as a faithful servant of the Catholic Church in its traditional stand on divorce; in the other guise, however, his words have

no more essential value than those of any other American citizen, lay or clerical. But Electricity and the brains of Marconi, De Forest, and countless others have given him a Delphic potency, which carries his words into 10,000,000 living rooms weekly—winged, disembodied, infallible as the Pope he patronized by occasionally quoting.

From a parish housing, in all, three dozen Catholic families comes a voice that has summoned to its active support at least 12,000,000 adult Americans—the number of correspondents whose names repose in his files. From a first broadcast in 1926, over a single local station in Detroit (the manifestation of a desperate wish to relieve his church of a debt burden by enlarging his flock), with a mail response of eight letters, Father Coughlin has catapulted to an independent network embracing 31 stations (certain of which have found it expedient to emphasize from time to time that his use of their facilities is paid for by himself, disclaiming responsibility for his utterances). A single broadcast has not infrequently brought half a million letters of approval within a week, or by far the largest response to any broadcast not offering free prizes. Though he claims never to have solicited money directly in his broadcasts, some magic power in his voice lures huge numbers of dollars from his devotees. Enough money, indeed, to build a $750,000 shrine that dwarfs the modest structure in which he began his career; to pay a weekly bill for radio time that amounted in 1934 (for the 27 stations he was using then) to $14,000 for each session, or $300,000 for the five winter months; to maintain a clerical staff of 220 persons, who open, sort, answer, and file his mail; to purchase a half-interest in the Detroit publishing plant where his discourses are prepared for distribution to 3,000,000 avid correspondents each year; to support such activities as the Radio League of the Little Flower and its contemporary offshoot, the National Union for Social Justice.

As Father Coughlin is the spiritual counselor to the American people, and Long the material, so General Johnson fits neatly into the necessity for a patriotic spokesman to complete the triangle . . .[10]

Conclusion

The large impersonal groups of the modern world necessarily must depend for control to a considerable extent upon agencies

---

[10] Irving Kolodin, "Propaganda on the Air," *The American Mercury*, July, 1935, pp. 293–300. By permission of the American Mercury, Inc., and of the author.

of mass impression. Only in this way can any degree of group rapport be established and maintained. The disadvantages lie in the fact that the individual, trained to respond to suggestion, is gullible. Though not entirely a puppet, he is capable of being swayed by the stimuli that reach him, often weighted with an impression of universality. If a thing is in vogue it makes a strong appeal. Many suggestible persons respond readily even to mild stimuli, such as found in stories of crime or suicide.

In a complex world, living becomes unduly complicated by the many enticing patterns of behavior which beckon the wayfarer. Often he does not know the source of their suggestion; many times he is not capable of evaluating their authenticity.

In a society with liberty of choice and freedom of action, the discerning individual finds it possible to choose a socially sanc-tioned course. The extent to which he may choose his own system depends upon the freedom which the chief instruments of diffusion enjoy. In some nations the channels are closely censored and patterns of life are ready made. All the masses need do is follow—or suffer the consequences. In democratic societies, many dissenting voices speak, and the individual is free to sift the chaff from the wheat if he can do so, or if not, to be led first here and then there to the extent of his financial resources and moral boundaries.

Publicity today has become a potent deterrent from wrong doing for individuals in the secondary group, whom the sting of primary group gossip cannot reach. They abide by the standards of their group in order to avoid unpleasant notoriety. The publicizing of embezzlement cases has put fear of public condemnation into the heart of many a public official.

Modern business and the big industries fear Senate investigations and resort to all sorts of devices in attempting to avoid them. There is little doubt that fear of unfavorable publicity is a dynamic factor in secondary group society in keeping groups and institutions as well as individuals in check. Corruption, vice, graft, and the misuse of public office would be even more common than now, were it not for fear of exposure by the press.

Publicity, however, is not an unmixed evil. Many a boy or girl or man or woman has had his entire life ruined [11] by the un-

---

[11] See Frank Tannenbaum, op. cit., pp. 19–22, for a discussion of the effect of dramatizing the first crime.

feeling, indiscriminate smearing of his name on the front pages of the city's newspapers, when perhaps he had committed only a first offense. On the other hand, the constant exposure of crime, tax evasion, and other trespasses of the law by the press is a powerful factor in enforcing control in the secondary group. In fact, the present regulation which makes it necessary to publish all violations of the income tax law, probably will prove as effective a device as any that could be instituted in making people careful that they represent fully and accurately their obligations to the government.

SELECTED REFERENCES

Abel, Theodore, "The Pattern of a Successful Political Movement," *American Sociological Review*, vol. 2, pp. 347–352. June, 1937.

Arnett, C. E., and Others, "Prestige as a Factor in Attitude Changes," *Sociology and Social Research*, vol. 16, pp. 49–55. September, 1931.

Bent, S., "Propaganda Rules the Waves," *Review of Reviews*, vol. 95, pp. 38–40. February, 1937.

Bernays, E. L., "Freedom of Propaganda; Constructive Forming of Public Opinion," *Vital Speeches*, vol. 2, pp. 744–746. September 1, 1936.

Black, Hugo L., "Inside a Senate Investigation," *Harper's Magazine*, pp. 286 ff. February, 1936.

Bossard, Joseph H. S., *Social Change and Social Problems*, revised edition, chaps. 5 and 6. Harper and Brothers, New York, 1938.

Churchill, W., "You Get It in Black and White; Newer Mediums Cannot Replace the Printed Word," *Colliers*, vol. 96, pp. 32 ff. December 28, 1935.

Cochran, M. L., "Movies and Young Criminals," *National Education Association Journal*, vol. 21, pp. 169 ff. May, 1932.

Editorial, "The Newspaper and Social Responsibility," *Christian Century*, vol. 48, pp. 830 ff. June 24, 1931.

Graves, W. Brooke, editor, *Readings in Public Opinion*, chaps. 9, 10, 14, and 15. D. Appleton-Century Company, New York, 1928.

Holmes, Joseph L., "Crime and the Press," *Journal of the American Institute of Criminal Law and Criminology*, vol. 20, pp. 6 ff. May, 1929.

Johnson, B., "Newspaper's Lost Leadership," *North American Review*, vol. 232, pp. 65 ff. July, 1931.

La Piere, Richard T., *Collective Behavior*. McGraw-Hill Book Company, New York, 1938.

Lasswell, Harold D., *Propaganda Technique in the World War*. Alfred A. Knopf, Inc., New York, 1927.

Lippmann, Walter, *Public Opinion*. The Macmillan Company, New York, 1932.

Lumley, Frederick Elmore, *The Propaganda Menace*. D. Appleton-Century Company, New York, 1933.

Nevins, Allan, *American Press Opinion, Washington to Coolidge*. D. C. Heath and Company, New York, 1928.

Pitkin, W. B., "Screen Crime vs. Press Crime," *Outlook*, vol. 158, pp. 398 ff. July 29, 1931.

Wallas, Graham, *The Great Society*. The Macmillan Company, New York, 1920.

PART IV

INSTITUTIONS AS AGENCIES OF SOCIAL CONTROL

CHAPTER 13

PROBLEMS OF THE AMERICAN FAMILY AS AN AGENCY OF SOCIAL CONTROL

THE DEVELOPMENT OF A PERSONALITY UNDER THE CONTROLS OF A CLOSELY KNIT FAMILY PATTERN: A CASE STUDY [1]

During the turbulent 1850's when sectional strife was drenching Kansas soil with martyr blood, many home builders came quietly in and established a culture which was to remain after the war clouds had cleared away. In two of these families we are particularly interested: my maternal and paternal great-grandparents.

My mother's family tree spread with four sturdy branches: Quaker, Puritan, Wesleyan, and Boone. If less conforming branches had grown there, they had been carefully pruned from the record. This family, together with some half-dozen of their group, brought with them a rigid set of mores which they projected on each succeeding generation. They had three ambitions: to till the soil, to establish homes, to spend eternity in Heaven. Their mores, their taboos, the whole of their existence was entangled with their religion. Mistakes, or deviation from the code was sin. There was no choice of conduct. Living the "well-defined" right way would be rewarded by persecution in this life and eternal happiness in the after life. Any other way of living was a life of sin to be punished by eternal torment. The Bible sins were well defined; equally so were smoking, drinking, card playing, dancing, pleasure on Sunday, and scores of others. If this way of life could be projected upon the individual by teaching the love of God, well and good; if not, it must be accomplished through teaching the fear of God. The wicked were struck dead or beset by dire misfortunes—the same misfortunes to the saints being considered merely a divine testing.

Their material existence was equally well ordered. The men farmed well; the women kept their houses immaculate. The homes

---

[1] A student's autobiography in the author's collection.

were warm with hospitality. Although there was "no compromising with the Devil," no borrowing of new immaterial inventions, there was no hate toward the out-group. To hate was to sin; therefore, the out-group, being lost in sin, was to be pitied and brought into the fold. Beauty was in spiritual perfection. Purity of line and color in the material world was insignificant. Knowledge was to be desired—insofar as it did not conflict with their social code. Logical thinking was promoted—as long as it did not disarrange the pattern. Fantasy thinking was a mark of great spiritual leadership when directed toward spiritual things, but a sure path to destruction if used in connection with "desires of the flesh."

My father traced his family back into Kentucky, but beyond that it faded into the past. In Kentucky they had owned land and slaves and were more concerned with living well in this life than in living long in the other. Beauty—music, art, nature—was important in their culture pattern, and to entertain in the lavish Southern manner was necessary to their happiness. Although they did not attempt to project their mores on the community, their more liberal attitudes certainly had much effect on the new culture. Relatively free from prejudice, they participated in the other frontier groups at the same time keeping themselves separate in many ways. Their home, so different from the utilitarian homes of the community, rose in gracious beauty against a wall of virgin forest. Its wide-spread velvet lawn (such a waste of good land) seemed to shut it off as a moat from inroads of conflicting modes of life.

My parents were the third generation of these pioneers. My mother lived by a code little different from that of her grandmother. My father, frail and sensitive, possibly to compensate for his physical weakness had established a reputation in the community as a thinker, a philosopher, and a nature student. Their home, distinctive with its spaciousness and beauty, its fine hospitality, and the diffusion of the two cultures, became the center of the spiritual and social activity of the community. The three older children grew up in this environment, giving the expected honor to their elders and participating in their own age group. At the time this group began to establish homes, the community was no longer isolated. Many moved away and diffusion of culture took place rapidly. Social contacts became "contaminated" with worldliness, and the small original group, now composed of the middle-aged and old, became more and more isolated.

The status of my parents, along with that of the other members of their group, began to fall. The new element considered them "old fogies" and were not interested in the fine things they had to give because of the rigid wall of taboos that had to be first surmounted. This, however, was not the only change. The soil no longer produced abundantly, and the fine old house was in need of repair. The spacious pantry shelves were no longer filled with great stores of food. My mother was broken in health, and my father, always frail, was now a semi-invalid. There were few young people and fewer children in the community, none in the neighborhood. Dancing, card playing, and the movies—still taboo in my group—replaced the singing school, literary society, camp meeting, and Sunday school which had provided social contacts before. At least three major events had disorganized the home, and my father and mother, with all their high ideals and ambitions, were left lonely and discouraged. This was the environment into which I was born.

What a perfect setup for projection! Through this frail, nervous little girl they would project their thwarted ambitions. My parents and the remnant of their group saw no other way for continuing their culture in the face of outside forces. I would reach perfection. I would be devoutly religious, kind, gentle, soft of voice and manner, a little lower than the angels. I would keep a household running smoothly, be a perfect seamstress, a renowned cook. I would sing and play and drink deeply of the joy of music. I would have a spark of genius to carry on to distant heights. I would have a deep and perfect understanding. "As the twig is bent, so is the tree," they reasoned; so by careful control of the stimuli they attempted to build up a set of conditioned responses to enable me to play the role they wanted me to play.

My pre-school years were spent in isolation from contacts with a play group. Participation was in my parents' group, and my role was that of an example, a reflection of their attitudes. Not only did I play this role, but I played a similar role in a group of imaginary people with which I kept in close contact—a group of fantastic children strangely old and wise. So deeply absorbed was I in these two groups, the real and the imaginary, that play-group contacts made during my first two years of school have left no impression. There is simply no recollection of the existence of persons other than the teacher and myself. Incidents related to my groups are remembered with considerable clarity. From the fact that I recall accurately my relations to my parents-age group during this period, we can draw the conclusion that since all pleasant things had come to me through contacts with adults, I was conditioned to anticipate that all future pleasure would come from this group; and, this being the case, I did not participate with my age group. I was quite definitely an introvert.

The second stage of my personality development came between the ages of eight and twelve. The first half of this period was spent in a frontier community in a western state. Here, far removed from direct contact with my old group, surrounded by new behavior patterns and exposed to new stimuli, my personality began to change. My parents, no longer aided by the relatives and friends, lost much of their influence. Here, experiments with "forbidden fruit" resulted in no loss of status. Furthermore, I began playing a role in a play group. Although still walled about with taboos and burdened with habits of conduct proudly referred to as "conscience" I was admitted to the group in almost full participation.

The pleasant responses received from these first out-group stimuli, coming as they did at the time when I first ventured out of my first we-group, developed a questioning attitude toward some of my mores and rigid behavior patterns, and started me on a quick swing toward extroversion.

The last two years of this period were spent back in the old home community. The neighborhood had changed rapidly, my parents being the only remaining members of the old group. Although the new neighbors were looked upon with friendly interest, the participation between the two was limited to business and secondary group relationships. During this time, in spite of the acceptance of out-group mores, I probably made the greatest progress in absorbing the culture of the two parental groups which were my heritage through many generations. The traditional web which had been thrown about me since babyhood began to close in. The bands from the past which were to bind my future grew stronger: filial duty, duty toward the family God, duty toward the family traditions—duty, always duty. These were, however, probably my happiest years. I learned to sew, to cook, to make things with my hands. I walked beside my father through bursting spring and dazzling fall; caressing silky buds, and thrilling to riotous color. We stretched quietly in cool grass to watch the squirrels scampering overhead; the lazy clouds banking above the horizon. And he talked to me, in that far-sighted way of his, of things that were and of what was to be; he talked to me of people, of what they thought and how they acted, and I, who had never known people, learned to see them in relation to their opportunities and their different cultural environments; he talked to me of justice and injustice and the influence I could have in bringing into our culture the political and economic theories which he considered essential to progress—theories which, ridiculed by society then, are now accepted; and when he died, at the end of my twelfth year, he left me with a heavy yet exalted realization of my duty to my mother, my God, and to my fellowmen.

The third stage of my personality was a stage of adjustment. At the age of thirteen I grew up physically and mentally, and developed a mature way of life which now began to set me off from my age group. I began to be left out of things. I neither carried a ribbon at the Maypole, nor qualified for parts in the country school programs. My physical maladjustment kept me from participating in the rough and strenuous games. My mores began to conflict with much of the social life as my age group grew older. This was particularly true in high school, where the strict taboos and old-group ideas began to force me to withdraw further and further within myself. Although I was still an ambivert, I was moving rapidly toward introversion.

There was one great compensation. Always eager to learn, I now became deeply interested in my school work, although, as in earlier years, I had no time for reading outside of school. Although my parents had always wanted me to learn from books, their attitude had been of the "learn to swim, but don't go near the water" type. "Get your work finished first" was their motto. Duties were piled high before me, and as a result of my early training I had no thought of leaving them uncared for. Strange it was that even after a long and busy life they had not learned that a busy mind creates more work than the physical machine can do, and that one of the virtues of life is to know where to make the sacrifice—what unfinished task will cost the least in satisfaction and happiness.

My high school period really began to be not so much one of adjustment as one of transition. It was like the lull before the storm, the marking of time before the march. Cut off from group contacts, unhappy through living in the past in which my mother lived, I placed my faith in the future, and in my fantasy thinking built the foundation for a future different than the past had been. There was a great deal of unhappiness to be sure, but through rationalization and day dreaming I lived apart. Left so often to my own thoughts, I was beginning to question, to reason, to choose. The bonds which held me so tightly to my primary family-group mores and patterns still held firmly, but I felt that with graduation, when I went out "on my own" they would be severed and I would begin living by new codes, would have new ideas, attitudes, and habits, which would make me a part of the society about me. Strange illogical reasoning to believe that a band so carefully tempered through the years would snap so easily! Each year had made my duty to dependents a heavier burden and I passed into another waiting period.

This fourth stage might be termed a stage of logical thinking. Less hysterical, more my own master, I began to adjust the accumulated culture traits into patterns of my own, my own philosophy of life. I began to think my own thoughts, and to express them rather frequently. Consequently, I lost status in my old group, and not being able to participate in my own age-group without causing too much unhappiness to those dear to me, I could not gain status in another group. My job after high school was in the old community, making it even harder to attempt a break.

I entered the fifth stage of development mentally and physically exhausted. During the period of rest necessary to rebuild my body, I cut loose from the old inhibitions and began to give expression to long expressed desires. Habits were difficult to break, but I found it could be done.

At the beginning of this fifth stage, the college period, I must leave my analysis. With new stimuli, fewer taboos, more opportunity for borrowing new patterns, I will no doubt form new habits, but, from the experience of recent years, it seems safe to conclude that I will never break entirely from the training of my childhood and of my youth.

From a study of my development, we may conclude that a personality may be shaped chiefly by the mores of a small group if that group is isolated by physical or taboo barriers, and that when this happens socialization in a larger group is difficult; that projection of the culture of an intimate "in-group" upon the child can be so effective as to practically eliminate the influence of "out-group" patterns and to make difficult the attainment of status in normal "out-groups;" that both fantasy and logical thinking have an important place in the forming of personality patterns; that perfect social adjustment for many individuals is out of the realm of possibility in a complex social world, but that a personality can readjust through compensation and limited participation in "out-group" patterns, and thus acquire reasonable satisfaction; and that an isolated rural child who is shown the "out-group" world from a distance will probably never see it from intimate contacts.

The foregoing account of the actual experience of evolving a personality within the family group illustrates effectively each major point developed in this chapter: (1) That the family as a sociological agency is the most important institution of control, in its permanent effects upon the shaping of personality; (2) that it is possible through an authoritative family pattern to impress upon the child by precept, example, and if necessary, by discipline, the major codes and habit patterns of his society as they are conceived by the parents and selectively presented by them; (3) that latent patterns often are at work in the family situation and become important influences in control. Through projection the parent may try to realize his own ambitions through his children, as did these parents through their youngest daughter; (4) that the family may fail in certain respects as an agency of control. Chief among its failures is the one illustrated in this case, that of developing a personality in a mold too narrow to provide a sufficient background for successful living in the general culture in which the child will, with increased maturity, have to function.

THE IMPORTANT PLACE OF THE FAMILY AS AN AGENCY OF CONTROL

With the shift in recent years from a biological to a sociological emphasis on personality, there has come an increased appreciation of family patterns as a factor in fashioning the child's personality. It is now recognized that the family passes on not only the biological heritage, but the cultural heritage as well; that the child's tendencies toward introversion, extroversion, honesty, reliability, truthfulness, conservatism, timidity, aggressiveness, and other traits are not so much matters of biological capacity as of early conditioning in the family.

Experiments in child psychology have pushed the learning personality-forming processes back toward infancy. Now, we go so far as to assume that many basic personality traits are firmly imbedded by the time the child has reached the age of two or three years. If this be true, the effectiveness of the family in conditioning the child's personality and in implanting within him controls that will be potent in his social life is of outstanding importance.

Because of its primacy in the experience of the individual, it has the best opportunity of any institution to make its pattern felt. Because of its intimate nature, experiences are such that they make deep impressions. Added to these facts is the supplemental one that the individual in infancy and early childhood is more sensitive to stimuli than he is later, so that experiences register more deeply. Moreover, the family situation, because it constitutes the complete experience world of the small child, ordinarily presents a uniform and consistent set of experiences, which is so constantly repeated that response channels in the nervous system become well grooved.

In what other respects is the family unique or important as an institution of regulation? First of all, its motives are without parallel. The permanent family is built about the biological need for child care and the sociological need for legitimate parenthood. For these reasons the family probably operates as the least selfish of our social institutions, tending to keep the welfare of its helpless members in mind in the exercise of all of its controls. The virtues of affection, tolerance, patience, self-sacrifice, and love predominate more than in other institutions. Patterns of authority designate the limits within which the unshaped personality can express itself. It is perhaps for this reason that Thomas has referred to the family as the agency which operates by the ordering and forbidding technique.[2] As the child matures in age and experience, and as his habits become more fixed, the authority pattern is gradually relaxed and the youth is allowed greater freedom of choice and self-direction. This becomes the logical step in his transition to an independent world where he is no longer subject to the control devices of the family.

The degree of success which a family will attain as an agency of social control probably varies radically with the locality. If the

---

[2] W. I. Thomas, The Unadjusted Girl, pp. 70 ff.

family lives in a community where traditions of the community and neighborhood are in harmony with those of the family, its task of control is greatly lessened because the community shares the responsibility.[3] On the other hand, if the community patterns differ markedly, the family's problem is greatly increased because the child usually wavers back and forth between family patterns and those of the community, a condition well illustrated in the case study at the beginning of this chapter.

The problem of control varies greatly within the family also. Some families are well integrated; others are not. Lack of integration within the family frequently results in child delinquency, as has been indicated by many studies. If the family fails in its control function, and if other institutions do not absorb this responsibility, then the child is likely to flout all social regulation. In areas undergoing rapid change, such as in our industrial centers, in Russia, or in coast cities of China, families face more formidable problems of regulation than families in static societies where family patterns are fortified by age-long traditions and customs.

The family itself as an agency of control is effective only when it is fairly well integrated, and where its own goals and purposes are clearly defined. In a society like our own, where divorce rates are exceedingly high, and where the two parents sometimes have different goals in life, the possibility of the family's acting as an effective agency of control is greatly decreased. Perhaps it is because of this fact that the family is gradually sharing its problems of social control with agencies outside the home. The school is taking over more and more responsibility for character training and for conditioning the child to proper habits, even personal ones such as cleanliness, courtesy, and truthfulness. The supervised playground, the Sunday School, the nursery school—all of these agencies are absorbing those functions of control which the home no longer is competent to perform alone. Not only is the family an agency of control but, like other institutions, it is susceptible to the general cultural milieu which determines the particular role that it will play as an agency of control.

---

[3] Chaffee's description of the common patterns of family and community in the Amana Colony is interesting in this connection. Refer to her account, pp. 151, 152.

The Authority Pattern in Family Life

Precept and example almost always loom large in the family circle, but larger in a patriarchy or matriarchy than in the so-called democratic family. The unruly Hebrew child, according to the Mosaic Law, was stoned to death. Roman patriarchs had the power of life and death within their families. In the American family, precept and example function to a great extent, but a degree of authority is always present. That authority is very desirable in the experience of the child, I think, cannot be denied by those who understand human nature and the necessity that it fit into the group environment. Undisciplined human nature will not long be tolerated in a civilized society.

Margaret Mead, in her study of New Guinea, as has been indicated in another connection,[4] has revealed the fact that children raised in that primitive environment, where childhood is entirely unregulated, and where few habits needed for adult life are inculcated into the personality, look upon maturity with a great degree of pessimism, and during the rest of their lives mourn the loss of childhood.

Discipline is essential in the family pattern. It is a part of human experience to learn to conform, to learn to harness biological drives in the interest of social welfare. Society is built on this principle, and can be maintained only as long as it remains in operation.

But even though some authority is necessary, too much is disastrous. Students of child psychology have shown that if the authority pattern is made too imposing, if the child's individuality is too much suppressed, if reality is made too overwhelming, the child must take refuge in perhaps unwholesome means of releasing tensions and giving vent to his feelings of frustration. He may rebel, or he may resort to day dreaming and fantasy creation, living more and more in an imaginary world in which he always plays either the hero or the poor persecuted sufferer.[5] Both are harmful from the standpoint of personality development.

The fear element may become too prominent under the authority pattern, so that the child develops a sense of insecurity,

---

[4] Mead, *Growing Up in New Guinea*. See p. 143 of this book.
[5] For a more extensive discussion of this problem see *The Child: His Nature and His Needs*, M. V. O'Shea, editor.

and habits of submissiveness that hinder him in his later social adjustment. The authority pattern is most normal when it achieves a balance between freedom and discipline.[6]

Modern disciplinary philosophy assumes that the adult may transcend the ordering and forbidding technique, and even control the young child in the family situation by motivation, leading the child to do the things the adult wants done without using his superior force and without making authority obvious. This is a part of the ideal of the democratic family, that the child shall learn to participate as an individual in the family situation, that there shall be a give-and-take relationship in which the parent, because of superior wisdom and experience, directs but does so without the obvious manifestations of authoritative patterns.

CONTROL BY LATENT PATTERNS IN THE FAMILY

Because the family is interested primarily in the child, the attention directed toward him may unconsciously lead to control for purposes of exploitation, the parent reaching the point where he thinks he is doing a thing for the welfare of the child when actually he is doing it to satisfy some hidden motive of his own; it may be some thwarted ambition he tries to realize in the child, or it may be that he projects his own ideal life onto his children, as did the parents in the case study. Their child must be righteous, good, kind, industrious, musical, cultured. This process of realizing one's interests through imposing them upon others, known as *projection*, is a perfectly natural phenomenon and is possibly far more common in the family than is recognized. Generally, it is desirable and works no hardship; that parents seek to immortalize through their children unrealized hopes and ideals is normal and wholesome. Only when they try to control the child against his natural interests is projection undesirable.

It may be more common in its worst forms in the American family than elsewhere because many women here have faced the alternative of a career or marriage, and have chosen marriage only to regret it later. Thus an ideal situation is provided for projecting unfulfilled ambition upon the child. Sometimes ideals are

---

[6] The way in which a well-knit family pattern can lead to the development of a personality which may be entirely too well integrated for the good of that person as he shifts to another environment was well exemplified in the college student's autobiography quoted in the introduction to this chapter.

imposed and standards of achievement set which he has neither the capacity to realize, nor the ambition to fulfill.

From experience with college youth, and from collecting and reading a number of student autobiographies the writer has been led to believe that vocational interests are very frequently projected upon the child, sometimes in a disastrous way, because often he is entirely unfit for the vocation of his parents' choice.

Kimball Young has discussed the problem of projection as a vital one in our culture. A part of his argument follows:

The child, rather than developing his talents and interests out of innate trends and through normal development in various social media, is brought under the domination of a fixed idea of the parent. Too often the parent has harbored some unfulfilled desire or ambition for fame, money, education, social status, or what not which is worked over on to the child.

We know full well that parents live in their children quite as do the children in them. "Identification," as it is often called, is by no means a one-sided affair. Not long ago in discussing with a mother a certain regimen for children, she remarked regarding some indulgences which she had granted them, "If I have to have the children, I don't see why I shouldn't enjoy them." It has, of course, been long recognized that many mothers derive a distinct erotic pleasure from nursing their babies. But we should not imagine that any pleasure which a mother may take in her children ends there. It is evident everywhere that women do look upon their children as their own in a very intimate, dare one say selfish, sense, in which their own delight in caring for, playing with, and planning for the child becomes highly significant for themselves.

Not only mothers but fathers find tremendous satisfaction in watching over and planning for their children.

Thus, for parents there is afforded them in their children an easy duplication of another childhood and youth, wherein their own ambitions, plans, and desires may be thrust upon the next generation. The motives for this projection vary greatly, for the particular type of ambition projected upon the child depends, certainly, upon the specific history of the parent.

Projection is perhaps more or less inevitable in a society of open classes where there is intense desire to improve the family status in each succeeding generation.

The problem of projection in parent-child relationships is self-evident. The more spontaneous development is interrupted to give place to the formulation of life-organization in terms of patterns possessed by the parent that may not be altogether wholesome and sound for the child.[7]

It is in a rapidly changing social order that projected parental patterns often interfere seriously with the adjustments of youth, for parents usually try to perpetuate the values of an age that is passing; youth must live in the new. This fact, most strikingly illustrated in the adaptation of the immigrant child to the new culture, is true of all situations in which culture patterns are changing. The following selection portrays immigrant adjustment.

Vocational adjustments are often complicated when the parents project their ambitions upon the younger generation. Particularly has this been true of the Japanese in Hawaii. The majority of them came to work on the sugar plantations with the intention of accumulating sufficient savings to assure a comfortable livelihood and a higher social station in the homeland. Being accustomed to the low wages of the Orient, the earnings of the plantations seemed to offer a fair opportunity for acquiring a competence. Many have returned, but the majority, in spite of unremitting toil, have not been able to accumulate enough to assure a life of comfort in the old country. With their ambitions unrealized, many hoped to see their dreams come true in and through their children.

The full significance of this situation cannot be understood apart from its oriental background. Japan is not far removed from a feudal regime in which distinctions in class and social rank were important. The immigrants lived in their old memories and planned to return to the homeland to acquire a superior status in an aristocracy; they were not aiming at the attainment of equality in a democratically organized society. Many have concluded that it is no longer possible to return to positions of dignity in their home communities. They cannot win recognition and status in America, but there is hope of gaining vicariously through their American-born children what

---

[7] Kimball Young, "Parent-Child Relationships: Projection of Ambition," *The Family*, 1927, vol. 8, pp. 67–73; also appears in his *Source Book for Social Psychology*, pp. 374 ff.

they had failed to do for themselves. Since certain limitations are placed upon the younger generation on account of race, the parents look to education as a means of betterment.

The projection of ambitions has not ended with an encouragement toward securing an education; very often it has been carried over into advice relative to the choice of an occupation. In this connection the tradition of the Orient, particularly of Japan, becomes evident. The parents are desirous that their children turn to occupations that will reflect credit upon the family name. If they are not sufficiently ambitious to rise above the occupations open to their parents in Hawaii, they are considered failures and as such bring discredit to the family.

Some parents choose vocations for their sons and daughters against the better judgment of the children. A number accept the parental choices as temporary expedients, but hope to make readjustments later. Some are torn between duty to their parents and obligation to themselves. Others rationalize the situation and endeavor to make the best of the vocational choices made by their parents. A Chinese girl in Hawaii, who had been projected into the teaching profession by her mother, found consolation in the fact that she would have a long summer vacation for rest and travel. Some gradually become interested in the parental choices; some even become enthusiastic about their future.

When parents project their ambitions upon the child, there is no normal development of the child's own interests and talents. He does not select his own patterns and work out his own life organization; his course is directed by fixed ideas of his parents. With oriental parents, living in memories of the old country and not understanding their Americanized children, this parental domination often accentuates the problems of the young people. Not all parents, however, make the occupational choices for their children. Many provide opportunities which arouse and develop in a normal way the children's own interests and ambitions. While the parents, in projecting their ambitions upon the children, are interested in satisfying their own thwarted wishes, they are not unmindful of the status of the younger generation. The problem lies in their analysis of the situation from their own point of view and not from that of the children.[8]

---

[8] William C. Smith, *Americans in Process*, pp. 110, 111, 112. By permission of the author.

FAILURE OF THE AMERICAN FAMILY AS AN AGENCY OF CONTROL

There are many reasons for thinking that in our culture, where the functions of the family are changing, it is failing as an agency of control. Nevertheless it still remains the most effective agency we have.

Our democratic philosophy of life gives the parent a less prominent place in control, because we assume that the child should be given considerable liberty and self-direction, more than most societies have permitted. In fact, many parents feel that they are unfair to the child if they interfere in any way with the development of his individuality. The modern-day parent tries to govern by motivation rather than by command, by subtlety rather than by superior force, by winning confidence rather than by using their advantage of superior age and experience.

Far more important than these rather external factors, however, is the fact that in the world today many parents themselves lack definite established patterns of life to pass on to the child. The adult lives in a complex world, a world reflected in his personality, his values, and his extra-home activities.[9] It is hard for the parent to insist upon an authoritative pattern of morals or religion when he himself holds no absolute standards. As a consequence, he frequently presents several alternatives, expecting the child to choose his own course, a thing which no child is capable of doing. "Teach him no religion; let him choose for himself" is commonly heard. Should parents expect the immature child to do what they as adults have found themselves incapable of doing? What child has the ability to choose a religion for himself in a complex culture like our own, or to choose a moral code in the absence of established moral standards in the home?

Likewise, some parents have gone to the extreme of thinking that a child should make up his own mind regarding his life vocation, without any parental advice. Fortunately, in this realm the child usually is given enough experience with various activities in the school system to arrive at some idea of his abilities and interests.

---

[9] For an excellent analysis of changing family functions see W. F. Ogburn's discussion in *Recent Social Trends in the United States*, pp. 664–679.

It is certainly true that we live in an age when a child should develop the power of discrimination in the field of morality so that afterwards he will be able to decide for himself. On the other hand, no one ever develops those standards from within; rather he must acquire them from outside himself. Leaving moral guidance entirely to the "instinct of youth" is hazardous from the standpoint of a well-ordered social system or a well-ordered individual life.

The family fails as an agent of control frequently because it fails as a family. It has long been known that children and youth in broken or disorganized homes come far short of developing effective standards of control as compared with normal families.

The fact that the family has taken on an epicurean tinge in which pleasure looms much larger than duty, is developing a situation in which the interest of the child may not be the primary concern. Rather an interest lies in happiness for the adult. The child in many cases is accidentally produced, due to faulty birth control techniques, and so starts life as an unwanted guest in the home. Parents may shuffle him aside and follow necessary interests in the vocation, or selfish interests in the climb to social status. He may be left so much alone that he develops a feeling of insecurity and uncertainty about his environment, not having any definite standards by which he can chart his course.[10]

There has been a general breakdown of controls outside the family which has influenced family patterns. The family itself is enmeshed in the cultural ideology of its time.[11] In our culture numerous changes in the fields of technology and ideology have made their inroads on the family, encroaching upon its functions, changing its outlook and challenging some of its foundations. The general culture no longer decrees that the family be stable if members composing it want it to be otherwise.

Another reason why the family is failing as an institution of control is that motives for marriage do not very well co-ordinate with family functions. We build marriage on romance alone. Courtship furnishes a glorious holiday for romantic expression. Marriage is designed for human happiness, frequently an ethereal

---

[10] Compare James S. Plant, *Personality and the Cultural Pattern*, chap. 7.
[11] Joseph K. Folsom, *The Family*, pp. 552 ff.

and impractical happiness having little relation to the realities married life must necessarily involve.

While it is true that the ultramodern family living in the urban apartment house has lost many of the functions of control that the family once exercised, actually the average couple which expects to have children must also expect to face a number of problems both of adult and child discipline if their family is to succeed as a permanent and regulated unit. Success in romance is no assurance of the possession of the enduring personal qualities essential to well-regulated family life. As romances are conducted under modern conditions, youth has little opportunity to evaluate the other person from the viewpoint of his capacity to fit into a domestic situation. Courtship in our mobile society is for the most part carried on outside the family situation, and it takes considerable imagination for the average youth to think of his partner as a member of a home.

It is probable that a great number of marriages are entered into without the practical aspects of marriage ever having been discussed. It used to be that the child grew up in an adult society where he participated in the experience of an adult world and acquired mature standards of value. Today young people increasingly live in a youth group where adult values are viewed with considerable skepticism. This has a bearing on conduct prefatory to marriage as well as on conduct in the family. It undoubtedly contributes somewhat to the failure of the American family as an institution of control.

In our conglomerate population, a mixture of all nations, a great number of people who marry have dissimilar backgrounds and interests. This frequently means a lack of uniformity in the family pattern, so that the child is faced, to a measure at least, with two rather diverse worlds of values, as is the case where Protestant and Catholic marry and each maintains his faith.

The failure of the family as a controlling agency in the complexities of the urban environment are well known. The most extreme example of this breakdown is observed in the failure of the immigrant family to maintain control over the second generation. The parent, believing as he does in old world standards, fails miserably in trying to impose them upon youth who live in an American world. Because the immigrant child typifies in such an impressive manner the individual who bridges distinct family and neighborhood patterns, selections illustrating the adjustments of immigrant children are reproduced.

CONFLICT OF FAMILY PATTERNS IN A CULTURALLY MARGINAL GENERATION [12]

The American-born children of oriental ancestry have made contacts with several types of family life. There has been no standardized oriental pattern to follow. In some homes the oriental pattern has been followed with slight variations, but in most instances there has been considerable disorganization and a certain amount of reorganization to fit the new conditions. The young people have made contacts with the occidental family system. As they have tried to steer their course through this uncharted sea, they have broken with many of the oriental practices.

The young people, who have become imbued with democratic ideas, object to the old-fashioned, autocratic family control. The native-born girls, who observe the freedom of American women, are doing much to break down the idea of male domination. They consider themselves Americans and are unwilling to acquiesce in an arrangement which would reduce them to a perpetual minority. Many oppose their parents and argue against their ideas. Some girls are not even satisfied with a status of equality. They state in no uncertain terms that they desire to be the dominating heads of their households. This is not mere idle talk, for some of the women are carrying their ideas into practice. This is made evident by an immigrant Japanese:

> You know, my wife, she used to help me all the time; bye an' bye she catchum baby, then she not help me so much. Bye an' bye she catchum 'nother baby, then she say to me, "I no help you no more." I say, "Yes, you will." She say, "No, I won't; I American citizen." This afternoon, my wife, she telephone me, "You come home." I say, "I no can come, truck gone, I no can come." She say, "You come home!" I go home. Truck gone, I walk home.

Many boys advocate greater freedom for the women but they are unwilling to go as far as the girls; they are not ready to surrender completely the idea of male superiority.

---

[12] William C. Smith, *Americans in Process*, pp. 227–235. By permission of the author.

The girls of oriental ancestry are not willing to submit to a system under which the mother-in-law dominates the young wife; they do not want to live with mothers-in-law or other relatives according to oriental custom. Wherever possible the young people move out of the crowded tenement sections. The rapidity of the movement, however, is determined in considerable measure by the economic situation. While the young people prefer to live under their own roofs, oftentimes the economic circumstances will not permit.

Many of the young people are outspoken against the idea of parentally-arranged marriages. Many refuse to accept the arrangements made by their parents. Financial independence, particularly among .he Chinese of Hawaii, has been an important causal factor. Many Chinese women feel free and independent now that they are wage-earners. Some go to extremes in order to make the emancipation complete; they marry men distasteful to their parents just to parade their freedom. Some have left their homes to avoid marriage with men selected by their parents. Some have declared that they would do as they pleased—but when the time for marriage arrived, the parents took matters in hand and settled all. The parents may adopt American dress quite readily, but the attitudes relative to family matters are deep-rooted and change less easily.

The young people have seen parentally-arranged marriages go on the rocks and this has conditioned them against the system. A young woman related her own story:

> At thirteen years of age my father married me off to a wealthy middle-aged man who seemed like a father to me. Naturally, I was taken from school, which I regretted very much. At every opportunity I read my books and always watched the other children going to and from school with envy. I always felt as though I belonged to them. I did not dare to tell this to my parents, not even to my mother, as it is against our religion to entertain even a thought of disobedience to one's husband. This feeling, however, became very intense within me and at last, after three years, I decided to leave him. There was much anger and consternation, but I was determined. I had read of American wives acting in this manner under such circumstances and I still feel it is right. I defied anyone to interfere any further with my actions. Some time later I met a student at the night school which I attended. . . . On further acquaintance we found our view of life very similar and decided to marry.

Many young women set high standards for their future husbands. If such are not found they will not marry. This is quite revolutionary when we consider that bachelors and spinsters have no place in the oriental scheme of life. A considerable number of young women are not marrying, or, at least, they are postponing marriage. They are not remaining single because of inability to marry. According to one writer, "The American-oriental flapper is the most courted woman in the world, for she is wooed not only by the 'sheiks' of her own age but by the tens of thousands of oriental bachelors on the Coast, who can no longer import wives from their home country."

Although many have broken with the old traditions there is, nevertheless, a marked family solidarity. The familial sentiments of many young people are strong. Because of this many deny themselves rather than disappoint their elders. Many make definite plans to care for their parents in old age. The parents have sacrificed to give them a start in life. In return they bend all their energies toward making their elders happy. Some save in order to build comfortable homes for them. Some, desirous of preparing for professional life, give this up and turn to vocations with a more immediate income. Even where home relationships have not been happy, there are young people who care for their elders and make sacrifices for them.

The young people are setting the occidental family before themselves as an ideal to be followed. Many indicate a decided preference for western practices; some even go to extremes in carrying them out. In the discussion of love affairs, there is a great difference between Orientals and Occidentals. Orientals do not have love affairs; hence they are often shocked by the freedom with which Americans discuss such matters.

Very few of the young people have had sufficient contact with American family life to pattern after it, but they are eager to learn from every available source. Books, magazines, and Dorothy Dix's column in the newspaper are read with avidity. Some have learned by working in American homes. Many of their ideas are acquired in the moving-picture theaters.

Many young people are in a difficult situation. They have not learned the technique of American courtship which differs greatly from the oriental practice where the go-between, or match-maker, plays such an important role. When they try to adopt Western methods they find no adequate guide-posts to direct them, and in this period of transition many suffer heartaches. But even if they had made the occidental mode of courtship their own, they would still encounter difficulties. Most houses of the Orientals are not of such size and character that the daughters could conveniently and with appropriate dignity entertain young men friends. More important, however, are the parental attitudes which are encountered. If a boy calls on a girl, the parents consider it a serious matter and that marriage is almost certain to follow. According to many of the older Chinese in the United States, disaster lurks in the automobile rides of young American couples. The young people hear these ideas expressed in their homes. Since many of them do not fully understand American customs, standards, and ideals, an automobile ride not infrequently leads to a forced marriage.

The Breakdown of Control in the Immigrant Group with the Decay of the Large Family [13]

The general background of the disorganization of the marriage-group among Polish immigrants is the decay of the large family, the weakness of the Polish-American community and the novelty of the American legal standards. Marriage as a social institution was a part of the wider family institution. The large families of the husband and of the wife, whatever rivalries and conflicts there might be, were both interested in preserving the conjugal bond which was much more their work than that of the individuals concerned and which had led to a detailed adjustment of the economic and social affairs of each family and could not be broken without undesirable consequences for each of them. Each family, therefore, took care to enforce all the traditional rules of behavior upon its own married member and at the same time was ready to defend this member against any break of these rules committed by the other party. And whenever the large family itself overstepped the principles for which it was meant to stand or was unable to influence the marriage-group, the community exercised its rights of control over both the marriage-group and the large family. The traditional system was sanctioned by the entire social milieu of the married couple, including the

---

[13] From William I. Thomas and Florian Znaniecki, *The Polish Peasant in Europe and America*, vol. 5, pp. 221–224. By permission of Chapman and Grimes, publishers.

church and the state, whose rules in this one respect were in harmony with those recognized by the peasant community.

Now, as we have already seen, in this country the large family is no longer a real social body with concrete common interests—for usually only a few members have immigrated and these are often scattered over a vast territory. The community has also only a small stock of old traditions left and cannot efficiently enforce even these unless the individual chooses to participate actively in common life. Further, in spite of the great vitality which the parish has as a social institution the authority of the church as a religious institution is much weakened, perhaps for the very reason that the existence of the Polish-American church depends on the free will of the congregation. And the state, even if it tries to uphold the marriage-group, does it in a way which does not harmonize at all with the traditions of the peasant and far from preserving, rather weakens, as we shall see, the institutional meaning of marriage in the eyes of the immigrant. As a result marriage almost ceases to be a social institution, and the old socially sanctioned attitudes upon which the strength and permanence of the conjugal bonds were based lose most of their practical influence.

Under these circumstances marriage rests almost exclusively upon temperamental attitudes of the individuals, not upon their obedience to social rules. Sexual desire, maternal instinct, in a much smaller measure paternal feeling, desire for response and desire for security are practically the only powers which draw and keep the couples together. Our documents will show that none of these attitudes is sufficient to form a permanent basis for the family. And it is much more difficult for immigrant society to substitute new social ideals and norms for the crumbling old institutional foundation of family life than to create substitutes for the traditional economic life-organization. The abstract principle of duty has little if any practical influence unless derived either from concrete social rules or from some form of religion. Love as a cultural product with its idealization of the entire personality and consequent permanent attachment to the exclusion of all other individuals is rare in general and particularly rare among the peasants with their traditional subordination of the individual to the group. Economic ideals, when they exist, contribute, indeed, to the maintenance of family life in general, since the immigrant can seldom imagine an economically perfect life without a family. But this does not guarantee sufficiently the stability of marriage, for in any particular case a man may prefer to establish a new family rather than stay with the old one. Moreover, conjugal trouble reacts unfavorably, as we know, upon economic life. The social progress of the marriage-group, an active and prominent participation in Polish-American life which attracts to it the attention of the community, and the advance of the young generation are indeed positive moral factors insofar as they frequently prevent an open breakdown of the marriage-group; but their action is limited to a minority of the immigrants and is appreciable only when the marriage-group has already begun to achieve a certain social prominence, i.e., when the parents have passed the "stormy period" of youth. Besides, in view of the tacitly accepted principle of Polish-American society not to interfere too much with the private life of socially useful members, a very far-going real demoralization may subsist under the appearances of respectability. The nominal standards of respectability are, of course, still kept up by the leading circles but with the exception of a small number of intellectual immigrants who have brought with them a general and more or less rationally motivated idealism, and of those members of the younger generation who are in close touch with such American circles as have preserved the traditional family mores intact, these standards seem to be merely a respected survival whose most real, though unavowed function is to import to the eyes of society a kind of scandalized interest in those cases in which they are openly broken.

The moral status of the average Polish-American individual or marriage-group in matters of conjugal life can be thus briefly characterized as that of a very unstable balance of temperamental attitudes and personal habits, which determines whether the traditional social schematization—now almost reduced to a mere form—will be preserved or not. As long as the natural tendencies and habits of the man and of the woman work more or less in accordance with this schematization, their relation is still defined as of old, since it is easier to accept the ready and usual definition than to work out a new one. But there is no social prestige behind this definition and no higher motive which would induce the individual to accept and maintain it when it disagrees with his temperament and habits. Therefore, any cause producing disharmony between the old social schemes and the individual's natural or habitual tendencies may lead him to reject the traditional definition and either prevent him from establishing a conjugal relation where according to all the social rules it should be established, or make him break a conjugal relation already existing. The cause may be some influence producing in the individual new attitudes incompatible with the elementary conditions of conjugal life in general, or it may be some agency modifying the specific traditional scheme of conjugal life in a way which makes it seem no longer acceptable to him. . . .

To a lesser extent all children absorbing the culture pattern of an external world different from the family pattern must face adjustment problems similar to those of the immigrant child. In fact, any mobile family in American culture is likely to meet them to some extent, whether they move to a community of different character, or whether they move vertically from class to class, social or occupational, where new standards are involved.

Conclusion

The family lays the cornerstone of personality and develops lasting life-patterns, which, if they conform to those of the community, prepare the child for normal social living. If they are inadequate the child will be unable to adjust properly unless assisted by some other agency. Discipline, precept, and example play a prominent part. The "ordering and forbidding technique" is frequently employed. As soon as the child has free motion and begins to pull, tear, pry, meddle, and prowl, the parents begin to define the situation through speech and other signs and pressures: "Be quiet," "Sit up straight," "Blow your nose," "Wash your face," "Mind your mother," "Be kind to your sister," and similar admonitions. This is the real significance of Wordsworth's phrase, "Shades of the prison house begin to close upon the growing child." [14]

In our complicated social system, with its emphasis on competition and individual success, most parents have many unfulfilled wishes, often centered in vocation. He projects these wishes upon his child, and through him tries to gain a vicarious satisfaction. If he loves his work he may train his children to follow this profession, even going so far as to insist that they enter it against their wishes. There is no harm in such projection as long as it is in line with the child's temperament; in fact, the parent can legitimately go a long way in determining the child's interest.

---

[14] W. I. Thomas, *The Unadjusted Girl*, p. 43.

But if the child lacks natural aptitude such a projection is inevitably futile, and often harmful.

However, we are not concerned here with the justice or the injustice of projection, but simply indicate that it often is a subtle factor in controlling the vocational choice of the child. In a similar manner parents project their ideas and morals, their religion, and political loyalties upon their offspring. To a certain extent all training is the projection of elements of culture upon the child. This is the essence of the process of passing on the subtler elements of the culture heritage.

In our world of rapid change parental patterns often prove inadequate controls because many parents have no definite standards; others fail to keep pace with changing times; still others have interests other than child training uppermost in their minds. Outside agencies are usurping realms of control on which the family once held a monopoly. With all of this, however, the family is still an indispensable agent of social control.

SELECTED REFERENCES

Burgess, E. W., "Family Tradition and Personality Development," *Proceedings of the National Conference of Social Work*, pp. 329–332. 1928.

Cavan, R. S., "Relation of Home Background and Social Relations to Personality Adjustment," *American Journal of Sociology*, vol. 40, pp. 143–154. September, 1934.

Chapin, F. Stuart, *Contemporary American Institutions*, chaps. 6 and 7. Harper and Brothers, New York, 1935.

Chapin, F. Stuart, *Cultural Change*. D. Appleton-Century Company, New York, 1928.

Dane, C., "What Is Love? Is It What We See in the Movies?", *Forum*, vol. 94, pp. 335–338. December, 1935.

Dowd, Jerome, *Control in Human Societies*, chaps. 18 and 20. D. Appleton-Century Company, New York, 1936.

Folsom, Joseph K., *The Family*, parts 5 and 6. John Wiley and Sons, Inc., New York, 1934.

Hoffman, W., "Effect of Increasing Divorce on Family Life," *Current History*, vol. 30, pp. 876 ff. August, 1929.

Keller, A. G., *Brass Tacks*, chaps. 6 and 7. Alfred A. Knopf, Inc., New York, 1938.

Keller, A. G., *Man's Rough Road*, part 4. Frederick A. Stokes Company, New York, and Yale University Press, New Haven, 1932.

Landis, Paul H., "Control of the Romantic Impulse through Education," *School and Society*, pp. 212–215. August 15, 1936.

Landis, Paul H., and Judson, T., *Social Living, Principles and Problems in Introductory Sociology*, chap. 13. Ginn and Company, Boston, 1938.

Mead, Margaret, "Broken Homes," *Nation*, vol. 128, pp. 253 ff. February 27, 1929.

Mead, Margaret, *Growing Up in New Guinea*. William Morrow and Company, New York, 1930.

Mowrer, E. R., *Domestic Discord*. University of Chicago Press, Chicago, 1928.

Mowrer, E. R., *Family Disorganization*, chap. 13. University of Chicago Press, Chicago, 1927.

Mowrer, E. R., *The Family*, chap. 9. University of Chicago Press, Chicago, 1932.

Mowrer, Mrs. Harriet R., *Personality Adjustment and Domestic Discord*. American Book Company, New York, 1935.

Ogburn, William F., "Our Social Heritage," *Survey Graphic*, pp. 277 ff. December, 1927.

Plant, James S., *Personality and the Cultural Pattern*, chaps. 7 and 10. The Commonwealth Fund, New York, 1937.

Recent Social Trends in the United States (selection by W. F. Ogburn), pp. 664–679. McGraw-Hill Book Company, New York, 1933.

Reuter, E. B., and Runner, J. R., *The Family: Source Materials for the Study of Family and Personality*. McGraw-Hill Book Company, New York, 1931.

Richards, E. L., "Discipline and Adjustment," *Education*, vol. 54, pp. 403–409. March, 1934.

Sarvis, Maude Taylor, "Can Romance Sustain Marriage?", *Christian Century*, vol. 48, p. 1309. October 21, 1931.

Smith, William C., *Americans in Process*, pp. 110 ff., 227 ff. Edwards Brothers, Inc., Ann Arbor, 1937.

Stern, Bernhard J., editor, *The Family Past and Present*. D. Appleton-Century Company, New York, 1938.

Thomas, W. I., and Znaniecki, Florian, *The Polish Peasant in Europe and America*, vol. 2, pp. 288–295; vol. 5, pt. 2, chap. 3. Chapman and Grimes, Boston, 1918 and 1920 respectively.

Thomas, William I., *The Unadjusted Girl*, pp. 43 ff.; pp. 70 ff. Little, Brown and Company, Boston, 1923.

Wolfe, W. B., "Romance versus Marriage," *Forum*, vol. 86, pp. 166 ff. September, 1931.

Young, Kimball, "Parent-Child Relationship: Projection of Ambition," *The Family*, vol. 8, pp. 67–73. 1927.

CHAPTER 14

PROBLEMS OF THE CHRISTIAN CHURCH AS AN INFLUENCE IN SOCIAL CONTROL

SUPERNATURALISM AS A FACTOR IN CONTROL: A CASE STUDY [1]

I was reared in a family in which faith in an omnipotent being who is directly interested in our welfare was readily accepted as fact. The Holy Bible is an irrefutable religious authority. Although God is omnipotent, it is pretty generally conceded by all members of the family that he governs the universe by certain rigid rules and regulations. If, however, conditions warrant, i.e., a desperate situation arises and the family prays to have the danger averted, we believe that God will cut through all existing universal laws to save us from the insurmountable difficulties which exist. But we also believe that we must do everything in our power to meet the emergency.

I hold most of those beliefs, somewhat modified, as they were given to me. This religious approach to life has colored all of my subsequent career, especially having shaped my mores. For, reared in a locality which has a unique religious attitude such as I have described, I have naturally absorbed that culture pattern and in consequence of my scientific training have evolved a religion which is a strange mixture of science and religion. My family environment led me to recognize that certain meteorological factors caused rain. My religious beliefs cause me to believe that if the need of rain was felt in South Dakota and the people of a community faithfully prayed for rain it would be forthcoming in spite of the meteorological conditions. Or rather I should say that God would arrange the meteorological conditions so that it would rain.

Although I tend to be an agnostic when considering the ultimate destiny of man and the existence of a supreme deity, I derive an immense amount of comfort from prayer, and my faith in a God who

---

[1] Selections from a student's autobiography in the author's collection.

236

is willing to help whenever I am in trouble. This faith has given me the strength to live in the way that I believe to be morally correct even when it is apparent that I lose in a social, economic, and physical sense by so doing. There is no doubt that I could gain much in the way of social benefit here at college if I were to dismiss some of my religious beliefs and "jump into the swim." I recognize this but refuse to do so because I believe that the loss from the standpoint of mental peace would be greater than the gain from physical satisfaction.

This strange religious approach to life has very naturally colored my attitudes toward many business and pleasure practices which characterize our everyday world. Because of this training I do not believe in taking an unfair advantage of another in competition. I have tried in my school work to give other students an equal opportunity with myself. At times I think that I have failed in this attempt, but that is neither here nor there, for the success of my attempt is no criterion of my beliefs. In debate, speech, and other extracurricular activities I have tried to be fair and square with my competitors.

My more rigid taboos are, as would be expected, against dancing, drinking, gambling, smoking, and indulging in illicit sex relations. I do not condone these practices because I believe that indulgence in them by whole communities will lead to the eventual destruction and disintegration of our family and community life, features very desirable if our present culture pattern is to continue to exist. My logic and line of reasoning supporting my beliefs are too involved and complex to present in a paper of this volume.

This selection from a student autobiography suggests the extent to which one's religious belief may affect his social conduct. From a purely sociological viewpoint, religion probably has been of greatest significance in human culture because of its influence in social control. Dealing with the inner life of man, and connecting man with those powers which he conceives to control life and the universe, religion possesses potentialities for regulating man's conduct to a remarkable extent. Because of its universality and its deep grip on humanity, it is everywhere a controlling institution of prime importance in human affairs.

Few social institutions have capitalized so fully as has religion on the appeals to which man is susceptible. It has set before him the highest goals which the human imagination is capable of grasping. It has led him to sublimate many present desires for future gain. Religion has the capacity to draw upon the dynamic emotional qualities of the human spirit, and through ritual and symbolism to help man focus his emotions so firmly upon the ends to be sought that habit formation builds rigid character to fit the religious scheme. It has made use of testimonial and confession. It has capitalized on mob spirit and made use of suggestion, even at times approaching the stage of mental telepathy. It has developed skilled orators and used them in winning masses to its cause. It has developed song and hymnology to be employed in its interests. It has often shown remarkable capacity to weave man's spiritual and emotional life into an integrated pattern centered about great moral, social, or eternal ideals.

Today we think in terms of a relative morality, of a discovered truth developed through experience, and of codes and concepts of truth as numerous as the tribes of men. But for centuries man believed that a divine law permeated the moral universe, that there was an absolute truth which had been revealed to man. Locke, in his essay on human understanding, commented concerning this divine law:

. . . That God has given a rule whereby men should govern themselves, I think there is nobody so brutish as to deny. He has a right to do it; we are his creatures; he has goodness and wisdom to direct our actions to that which is best; and he has power to enforce it by rewards and punishments of infinite weight and duration in another life; for nobody can take us out of his hands. This is the only true touchstone of moral rectitude; and, by comparing them to this law, it is that men judge of the most considerable moral good or evil of their actions; that is, whether, as duties or sins, they are like to procure them happiness or misery from the hands of the ALMIGHTY.[2]

THE CHRISTIAN CHURCH AS AN INFLUENCE IN SOCIAL CONTROL IN AMERICAN SOCIETY

Christianity as represented by the church as a social institution has been unique in America chiefly because of the numerous de-

---

[2] John Locke, *An Essay Concerning Human Understanding*, p. 475. By permission of the Clarendon Press, Oxford.

nominations that have sprung up to express divergent points of view. We have in the United States more than 200 distinct religious denominations, practically all of which are of Christian origin and of Christian profession.

At the one extreme the Christian church remains in philosophy fundamentally what it was throughout the Middle Ages—a God-centered or eternity-centered institution concerned primarily with the ultimate values of human destiny. Churches approaching this extreme are interested in the salvation of the individual's soul because salvation is essential to his eternal well-being. This group puts much emphasis on eternal life and related problems of human destiny. The first and consuming concern of the individual is to regulate his relations with Deity in such a manner that he is assured of Divine favor. Ultimate rewards and penalties are prominent in the controls of the religious group. Churches at this extreme do not always lack a moral emphasis but the moral emphasis is secondary.

At the other extreme of the Christian system in America today are the religious bodies which have become primarily morality- or society-centered. A large number of the so-called liberal churches still consider relations with Deity important but think that man works out these relations in large by achieving proper relations with his fellow men. The trend of Christian thinking for centuries has been toward a social emphasis.

Churches range all the way between these two extremes in fundamental goals, and, consequently, in methods of approach to problems of human conduct. Those interested fundamentally in man's relation to God employ certain devices of social regulation; those interested primarily in Christianity as it affects man's relation to man, that is, in Christian morality, use other devices of control.

Diversity of Control Patterns and the American Culture Setting

The diverse patterns of the American church are in part a product of the diverse patterns of American society. We are a mixture of many nations and of many creeds. We have been a land without rigid traditions and without an established church. We have fostered religious liberty, which means religious individualism. Every man chooses whether he will worship with the upper classes or the lower classes, whether he will worship with the conservative or the liberal, whether he will be concerned primarily with his relations to God or with his relations to his neighbors, or in fact, whether or not he will be concerned about religion at all. Even though we have universal education, there is a great range in the intellectual level of the American population. There are many people who must still be appealed to on a fairly primitive level if religion is to mean anything to them. Their religion must be highly emotional if they are to have any interest in it and if they are to obtain any satisfaction from it, or, for that matter, if they are to be controlled by it. There are others of the super-sophisticated classes who are interested in a metaphysical approach to the universe and in a philosophical concept of man and human relations. Obviously the goals of life presented by the church to control these various groups must be different.

The following descriptive analysis begins with those means of control more prominent in the eternity-centered churches, which minister to the lower social classes and tend to be emotional in their appeal, and follows with a discussion of control as exercised by the so-called liberal churches which have been labelled "morality-centered."

Controls Employed Chiefly by the Eternity-Centered Christian Church

Many religious bodies in our society, and probably most of those influencing the lower social classes, especially those appealing most deeply to submarginal groups which are deprived of many of the better things in life, tend to be centered in eternal values, to be interested primarily in man's relation with God and only secondarily in man's relation with man. Their main concern is to see that man assures himself of a safe place in the world hereafter.

Some of the chief control devices employed by these groups are outlined below. It is true that some of these appeals are used in most Christian churches, but they are not so prominent in many modern Christian church bodies.

The appeal to authority. Religion in the past was an important controlling factor because it spoke with the voice of authority, the voice of God. To a lesser extent this is still true. In certain circles today the dictates of the minister are not to be questioned.

The practice of appealing to absolute authority for answers to all questions of divergent behavior has proved a powerful force in the regulation of human behavior. The appeal may be made through universally accepted traditions, or through the word of those supposedly gifted with superhuman powers. To the group which accepts them, the precepts become infallible guides to the proper course. Everywhere such precepts have been stabilizing and integrating factors in human society.

Many religions of the world have had sacred books which were considered to be the product of divine revelation, and which mapped out lines of proper conduct and thought. Thus, religion has often come to have the final word in moral sanction, and to be the final court of appeal on all questions dealing with right and wrong. When society reaches a period in which the authority of its sacred books is challenged by the larger portion of its members, an important means of enforcing social control disappears.

The operation of other-worldliness as a control device. The other-worldly appeal in religion has been an effective control device, not only in making a person conscious of the effect of misbehavior in this life or the life hereafter, but also in consoling him in times of social conflict with the promise of heavenly rewards. Faith in the other world has helped him to resign himself to an unequitable social order.

This theme, present in the thought of many submerged classes who find solace in religion today, has been dominant in the experiences of many peoples. King David, centuries ago,[3] described the prosperity of the wicked, their haughtiness, pride, and corruption, and then confessed, "I was envious at the foolish, when I saw the prosperity of the wicked." But then he went up to the "sanctuary of God," and he said, "Then understood I their end. Surely thou dids't set them in slippery places: thou castedst them down into destruction." Hope thus revived and he was ashamed that he had thought of disobedience and rejoiced in the assurance that "Thou shalt guide me with thy counsel and afterward receive me to glory." Such resignation to one's circumstances makes for order in society.

---

[3] Psalms 73.

The appeal to personal adjustment. In much hymnology, in many sermons, and in many scripture passages is found the appeal to peace for the troubled soul. In a world wherein the great lower strata of society knows conflict and trouble, an appeal to peace of mind and soul has tremendous significance. As culture becomes more intricate, the stress and strain which each individual, because of conflicting group patterns, embodies in his own personality lead to much difficulty in personal adjustment. The evangel of peace who can give a clear-cut, simple formula for bringing perfect inner adjustment that will make one right both with God and with man will always have a following among those in whom he can inspire faith.

The appeal to hope has always elicited a hearty response from the masses. Man, being the one and only creature, as far as we know, who concerns himself with the future, is subject to mental anxiety which often tests him to the utmost. A gospel of hope, which will assuage his torment by giving assurance that things will work out for the best does much to bring peace and mental security. Again and again the Bible passage, "All things work together for good to them that love God, to them who are the called according to his purpose," [4] has been employed to bring consolation to those who see life blighted by some social or natural catastrophe. This gospel of hope often plays upon man's desire for immortality, bringing to him the promise that righteous living will assure a future life which will perpetuate for him the finest things he has experienced in his present existence. All such influences, in that they help men to adjust to the existing social order, make for control.

The appeal of duty. The stoic appeal of duty may loom large in religious control. The development of conscience is a part of the religious program. Religious conscience, being of social origin, is built by establishing religious standards and loyalty to them. Among Christians, that which the group defines as right becomes the standard for habits and attitudes; variation from it is sin and brings a sense of guilt. In religious parlance this latter is referred to as a guilty conscience, conscience being considered the inner monitor which guides one in his conduct, showing him the right and the wrong. If training has been thorough, and only one set of standards has been presented and accepted,

---

[4] Romans 8:28.

one can depend upon conscience to direct him in the way of truth and right as conceived by his religious group. Only for such individuals can conscience be an unerring guide, pointing the way of duty.

The sense of duty is much more far-reaching than has been implied in this discussion. The religious message usually defines not only standards regulating one's actions as they apply to specific acts in social relations, but also one's duties to God. The discharge of these duties, which include the necessary obeisances, such as prayer and worship, and, in their highest social expression, service to one's fellow men, is necessary to a clear conscience.

Control by prophecy. A new date for the end of the world is set every few years, and almost always by some religious leader. Other dire and catastrophic events—wars, famines, troubles to vex the earth—have been foretold since time immemorial. Occasionally desirable events are predicted; in Christian literature the millennium of peace has been prophesied.

Prophecies on the part of religious leaders are sometimes meant to control their followers, and whether such is the intent or not, they have the practical effect of doing so. In college autobiographies collected by the author, some students confess hours of terror in their childhood and early youth when, during thunder storms, they thought the end of the world had come. Apparently such fears still operate among certain groups in our culture.

Fear and hope have been stimulated by prophecy throughout the ages. The man who fears the future is not likely to adopt a devil-may-care attitude. The man with hope to be realized adjusts his conduct so that he may experience its fruition.

Everlasting life. Man has seldom been content with terminating life at the grave; rather he has conceived of things beyond. Often the nature of that life hereafter is thought to be dependent upon one's conduct in this world. Thus religious people are motivated by the rewards and punishments that will result from their behavior during their period of mortality. At times in the history of the Christian Church the preparation for this afterlife has been the one consuming purpose of the devout, and always the evil doer has been threatened with the sin's dire consequences to immortal existence.

That such beliefs are dynamic factors in human conduct cannot be denied. And in cases where the road to better things hereafter is paved with humanitarian service on earth, these beliefs become forces of the highest type in social control. One cannot say so much for monastic seclusion motivated by a desire to escape the taint of the common ways of men in order that one may not pollute his soul.

Conversion. That religion has power to convert men from bad to good has been demonstrated widely in the experience of evangelism. Many hardened sinners have had their lives entirely transformed through the dynamic influence of an evangelist's message,[5] and have been made susceptible to means of control which were formerly ignored. Some have overcome habits which, without the power of religion, they could never have broken.

Evangelism. Evangelism has in the past been a potent force in America.[6] It still is, but its power today rather than being among all classes is chiefly among the dispossessed social classes. In our present culture the more sophisticated groups ordinarily are reached, if at all, by religious education, formal ritual, ceremony, and sermon. It is the suppressed masses that flock to hear the message of the revivalist. Perhaps the popularity of the evangelist among the culturally submarginal group grows in part out of the fact that he presents values of a spiritual nature to down-trodden peoples, which help to compensate for the lack of material goods. That this fact has a dynamic influence on human behavior, and tends to regulate the masses in an orderly manner no one can doubt. Such a religious philosophy has done much to provide social control for migratory laborers, many of whom are of the Pentecostal faith, who ordinarily are largely removed from the regulative system of any community. Resignation because of religious belief probably has hindered labor organizations among farm workers; religion consoles them in their present state of living.

To the extent that the revivalist group deals with real conflicts and real personality maladjustments and works out solutions it is a constructive force in the social order. However, the technique of the revivalist is usually to develop a sense of guilt and sin in the

---

[5] See for instance Frederick M. Davenport's *Primitive Traits in Religious Revivals.*

[6] R. L. Duffus' "Moody: Showman of the Sawdust Trail," *Reader's Digest,* June, 1937, pp. 75 ff. gives a popular summary of revivalism in America.

patron as a prerequisite to conversion, the effect being to heighten personality conflict. Many victims do not seek a remedy for their suffering, and many of those who do are unable to find a long-time method of satisfactory adjustment. Those who can be saintly undoubtedly find peace and perfect adjustment to those elements of the social order which have troubled them. The testimony and experience of many who have been transformed by the revival leave no doubt as to the supreme satisfaction and the integration of personality which they have achieved through evangelistic religion. The social righteousness of these individuals, and their ever consistent behavior must convince even the skeptic of the effectiveness of inner motivation growing out of a great religious purpose. The fact that these patterns, being confined to the in-group, often call for a very narrow exercise of social morality does seriously limit the social usefulness of such controls, but it does not gainsay their powerful influence in regulating behavior.

The Christian model. No small part of the power of Christianity to control, both in the realm of religion and of morality, grows out of the fact that it provides a model after which behavior may be patterned. Christ is a perfect model after which the Christian followers can build character. In some generations this saintly character has been more social than in others. But be that as it may, millions of people, in trying diligently to emulate their model, have become self-disciplined, and as a consequence many problems of social discipline have been avoided throughout the Christian world. In spite of what may be said about disillusionment, the decline in the importance of religion, and the loss of faith among the masses of our urban-industrialized world, millions of youth in America still try to pattern their lives after the life of Christ as interpreted to them by their religious leaders. Millions of adults with greater or less degrees of confessed faith still strive to imitate the example of Christ. In so doing they find motives for an orderly social life without the necessity of external restraints.

THE SHIFT OF EMPHASIS IN SOCIAL CONTROL IN THE MORALITY-CENTERED CHURCH

A number of the more liberal Christian churches in America have developed a primary interest in man's social well-being, and have tended to minimize the importance of preparation for the world hereafter. Religion is employed to inspire the Christian follower to develop Christian moral character. These churches attempt to control the individual in line with the highest purposes of which man seems capable here on earth. Interest at all times tends to be in Christianizing the present social order. One maintains proper relations with Deity through the practice of Christianity in social relationships.

In such churches a new type of appeal becomes important. The emphasis upon Christ as a model is prominent, as it is in the case of more conservative denominations, but He is held up as the model of Christian social service rather than as the model of the perfect Divine character. There is also an appeal to authority but not authority in the absolute. The Christian social act is good because it is practical in human relationships. Personal adjustment is important because man finds adjustment in working out his relation with his fellow men on the basis of the golden rule. Duty is approached, not in the stoical sense, but through the service motive. One learns to achieve his highest personal happiness through discharging certain obligations to society and its members. Justice becomes not a stern concept based on absolute truth, but a constantly changing relationship. One must understand the trend of social life in order to be able to understand what justice is in any particular situation.

Control by prophecy in the older religious sense has practically disappeared in the modern church. Men now see visions and dream dreams of a better social order, or of a Utopia that man creates through Christian influence, rather than a Utopia that is handed down from Heaven. Some even go so far as to see everlasting life in a new light, conceiving of man as living on through his influence on the social group rather than thinking of eternal life chiefly in terms of streets of gold and eternal pleasure.

Control by conversion tends to be replaced by control through education. The modern church has come to see that character has continuity, that ordinarily Christian character is not achieved by a transforming emotional experience but by the building of habits and attitudes, and by the practice of right deeds. Stress is upon character formation rather than upon instantaneous transformation. As a consequence of this change in philosophy the emphasis on evangelism has declined, and the emphasis on religious education and religious activity has increased. Little is said about the soul's salvation, but there is much emphasis on saving the social order, and on saving certain groups who seem to have been worsted under the present social order. There is less emphasis on the revealed truth of sacred books, and more of a quest for an understanding of means of rendering social service in a secondary group world. There is less emphasis upon purity in the abstract, but more emphasis upon the doing of deeds which in themselves will exhibit high purpose. There is much less talk of uncleanness and sin and more attempt to remove social conditions that in themselves produce uncleanness and sin. This seems to be the trend of the more liberal church which shifts its emphasis toward a social gospel. Its central focus becomes social action motivated by Christian influences, rather than eternal salvation.

The appeal to social justice in modern religion had its beginnings, insofar as the Judaistic-Christian lineage is concerned, in the minor prophets of the Old Testament. The primary emphasis gradually shifted from the holiness and severity of Jehovah and concern over one's duties toward Him, to an emphasis on God as the Father and to an interest in righting the wrongs in human relations. This interest in social justice reached a high level of expression both in the example and in the teachings of Christ, but only in the last few decades has it become a major consideration of the Christian Church in the West. The appeal to social justice made in the pulpit and in the religious press, challenges many youths to idealism, courage, and self-sacrifice. The missionary spirit has never been allowed to die. The motive given men to sacrifice themselves for what they thought was the social good has been an important controlling power in human affairs.

Obviously, the Christian Church, to the extent that it assumes a social form, proves a powerful restraining and directing influence in human relationships. In making the measure of man's religious perfection his effectiveness in getting along with his fellow men, it makes for moral living. "Forgive us our debts, as we forgive our debtors," is a dynamic social ideal.

The conscientious Christian who is conditioned to a moral type of living finds religion an element in his social behavior. His group expects certain things of him because he professes to

be a Christian—fair dealing, kindly attitudes, love, tolerance, forbearance, mercy, to mention but a few of the Christian ideals.
He expects much of himself also. Such ideals are powerful leav-
ening influences in human relationships throughout Christen-
dom.

DIFFICULTIES OF MORAL DEFINITION FACING THE MORALITY-CENTERED CHURCH

One of the greatest difficulties the modern church faces is that
of making religious principles as effective in the more impersonal
relationships of the great society, with its secondary group relations, as they have been in the primary group with its intimate
face to face contacts. The task of defining the right will always
be a difficult one; it is so much more simple to know that giving
a cup of cold water to the thirsty wayfarer is the right thing to do
than it is to know which nation should have wheat in a great war,
or whether all nations or perhaps none should have it. One of
the almost insurmountable difficulties of a secondary group morality adapted to the great society is that it takes an immense
amount of study, some rationalization, and occasionally some
guessing, to judge what is moral, and in the end that judgment
may have been so colored by propaganda and the general cultural
compulsives of the time that it is entirely biased.

The moral principles of Christianity are applicable to social
living on any scale, as are those of other great religions. Such
practical use of them as was made by Christ and the Apostles,
however, was chiefly in the world of primary group relations.
There is little question about what is right in most of these
personal relationships; perplexity reigns because we are living
today in a world in which impersonal, large-scale dealings are
becoming commonplace.

One author suggests a solution [7]—that the Christian church
avoid pronouncement on specific issues which do not properly
fall within its authority and on which one must have specialized
knowledge and training in order to form a sound judgment, that
it leave action in these fields to individual Christian men who
are competent to speak with authority on particular problems,

---

[7] Alfred E. Garvie, *The Christian Ideal for Human Society*, pp. 402–403,
Richard R. Smith, Inc., New York, 1930.

but that the church see to it the Christian spirit pervades the local community and its actions.

THE SOCIAL APPEAL AND CHURCH INFLUENCE

The socially minded church that is interested in contemporary problems, while it appeals to sentiments of the modern mind, sometimes has difficulty in maintaining its hold on the individual because there are so many other organizations in our society which make the same appeal and which claim no direct religious motive. For instance, social work has developed and gives expression to service motives such as the church once fostered through its charity program. Numerous types of social legislation and social action now sponsored by the state and by civic groups provide an outlet for the expression of a high type of social service motive. It is probably for this reason in part that we no longer consider it essential for a man to participate actively in the church in order to be a "good" man, or in order to be a moral man. Control by the social service motive has come to be a powerful influence in contemporary affairs, and the church cannot claim a monopoly upon this concept, as it always has upon concepts traditionally used by religion in achieving control over adherents. Most churches still hold, however, that spiritual influences are essential to completely moral living.

In other realms beside the sphere of social service, sectarian institutions have encroached upon what was once church territory. The church is no longer the principal institution in the experience of the people. Educational institutions have acquired more influence among many than has the church. Even recreation has become an activity in the modern world that probably consumes more time of the masses than does religious exercise. In our nation today over half of the population claims no church affiliation. One cannot say that all of this group are free from the controlling influence of religion, but neither can one say that many of those who claim church affiliation are gripped by the controls of the church. This is not to be interpreted as meaning that religion is not a potent force in control today. With many of those whom it influences there is still no greater force in regulating conduct, but the church probably does not dominate the thought and life of the nations of the Western world to the extent that it once did.

Religious Disillusionment as an Aspect of Diverse Institutional Forms in an Open Class Society

We hear a great deal of the decline of religious influence, and undoubtedly there has been considerable decline, especially in the influence of certain types of church bodies on social control. As has been intimated, the trend has been away from appeal to absolute and ultimate values, to social and temporal values. This trend in the progressive church reflects to some extent the trend in the development of the modern mind. Sophisticated groups no longer think in terms of the old appeals of religion, and no longer respond to these appeals. They even rebel against religion on this basis. This does not necessarily mean that they revolt against religion as such or against the church, but simply against the church as represented by certain denominations.

Because our society is highly mobile in a vertical sense and individuals climb freely from lower to higher classes, and from an uneducated to an educated level, many individuals reared in childhood in primary groups which were under the domination of an other-worldly-centered religious body, upon drifting away from the influence of this group, come to think of life in different terms from those which their church employed. Their revolt against the church may involve a revolt against all religion, as they tend to interpret all religion to be of the type they have known in childhood and youth. This kind of revolt is frequently manifested among youth on the college campus or in the urban environment. Many of these individuals eventually find a place in social-minded churches but others entirely divorce themselves from church activity.

There are psychological and social problems involved in such revolt. Does a loss of faith cut man loose from his moral moorings and leave him a ferocious animal, or does he have sufficient restraint of a social nature to keep him behaving much as he did before the religious motive was destroyed? This is a question which our age has not had sufficient experience to answer fully. There is no question but that a great many people, in cutting loose from old faiths, have suffered such disillusionment that they have been led to pessimism, personality disintegration, and in some cases to suicide. Many lives which at one time were motivated by a dynamic urge no longer have the old motivation of faith. It is no doubt difficult for many to revert from a great faith without dropping temporarily into despair, superstition, or cynicism. The shifting of attention, from what was conceived to be eternal truth to the cold realities of a machine world, necessarily develops something of the sense of futility. Although it requires strong character to lose faith without going morally bankrupt, no doubt many do eventually find in social motives something to replace the former belief in an authoritative religious code.

Certain groups in our society may have compensated for religious losses by an intense type of intellectual sophistication which has robbed them of moral and spiritual values.[8] With this loss of the religious attitude has developed a habit of mind which leads to the debunking of everything which once made life worthwhile. The result tends to be moral confusion frequently accompanied by a dampening of public spirit and altruism—the loss of the sense of "I ought" and "I must" and the development of a selfish desire for sensual satisfaction, for living in the immediate present, for serving oneself rather than one's fellows. Some, having lost religious faith, become disillusioned and no longer find a motive for social living. Do people who have never had a faith suffer equally? There are without doubt other bases on which a sense of social and moral responsibility can be founded.

When the white man invades a primitive civilization he disregards the native's taboos, breaks their laws, defies their gods, and profanes their sacred objects, without experiencing the curses that are supposed to follow such conduct. Soon taboos, ritual, divine law, and other agencies of control are powerless, for, in the realm of the supernatural, when belief is gone its regulative force is spent. This loss of faith has been considered a disintegrating force in primitive cultures, and may have a similar effect in advanced cultures.

CHRISTIAN INFLUENCES AS CULTURAL COMPULSIVES

The Christian church, because it has stood for certain basic human principles, and because it has preached and practiced to a greater or less degree in different periods certain moral concepts, has been an influence in determining the trend of cultural de-

---

[8] See Walter Lippmann's *Preface to Morals*. See also Frank Hankins' *An Introduction to the Study of Society*, pp. 519 ff.

velopment in the Western World and consequently in shaping the life philosophy of Western peoples. It is therefore likely that the church as an institution has had a much more pervasive influence than can be appreciated from a description of phases of its attempt to control in specific realms.

Christian concepts, like the concepts of several other religions, are dynamic with social power, and many basic religious principles are fundamental in any system of social relations. Religion has great cohesive power. For example, communistic colonies have been held together best by religion. In fact, most of the communistic colonies in rural America have been founded for religious purposes.[9] This power of religion to control and integrate a group by religious mores is most clearly demonstrated in the long history of the Jew, who, while living in the midst of other cultures, has maintained his own way of life. The emphasis of the Christian Church on the universal brotherhood of man has potential power for cohesion of inter-racial and international groups.

Certain ideas that have originated in connection with religious institutions have been dynamic in their effect on economic and political institutions. We have referred elsewhere [10] to the effect of Protestantism on the development of capitalism and democracy. It must be recognized that capitalism and democracy also had their effect on the development and growth of Protestantism. It is impossible to measure these general effects of the Christian church as an influence in social control, but undoubtedly they have been and are pervasive in Western culture.

CONCLUSION

In a nation of voluntary church affiliation, possessing no state church and having a heterogeneous population and culture, denominational stratification on the basis of such factors as wealth, educational qualities, and levels of emotional appeal is necessary if all groups are to be brought under the scope of church control.

Religion of an other-worldly character, because it operates in the realm of motives, has been an effective agency of control in human affairs. Having supernatural sanctions, and holding before man the ultimate goals of human existence as particular

---

[9] See again a description of life in the Amana Colony, chapter 15.
[10] Chapter 8.

cultures conceive them, it becomes dynamic in shaping conduct. Christianity, when given a social emphasis, in setting before its followers a perfect, albeit human, model has given man an ideal pattern. In making social conduct a prerequisite to divine favor man has been given a social purpose that, when followed, becomes a highly constructive influence in social control. Periods of religious disillusionment require that many seek a new basis for "right" conduct, or stray from established codes. Such periods put greater burdens for social regulation upon other agencies, for as Beach has said,[11]

The history of mankind and its behavior reveals clearly the fact that religion has always been one of the chief agencies which hold a society together. And while it has also often been a condition obstructing necessary change and so leading to social decay, it has been equally at times a vital moving power for the overthrow of evil and for social reconstruction in the face of degenerating forces.

SELECTED REFERENCES

Beach, Walter G., *Social Aims in a Changing World*, chap. 8. Stanford University Press, Stanford University, 1932.

Bell, B. I., "Present Status of Religion Among Thinking Men," *Scribner's Magazine*, vol. 96, pp. 340–344. December, 1934.

Cavanaugh, F., "Modern Sociology," *Commonweal*, vol. 18, pp. 156–158. June 9, 1933.

Chapin, F. Stuart, *Contemporary American Institutions*, chaps. 11 and 12. Harper and Brothers, New York, 1935.

Clark, John Maurice, *Social Control of Business*, pp. 254–256. University of Chicago Press, Chicago, 1926.

Cooley, Charles H., *Social Organization*, chap. 32. Charles Scribner's Sons, New York, 1909.

Curry, B., "When Religion Fails," *World Tomorrow*, vol. 16, pp. 90–91. January 25, 1933.

Davenport, Frederick Morgan, *Primitive Traits in Religious Revivals*, pp. 75–81. The Macmillan Company, New York, 1905.

Dieffenbach, A. C., "Breakdown in Religion," *Current History*, vol. 38, pp. 406–413. July, 1933.

---

[11] Walter G. Beach, *Social Aims in a Changing World*, p. 123. By permission of Stanford University Press.

Dowd, Jerome, *Control in Human Societies*, chaps. 21 and 22. D. Appleton-Century Company, New York, 1936.

Editorial, "After the Social Gospel?", *World Tomorrow*, vol. 16, pp. 654 ff. December 7, 1933.

Ellwood, Charles A., *The Psychology of Human Society*, pp. 401–406. D. Appleton-Century Company, New York, 1931.

Ellwood, Charles A., *The Reconstruction of Religion*. The Macmillan Company, New York, 1925.

Fiske, C., "Morals and the Church," *Current History*, vol. 33, pp. 322 ff. December, 1930.

Graves, W. Brooke, editor, *Readings in Public Opinion*, chap. 8. D. Appleton-Century Company, New York, 1928.

Hankins, Frank H., *An Introduction to the Study of Society*, revised edition, chap. 22. The Macmillan Company, New York, 1935.

House, F. N., *The Range of Social Theory*, chaps. 18 and 19. Henry Holt and Company, New York, 1929.

Howe, Q., "Twilight of the Gods," *Living Age*, vol. 345, pp. 132–141. October, 1933.

Hutchinson, P., "Future of Religion," *Forum*, vol. 89, pp. 226–231. April, 1933.

Hutchinson, P., "Religion versus the World We Live In," *Forum*, vol. 89, pp. 81–87. February, 1933.

Keller, A. G., *Brass Tacks*, chap. 5. Alfred A. Knopf, Inc., New York, 1938.

Keller, A. G., *Man's Rough Road*, part 3. Frederick A. Stokes Company, New York, and Yale University Press, New Haven, 1932.

Lazaron, M. S., "Confusion Less Confounded," *Survey*, vol. 68, pp. 346–348. August 1, 1932.

Link, Henry C., *The Return to Religion*. The Macmillan Company, New York, 1937.

Lippmann, Walter, *A Preface to Morals*. The Macmillan Company, New York, 1929.

Locke, John, *An Essay Concerning Human Understanding*, pp. 475 ff. The Clarendon Press, Oxford, 1894.

Luccock, H. E., "Preaching in an Age of Disillusion," *Christian Century*, vol. 47, pp. 937 ff. July 30, 1930.

Magner, J. A., "Basis of Morality," *Catholic World*, vol. 132, pp. 400 ff. January, 1931.

McDowell, J., "Can America Endure Without Religion?", *Missionary Review*, vol. 54, pp. 684 ff. September, 1931.

Miner, J. R., "Do the Churches Prevent Crime?", *American Mercury*, vol. 25, pp. 79 ff. January, 1932.

Mowrer, E. R., *Family Disorganization*, pp. 278–279. University of Chicago Press, Chicago, 1927.

Niebuhr, R., "Moral Man and Immoral Society," *World Tomorrow*, vol. 15, pp. 565–567. December 14, 1932.

Plant, James S., *Personality and the Cultural Pattern*, chap. 16. The Commonwealth Fund, New York, 1937.

Read, C. F., "Religion and Mental Hygiene," *Survey*, vol. 69, pp. 256–257. July, 1933.

Recent Social Trends in the United States, chap. 20. McGraw-Hill Book Company, New York, 1933.

Richelsen, I., "Now That I No Longer Believe," *Scribner's Magazine*, vol. 92, pp. 100–101. August, 1932.

Saint Augustine, *Confessions*, vols. 1 and 2. G. P. Putnam's Sons, New York.

Schweitzer, A., "Religion in Modern Civilization," *Christian Century*, vol. 51, pp. 1483–1484, 1519–1521. November 21 and November 28, 1934.

Sockman, R. W., "Vanishing Sinner," *Harper's Magazine*, vol. 161, pp. 676 ff. November, 1930.

Stelzle, Charles, "The Evangelist in Present-Day America," *Current History*, vol. 35, pp. 224 ff. November, 1931.

Sullivan, W. L., "Our Spiritual Destitution," *Atlantic Monthly*, vol. 143, pp. 373 ff. March, 1929.

Tawney, R. H., *Religion and the Rise of Capitalism* (Scott Holland Memorial Lectures). John Murray, London, 1929.

Weber, Max, *The Protestant Ethic and the Spirit of Capitalism*, translated by Talcott Parsons. Charles Scribner's Sons, New York, 1930.

CHAPTER 15

FORMAL EDUCATION AS A SOCIALIZING AGENCY

Formal education is usually much less emotionally charged than religion and much less effective than the family, in implanting deep-set patterns of behavior. Yet it is everywhere recognized as a means of shaping personality to fit the social order, and also as an agency for developing restraints in the individual so that he will conform to the culture patterns of his time.

EDUCATIONAL AIMS AS GOALS OF SOCIAL CONTROL

Today we hear much of educational aims. We think of preparing youth for the responsibilities which he will face in a democracy. We want him to develop a broad social morality that will lead him to consider the interests of others in relation to his own. We want to mold his individuality in line with social purposes. Much of our moral theory, which is shot through and through the school system in all of its aspects, aims in this direction. Through education we try to develop the desire to be of general social helpfulness, to train the emotions, the impulses, the passions of youth, so that they will conform insofar as possible with the better social codes of our society. We try to inculcate a respect for law, a loyalty to ideals. We expect the school to develop a person who will be adaptable, who can readily adjust himself to the rapidly shifting scenes of our culture without losing his equilibrium; to develop an elastic sort of person who will not break under the processes of social and cultural change, nor lose his direction in moving from one environment to another.

Modern educational methods are aimed at teaching children codes of conduct, rather than placing emphasis upon discipline as such. In the final analysis, the aim of the school is always to develop an individual who will fit into the social order of his time. The means differ with the time and place.

. . . The school system of a nation is an attempt on a large scale to control individuals and the future of the nation by educating minds, developing characters, and prescribing techniques to order and according to plan. It is a part of the bigger system of society and social control, and follows the pattern and drift of the larger society. In a conservative society the processes are conservative; in a radical society they are radical. Contrast, for example, the schools of the United States and Union of Soviet Socialist Republics.[1]

BIOLOGICAL PLASTICITY EXTENDS HUMAN MODIFIABILITY

Educational theory has made much of the plasticity of the human mind, and also of the permanence of well fixed habits. It is assumed that the school should take advantage of this plasticity by shaping habits in the child that will conform to the culture in which he is being prepared to live when he reaches maturity.[2]

Ellwood has said that education furnishes the most "subtle and ultimate" form of social control available to society, because it develops habits and forms character. It is, he believes, the first means of socializing the individual, of developing in him a consciousness of society. Because it begins early, and because it works so effectively in implanting attitudes and values, it can work transformations which other forms of social control cannot realize.[3]

That formal education may be used for many purposes in a complex society is generally recognized. Clark suggests several possibilities:

. . . Education may fortify class prejudices or break them down, rouse mental independence or lull it to sleep. It can go far to make bigots or adaptable co-operators, docile subjects or capable citizens, to spread a gospel of democracy or service, or to cultivate a self-centered and self-satisfied snobbery, either of abstract culture, aristocratic privilege or comfortable middle-class complacency. It has been controlled in the interests of the church, of a militaristic aristocracy, of communism, and atheism, and often it has worked wonders.[4]

---

[1] John M. Gillette and James M. Reinhardt, *Current Social Problems*, p. 639. By permission of American Book Company.
[2] E. A. Ross, *Social Control*, pp. 163 ff.
[3] C. A. Ellwood, *The Psychology of Human Society*, pp. 410–413, D. Appleton-Century Company, New York, 1931.
[4] John M. Clark, *Social Control of Business*, p. 252. By permission of the University of Chicago Press.

CONTROL OF BIOLOGICAL FACTORS BY EDUCATION

In our time, the emphasis is upon environmental rather **than** instinctive factors, and it is assumed that many traits which, in the past have been thought to be essentially biological, are actually susceptible to regulation by inculcating habits, standards, and ideals through education. Many examples could be cited. The one developed in the following paragraph suggests that education may be used to implant standards and motives by which the person will come to guide the direction of his romantic impulses, even to the extent that mating becomes a matter of intelligent choice rather than an instinctive-emotional gesture.

Control of the romantic impulse through education.

. . . I contend that methods of selecting mates are a matter of custom and that romance need not be sanctioned by marriage custom; that our present romantic notions have a bearing on our high divorce rate; that although back of all romance is the sex impulse, romance is subject to control and direction and in our society may be made to conform to the interests of a more permanent family.

Abraham and Sarah chose Isaac's wife, and Isaac married her on faith. China boasts of a civilization with centuries of human experience in the background. Chinese fathers have always reserved the right to select the brides for their sons, and frequently the marriage ceremony has been the occasion of the first meeting of bride and groom. In primitive tribes custom decrees that the maternal uncle, the parent or other adults make the matches. Royal marriages in Europe have usually been arranged primarily for political purposes, with little regard for romantic implications.

There is considerable evidence that leads us to suppose that our worthy ancestors in America held romance in less esteem than parents do at the present time. They saw to it that the son's "gal" was more than a "lazy good-for-nothing" who could not so much as bake biscuits and were shrewd enough to see that the daughter was courted by a lad whose father had at least an "eighty" or, better still, a "quarter section." Practical considerations loomed large in the choice of mates in the stable rural society of yesterday. Parents desired that mates be chosen for qualities which were likely to wear well and not for a romantic holiday.

On what grounds can we hold that marriages based on romance are causal factors in the divorce rate? The weaknesses of romance as a basis for marriage are numerous. It is too personal and selfish to be highly social. It is too individualistic, making the family an experimental venture in disregard of state and racial interests. It is highly emotionalized and, at best, idealistic. It is chivalrous but not practical, being tainted with the unearthly, the spiritualistic, the intangible. It seeks bliss, supreme pleasure, and tries to force existence in a realm of ecstasy where people are capable of living for only short periods of time.

Marrying on a romantic basis only is comparable in many respects to going to college to have a good time—to have dates, to dance, to play cards, to play football and to join a fraternity. Such collegiate attempts end with a failure at the end of the first quarter, probation at the end of the second quarter and home at the end of the third.

I am not a worshipper of the stoical endurance of our pioneer fathers or the submissive grace of our grandmothers, exhibited in keeping the marriage bargain whether it yielded satisfaction or misery. This avoidance of divorce may develop great patience, tolerance and the other graces of the meek; I doubt, however, that it is a mark of wisdom to endure, especially when children are involved. Public opinion on the divorce question has changed in the direction of greater liberty. This we must recognize. But the greater liberty makes the more pressing the problem I am presenting. Shipwreck in marriage is no less a catastrophe now when it ends in the divorce court than it was in our Puritan days when passive endurance covered the fact from the outside world. Indeed, the disillusionment that unhappiness in marriage causes nowadays is much more pronounced in that we seek happiness so intensely.

It may be more than a coincidence that America, the land of romantic marriages, has the highest divorce rate of the nations. One could hardly say that the uncontrolled romantic impulse is the sole cause. Perhaps underlying causes that permit the free exercise of the romantic impulse are also factors in the divorce rate.

A permanent family must supersede the natural sex urge in many respects. The family is largely an artificial invention that is made possible by restraints and taboos imposed upon natural impulses. It therefore presupposes that the artificial standards which society sees fit to maintain supplement animal attraction in choosing a mate. But I would not be the one to recommend that we do away with romance in mating. I favor human happiness in every conceivable form—especially in that highest expression we call love. I have a feeling, rather, that we might conserve more of it by a greater degree of control over the romantic impulse.

. . . we need to temper the romantic impulse in youth, as we do other human impulses, by instilling in their minds certain ideas that will restrain and guide their emotions. We need to more fully socialize this impulse as we have socialized hunger, for instance. Eating has become a fine art with us as compared to its practice among savages and infants. We control the hunger drive by etiquette and by our notions of the balanced ration and regular meals. The organic drive is still there, but in civilized society we try to act as though it were not.

We need to make romance a little finer art than it has been—to raise it to a new plane of understanding. In this manner we might regulate romantic love in the interests of a more permanent family unit and a better race. Parents could do much in this training in the art of romance by building up certain standards by which the youth could guide his selection of a mate, but reforms in custom more often begin in the school than in the home. . . .[5]

Among the solutions offered are the following: That we train youth to consider the eugenic aspects of marriage; that we enlighten them concerning the economic responsibilities of the family; that we give them some insight into the family as an institution, leading them to recognize that marriage is more than a romantic gesture; that we lead them to appreciate that, once a couple becomes married, they become a family and must fit into a great number of institutional situations in which non-family groups do not participate; that we help them to understand that a common background along certain lines is essential to effective comradeship over a long period of years; that we teach them to restrain the romantic impulse by enlightenment concerning factors that are likely to be important to an enduring family relationship, such as marriage as an institution presupposes.

---

[5] From Paul H. Landis, "Control of the Romantic Impulse Through Education," *School and Society*, August 15, 1936, pp. 212–215. By permission of the Science Press.

The School as an Agency for Socialization in Contemporary Society

Time was when the church was looked upon as the chief agency of socialization, and when the state depended upon the church to prepare for it a loyal group of subjects. But now, with increasing emphasis, we hear the school mentioned as the chief instrument by which society attains an orderly system of life. Not only do governments look to the schools to instruct their people in civic duties, but also they ask the schools to assume the responsibility for training in proper habits, when the home fails to do so. The schools are expected to compensate for the failures of both home and church, in teaching morality. For more than a century the trend has been to increase the functions of the school as an agency of control. With our present knowledge of personality formation and the way by which social control is achieved through the shaping of personality, the burden is sure to fall even more heavily on that institution in the future.

Social education is rapidly becoming a primary function of the school, and rightly so. At long last we are recognizing that in a practical way, through education, we can make human nature that will fit the society we want, rather than teach the child a selected mass of the more formal cultural heritage which, because of certain established traditions, has come to be considered important.

The educative process described in Part Two of this book has in the past been achieved to a considerable extent by chance, through the natural experience of the child growing up in society. While this will always be true to a certain degree, the school can and is modifying its methods and aims to suit social objectives more fully than before.

Education and the State

Interestingly enough, the school now holds a position in relation to government not far different from that held by the Church during the Middle Ages. Then, church and state were joint public institutions. Today, in most modern states, church and state are separate. Education, on the other hand, has become a state function. It is publicly supported and used as a tool of government. As such it enjoys unusual prestige, and also is in a position to act as a powerful agent of control, shaping the individual for the political order. In democratic societies, the function of control is broadly conceived, and the individual is shaped for an individualistic social order. He is trained to consider alternatives, and to exercise choice and initiative. In autocratic societies, education becomes narrow-gauged, and is used as an instrument of indoctrination.

EDUCATION FOR POLITICAL INDOCTRINATION

If only one system of thought is presented to the youth, if the stimuli are made uniform, there are almost no limits to the extent to which his personality may be shaped to fit the prevailing system of social thought. No doubt this is one reason why formal education has long been considered a fundamental part of political control.

Universal education—physical, mental, and moral—is absolutely necessary if a nation is to realize its full military and economic strength. Napoleon believed education to be the most important of all political questions. If the child were not taught what to be, the state would be subject to disorder and change. The state rests on the common culture, common convictions, and common ideals of the people. Under Napoleon, the school master had to take an oath to teach in such a manner that his students would become devoted citizens of the Napoleonic dynasty. The French republic, in 1882, because of strong nationalistic motives, changed its school curriculum so that civic morality, rather than religion, was emphasized. The purpose was to socialize the pupils for French nationalism and Republican politics. The teacher was required to teach the good old-fashioned morality, nothing philosophical or theological. The duty of the citizen to his country was emphasized; the pupils were taught that they must sacrifice time, money, even their lives, in order to preserve their beloved French institutions, language, and traditions. Wrongs that France had suffered at the hands of Germany were used to revive old hatreds. The child was made to feel that he ought to be glad to be a Frenchman, and honored to share in her glorious past, present, and future. The constancy and solidarity which France exhibited in the World War was probably due in part to the fact that French children for a generation had been trained in civic virtues. French history was taught in such a way as to increase the child's love for his country. He was made to feel personal sorrow for her misfortunes. National weaknesses were admitted, but only as temporary setbacks in the triumphant march to greater glory.

William II used the Prussian schools in combating the spread of socialism and communism. They taught that not only was social democracy against God and religion, but also that it was impracticable and dangerous to society and to the individual. The state alone could protect individual rights. Had not the Prussian kings always worked to improve the social welfare? Statistics were used to show how working class conditions had improved under their care.

The educational system of the German Empire inspired emotional patriotism to a high degree. Poems, set to stirring music recalling national virtues, for over a century were used to build up the spirit of solidarity. The teaching of German history established such a set emotional bias that the German mind resisted anything contrary to the bias. Geography was taught so as to build up the idea of a Germany surrounded by enemies. Local topography was taught with the purpose of making the student love the very ground on which he walked. Geography showed him the necessity of national economic and military policies. The net result of the German system was that the child learned thoroughly what the government wanted him to learn.[6]

Many governments place faith in education as an agency for developing the attitudes and restraints considered essential in the citizen. This is a confessed purpose of our own state educational system and that of most modern nations. To a considerable extent we indoctrinate youth in favor of democracy, nationalism, and patriotism. Much less emphatic are we, however, in this than are many nations of the world. We indoctrinate but at the same time present other points of view and allow comparative freedom of expression in the classroom. In Russia, Germany, and Italy, and to a lesser extent in many other European states, the school room as well as the radio and press are under the control of the state so that youth is indoctrinated with the national political philosophy and that alone. The *New Russia's*

[6] Edward H. Reisner, *Nationalism and Education Since 1789.*

Primer,[7] for instance, puts before the child fragments from a book supposedly written fifty years hence when communism has brought its great rewards. It describes a great machine civilization not unlike that in America, but without the American social problems that have grown out of our machine civilization.

The possibilities of political indoctrination through state systems of education have already been discussed. The following selections illustrate dramatically how some nations are using education to the ultimate degree as an agency of control at the present time.

Fascist education.

A look at the textbooks used in Italian schools is sufficient for an understanding of the spirit with which the Fascist regime carries on the education of children and youths. Textbooks are prepared by a government commission and are the same in all the schools. It is the scope and purpose of educators to make Fascists; to create men does not concern them.

Let us begin with the primer. This book is nothing more than a means of influencing the intellectual and moral make-up of the child. The child, when it begins to spell, finds on the very first page of the speller the words: "Duce"—*Fascismo-Mussolini.* On the last pages of the speller the following words are found: "For Mussolini eia, eia, eia, alala," and again, "We children must salute the King, Mussolini, and our own great country, Italy." "Italy is the greatest of all nations." "Italian soldiers fear nobody."

The book is full of pictures which represent Fascists in black shirts, the fasces of lictors, and armies and soldiers. The child of six must immediately become accustomed to armies and armed men. Look at the book used in the first grade. The pictures and illustrations are very numerous and show, for example, a large regiment, a Fascist militia of men on guard, and a warship. Many short stories are included for the edification of the children. Here is one of them. A little girl of six received a doll as a gift. Her little brother had received some lead soldiers. The little boy said: "I can't understand what pleasure you girls find in playing with dolls." In answer the little girl said: "I can not understand how you boys can get any fun out of the lead soldiers." At this point the nurse intervenes and

---

[7] M. Ilin, *New Russia's Primer,* pp. 143–162, Houghton Mifflin Company, Boston, 1931.

says: "My dear children, everything is exactly as it should be, for you, my little boy, ought to know that if little girls did not love their dolls so much you boys would not have so many soldiers." "And why is that?" said the youngster. "Because little soldiers are the children of dolls." Such is the wisdom of the nursemaid, who reveals the purpose of women to produce soldiers and many of them, and the duty of men to be soldiers, always ready to kill and to be killed.

In the reader of the second and third grades further progress is made. Sentences like these may be found: "Italy is very beautiful, Italy is very powerful, and fears no one."

"Social" education of the children is not neglected either. Judge for yourself. In the reader of the third grade we find that the "workers of the period previous to Fascism (that is the free workers who were liberally organized) were a gentry who had no desire to work and they declared (horrors!) that the rich exploited them." "On the contrary," continues the book, "the rich labor more than any other group, and without getting any advantages from it."

The reader of the fourth grade speaks of the Fascist revolution and makes clear to the children how the "Duce" saved Italy from the abyss of Bolshevism.

Speaking of the last war, three or four persons are indicated as its heroes, among them Mussolini. This is the same Mussolini who was accidentally wounded during drill and who spent only several weeks in the trenches.

As we go on from grade to grade we find this education for Fascism emphasized and carried through. Mussolini himself indicated some time ago what ought to be the motto of the Italian school children: "The text book and musket make a perfect Fascist." [8]

Education in Germany.

The reform of German education in the light of the National Socialist Revolution is proceeding apace. . . . The most important aspects of an educational system are the spirit in which it is conducted and the aims which it seeks to promote.

. . . Hatred is inculcated against the suspected enemy within and the former enemy without, from the earliest childhood up, with such venom and barbarism as the world has not yet witnessed. There

---

[8] Francesco F. Nitti, "Special Correspondence," *School and Society*, vol. 36, No. 939, pp. 824, 825. By permission of the Science Press.

must be spiritual degeneracy somewhere if as early as the elementary school period children are taught to hate other children, whether Jews, Socialists or Communists; there must be something warped in a mentality that recommends that fairy tales should be used to spread such hate—that the wolf in "Little Red Riding Hood" and in "The Wolf and the Seven Little Goats" is the Jew in disguise, and that the witch in "Hänsel and Gretel" represents the French! Man's inhumanity to man is as nothing compared with the tyranny of children against children, which is directly encouraged and which irretrievably sears the souls of its victims.

The teachers are everywhere made conscious of their new duties in the new social order. They have had, of course, to surrender those notions of democracy and professional leadership for which they have struggled in Germany since 1848.

It is not necessary to repeat here the falsification of history, of the Nordic and Germanic theories, of the race theory and so on. . . . Whatever the official pronouncements on the desire for peace and on disarmament may be, here is first-hand evidence of the kind of militaristic indoctrination and war propaganda which is going on in the schools, with techniques, in comparison with which the propaganda and indoctrination of the Imperial period were infantile. For, more than ever, the whole of German life has become a school and there is no aspect of it—social, political, economic, scientific, literary, or esthetic—which has not been *gleichgeschaltet* or co-ordinated with the fundamental purposes of National Socialism.[9]

Political education in Russia.

A comparative study convinces that so far as educational principle and practice in political education is concerned, Soviet Russia offers no great contrast to Prussia (before the war), Italy and other more or less autocratic states of the west, of past and present time. . . .

The *raison d'etre* of strict and thorough indoctrination in the field of social science is found in these facts: a new regime has replaced the old, not by gradual transition and evolution, but by revolution; any new regime, and especially a quite radical one, is for the time being, at least, on the defensive; besides, the new regime professes

[9] I. L. Kandel, "The New German Nationalism and Education," *School and Society,* May, 1934, vol. 39, pp. 553–555. By permission of the Science Press.

motives, holds notions, that were long suppressed and which it hopes to make permanent. Indoctrination is at once its defense, building strong the walls against the well-known old foes within and those without; little support can be expected from aged disciples, but the young are ready, pliant, strong. The way is clear, the means well known, and every "advanced" nation uses them to-day, whether avowedly or not.

"School must be life" is a dictum accepted generally by educational leaders in Russia; and political life can not be separated from the rest of it and excluded from school. "Our task in the schoolworld," said Lenin, "is to overthrow the bourgeoisie and we declare openly that the school apart from life, apart from politics, is a lie and a hypocrisy." In other countries, he pointed out, cultural education apart from political life had been an ideal, but one which, he averred, was not honestly adhered to. This idea of non-political or neutral education is but a hypocrisy of the bourgeoisie—a means of duping the masses. "In all the bourgeois states, the bonds which unite politics to education are very slender; but if bourgeois society does not recognize it, it does, nevertheless, educate the masses by means of the church and by means of all the organizations which rest on private property."

Lunacharsky, Shatsky, Pistrak, Krupskaya—in fact, all leading educators of Russia—believe in the necessity of political education. Of more import than that is the fact that it is practiced everywhere in Russia to-day. It begins in earliest youth for those who go to school or preschool institutions and is likewise provided for adults whose education has been neglected. "The entire work (in the pre-school institutions) is carried on in the mother tongue and has as its purpose the development of a materialistic conception of the world, creative activity and collectivistic habits of life." A similar purpose, though stated variously, is found in all Russian schools. The Unified Labor School aims at "the education of children in the ideas of collectivism, that they may be accustomed to live, learn and work collectively."

More than two thousand years ago a certain wise man, having explained how the ideal state was to be organized, directed and maintained, was faced by the problem of first establishing belief in the new system. He recognized clearly human dislike of innovation; therefore there must be careful preparation for its acceptance. His solution, like those of many others who have proposed what they considered "perfect" or "nearly perfect" systems for the benefit of their fellows, was a resort, to "a single spirited fiction whereby we may bring even the rulers themselves, if possible, to believe it, or if not them, the rest of the city." A skeptical listener, seeing difficulties in this solution, queried, "Can you suggest any device by which we can make them believe this fiction?" and received the candid reply: "None at all by which we could persuade the men with whom we begin our new state, but I think that their sons and the next generation and all subsequent generations might be taught to believe it."

The problem of social control was faced frankly. Systematic indoctrination of youth was to accomplish the firm establishment of the new social order. Modern statesmen, though oft inclined to ridicule the ideas of mere philosophers, have nevertheless succumbed to them, whether for good or evil. Thus Western nations began to regiment the thinking of their nationals in more or less vigorous fashion through organized schools. This development was earlier and more vigorous in some lands than others. In purely autocratic states and dictatorships the purpose of indoctrination was much more frankly avowed, clearly stated, effectively performed. Prussia became leader and teacher of her sister German states, of Europe and America as well. Czarist Russia copied western tactics. "The aim of the government in the education of students," as one ancient set of instructions declared, "is the training up of faithful sons of the Orthodox Church, loyal subjects of the Czar, good and useful servants of the Fatherland. . . . The soul of education and the supreme virtue of the citizens is humility. . . ." Our friends and neighbors in Soviet Russia have plenty of good (or bad) precedents to guide their practice.[10]

Formal Education as Selective Participation in Social Experience

Formal education consists in teaching the child to participate in those selected parts of human experience that are considered of superior importance to character, life and happiness. In this manner it is used as a tool for social progress. We put a better

---

[10] Thomas Woody, "Political Education in Russia," *School and Society*, December, 1928, vol. 28, pp. 665–666, 672–673. By permission of the Science Press.

construction on past history than it deserves; we emulate people who have done noble things, and select for presentation chiefly their admirable ventures. We teach those skills, habits and routines which are considered most useful socially. In other words, by selective participation in group activities, we make the child what we think he ought to be. By giving him the best we know, we try to make him an improvement over the adult generation. The next generation is expected to exercise more virtues, to suppress more evil tendencies, to measure up to more ideals than we have.

UNIVERSAL EDUCATION AS AN AMERICAN SOCIAL VALUE

One of the major implications of the school as an institution for control in American life is that, first, it stands for all that democracy stands for—universal opportunity and social equality. Second, it stands for enlightenment—learning. It is a token of the respect that American civilization pays to knowledge. Third, it stands for an equalization of privilege because it is assumed that education is the chief method of vertical mobility, that one achieves privilege as he reaches the pinnacle of the social system through the school system. By opening the public school system to every man, we keep alive the fundamental tradition of an open class system. Fourth, it stands for specialization. We assume that in a complex society numerous specialized functions need to be performed, and that these functions can be performed effectively only through an educated public. Fifth, it stands for our political tradition, that every man having a right to vote should be able to vote intelligently if the nation's issues are to be settled in a rational manner. Sixth, it stands for progress in the American mind, for we assume that the way forward for our civilization is through the development of the intellectual level of the entire citizenry of the nation, not through lifting of a few to a great pinnacle and degrading the rest to a status of slaves, who by strenuous toil create leisure for the masters whom they serve.

The American school system as a phase of control in our institutional life is significant primarily because of these basic cultural values which it incorporates in its curriculum and general policy, but more especially because the public school system has come to stand for these values in American civilization. It has become an emblem of American social values and major cultural goals.

CONCLUSION

Because the child is plastic and because habits once well formed become mechanistic, there lies within the power of any state the possibility of developing its children and youth into citizens who measure up to its standards. All modern societies make much of this fact. Most primitive societies have acknowledged it, if not through formal education, then through some kind of formal initiation ceremony taking place during the period of adolescence.

That education even has the power to transform and redirect biological impulses and to redefine traits that once were given a biological meaning, has been adequately demonstrated by various works in our time. By far the most extreme use to which education has been put is that of employing it for purposes of political indoctrination under totalitarian states. Its use here has been so effective that in the period of a few years the political philosophy of entire nations has been altered. Thus, the philosophy of Russia, in from fifteen to twenty years, has been completely transformed through an effective system of education; Italy and Germany, with a different philosophy to perpetuate, are well on the way to the same goal.

SELECTED REFERENCES

Benjamin, Harold, editor, Education for Social Control. American Academy of Political and Social Science, Philadelphia, 1935.

Bossard, Joseph H. S., Social Change and Social Problems, revised edition, part 2. Harper and Brothers, New York, 1938.

Breed, F. S., "Preface to Moral Training," School and Society, vol. 32, pp. 273 ff. August 30, 1930.

Chambers, M. M., "Inculcating Respect for Laws in the Schools," Education, vol. 52, pp. 356 ff. February, 1932.

Clark, John Maurice, Social Control of Business, pp. 252 ff. University of Chicago Press, Chicago, 1926.

Dewey, John, Experience and Education. The Macmillan Company, New York, 1938.

Dowd, Jerome, Control in Human Societies, chap. 16. D. Appleton-Century Company, New York, 1936.

Eddy, Sherwood, *Russia Today*, pp. 105–108. Farrar and Rinehart, Inc., New York, 1934.

Editorial, "Indoctrination by Default and Indirection," *School Review*, vol. 43, pp. 721–723. December, 1935.

Frank, G., "Education and the Social Welfare," *Vital Speeches*, vol. 2, pp. 453–457. April 20, 1936.

Gillette, John M., and Reinhardt, James M., *Current Social Problems*, pp. 639–644. The American Book Company, New York, 1933.

Glueck, E. T., "Family, the School, and Crime," *Vital Speeches*, vol. 1, pp. 516–520. May 6, 1935.

Graves, W. Brooke, editor, *Readings in Public Opinion*, chap. 7. D. Appleton-Century Company, New York, 1928.

Harper, Manley H., *Social Beliefs and Attitudes of American Educators*. Teachers' College, Columbia University, New York, 1927.

Howerth, I. W., "School as a Social Institution," *Education*, vol. 45, pp. 586 ff. June, 1925.

James, William, *The Varieties of Religious Experience*. Longmans, Green and Company, New York, 1903.

Kandel, I. L., "The New German Nationalism and Education," *School and Society*, vol. 39, pp. 553 ff. May, 1934.

Melvin, A. G., "Education or Revolution," *School and Society*, vol. 39, pp. 509–511. April 21, 1934.

Nitti, Francesco F., "Fascist Education," *School and Society*, vol. 36, pp. 824–826. December 24, 1932.

O'Shea, M. V., editor, *The Child: His Nature and His Needs*. The Children's Foundation, New York, 1924.

Plant, James S., *Personality and the Cultural Pattern*, chaps. 11 and 18. The Commonwealth Fund, New York, 1937.

Prucha, L. C., "Is Adult Education Indoctrination?", *School and Society*, vol. 42, pp. 93–94. July 20, 1935.

Recent Social Trends in the United States, chap. 7. McGraw-Hill Book Company, New York, 1933.

Reisner, Edward H., *Nationalism and Education Since 1789*. The Macmillan Company, New York, 1922.

Richards, E. L., "Discipline and Adjustment," *Education*, vol. 54, pp. 403–409. March, 1934.

Smith, W. B., "Education of the Emotions," *Educational Review*, vol. 72, pp. 88 ff. September, 1926.

Snedden, D., "Education and Social Change," *School and Society*, vol. 40, pp. 311–314. September 8, 1934.

Stratton, G. M., "Black Beast in Our Education," *Scientific Monthly*, vol. 29, p. 546. December, 1929.

Tannenbaum, Frank, *Crime and the Community*, chap. 3. Ginn and Company, Boston, 1938.

Tolson, C. A., "Youth and Crime," *Vital Speeches*, vol. 2, pp. 468–472. April 20, 1936.

Washburne, C., "Science and the Free Personality," *School and Society*, vol. 44, pp. 734–736. December 5, 1936.

Woody, Thomas, "Political Education in Russia," *School and Society*, vol. 28, pp. 665 ff. December 1, 1928.

CHAPTER 16

ECONOMIC FORCES PROMOTING SOCIAL ORDER AND DISORDER

The Discipline and Destiny of the Job [1]

For simple folk the meanings of daily life flow in large measure from the logical and chronological continuums and climaxes, the sequence patterns of which may be compound (rather than complex) in any order. For instance, the harnessing of the team after breakfast on Monday morning means a sojourn to the fields, where logically continuous activity will take place till noontime and after noontime till evening, when the unharnessing of the team will lead up to the doing of small chores till supper or bedtime. The finishing of some or so much work furnished the immediate climax or point which was looked forward to, the point of sleep provided the closing of the paragraph or chapter. But in daily life evening looks forward to dawn, sleep to awakening. Monday night is the frontispage to Tuesday morning. And so throughout the week is the continuum that moves toward the Sabbath—a larger climax in the immediate daily round, and generally as well, itself a unit in the succession of Sabbaths and Special Sabbaths in the Appalachian culture looking forward to the eternal Sabbath of the Soul. The finishing of so much work in the fields on Monday was itself an event in the succeeding amounts of work to be done until the winter plowing should be finished; but the end of winter plowing was significant because it meant readiness for springtime planting. The end of planting looked toward the growing and cultivating season which itself looks toward maturity and harvest time. Harvest is then the grand climax in the annual activity. But harvest means abundance or leanness of subsistence until the next harvest. Any surplus is put away for rainy weather, for retirement from the active life, to help eke out a living

---

[1] Reprinted from Matthews: *Experience-Worlds of Mountain People*, pp 42, 43, by permission of Columbia University Press.

in the feeble days of later age, or to give the children a start educationally or financially.

So the meaning of any event comes from its relation to a continuum with successive climactic points, or from its comparison with some sensed entirety.

THE SIGNIFICANCE OF WORK TO SOCIAL CONTROL

Even in our day of short laboring hours, work consumes more time than any other life activity, with the possible exception of sleep. There is a discipline about work which does more to keep system and order in society than we ordinarily think. Though the average individual spends only eight hours a day at the job, that job looms large on his horizon.

In all societies, work in one form or another has occupied a considerable part of the waking time of members, and is ordinarily within the bounds of the social codes. Work entails habit formation and the development of routine patterns of living. Having work means that one's time is occupied; it is "idle hands that find evil tasks to do."

The Lynds, in *Middletown*, [2] paint a realistic picture of the day to day struggle of men for bread in an industrial order. They say that if one prowls about the streets at six o'clock in the morning, he will see lights in the kitchens of working men; their day has begun. Seven out of every ten gainful workers are in the great working class which must leave home sometime between six-fifteen and seven-thirty in the morning. Those of the business groups leave sometime between seven-fifteen and nine o'clock. Women, too, must rise early to prepare breakfast for their families. Household tasks occupy them a good part of the remainder of the day, especially in those homes where there are children. The gainfully employed women work eight hours or more a day, sometimes at hard labor. The reward of all these workers is nearly always money, which they must have in a commercial society in order that they and their families may live and carry on the ordinary social activities which make up life in Middletown. Thus the years go by, each person expending his best energies in order to obtain necessary funds to purchase the economic goods and satisfactions that are prominent in Middletown's culture and social life.

---

[2] See pp. 23, 53, 80–84, 87.

In contrast to the industrial and business classes of Middletown are the common working classes of the rural areas of our nation, who are much nearer the soil and who generally have a larger proportion of their time consumed in work activities. The extent to which work dominates daily habits of hill folk in the Southern Appalachians, where a somewhat primitive agricultural system prevails, was vividly presented by Matthews in his description of the experience-worlds of mountain peoples quoted at the beginning of this chapter. The daily routine of most of our rural people throughout the nation is a round of toil, from before dawn until after dark. The farm operator begins his day with chores, proceeds to do a day's work in the fields, and returns to chores at the end of the day. Preparing meals and often doing chores, washing, ironing, patching, gardening—these activities consume ten, twelve, even sixteen hours a day for the wife in the farm household. In about six cases out of seven in our nation she has none of the ordinary conveniences of the urban home made possible by running water and electricity.[3] Even farm children know the discipline of work. For them, chores precede the school day in the morning and end it again in the evening. Weekends, holidays, and summer months often find them following the same work routine as parents, insofar as their strength permits.

Work mores are prominent in the thought as well as in the action patterns of rural America. People who work long and hard are respected. There is no place for the loafer or drone. One who quits a job loses respect. There is no place for the striker. Much rivalry centers about work. Even the immature youth will keep the long hard pace of the harvest crew, in order to avoid the humiliation of having it known that he was not equal to the job. The city dude who comes to work on the farm is initiated to work and the work mores by being put through the paces to try his stamina. If he proves equal to the job, he is accepted; if he proves unequal to it, he becomes the butt of the community's jokes, the embodiment of all that "city pansy" stands for in the rural mind.

---

[3] The United States Census for 1930 showed that only 15.8 per cent of all farms had water piped into the dwelling, and that only 13.4 per cent of the dwellings were lighted by electricity.

Unemployment and Personal Frustration

Problems of social control have multiplied in the urban-industrial world with the decrease in the length of the working day and the development of widespread unemployment. Because it is assumed that "idle hands are the devil's workshop," recreational activities have been developed to occupy the leisure time of both youth and adult.

It has long been known that crimes against property increase in times of depression, when socially sanctioned ways of making a living are blocked. Studies of the unemployed made during the depression of 1930 to 1935 revealed most strikingly the extent to which the personality of modern man, and his whole social orientation is centered in his job.[4] Unemployment blocks channels of activity and causes frustration; if it be prolonged, few individuals can retain their mental equilibrium. People feel lost without their accustomed work; they no longer are an integral part of the social system. A sense of hopelessness develops in the jobless person; gone is his optimistic outlook; gone is his chance for vocational advancement; despair and futility creep into his thoughts. With the loss of contact with friends, social institutions, and other influences that have been the ballast of his personality, a new "looking-glass self" develops—a castaway, a failure, a disgrace to friends, a disappointment to himself.

In addition to the group of workers caught by the depression, there were thousands of youths who finished school, reached an employable age, but found no employment. Many in this group failed to develop the disciplinary habits of work during the formative years of young manhood, when one ordinarily acquires a sense of economic self-sufficiency. As a future consequence, this group will increase problems of control for the community and the state, for among them are youthful hoboes, loafers, and ne'er-do-wells.

Pecuniary Valuations as Forces in Control

Underlying work, this more obvious factor of social control in the sphere of economic activity, there are pecuniary values which do much to motivate conduct, especially in a highly commercial-

[4] E. Wight Bakke, *The Unemployed Man*. See also James Reinhardt, *Social Psychology*, chaps. 13, 14, 15.

ized age like our own. Though important, these values have been discussed comparatively little, the greatest contributions having been made by Thorstein Veblen and Charles H. Cooley. E. A. Ross also has contributed something to the theory of pecuniary valuation.

Veblen. Thorstein Veblen, in that almost romantic economic work, *Theory of the Leisure Class,* has shown how great wealth makes possible a conspicuous use of leisure which raises one's self-feeling and increases social prestige. Conspicuous consumption, which consists in the extravagant expenditure of funds for goods, is another type of display bringing great satisfaction, and at the same time calling forth from the masses an admiration almost akin to worship. Emulation is at the root of the desire for ownership; the accumulation of pecuniary goods is a prerequisite to leisure, to extravagance in tastes, dress, and to display, all of which values men in a predatory capitalistic order respect very highly.

Ross. E. A. Ross has shown that wealth in itself is latent social power and not just economic power, because those who have wealth soon convert portions of it into "political power, legal privilege, and invidious social preference and exemptions, all serving to mark them off from the rest of the community." [5] Invariably, wealthy persons tend to overthrow the primitive state of equality, and to foster social distinctions by virtue of their riches. Great fortunes exempt their possessors from the necessity to work, and enable them to "bedazzle with a splendid style of living" and to "command ennoblement." Soon the idea is accepted that this wealthy dominant class is set apart because of inherent capacities and virtues which the masses do not possess. The generation which inherits wealth has even more prestige than the parents who struggled to acquire it. Prestige accumulates as wealth is handed down to succeeding generations. Now, as always, patriarchs of fame are those who have acquired many cattle, great herds of sheep, many acres of land, or great bank accounts.

Cooley. By far the most penetrating analysis of the economic sphere as an agency of control is that made by the late Professor

---

[5] See E. A. Ross, *Foundations of Sociology,* pp. 218–219, The Macmillan Company, New York, 1905; also *Principles of Sociology,* pp. 318, 334, 335, D Appleton-Century Company, New York, 1920.

Charles H. Cooley, who discussed at length the subtle and far reaching influence of pecuniary valuation as it operates in the modern world. [6] He considered pecuniary valuation as a general social process, the value of a particular article of goods depending entirely upon the opinions and customs that prevail within the group. For instance, wheat bread has a particular value in our culture, whether it has merit from a hygienic standpoint or not. In Germany, beer likewise has a peculiar significance. The value of these goods is a matter of their being in vogue. To a considerable extent, the thing that is in vogue in our time is so because of psychological processes stimulated by advertising. Pecuniary values exist because of special institutional developments which have created them over a period of time. They are not universal; they are not necessarily essential to human nature; but they exist in the system of exchange because of their meaning in terms of current experience. The mechanisms of the market actually have developed and defined them.

Cooley considers the market, that is, the system of exchange, as much an institution as the state or church; in fact, in modern life it may even come to overshadow these other institutions. The market, a vast and complicated system deeply rooted in the past, has grown enormously in recent times, developing incalculable prestige. One cannot explain a fraction of it by the working of natural wants. He must take into account the ability of this market to increase artificial wants, and to regulate the individual in line with these created wants.

In general, people tend to conform to institutionally created desires, although some, either because of natural endowment or because of unusual situations, depart from the type, perhaps initiating new economic tendencies that grow and destroy the old type. The non-conformist frequently represents human nature values as contrasted to institutional values. Revolt often leads to more humanized expenditure in the field of monetary relations, so that now many things that were considered indispensable twenty-five years ago are no longer demanded, and other things which were unthought of twenty-five years ago are today essential items in every household budget. Cooley calls

---

[6] Charles H. Cooley, "The Institutional Character of Pecuniary Valuation," *The American Journal of Sociology*, January, 1913, vol. 18, pp. 543–550.

attention to the unconscious nature of domination by pecuniary values and our willing acceptance of their worth, and concludes:

We have to recognize, then, not merely that pecuniary value is, in general, a social value which derives from the social development of the past, but that it is the outcome, more particularly, of a special phase of that development, namely, the comparatively recent growth of industry and business, including also the growth of consumption. This is the special institution from which, for better or worse, the pecuniary values of to-day draw their character, very much as ecclesiastical values draw theirs from the history of the church. The phenomena of any institution are moulded in part by the general conditions of the time, but they are moulded especially by their particular institutional antecedents, which may be somewhat incongruous with the more general conditions. If you attend a service of the Established Church you become aware of points of view which may seem to you, as a man of to-day, absurd and incomprehensible, except as you know something of their history. The same may very well be true in the pecuniary world, though we may not notice it because we are more used to it, because we are ourselves members of this church.[7]

THE POWER OF PECUNIARY VALUATION IN A NON-PECUNIARY REALM

Having defined the pecuniary values and traced their origin in economic institutions, Cooley shows that the purpose of money valuation is to standardize other values by providing a common measure.[8] Money makes it possible for many sorts of values of a non-pecuniary character to work freely in the social system. Pecuniary value comes to be a powerful social force, so that one who accumulates so many dollars can through them manipulate a great number of other social values, can demand numerous services and regulate certain affairs in the social system to suit his taste.

Actually then, economic valuation far transcends in significance the economic aspect itself. It makes possible the participation of the individual in numerous phases of life. It provides a universal medium through which an individual shares in the

---

[7] *Ibid.*, p. 550. By permission of the University of Chicago Press.
[8] Charles H. Cooley, "The Sphere of Pecuniary Valuation," *The American Journal of Sociology*, November, 1913, vol. 19, pp. 188–203.

total life of the society. It is true that not all values can be reduced to pecuniary terms, but a great number can, to the extent that pecuniary factors come to regulate social activity. Even a thing like honor, which many would place outside of the pecuniary realm, is frequently affected by it. Many an individual denies himself pleasures in order to pay a debt and maintain his honor. Others buy and sell honor with money. So even very subjective factors in personality become regulated by financial value. Beauty in the form of art, music, and literature, is to some extent tied up with the pecuniary market.

He concludes then, that while pecuniary values do not involve all of our behavior, certainly they are an important influence in control in many realms which we usually consider entirely free from economic considerations.

Possibilities of Constructive Social Control Through the Pecuniary System [9]

Notwithstanding the insufficiencies of pecuniary valuation, the character of modern life seems to call for an extension of its scope: it would appear to be true, in a certain sense, that the principle that everything has its price should be rather enlarged than restricted. The ever-vaster and more interdependent system in which we live requires for its organization a corresponding value mechanism, just as it requires a mechanism of transportation and communication. And this means not only that the value medium should be uniform, adaptable, and stable, but also that the widest possible range of values should be convertible into it. The wider the range the more fully does the market come to express and energize the aims of society. It is a potent agent, and the more good work we can get it to take hold of the better. Its limitations, then, by no means justify us in assuming that it has nothing to do with ideals or morals. On the contrary, the method of progress in every sphere is to transfuse the higher values into the working institutions and keep the latter on the rise. Just as the law exists to formulate and enforce certain phases of righteousness, and is continually undergoing criticism and revision based on moral judgments, so ought every institution, and especially the pecuniary system, to have constant renewal from above. It should be ever in process of moral regeneration, and the method that

---

[9] Charles H. Cooley, *Ibid.*, pp. 202–203. By permission of the University of Chicago Press.

separates it from the ethical sphere, while justifiable perhaps for certain technical inquiries, becomes harmful when given a wider scope. As regards responsibility to moral requirements there is no fundamental difference between pecuniary valuation and the state, the church, education, or any other institution. We cannot expect to make our money values ideal . . . but we can make them better, and this is done by bringing higher values upon the market.

To put it otherwise, the fact that pecuniary values fail to express the higher life of society creates a moral problem which may be met in either of two ways. One is to depreciate money valuation altogether and attempt to destroy its prestige. The other is to concede to it a very large place in life, even larger, perhaps, than it occupies at present, and to endeavor to regenerate it by the translation into it of the higher values. The former way is analogous with that somewhat obsolete form of religion which gave up this world to the devil and centered all effort on keeping out of it, in preparation for a wholly different world to be gained after death. The world and the flesh, which could not really be escaped, were left to a neglected and riotous growth.

In like manner, perceiving that pecuniary values give in many respects a debasing reflection of life, we are tempted to rule them out of the ethical field and consign them to an inferior province. The price of a thing, we say, is a material matter which has nothing to do with its higher values, and never can have. This, however, is bad philosophy, in economics as in religion. The pecuniary values are members of the same general system as the moral and aesthetic values, and it is part of their function to put the latter upon the market. To separate them is to cripple both, and to cripple life itself by cutting off the healthy interchange among its members. Our line of progress lies, in part at least, not over commercialism but through it; the dollar is to be reformed rather than suppressed. Our system of production and exchange is a very great achievement, not more on the mechanical side than in the social possibilities latent in it. Our next task seems to be to fulfil these possibilities, to enlarge and humanize the system by bringing it under the guidance of a comprehensive social and ethical policy.

CONTROL AS PRACTICED BY BUSINESS

We can hardly think of the economic sphere today without thinking of business activity and the controls exercised over our daily lives by business. We live in a time when each great industrial enterprise and business institution goes out of its way to influence the public. Lobbyists paid by the great industries fawn upon or threaten the legislator, as the case demands, scrutinize every state and national measure to see whether it affects their vested interest, and are perpetually vigilant to see that those measures which favor their cause are passed, and that those which jeopardize it are killed. Tremendous sums are spent on advertising by modern business concerns, in order to cajole the public into buying the particular product or products sponsored.

The control exercised by business through advertising is always motivated by a desire to exploit. Sometimes this desire is less obviously predatory than at others, but always at the bottom is the idea of making a profit at the expense of the customer, who is the target of the entire system of control.

Advertising stimulates desire and hastens diffusion, the idea being to control the buyer in such a manner that he will patronize the business. But often it goes a step further and controls desire itself. New desires break old habits. New habits bring new customs, for the breaking of old habits develops a responsiveness to change and progress. The stubborn resistance of cultural inertia tends to be destroyed in the *milieu* of modern advertising, in which change becomes king.

Advertising is no small factor in the shaping of good and bad tastes, and in the determination of social values in the sphere of material goods. It lifts many very ordinary products above the prosaic and the commonplace, weaving about them an air of romance and mystery. It creates a veritable fairyland in which modern man, if he has the necessary wealth, can play.

Often we are inclined to look upon this whole field of control as undesirable and perhaps vicious, but quite to the contrary, it is not an unmixed evil. Modern female charm and the projection of youth into older age should be attributed to a large extent to contemporary advertising of beauty culture products. Personal hygiene, the perfection of diet, the universal knowledge of vitamins, the practice of certain fastidious habits, all of these notions and thousands of others have been assimilated by the masses through the advertising medium.

More than we realize, the modern advertiser has become an agent of education, disseminating both the best and the worst in our culture. The old passes; the new comes quickly. Popular tastes, best sellers, modes, styles—some good and some bad—sweep the American cultural sea because of advertising.

Advertising now has made use of most of the same control devices that through the centuries have been employed by religions. It has likewise appropriated many of the techniques of education. There are no limits to the ingenuity of the advertiser. He associates the name of his goods with beautiful music in a radio theme song; he hires a splendid voice to describe the fabulous worth of his wares; he associates his goods with the cultural, the artistic, the pleasurable, the sensual, the great, the beautiful, the humorous. The only limit to suggestiveness is public tolerance, and that, apparently, is limitless.

Advertising today plays upon more fears than does religion. They are not fears concerning the world hereafter, but rather the personal, social fears so easily stimulated in those who desire to live circumspectly and to command the admiration of their social group. The fear of body odors; in women the fear of a thick shadow that marks matronliness and age; the "pink tooth brush," that hypochondrial fear which, if realized, betrays the hastening of toothless old age; "even your best friends won't tell you," that fear of social isolation—all these fears are taken advantage of by manufacturers and advertisers.

Advertising has been discussed extensively in both scientific and popular literature, and its deliberate attempt to control through appealing to almost every motive of man—thrift, beauty, fear, hope, comfort, status, friendship, love, to mention but a few—is so generally recognized that further comments here are unnecessary.[10]

The Folklore of Capitalism

T. W. Arnold, in his penetrating analysis of the protective symbolism which has accumulated around our economic system,[11] shows how we in our nation have developed the ideal that the great corporation is endowed with the same rights and prerogatives as the free individual; in fact, that this philosophy of rightful authority on the part of the great corporation is almost

---

[10] The use of modern means of diffusion for advertising and other purposes has been discussed in Chapter 12.

[11] T. W. Arnold, *The Folklore of Capitalism.*

akin to the divine right of kings which prevailed in the early centuries. While we ordinarily do not recognize the fact, he says that we really have an industrial government which our judicial institutions are designed to serve. This myth surrounding our economic institutions, until very recently, has been so effective in controlling the thinking of individuals that even the masses have come to feel that the freedom of the great corporation to work out its own destiny is imperative to the rights of the individual and to the progress of national life, just as was the future of the church and ecclesiastical organizations during the Middle Ages generally identified with the success of the nation.

This personification and defense of a great corporation is entirely irrational, except as one views the system through the symbols which it has created. While even politicians and legal thinkers do not view private business as the essence of government, actually these organizations control credit, the prices we pay for public services, and the security of the individual. "Paternalism, bureaucracy, regimentation, arbitrary control" are terms, he says, which we do not ordinarily apply to our regimented industrial structure. The United States has two coördinated governing classes—business, which builds our cities, manufactures and distributes our goods, and holds automatic control over the life of the millions; the other sphere which we call government, but which in reality is concerned largely with preaching, and which is so caught in the mass of symbolism that it accomplishes little, except at times when the undercover political machine cuts through the symbolism and, unhampered, works a cure.

He holds that there is little question where temporal power actually lies. It is not in government but in business, and rarely can government compel business to come to its knees. Until very recently the government at Washington was tremendously interested in and satisfied to confine its organized activities to what Arnold calls preaching. Men were slow to realize, and still are, that the control of large corporations is actually a part of our government, that these corporations are not comparable to individual owners of industries.

In this work Arnold has uncovered some of the ways in which the great industrial corporations defended by well-founded traditions and rationalizations, have built a regulative system, which in our capitalistic society has been in the past, and probably still is, more powerful in influencing human affairs than government itself. The system of definition has been so effective that those governing did not recognize the source of authority. Undoubtedly many people in certain states, if they realized that certain large corporations were actually back of much legislation, would come to view this problem with a different attitude.

CONCLUSION

Work, that important disciplinary factor in the experience of man, is one of the chief forces of social control. Because man's time is consumed in the processes of food-getting and satisfying other material wants through work, he finds no time to stray from the beaten path, and in work, ordinarily, he develops habits of restraint and patterns of action that conform to social patterns. But man's life in the economic sphere often leads him beyond the point of work for the satisfaction of basic wants. When necessities are achieved, luxuries are sought. Social satisfactions are then made possible by the acquisition of more property than others in one's group possess. Pecuniary values come to stand for a myriad of social values associated with high status. So one uses his goods in ways that make conspicuous the fact that he has an abundance of them—indulging in conspicuous leisure, conspicuous consumption, and conspicuous giving, all of which are socially sanctioned. These pecuniary values become the measure of success, the yardstick of personal worth, the goal of achievement.

Much less fundamental, yet of great importance, is the attempt in our time of organized business and industry to control the individual in such a manner that he may be exploited for profit. This deliberate and conscious system of control in extensive operation today overlooks scarcely a human motive, value, or goal of life, in the attempt to win patronage. But the control of business does not cease with cajoling the customer into buying. Great corporations have assumed much of the responsibility for government, seeing that the interests of "the people" are always identical with those of their corporation.

SELECTED REFERENCES

Arnold, T. W., *The Folklore of Capitalism.* Yale University Press, New Haven, 1937.

Arnold, T. W., *The Symbols of Government.* Yale University Press, New Haven, 1935.

Bakke, E. Wight, *The Unemployed Man.* E. P. Dutton and Company, New York, 1934.

Chase, Stuart, "Advertising: An Autopsy," *Nation,* vol. 138, pp. 567–568. May 16, 1934.

Clark, John Maurice, *Social Control of Business.* University of Chicago Press, Chicago, 1926.

Cooley, Charles H., *Social Process,* part 6. Charles Scribner's Sons, New York, 1918.

Cooley, Charles H., "The Institutional Character of Pecuniary Valuation," *American Journal of Sociology,* vol. 18, pp. 543–550. January, 1913.

Cooley, Charles H., "The Progress of Pecuniary Valuation," *Quarterly Journal of Economics,* vol. 30, pp. 1–21. November, 1913.

Cooley, Charles H., "The Sphere of Pecuniary Valuation," *American Journal of Sociology,* vol. 19, pp. 188–203. November, 1913.

Corbett, Elizabeth, "The American Legend," *The Century Magazine,* vol. 117, pp. 303–310. January, 1929.

Dowd, Jerome, *Control in Human Societies,* chap. 17. D. Appleton-Century Company, New York, 1936.

Falk, Alfred T., *Short Talks on Advertising,* third series. Bureau of Research and Education, Advertising Federation of America, 1935.

Fleming, P., "Advertising Terror," *Living Age,* vol. 346, pp. 87–88. March, 1934.

Graves, W. Brooke, editor, *Readings in Public Opinion,* part 3. D. Appleton-Century Company, New York, 1928.

Keller, A. G., *Brass Tacks,* chaps. 2 and 3. Alfred A. Knopf, Inc., New York, 1938.

Keller, A. G., *Man's Rough Road,* part 2. Frederick A. Stokes Company, New York, and Yale University Press, New Haven, 1932.

Knight, Frank H., "The Newer Economics and the Control of Economic Activity," *Journal of Political Economy,* vol. 40, pp. 433–476. August, 1932.

Laird, D. A., "Why Do We Buy?", *Review of Reviews,* vol. 91, pp. 32–35. January, 1935.

Lynd, Robert S., and Lynd, Helen Merrell, *Middletown,* pp. 23 ff. Harcourt, Brace and Company, New York, 1929.

Matthews, M. Taylor, *Experience-Worlds of Mountain People,* pp. 42 ff. Columbia University Press, New York, 1937.

Orman, F., "Advertising in a New Era," *Review of Reviews*, vol. 83, p. 93. April, 1931.

Plant, James S., *Personality and the Cultural Pattern*, chap. 17. The Commonwealth Fund, New York, 1937.

Reinhardt, James Melvin, *Social Psychology*, chaps. 13, 14, and 15. J. B. Lippincott Company, Chicago, 1938.

Stocking, Collis A., "Advertising and Economic Theory," *The American Economic Review*, vol. 21, pp. 48–54. March, 1931.

Tawney, R. H., *Religion and the Rise of Capitalism*, (Scott Holland Memorial Lectures). John Murray, London, 1929.

Veblen, Thorstein, *The Theory of the Leisure Class*. The Macmillan Company, New York, 1905.

Wallas, Graham, *The Great Society*. The Macmillan Company, New York, 1920.

Weber, Max, *The Protestant Ethic and the Spirit of Capitalism*, translated by Talcott Parsons. Charles Scribner's Sons, New York, 1930.

Wilder, Robert Holman, and Buell, K. L., *Publicity; A Manual for the Use of Business, Civic, or Social Service Organizations*. The Ronald Press Company, New York, 1923.

Young, J. W., "Professor Looks at Advertising," *Good Housekeeping*, vol. 100, pp. 86–87 ff. May, 1935.

Young, Kimball, *An Introductory Sociology*, chap. 27. American Book Company, New York, 1934.

Young, Kimball, *Source Book for Sociology*, chap. 27. American Book Company, New York, 1935.

CHAPTER 17

GOVERNMENT AND LAW AS REGULATIVE AGENCIES

AUTHORITATIVE ASPECTS OF GOVERNMENT AND LAW

"There must be," observes Malinowski, "in all societies, a class of rules too practical to be backed up by religious sanctions, too burdensome to be left to mere goodwill, too personally vital to individuals to be enforced by any abstract agency. This is the domain of legal rules." [1]

Aristotle described man as a political animal by nature, and conceived the state to be the one institution vested with sovereignty. [2] "Government alone is the common instrument of all the people, the common agent of the final sovereign," as a contemporary expresses it. [3] It is true that even in very democratic societies the state is the ultimate authority in many spheres of activity, and it exercises its sovereignty over many realms of behavior. In a society like our own, where the state provides many services, it comes to direct by setting standards, by sponsoring and encouraging activities, and by developing numerous regulations which act as guides to behavior.

In the development of laws, it determines codes and penalties for violation; it regulates, it promotes, it prohibits. As an agency of formal, conscious, deliberate social control, the state has no peer among social institutions. However, because in most countries this control is conscious, deliberate, and formulated, it is perhaps not as effective in motivating the individual as those controls exercised by more intimate institutions. Moreover, there is always a compulsory element about controls developed by the state, so that a good many citizens feel that one can do

---

[1] Quoted by T. V. Smith in "Custom, Gossip, Legislation," *Social Forces*, October, 1937, p. 24.
[2] *Aristotle's Politics*, translated by Benjamin Jowett.
[3] David C. Coyle, et al., *The American Way*, p. 15.

whatever he can "get by" with. Rather than a conscientious observance of law, an observance motivated by fear of penalty is developed. In such a case the control device becomes external and tends toward superficiality.

In the modern state, with its highly complex system of organization, laws, because they are the chief means of organized group control, multiply very rapidly; some of our states have as many as 15,000 of them on the statute books. Municipalities must print entire booklets containing their traffic regulations. Every legislature and national congress faces repeated requests from interested groups for the passing of restrictions or for the granting of privileges.

As new material culture accumulates, new laws and restraints are necessary. As secondary group contacts increasingly come to characterize experience, more and more regulations of a legal character appear to be essential, in order to maintain the minimum standards of social justice. It becomes illegal to do many things, and it becomes equally illegal to neglect certain responsibilities.

In our society it is customary to command respect for law through imposing both physical and financial penalties. It is these laws and their penalties which maintain the social structure of the modern political state. Law, then, becomes the chief tool by which governments control.

Modern governments, in the field of promotive control, have come to sponsor social legislation more and more. Governments now preside over social relationships and take care of social adjustments for a considerable number of individuals, groups, and classes. Social legislation is looked upon as one of the chief tools for bringing about social justice.

Government today thinks nothing of taking from wealthy individuals or groups, and distributing the benefits among the masses. One of the chief tools for such a procedure in a capitalistic society is taxation. At other times, however, vested interests may manipulate the government so that it operates to their advantage by extending privileges or granting exemptions.

IDEALS AND AUTHORITY

Governments rule most completely when they are able to penetrate beyond the mere regulation of overt and external acts into the control of individual attitudes, motives, beliefs, and intentions. In most nations of our time, governments are attempting to do this by regulating means of communication. The press and the radio, especially the latter, in most countries of the world, are now completely under state control. A government may so effectively control by such means that it eventually wrecks itself. Complete suppression usually results, sooner or later, in the revolt of the masses.

Modern dictatorships furnish excellent examples of the development of extreme ethnocentrism and loyalty to a country. They attempt to control religion, morality, and education; in fact, as we have seen,[4] their education has degenerated into what is very obviously indoctrination. Certain religious groups with interests counter to those of the state are suppressed or destroyed, and educators, public leaders, and scientists are ruthlessly slaughtered or suppressed, if they dare to oppose the interests of the state. The "great ideal" of any dictatorship is always enforced by an iron hand, directed by a tenaciously intolerant loyalty to the purposes of the state as the supreme goal of human endeavor.

In times of war, when heroic ideals captivate the masses, the living fire of a fanatical patriotism grips even the most democratic of nations, and bigotry, brutality, and absolutism are enthroned. One need go no further than our own nation to be impressed with the truth of this generalization, for in the days of the World War, when we were "saving the world for democracy," we suffered willingly such regimentation as only dictatorships practice in times of peace. The blades of guillotines and the points of bayonets are kept brightest, the dark caverns of prisons are kept most crowded, at the same time that the masses are uttering the passionate cry, "Liberty, equality, fraternity!"

Ideals in the governmental sphere can become so all-consuming, when they reach the point of mass hysteria, that complete and unmerciful authority is employed. In-group loyalties become exaggerated, national ethnocentrism reaches its height, racial myths are revived, minority groups of a different cultural ethos or racial stock are persecuted; all of these influences serve to intensify the ideal.

---

[4] Chapter 15.

INCREASING IMPORTANCE OF GOVERNMENT AND LAW IN THE FIELD OF SOCIAL CONTROL

The informal control devices of primitive societies long ago ceased to be sufficient for the regulation of modern man. Though some of our institutions are waning in influence as agencies of social control, for instance, the family and the church, not so is the state. As civilization becomes more complex the importance of the state increases. Bernard comments:

. . . the state is of rapidly increasing, not of diminishing, importance in modern life. It could not be otherwise, for in a highly complex society there must be some general clearing house for social control and policy making. The state is the only institution capable of performing this function that stands for the whole people. If business should capture the state, as once the Church held it, it would still be the state that would function as the agent of business, as once it served the Church.[5]

The inevitability of this extension of government control is stressed by Marx, who says,

Mutual interdependence is the keynote of modern society. The range of personal risks which do not somehow involve a common risk, is permanently shrinking. Consequently the system of common precautions aiming at adequate insurance against common risks, whether we call it social security or governmental interference, is growing more elaborate, decade by decade.[6]

WEAKNESS OF LAW AS A CONTROL DEVICE IN CONTEMPORARY SOCIETY

One of the major problems at the present time, in the field of law as an arm of government, seems to be that it does not discharge its functions very effectively. The schoolroom tries to justify law and to teach law observance. Every child is taught that a good citizen invariably obeys the law. Yet much of our law is so ill-conceived, and much of our legal procedure is

---

[5] L. L. Bernard, "The Field of Political Sociology," *Journal of Social Philosophy*, January, 1938, vol. 3, pp. 124–138.

[6] Fritz Morstein Marx, "Propaganda and Dictatorship," *The Annals of the American Academy*, May, 1935, p. 212. By permission of The American Academy of Political and Social Science.

such a hodge-podge of tradition and outmoded ritual that few Americans who have had any experience with it respect it. We teach observance because it is good theory; yet a man could scarcely live in urban society and fully conform to all its laws.

In the fields of court procedure, criminal prosecution, and law enforcement in general, people have lost faith in the system because the system has lost sight of its own goal.[7] No institution can maintain its prestige regardless of the amount of formal training its members receive, when it ceases to serve well the society that supports it. Experience, observation, and public opinion weigh the modern legal-judiciary system and find it wanting in effective social control.

The legal profession, the jury system, and democratic court procedure originated in a great epic of human history. They were liberating forces in a period when man was breaking away from the divine right of kings, from absolute authority in the hands of monarchs. But these circumstances no longer exist. This system, which was designed to protect the people from encroachment of their rights, became the tool of special interests. We are resigned to the fact that the average jury is selected on the basis of ignorance, that the successful criminal attorney is the man with the most perverted conscience, that the average trial is conducted as a combat between attorneys, and that the man who is successful in winning the jury wins the case. We think of legal procedure as a battle of wits by the attorneys, and not as a sound method for determining guilt or innocence. It is true that in cases it still serves to fix guilt or innocence, but actually most evidence comes from factors outside of the legal process as such.

Law specifies the penalty for disobedience, and usually in quite specific terms. Thus it not only sets a standard for behavior and provides a guide to legitimate conduct, but it provides the measure of punishment to be meted out in case of insubordination. Students of criminology hold that severity of punishment is much less effective as a deterrent to lawbreaking than *certainty* of punishment.[8] The irony of the situation in America is that

---

[7] See Richard La Piere's discussion of "legal absolutism," in *Collective Behavior*, pp. 411–413.

[8] Neither certainty of apprehension nor severity of punishment are adequate for purposes of control. See E. H. Sutherland, *Principles of Criminology*, chap. 17, J. B. Lippincott Company, 1934.

(1) our police are much less effective in apprehending the violator than in some nations, and that (2) once the offender is seized, the judicial system is so lax that the chances of conviction and punishment are not great. Cumbersome court procedure, delays until public ardor has cooled, ignorant juries that can be manipulated by lawyers versed in psychological chicanery—these and similar factors hinder conviction and punishment of the guilty. The breakdown of control as it applies to law and crime can justly be laid in part to the phases of the legal institution which have to do with seeing that penalties are administered to law-breakers.

One of the healthful symptoms of the times is the widespread attack on the judicial system and some few attempts at revision.[9]

The Authority of Stateways Compared to that of Folkways

Under ordinary circumstances, law is effective only if backed by custom, tradition, and favorable group opinion. When lacking in these sanctions it is entirely an external device, and as such, rules only overt behavior. Custom is an indispensable aid to control in any society, regardless of the number of laws which may be passed. Regulation of behavior by custom, tradition, gossip, and group opinion, moreover, always precedes the passage of laws. Certain customs in a complex state eventually become incorporated in law, and sometimes the law itself attempts to regulate matters of custom by the means at its disposal. It is when these two influences, custom and law, cross that one sees the relative strength of the two.

Legislation may encounter great difficulty in attempting to modify custom, as has been well elucidated by Odum, in his "Lynchings, Fears, and Folkways," in which he shows that stateways are often unable to compete in influence with folkways. Commenting on this fact in relation to lynching, he says:

. . . The fear which militates against vigorous protest and action is of course a product of the folkways. "Every time, the folkways will defeat the stateways if they are against the stateways." The special report on lynchings says: "The lynching method is a recognized

---

[9] T. W. Arnold, *Symbols of Government*; Jerome E. Ellison, "Justice Shifts into High," *Reader's Digest*, July, 1938, reprinted from Weekly Magazine Section, *Christian Science Monitor*, June 15, 1938; "Justice Moves Like a Fire Brigade," *Reader's Digest*, February, 1935, p. 52 ff.

custom in many communities. Hence, church members and civic leaders, instead of taking a determined stand against mob violence, often yield to it either by silence or by apology." What the outside observer does not see is that the folkways are so strong that the enforcement of law by local or State forces would mean literally civil war in the community. The folkways have ruled continuously since the days of reconstruction. Progress is being made, but it is in proportion as the folkways are being changed by education, publicity, civic appeal, and courageous leadership. . . .[10]

Control by the Extra-Legal Invisible Government

It has long been recognized that what one sees operating in the governmental sphere is not always the government. Lincoln Steffens, in his exposures of graft during the early part of the century,[11] has shown that buried beneath the legal structure is what F. Stuart Chapin has called an invisible government, functioning according to a plan of its own. Chapin describes elected officials, regular governmental procedures, laws, and regulations as the manifest pattern of government, but also calls attention to latent patterns of government, those that act beneath the surface unobserved. He shows that actually we are controlled by this latent government much more than we recognize.

Political corruption had become a social process and not a temporary lapse. It is easier to state than to prove the contention that, while these examples of the invisible government may have been all too true a generation ago, they are now events of the past. In fact, if one may judge from the exposures made during the Seabury investigation into New York City government in 1932, as well as elsewhere among American cities, there has been scant progress in the purification of local government and politics. In any event, it would seem the safer course to expect disclosures of corruption to follow upon impersonal investigation almost anywhere in the realm of local government than to be oblivious and complacent in our political ignorance. It would seem far more realistic to take the position that political corruption is a deep-seated social process, pathological to be sure and undesirable on all counts, but nevertheless a force to be everywhere

---

[10] From Howard W. Odum, "Lynchings, Fears, and Folkways," *The Nation*, December 30, 1931, vol. 133, p. 720. Reprinted by permission.

[11] *The Autobiography of Lincoln Steffens*, pp. 376, 379, 408–421, 427–428, 431–433, 446–449.

reckoned with, than to shy away from unpleasant facts and to live in a world of idealistic political wish-fulfillment.

All of these considerations would seem to establish the principle that the analysis of political institutions should go deeper than the legalistic surface described in law and charter. As a matter of fact, the three patterns of political institutions in contemporary America overlap one another. The legalistic pattern of government overlaps the quasi-legal party system, and this in turn overlaps the extra-legal pattern of the invisible government of the underworld.[12]

The latent patterns of government may take many forms, depending on the situation, such as the rule of mobs and gangsters who control affairs by intimidation, murder, and force, or the rule of grafters who manipulate municipal or national affairs with an eye to making money for their inner circle.

Thurman W. Arnold, in discussing the traditional and symbolic nature of government, [13] has stressed the fact that externally it must represent for Americans an ideal system in order to command the necessary respect to rule, but that in actuality government, in order to be effective, progressive, and constructive, must violate these symbols by developing an under cover system of action which often disregards the professed principles "in hidden and covert ways." He cites the interesting fact that the most corrupt administrations in city government have often brought great benefits in terms of constructive public action.

For example, the public works program of Chicago was accomplished by an under cover machine, and in the city of New York inarticulate groups were often protected by Tammany Hall. Arnold suggests that the practices of exploitive administrations have often made for progress, that they have paved the way in this country for a great industrial feudalism.

In the field of American local politics, the ward boss works a game all his own. Though he may not have in mind personal economic gain, he is definitely interested in keeping his own gang in power so that advantages may come to it. One of the most interesting analyses of the extra-legal government that has come to the author's attention is a frank, humorous, homely

---

[12] F. S. Chapin, *Contemporary American Institutions*, pp. 36–38. By permission of Harper and Brothers.

[13] T. W. Arnold, *Symbols of Government*, chap. 10.

account of Plunkitt, in which he tells of his practice of "honest graft" as a district leader for Tammany Hall during the early part of the century.[14] He describes at considerable length honest graft and shows how it works, boasting frankly "I seen my opportunities and I took 'em."

His party was in power and was going to undertake a great amount of public improvement. He was told that the city was planning to lay out a new park. He saw his opportunity and took it by going to the site and buying up all the land in the neighborhood. As soon as it became publicly known that a park was going to be built, everybody rushed to get the land which nobody wanted before. They found that Plunkitt had it. "Ain't it perfectly honest to charge a good price and make a profit on my investment and foresight? Well, that's honest graft."

Similarly, if a bridge were to be built, Plunkitt was tipped off and bought the property that would be needed for the approach, selling it at his own price later when the public must have it. He said, "It's lookin' ahead, just like they do in Wall Street in following the coffee or cotton market." He not only called it "honest graft," but confessed he was looking for it every day.

The city was to sell several hundred thousand granite blocks. He knew that there was going to be considerable competition and that the price at the auction would be high. He got in touch with all of the men who were going to buy blocks and agreed to give each of them the number they wanted for nothing. The auctioneer asked for a bid on 250,000 fine paving stones. Plunkitt bid $2.50 and got the lot. By such "honest graft," and without stealing a dollar from the city treasury, he boasted that he had gotten rich.

He kept in power by keeping in touch with the people in his district—by what he called "studyin' human nature and acting accordin'." He claimed that one could not study human nature in books or in college. One had to go out among the people and learn the real needs of the public, in order to serve these needs.

If Plunkitt heard of a young man who was proud of his voice he invited him to join his Glee Club. The young man became a follower of Plunkitt for life. If a young man was good at base-

[14] W. D. Riordon. *Plunkitt of Tammany Hall*, pp. iii–vii, introduction; 3–10, 40–53, 110–174.

ball on the vacant lot, he was brought into his baseball club.
If Plunkitt heard of a family in need, he went out and helped
them. He was at a fire in his district as soon as the fire engine
was, and comforted the victim by buying him clothes and helping him to get started again. "You can't tell how many votes
one of these fires bring."

Plunkitt always worked on the philosophy that the poor are
the most grateful people in the world and that they have many
friends. Of course, as in the case of all political machines, there
was the job for the "deservin'" man. And he saw to it that
every one of the children knew Uncle George Plunkitt and came
to understand that Uncle George and candy meant the same
thing.

Not infrequently this extra-legal government plays a dominant
part in state and federal legislation. Every bill affecting the
interests of any large group must run the gauntlet of lobbyists,
which group has been aptly dubbed, the "Third House." This
group probably gives the average legislator more information
than any other, on which to base his vote on bills before him in
the legislature. One Senator, in discussing crooks in the legislature,[15] suggests that bribes are often given to legislators for the
passing or not passing of certain measures. He introduces his
discussion with these paragraphs:

Is your district representative in your State Legislature crooked?
Does he accept money to vote for or against certain measures? And
if so, has he a good chance of getting away with it?

As a State legislator myself, I must confess that the odds are about
even on affirmative answers to the above questions. My belief is
based on a good many years of experience as a member of a legislature
in one of the larger States of the Union, and on careful observations
in other States. While my samplings cannot be taken as scientifically accurate for all, I am certain they represent an average which
will hold good for the entire nation.

Putting summary ahead of detail, I may say that ten per cent of
legislators come perilously close to being racketeers; twenty-five per
cent are primarily venal in their attitude toward such legislation as is

---

[15] A State Senator, "Crooks in the Legislature," *The American Mercury,*
July, 1937, pp. 269–271. By permission of the American Mercury, Inc., and
of the author.

capable of being turned to advantage; another twenty-five per cent will accept money for their votes on bills which do not vitally affect the general public and in which they have no personal interests; another twenty-five per cent, who do not accept money, are moved often by personal and group relationships, including retainers, business arrangements, political advantage, patronage demands, etc.; and about fifteen per cent are, or think they are, above suspicion of judging legislation other than on its merits—although I never have met one who could take an utterly detached viewpoint even when unconscious of personal interest. Unadulterated altruism has yet to come within my purview.

Paradoxically, some of the crookedest legislators in my State are among the ablest in their consideration of measures. You'd have to know them to understand that. And also you have to remember that most legislation does not involve the employment of money. There usually are not more than a dozen or so productive "money bills" in a regular session, and few of these are of major importance to the people. Most money bills involve legislation desired or opposed by special groups, who have sufficient means to swing votes.

Lobbying is not an unmixed evil. One author speaks very favorably of the lobbyist, indicating that he is a legitimate tool for educating the congressman, who is usually grossly ignorant on most bills. He says in part:

The lobby must be included as an important part of the legislative machinery and as having much to do with influencing administrative action. It may properly be called a "third house" or an "assistant government" but not an "invisible government." The important lobbying activities today are not done under cover; perhaps not as much as are the activities of the elected representatives.

The question of the desirability or undesirability of the lobby institution as an important part of the system of government arises. Does it perform services or is it detrimental? Before an appraisal of the institution can be made some of the important effects resulting from its existence should be noted.

Lobbyists have had some important effects on the work of legislators. In the first place they render service to legislators and administrators by acting in an advisory capacity. As advisers they introduce facts, viewpoints, and considerations which otherwise would be overlooked or would be beyond the legislator's capacity to acquire. Through the activities of lobbyists legislators have a supply of information and counsel which would require endless time and expense should they themselves have to acquire it. It is as advisers that lobbyists render their greatest service. If they act in good faith as advisers they help to bring public opinion to bear upon legislators and serve a useful function in the process of representative government.

One of the chief duties of lobbyists at legislative centers is to serve as the eyes of the interest which they represent. They keep the constituents of legislators informed of what takes place. It has been pointed out by students of public opinion that if representative government is to function properly some means must be devised of translating complex governmental questions into simple formulas so that the people generally may arrive at decisions on such matters. That function lobbyists perform. They not only reduce questions to simple proportions but show constituents how the proposed solutions of the question would affect their interest.

And there is another important point to notice. Without lobbyists the representation of an individual consists in helping to elect his legislative representatives. If the candidates for whom he votes are not successful there is no representation according to his choice. The individual finds a new method of representation at hand through lobbyists—a method of helping to direct representatives after they are chosen. That method lies open whether or not his vote has helped to elect representatives. It is a method of continuous representation, not only to determine whether legislators carry out the program on which they were elected but to give new direction as new problems arise. When this continuous method of representation is coupled with the work of lobbyists in translating problems to understandable proportions, there arises effective representation of a new order more influential in securing results in legislation than the old method of helping to place legislators in office.

There can be no doubt that lobbyists have brought the activities of legislators more into the open. Legislators now find that their legislative activity must be carried on under the close scrutiny of keen observers. There is little that goes on of any importance during a legislative session which escapes their attention. For nearly every important bill there are lobbyists on each side keeping an eye on every action of the legislators. Constituents would have much less information about the activities of their legislators were it not for the surveillance of legislative sessions by lobbyists. The growth of the lobby institution has played an important part in decreasing invisible government, so much complained about three or four decades ago.[16]

It has become increasingly clear to the general public that in the field of international relations as well as in national, state, and local affairs, there is an invisible government that has much to do with controlling our national destiny. The extensive publicity given the Senate munitions inquiry during the early thirties revealed at least a few of these undercurrent forces that operate in contemporary international affairs.

THE POLITICAL PARTY AND THE INVISIBLE GOVERNMENT

In our nation, and in fact, in most democratic nations, control of the government is in the hands of parties committed to certain stated issues, on the basis of which one or the other party comes to power and takes charge of law making and law enforcement for a period of years. In order to get into power and to retain that power, these parties are constantly on the alert to control the activities and interests of the voter in such a manner that their cause will be benefited. Behind party organization and underlying its publicized purposes is the pre-eminent desire to retain or gain control. This being the case, the forces of the invisible government frequently combine to keep the party in power. Thus the party may, and often does, become a mere tool in their hands.

CONTROL TECHNIQUES OF THE POLITICAL PARTY

Since political parties in our nation are constantly struggling for control of governmental functions, they exercise numerous control techniques in an attempt to maintain a favorable position in the public mind. Some of the more important devices are here discussed.

Myth making. Leadership in any field consists to some extent in the creation of a fictitious ideal out of the common clay. Cooley [17] has indicated that mankind tends to build up about its leaders myths which constitute the essence of fame. In the hero,

---

[16] Edward B. Logan, "Lobbying," *The Annals of the American Academy of Political and Social Science*, 1929, pp. 78–89. Reprinted by permission.
[17] Charles H. Cooley, *Social Process*, chap. 11.

group members tend to embody all of the virtues which they themselves conceive in their wishful thinking. The leader in this way becomes perfect, the incarnation of all that is considered good and great.

In the field of modern politics the process of myth making has been exploited to its fullest extent. The clever politician is a family man, or at least he loves babies. Pictures are printed of him kissing his grandson or patting the head of the child of some down-trodden pauper. He is a great fisherman, trout preferably, but at least bullheads, and the public is informed of it when he catches a 6-inch trout. To secure the farmer's vote he needs to be a "grass roots farmer." In these commonplace events which are publicized widely in the newspapers of the nation, the leaders of our country are shown to possess the human traits, the human interests, the human sympathies common to us all. In this way we are able to identify ourselves with the men who represent all that we hold good.

At the same time that loyal party followers are building up the myths designed to increase the fame of their leader, the opposition is tearing them down. They cry "communism," show that he associates with Red agitators, that he has been seen in the presence of Wall Street capitalists, that he has had his picture taken with a Negro and must therefore be a traitor to our caste system.

This battle of myth making is continually going on in our country, as one party, through news, cartoons, editorials, and radio, tries to make its leader the hero of the public and keep him that, and as the opposition tries to destroy his fame and in the end replace him by one of their own party. Every political party employs highly paid publicity staffs whose business it is to make or break reputations.

The time was in America when the newspaper exercised a powerful influence in determining political success or failure, but today the radio seems to have surpassed the press, because of its superior effectiveness in swaying public sentiment.[18]

Since no man actually possesses all the virtues that may be attributed to him, it remains for history to decide which are the truly great men in the political sphere, as elsewhere. In after

---

[18] "The Press and the Public," *New Republic*, special section, March, 1937, p. 179.

years defects of character and personality, or the mistakes of administration are gradually patched up, great deeds and great words are immortalized. In this manner certain statesmen come to represent the best of the age in which they live.

Enemies of straw. It is desirable for the candidate for public office to have certain real or imagined issues on which to hinge his campaign. These issues can be made much more dramatic and effective if they are embodied in the person of a man or of a group, so if no real man exists, a straw man is often invented. In the Roosevelt-Landon campaign the Hearst papers invented a Red issue, identifying Roosevelt with communistic propaganda and suggesting the danger and threats of a communistic order to American life. This appeal might have been very effective if Hearst himself had not been held in great disrepute by the American public at the time.

Roosevelt has held before the proletariat and middle classes, the "forgotten man" who seeks a "more abundant life," and the sins of the "economic royalists," those money changers who are the arch enemies of society, who occupy the throne of vested interest, who are responsible for all economic sins, who threaten our common democracy. Even in our open class society much is made of class struggle.

Hitler made the Jew the scapegoat; Russia the Church and the royalty; the French revolutionist, the monarchy.

The appeal to achievement. In the American dual system of party politics the party in power often has the advantage because it can point to a record of achievement, thus making use of positive propaganda. The opposition party is forced to rely on a negative type of approach, a propaganda of attack. They cannot point with pride to a constructive record because they have been inactive for four or more years. Their appeal must therefore be chiefly destructive in character, an attempt to run down the administration in power, to blacken the character of the administrator, to indicate the unsatisfactory nature of the regime that has been in power and the inefficiency of the reforms that may have been initiated.

The appeal to tradition. The "grand old party" has carried an emotional appeal to many individuals, and indeed, any appeal to tradition is always effective in the political realm. But an even better method of gaining sympathetic response than the glorifica-

tion of an abstract thing like a party is the appeal to great characters of the past that have ennobled the party. The Republican
party during a campaign becomes the party of Abraham Lincoln,
of Teddy Roosevelt, of George Washington. The Democratic
party becomes linked with Jefferson, and its battle cry is for a
return to Jeffersonian democracy.

Manner of address. President Roosevelt begins his radio talks
with the phrase, "My friends," a salutation that, by employing
a homely pattern, wins the sympathy of his listeners, for this form
of address is one often used in the primary group world and
hence is associated with our most intimate relations. The genu-
ineness of his greeting calls forth a response in the hearts of
Americans everywhere. With a similar idea in mind President
Hoover constantly referred to "the American family" in his public
addresses.

The appeal to universality. The human being, living his daily
life in the presence of society and trained in the ways of the herd,
feels most comfortable when in the presence of others. It is little
wonder then that the appeal to universality finds a strong response in the heart of practically everyone.

Politicians, having learned the value of this appeal, try to create
previous to every election a sense of universality of interest in
their candidate. They realize that there are always a great many
people who do not care which way they vote as long as they vote
with the majority, and for this reason find it a useful bit of
strategy to predict an overwhelming majority for their candidate.

In recent years pre-election polls have been used as devices for
giving the public objective proof as to which candidate is the
most popular and therefore likely to carry the majority vote. But
much more effective than verbal statements or any objective
proof which may be mustered are many more subtle devices
which create in the public mind a picture of the candidate as a
man of universal interests and universal sympathy. Politicians
always seem to feel that it is necessary to indicate to the public
that their candidate knows life as the masses know it. If he can
be shown to have climbed the ladder from poverty it is much to
the advantage of the party.

The patronage pattern. Political machines are built by patronage. Party adherents feel that they have vested interests in the
outcome; many jobs are at stake. "To the victor belongs the

spoils" has been too true, even in an age of Civil Service reform. The loyal worker knows that if his party comes into power his own reputation will be enhanced, and he will be recompensed for his service with a remunerative public position. He is, therefore, motivated by fear in case of loss, and by the hope of reward in case of victory. To many, therefore, politics becomes a bread and butter affair. Americanization many times has been motivated by a desire to obtain a meal ticket via the ballot, and in many urban communities it has been a fairly certain route.[19]

It is at the point of patronage that many of the forces of invisible government enter the struggle for control.

CONCLUSION

Modern society places much faith in government and legal machinery for the maintenance of order. In less highly civilized societies, where the individual is under the scrutiny of his local group, the vigilance of custom and group opinion removes most of the necessity for law and formal government, but with the development of complex society the state and its multiplicity of laws becomes essential, replacing to a considerable extent the customs, mores, and traditions of the simpler cultures.

It is true that law, to be effective in any society, must be backed by custom and tradition, but in states resorting to law as the primary means of control these elements are latent rather than active. In our time government and law have become the most active agencies of rational control employed in secondary groups, bowing to custom only in rare cases where wide protest defies state authority, as for instance in the matter of lynching. Law becomes both a standard and a penalty, in that its establishment indicates to everyone what is expected in the way of orderly behavior, and its violation always carries a punishment which in itself is a means of control.

Invisible government is often a powerful factor in governmental control, the government coming to represent interested parties who desire legislation that favors their purpose of exploitation. Actually, today government has come to represent so many phases of organized group control that one is never quite sure in whose interest he is being regulated. We talk about

---

[19] Paul H. Landis, *Three Iron Mining Towns*, chap. 12.

control in the "interests of the people," in the "interests of the state," in the "interests of democracy," or some other ideal abstract principle, but as a matter of fact control is often exercised in the interests of the "third house" in our legislative assemblies, the lobbies, which may or may not represent our interests as "the people," and probably do not in most cases. Too often princes, potentates, presidents, congressmen, and mayors have, with a Machiavellian capacity for rationalization, identified the interests of "the people" with those of "the ruler" and have sought diligently to see that the people's interests were effectively realized along these lines. The great society is a complicated world in which authority must be entrusted to those who represent us. It is a world so complicated that it is often debatable whether governments make laws in the interests of humanity, of a "grand old party," of the industrial magnates, or of the nation's major financiers, but in whose ever interest it be, we must at least recognize that the modern state is a powerful agency for social control, and that without it chaos would inevitably reign.

SELECTED REFERENCES

Arnett, C. E., and Others, "Prestige as a Factor in Attitude Changes," *Sociology and Social Research*, vol. 16, pp. 49–55. September, 1931.

Arnold, T. W., *The Folklore of Capitalism*. Yale University Press, New Haven, 1937.

Arnold, T. W., *The Symbols of Government*. Yale University Press, New Haven, 1935.

A State Senator, "Crooks in the Legislature," *American Mercury*, pp. 269 ff. July, 1937.

Aswell, E. C., "Religious Lobbying," *Forum*, pp. 152–162. March, 1930.

Beard, Charles A., "Whom Does Congress Represent?", *Harper's Magazine*, pp. 144–152. January, 1930.

Bernard, L. L., "The Field of Political Sociology," *Journal of Social Philosophy*, vol. 3, pp. 124–138. January, 1938.

Bryce, James, *The American Commonwealth*. The Macmillan Company, New York, 1916.

Carter, H., "Spoils," *North American Review*, vol. 235, pp. 523 ff. June, 1933.

Cooley, Charles H., "Social Control in International Relations," *Publications of the American Sociological Society*, vol. 12, pp. 207–226. 1917.

Cooley, Charles H., *Social Process*, chap. 11. Charles Scribner's Sons, New York, 1918.

Coyle, David C., and Others, *The American Way*, pp. 15 ff, 140–171. Harper and Brothers, New York, 1938.

Dicey, Albert Venn, *Lectures on the Relation Between Law and Public Opinion in England during the Nineteenth Century*. The Macmillan Company, New York, 1905.

Douglas, W. A. S., "Chicago Circus," *Nation*, vol. 132, pp. 269 ff. March 11, 1931.

Dowd, Jerome, *Control in Human Societies*, chaps. 23–25. D. Appleton-Century Company, New York, 1936.

Ellwood, Charles A., *The Psychology of Human Society*, pp. 396–401. D. Appleton-Century Company, New York, 1931.

"Gangland and Its Foundation," *Survey*, vol. 64, p. 511. September 15, 1930.

Gerold, Katherine, "Our Passion for Law-Making," *Harper's Magazine*, pp. 700–705. November, 1928.

Gillette, John M., and Reinhardt, James, *Current Social Problems*, pp. 773–778. American Book Company, New York, 1933.

Graves, W. Brooke, editor, *Readings in Public Opinion*, part 4. D. Appleton-Century Company, New York, 1928.

Heer, C., "Taxation as an Instrument of Social Control," *American Journal of Sociology*, vol. 42, pp. 484–492. January, 1937.

Heinz, Heinz A., *Germany's Hitler*, pp. 243, 250, 282. Hurst and Blackett, Ltd., London, 1934.

Hitler, Adolph, *My Battle*, translated by E. T. S. Dugdale. Houghton Mifflin Company, Boston, 1933.

Johnson, Claudius O., *Government in the United States*, pp. 202 ff. Thomas Y. Crowell and Company, New York, 1933.

Jowett, Benjamin, *Aristotle's Politics*, a translation. The Clarendon Press, Oxford, 1908.

Kavanaugh, Marcus, *The Criminal and His Allies*. The Bobbs-Merrill Company, Indianapolis, 1928.

Keller, A. G., *Brass Tacks*, chap. 4. Alfred A. Knopf, Inc., New York, 1938.

Landis, Paul H., *Three Iron Mining Towns, A Study in Cultural Change*, chap. 12. Edwards Brothers, Ann Arbor, 1938.

La Piere, Richard T., *Collective Behavior*, first edition, chaps. 15 and 16. McGraw-Hill Book Company, New York, 1938.

Layman, Geoffrey, "An English View of Personal Rights," *Harper's Magazine*, pp. 763–773. November, 1929.

Lengyel, Emil, *Hitler*, pp. 219–225. The Dial Press, New York, 1932.

Logan, Edward B., "Lobbying," *Annals of the American Academy of Political and Social Science*, pp. 78 ff. 1929.

Machiavelli, Nicolo, *The Prince*, pp. 142 ff. E. P. Dutton and Company, New York, 1908.

MacIver, Robert, *Society*, pp. 358 ff. Farrar and Rinehart, Inc., New York, 1937.

Marx, Fritz Morstein, "Propaganda and Dictatorship," *The Annals of the American Academy of Political and Social Science*, pp. 212 ff. May, 1935.

Michael, Jerome, and Adler, Mortimer J., *Crime, Law and Social Science.* Harcourt, Brace and Company, New York, 1933.

Mowrer, Edgar Ansel, *Germany Puts the Clock Back.* William Morrow and Company, New York, 1933.

Odum, Howard W., "Lynchings, Fears, and Folkways," *The Nation*, vol. 133, pp. 720 ff. December 30, 1931.

Plant, James S., *Personality and the Cultural Pattern*, chap. 13. The Commonwealth Fund, New York, 1937.

Plato, *The Republic*, translated by Paul Shorey. G. P. Putnam's Sons, New York, 1930.

Pound, Roscoe, *Criminal Justice in America.* Henry Holt and Company, New York, 1930.

Pound, Roscoe, "Science and Legal Procedure," *American Journal of Psychiatry*, vol. 8, pp. 33 ff. July, 1928.

Pound, Roscoe, *The Spirit of the Common Law*, pp. 103 ff. Marshall Jones, Boston, 1921.

Recent Social Trends in the United States, chap. 25. McGraw-Hill Book Company, New York, 1933.

Riordan, W. I., *Plunkitt of Tammany Hall.* Doubleday, Doran and Company, New York, 1933.

Ross, Edward Alsworth, *Principles of Sociology*, first revision, chap. 57. D. Appleton-Century Company, New York, 1930.

Smith, T. V., "Custom, Gossip, Legislation," *Social Forces*, pp. 24 ff. October, 1937.

Steffens, Lincoln, *The Autobiography of Lincoln Steffens.* Harcourt, Brace and Company, New York, 1931.

Sullivan, Lawrence, "Our New Spoils System," *Atlantic Monthly*, pp. 189 ff. February, 1936.

Tannenbaum, Frank, *Crime and the Community*, chaps. 2 and 5. Ginn and Company, Boston, 1938.

Wallas, Graham, *Human Nature in Politics*. Houghton Mifflin Company, Boston, 1909.

CHAPTER 18

SCIENCE AND TECHNOLOGY AS AGENCIES OF SOCIAL CONTROL

TESTED KNOWLEDGE AND BEHAVIOR

Man, being a creature with an inquiring mind, always seeks some sort of explanation for whatever attracts his attention in the world about him. Myth and science give him the answer. This same kind of mind, never content with leaving things as it finds them, leads man to tinker with the things he sees about him and to make other things of them. Thus, through the inventive process, tools and eventually technology develop. Finally, man is capable of transmitting both idea and tool to his posterity. We therefore live and move in a vast realm of scientific theories and mechanical contrivances, an environment of tested ideas on the one hand and of invented devices on the other.

E. A. Ross once discussed enlightenment as a method of social regulation.[1] There are undoubtedly many kinds of enlightenment, but in the contemporary world we have come to look upon science as one of the most penetrating devices for illuminating the mind. Science, which is supposed to represent tested knowledge, even supersedes common sense, tradition, and mythology. In those realms where it has entered it has actually demonstrated its superiority to any of these. True, it has not penetrated a great number of realms effectively as yet, but where it has, it has proved to be enlightening.

People have come to accept science as authority. They identify it with knowledge and, to some extent at least, they are willing to make their practices conform to its findings. Thus, various types of behavior come to be shaped in line with scientific thought. Health practices conform to new knowledge, and new laws of health. Romantic marriage customs gradually are modi-

---

[1] E. A. Ross, *Social Control*, chap. 22, The Macmillan Company, New York 1929.

fied by new scientific ideology concerning the family and marriage. For instance, intelligent persons, once they know that
certain traits are passed on to offspring with fateful regularity,
tend to project romance against an hereditary background. The
close relationship between slums and delinquency as revealed by
sociological research furnishes a new argument for clearing the
slums and a new motive for political action in the field of social
legislation.

Instances could be multiplied, but these are sufficient to make
the point that science, because it is enlightening, often affects
behavior norms and acts as an important control device. One
cannot assume that scientific findings will always be made the
basis for scientific behavior patterns. This is far from true.
Regardless of how much evidence may be piled up to show that
drugs, drinking, or night life is unhealthful, many people continue to indulge in these things. No amount of scientific information can easily destroy a pattern that provides sensual satisfaction. Man probably never will live completely scientifically.
Perhaps he could not, and find happiness. None the less, he
often does respect scientific findings to the extent that he modifies his behavior according to them.

We usually think of science in the concrete sense, as worked
out in technology. It is in this aspect that its influences, direct
and indirect, on patterns of control are most effective in our
world.

The far-reaching effects of mechanical techniques on control
patterns can scarcely yet be comprehended by our time, when
new evidence piles up daily. The factory makes inroads upon
the home, destroying its controls; modern transportation devices
break down primary group solidarity, and work destruction on the
old primary group controls. The Sabbath is secularized by the
Sunday joy ride in an automobile, and the church loses its hold.
Patterns of courtship change. Mobility and leisure come. Notions of change and progress with their challenge to tradition
are projecting themselves upon the mental screen, blotting out
tradition. Man's way of living is changing because of the machines he has made.

While the initial effect of invention is often disruptive, and
many times extensively so, it is still the hope of the Western
world that this is only a temporary effect, that the long-time re-

sults will make for better living and more efficient social control.

Certainly science and technology have made for the extensive control of the natural environment in the interest of human welfare. While such activities are outside the field of social control as defined in this book, they suggest the possibilities of social control through social science.

TECHNOLOGY AS A FACTOR IN CONTACT, DIFFUSION, AND CHANGE

Before the advent of the modern era of invention, social change as we know it today was nonexistent. The normal course of events flowed smoothly from century to century with relatively little interruption by major inventions. True, a catastrophic change occasionally destroyed the normal run of events, but, except for tribal conquest which led to some borrowing, there was little disruption of the cultural structure as such. Today one new invention of a major sort, such as the steam engine or electricity, may completely transform the manner of life of a nation. Such changes are never confined to their own sphere, but reach into many aspects of man's life, changing long established patterns of behavior, challenging old forms of life, and leading to a long chain of other disturbing inventions.

Technology hastens not only the processes of invention, for one invention almost always leads to more, but also the rate of diffusion, by increasing the range of contact and at the same time developing a state of mind receptive to the product being diffused. Therefore, the tendency of technology is to be disorganizing in its effect upon individual habits and traditional systems of control over wide geographical areas.

One sees the profound effect of the diffusion of mechanical inventions upon an ancient form of life in oriental cities today, where Western culture is making its inroad into a civilization built on long established custom. Chinese footbinding, which has been so closely identified with oriental ideas of beauty, modesty, and propriety for women, as a custom would perhaps have persisted for centuries yet, had it not been for the coming of the factory system, which took woman from the home into the factory where she needed her feet. She defied male domination; she defied tradition, and with this defiance came new attitudes and standards concerning beauty in feet.

But change does not stop there. With the industrial employment of Chinese women are passing the old patterns of life.
Once she was restricted in women's apartments and refused the
opportunity of speaking to any man alone. During her lifetime
she observed three "obeisances." In childhood she obeyed her
father, during her married life, her husband, and after her husband's death, her son. And it was held with certainty that she
would obey her husband in the life hereafter.

Throughout Arabia, India, Egypt, and Syria, where woman
has lived under the veil as a matter of unwritten law—a patron
of ancient custom and a slave to her husband in marriage—
modern means of technology providing for travel and communication make it impossible any longer to keep out the influence
of Western civilization, where machines have liberated woman
and given her a place in the sun. This contact with the Western
world, with its emphasis on woman's freedom and her vocational
initiative, is bringing revolt so that many Moslem women are
casting off the veil and beginning to see ahead to a new life for
women.

Here in these oriental cultures one sees an assault of the machine on domestic and social systems such as the Western world
experienced two hundred years ago. A process of constant readjustment has been necessary since then. New relationships
and new customs have been developed, new definitions of relationships invented, and new forms of control initiated to take
the place of the old. We in the West have adjusted our system
of control to the new technology fairly well, as far as family and
social systems are concerned, and with regard to the relation
between the sexes. The new definitions call for a greater equality
between the sexes, a greater freedom for women, their greater
use of initiative, and their right to choice and decision.

These examples, dealing largely with the effect of modern
techniques upon family and social systems, are paralleled in every
phase of modern life, and their influences are felt in every institution of society. The church no longer faces the same world,
no longer preaches the same doctrines, no longer expects the same
type of behavior that it once expected. In the final analysis, the
aims of life are essentially the same, the goals of personality are
the same, but new definitions have been developed, made necessary by the coming of the machine age.

The problem of law enforcement also has changed radically. Criminals rapidly adjust themselves to machine techniques, capitalizing on modern invention even more rapidly at times than do law enforcement officials, although both are constantly searching for new devices, the criminal to exploit society more effectively, the public official to protect society from exploitation. Now we employ not only technological devices of a physical nature, but also those of a psychological and sociological character, in the study of crime and in the detection of the criminal.

THE EFFECT OF MECHANICAL INVENTION ON NON-MECHANICAL SPHERES OF ACTIVITY

Enough has been said to suggest that mechanical invention may be revolutionary in many non-mechanical phases of man's experience. Today even beauty culture and birth control wait on the development not only of scientific knowledge but of mechanical technology. The mechanical techniques modify patterns of control, bring in new definitions of propriety, and lead to the creation of new philosophies adaptable to the mechanical devices. Rationalizations, defending the type of behavior required by a mechanized society, come into being.

Technology has also created a chain of circumstances affecting problems of delinquency. It has been the chief factor in the growth of the large city with its impersonal relationships, its slums and other specialized areas where peculiar behavior patterns develop, many of them of a pathological character. It has been responsible more than any other one factor for the development of leisure, which is associated with problems of delinquency. In fact, many of our problems of control grow out of modern man's leisure time. Leisure brings freedom to do things outside the restricted activity of work, and breeds a state of mind which starts the individual on a quest for personal satisfaction. It encourages epicureanism, makes the pleasure motive loom large in life. It is this state of mind which releases social controls and leads to the venting of biological appetites and non-sanctioned desires.

A few selections are presented to illustrate further some effects of invention and the machine on behavior. Ogburn and Gilfillan suggest influences of inventions upon society:

The effects of invention on society are various degrees and kinds.
Perhaps the first effect of inventions is the change in the *habits* of
the persons using them, as in the case of peoples who use typewriters instead of pen and ink. When the persons whose habits are
changed are numerous then a *social class* is affected. Thus, there
grows up a class of women typists and stenographers, who have a
place in society in relation to other groups and classes. Another
effect is to change certain *organizations.* Thus the organization of
various businesses is affected by the use of typewriters. Sometimes
inventions have far removed effects on a *social institution* in the
sociological sense of the word. Thus, such an institution as the
family is affected by the employment of daughters, wives and single
women in connection with machines in offices and factories. Further
influences are those affecting *ethics* and codes of conduct which
usually lag behind the material changes. For instance, at one time
it was almost a moral precept that woman's place was in the home.
The appearance of women on the streets and in places of business for
many years slowly affected manners and customs closely related to
ethical codes. A final influence to be noted is that on systems of
thought or *social philosophies,* which also have a tendency to lag
behind other influences. Thus the inventions attracting women
away from the home may be an element in a social philosophy regarding the equality of men and women, feminism and social justice,
which is just beginning to be recognized by certain elements in the
population. The effects of inventions are as various, then, as are the
different types of social organization.[2]

Sir Josiah Stamp, in discussing the impact of science upon
society, suggests among other things the change that has come
in our attitude toward speed. He says:

We have seen in a few years that the human or social temperament has a much wider range of tolerance than we had supposed.
We can take several popular examples. The reaction to altered
speed is prominent. In the *Greevey Papers,* it is recorded that the
Knowsley party accomplished twenty-three miles per hour on the
railway and recorded it as "frightful—impossible to divest yourself
of the notion of instant death—it gave me a headache which has not

---

[2] From The President's Research Committee, *Recent Social Trends in the
United States,* 1933, pp. 161, 162. By permission of the McGraw-Hill Book
Company.

left me yet—some damnable thing must come of it. I am glad to have seen this miracle, but quite satisfied with my first achievement being my last." In the British Association meeting for 1836, an address on "Railway Speeds" prophesied that some day fifty miles an hour might be possible. Forty years ago we may remember that a cyclist doing fifteen to eighteen miles an hour was a "scorcher" and a public danger. Twenty-five years ago, thirty miles an hour in motoring was an almost unhealthy and hardly bearable pace. To-day the fifties and sixties are easily borne, both by passenger and looker-on. Aeroplane speeds are differently judged, but at any rate represent an extension of the tolerance. . . .[3]

EFFECTS OF INVENTIONS ON INSTITUTIONAL CONTROLS [4]

. . . Very many of the great inventions following the so-called Industrial Revolution have been machines affecting industrial and economic life, namely, gasoline engines, motors, steamboats, chemical and metallurgical inventions. Very often, then, the first great social institution affected by these changes has been the economic organization.

Later derivative effects impinge on other social institutions, such as family, government, church. Thus, the great economic changes that followed the power inventions modified the organization of the family. Women went to work outside the home. Children were employed in factories. The home gradually lost its economic functions. The father ceased to be much of an employer or manager of household labor, at least in cities and towns. There followed a shift of authority from father and home to industry and State. In cities homes became quite limited as to space. More time was spent outside by the members of the family. In general, then, these changes in industry reacted on the family life.

In a similar way inventions have impinged upon government. In some industries the nature of invention was to encourage monopolistic corporations dealing in services used by a large number of individuals or other corporations. Hence governments took on regu-

---

[3] From Josiah Stamp, "The Impact of Science Upon Society," *Science*, September 11, 1936, p. 237. By permission of the Science Press.
[4] From The National Resources Committee, *Technological Trends and National Policy* (selection by W. F. Ogburn), pp. 9, 10, U. S. Government Printing Office, June, 1937. Reprinted by permission of the National Resources Committee, and available at the Superintendent of Documents, Washington, D. C.

latory functions as in the case of the public utilities. Taxation measures shifted from general property, tariffs, and excises on consumption goods to taxes on personal and corporate incomes and on inheritances. In many other ways the government was forced to extend its functions, as in the case of interstate commerce. City governments, especially, had to assume many more activities than those exercised by counties, where wealth was produced largely on farms without the use of power machines.

Thus, the great inventions which first changed industry produced derivative effects on other social institutions, such as government and the family. Finally these, in turn, have produced still another derivative effect upon social views and political philosophies. The attitude toward the philosophy of laissez faire eventually undergoes change as more and more governmental services are demanded, despite professions of the old faith to the contrary. The philosophy regarding home changes too. It is not so clear under the new conditions of the machine age that woman's place is in the home or that the authority of paternalism in the family is exercised as wisely as it was thought to be in the days of our forefathers. Also attitudes toward recreation and leisure time change, with city conditions and repetitive labor in factories. That these attitudes are so slow to change and are often near the last of the derivative effects of invention may appear surprising. It is true that these new attitudes always appear quite early with some few advanced individuals, leaders, and martyrs. The social philosophies of the mass of citizens do not change so early. Observation seems to indicate that the ideational philosophies hang on, become subjects of reverence, and are in general the last to change in any large way.

In concluding the observations of the way technologies exercise influence, an invention may be likened to a billiard ball, which strikes another ball, which in turn still another, and so on until the force is spent. Changes are started on one institution which impinge on others, and those on still others. There is great variety in these sequences; but in the past in many important cases the change occurred first in the technology, which changed the economic institutions, which in turn changed the social and governmental organizations, which finally changed the social beliefs and philosophies. This conclusion does not preclude, of course, the importance and prevalence of other social forces originating from sources other than invention and following this or other sequences. . . .

Technicways in Contemporary Society

Howard W. Odum has advanced the hypothesis that behavior patterns which arise as a consequence of modern techniques are different in origin and character from folkways and mores which originated through a long-time process of evolution in non-scientific cultures. In a preliminary article he has suggested what he means by the term "technicways" and has indicated that these differ from folkways and mores. He has also shown the extensive development of technicways in contemporary culture. His discussion is suggestive of the extent to which what he calls technicways influence social regulation and change behavior patterns. A part of it is reproduced below.

. . . The principal assumption of this paper is that, in contemporary civilization, at least as it is found in Western Culture, the technicways, transcending the folkways and supplanting the mores, tend to so modify human behavior and institutions as to outmode the earlier, natural rate of societal evolution. In particular, the tendency is to accelerate the rate of change in behavior patterns as well as in technological processes, and therefore the rate of cultural evolution. The tendency may be further to modify the whole behavior and character of the people. Thus in his Revolt of the Masses, Ortega complains of the immorality of European peoples who accept all from science, give nothing in return, demand more and more, thus surrendering the evolutionary processes of the folkways, mores, and character conditioning.

The practical implications of such a postulate are two. One is that technicways, quick products of science and technology, resulting in multiple artificial patterns and stateways, susceptible of manipulation by minorities and by machine economy, by exceeding the capacity of the people and of their living institutions to adapt, will likely augment the incidence of societal disintegration. Illustrations are legion. The technicways which emerge from the mating of technology with super-capitalistic economy might give new dominance to economic determinism; or combined with super-political technics, give new dominance to dictatorship through such mass control as radio or security paternalism, or combined with super-cultural patterns give such dominance to hedonistic determinism as would preclude the natural reproduction of the race. So, too, technicways may tend to accelerate the rate of evolution in such areas as race, rural and urban culture, agrarian to industrial society, sex relations and population policies, war and class conflict, values and the arts, occupation and health, religion and morality. Whether the changes, so accelerated, are desired or interesting changes, or merely forced, mechanical changes, will affect the enduring equilibrium and evolution of society.

The second assumption of practical application, contrariwise, is that through social science and social invention, now possibly available for the first time, the *technicways* may be utilized through social planning to set the incidence for continuing societal evolution which will insure social survival through social mastery of physical technology. Here again, illustrations are legion. By the same token as above indicated in the acceleration of societal evolution, the *technicways* may be set to achieving fairer economic practices, better race relations, nearer parity and equilibrium between agriculture and industry, more effective methods of attaining peace, the reintegration of human values, and the long catalogue of proposed developments in the field of social amelioration and direction. Involved, of course, are such common historical concepts as keeping close to the people, education for adaptation, the mastery of machines by men, science in the service of society, liberty, equality, fraternity. . . .

. . . In contradistinction to the *folkways* which arise, no one knows where and how, the *technicways* emerge demonstrably through the incidence of science and invention and their use in the realm of social life. *Folkways* are customs and habits which grow up naturally to meet needs, and they ripen through sanction and maturity into mores. Not so *technicways*, which arise from the pressure of technological forces and procedures to impel conformity of individual and group to quick-changing patterns, regardless of empirical considerations or of mass sanction. Thus, "fashions" superimposed through the technics of advertising do not represent the tastes of individuals or groups, nor do they reflect the gradual evolution from one style to another. Such fashions are not folkways to meet needs but *technicways* to fall in line with pressure or gadgets of the market place.

Technicways, it should be re-emphasized, are not the ways of technology; they are not *technics*. *Technicways* are the *ways of adjustment to technology*, of adaptation to an age of science which, through invested capital, is becoming well-nigh universal in its application to human use. Thus the Century of Progress Exposition at Chicago in 1933 was not the picturization of a hundred years of science, as was originally postulated, but it was the story of what science through invested capital was doing to and for mankind. Many of the exhibits were frankly projected to emphasize "psychological obsolescence" from which would come quick turnabout to new practices.

It is in this distinction between technics or the physical incidence of technology and the resulting social processes that *technicways* find definitive place and meaning. Again illustrations are abundant. There is little difficulty in distinguishing between, on the one hand, the technics of moving pictures or the earlier *folkways* and *mores* of parents with reference to children and the movies, and the current *technicways* reflected in a weekly attendance of eleven million children, involving long and improper hours, at moving pictures, 80 percent of which feature crime, sex, "love." So far this is contrary to both *folkways* and *mores*, yet the attendance increases.

So, too, the technics of special advertisements and of the marvels of cigarette manufacturing are not synonymous with, but are the incidence of, those *technicways* of women smokers and of the public opinion which have transcended the slow-moving *folkways* and *mores* gradually built up through custom and "morality."

In the old order, the *stateways* grow out of the *mores* which emerge through the *folkways*. The order of emergence appeared to be: *folkways, mores, stateways,* modifying *stateways,* nullifying *stateways,* new series of *folkways* and *mores,* and so on, requiring *time quality,* as well as cultural character. The *stateways* are ways of organizational society, whether government or church or co-operative community, to meet the needs of sovereignty or control. Under the technological order, the *stateways* come more quickly through a simple succession of exploratory *technicways,* enduring *technicways, stateways,* in which there is neither time nor disposition for intermediary *folkways* and *mores.*

Another illustration in which *technicways* may be said to accelerate certain desired ends is found in the case of whites and Negroes riding together in the increasing bus traffic in the South. Bus travel transcends the railroad in many instances; but, two systems cannot be justified. At first no Negroes are permitted to ride. Injunction and mandate are threatened. The experiment of having both races accommodated is forced by the technology of the situation. The *technicways* win and the *stateways* are established in state and interstate rulings. Yet no new *folkways* and *mores*, by their very definition, could be responsible for this change.

Another illustration, involving an important set of *mores* may be cited. The older *mores* of war implied the necessity for struggle for the survival of the fittest, for the development of courage and character, and the contrariwise elimination of the weak and of surplus population. The new technics of war, as when a bombing plane drops explosives on army or city, is no respecter of strong or weak, making imperative the need for *technicways* of peace, or else new *technicways* of war, outmoding the honorable rules of battle, will likely emerge. The long, hard struggle to create new *mores* for peace is in contrast to possible *technicways*, growing out of scientific and financial technology.

Our next definition seeks to identify the folk society with the natural society in contradistinction to organizational society. These terms must, of course, be relative and must serve as premise or base for more definitive terms. Approximate and analogous terms will be used to carry the definition as far as possible and authentic usages in social theory will be appealed to for support. Thus the natural society is envisaged in contrast to the technological or artificial society; the folk society in contrast to the *state* society; while from the "authorities" the range will extend from Herbert Spencer's evolutionary processes to Veblen's automatic self-conserving changes in man-machine economy.

Here again we must boldly assume our postulates in the face of the oft-repeated assertions that it is not possible to identify the marginal lines between the natural and the artificial and that we have no scientific measurements for either. It is possible, however, to give quite satisfactory preliminary definitions which are sufficient for further examination of the postulates. Thus, the primary occupations, agriculture, hunting, fishing, lumbering, mining, are "natural" occupations in contradistinction to the several hundred types of activities, sheltering new classes of workers, as found throughout the fields of commerce, industry, office, clerical and social services. Or in the development of agriculture and mining, animate power of man and beast represent the "natural" primary occupation as opposed to the machine mass processes of later development. The subsistence farm stands in contrast to commercial farming. So, too, the rural is natural as compared to the urban, measured in terms of societal evolution from the first stages to those of metal and industrial civilizations. These are secondary and technical as opposed to primary and natural. . . .[5]

CULTURAL LAG AND PROBLEMS OF CONTROL

Ogburn, in discussing maladjustments in culture as they relate to machine technology, has advanced the thesis and demonstrated the proposition that machine technology tends to change more rapidly than related culture in the non-material sphere.[6] Chapin has produced further evidence to prove that the more rapid change of technological culture tends to put this material culture out of adjustment with the mores, controls, and general definitions that people live by. Eventually new inventions in the non-material realm tend to cure the maladjustment.[7]

Again and again in our culture this type of thing has happened. Women begin working in factories, the meaning of the family changes, the relation between the sexes is modified, and then years afterward we begin to adapt our philosophy of life, our system of ethics, our notion of morals, in fact, our entire system of control, to fit the new situations induced years earlier by the machine pattern.

New machinery in forestry, agriculture, and mining has developed a widespread program of exploitation of natural resources such as the world has never before seen. This exploitation goes on unhindered by legislation, unfavorable public opinion, and other controls that would check it, and on the positive side lead to conservation. Not until our resources approach the dangerous point of exhaustion do we become alarmed about reforestation, the conservation of soil, and of mineral resources, and begin to impose restrictions and to develop programs of positive action—fifty years later than we should have.

So also we build factories in which we exploit the human animal, maim him, develop dangerous machinery which sometimes takes his life. We set up an industrial system where men, women

---

[5] From Howard W. Odum, "Notes on Technicways in Contemporary Society," *American Sociological Review*, 1937, vol. 2, pp. 337–341. By permission of the American Sociological Society.

[6] William F. Ogburn, *Social Change*, Part 3.

[7] F. S. Chapin, *Cultural Change*, Part 3.

and children are exploited for the sake of profit. We develop an economic structure as a counterpart of this industrial system, wherein a man must work for money alone and depend upon money to buy him other values and services and goods in order that he may live. In every respect we rob him of security. His tools are gone; they have become a part of the factory system. His independence and initiative are gone; he is directed by a factory foreman. His contact with the soil and other resources by which he might have made a living are gone; he has had to become a city dweller. He is placed on an impersonal level where he has no contact with the employer. In fact, his employer often is not a man but an impersonal capitalistic structure, described nowadays as a "soulless corporation." In this new system of life we provide the individual with no economic protection.

Fifty to seventy-five years late we develop social legislation protecting women and children from exploitation under the factory system, protecting men workers against industrial hazards, by accident insurance and death benefit plans. Only very recently has the common man been given a measure of security through the development of unemployment insurance, pensions, and annuities.

Briefly, in the field of social control all of this means that we have not yet learned to harness technology effectively and quickly, so as to avoid the problems in human readjustment entailed in technological development. There is a lag in the mechanism of control which prevents the quick adaptation of the social system to the newly created necessities of a mechanical age.

A lag also frequently exists between various complexes of machine culture calling for new and more effective devices of control. More foresight in the realm of regulation is needed. We multiply the number of automobiles faster than we can widen city streets. We concentrate population more rapidly than we can improve water systems, sewage disposal systems, and other services essential to health in places where great aggregates of population assemble. We develop new means for the propagation of ideas long before we develop effective restraints on the kind of ideas that should be propagated.

We develop an efficient technology in medicine but are still trying to operate under the old system of private payments at the terrible cost of more than 200,000 needless deaths per year.[6] The irony of the situation is that the American Medical Association is the most militant enemy of health insurance and socialized medicine—group payment plans that would put the new technology within the reach of the multitude who annually pay for poverty by sickness and death. This is an amazing lag, in a nation that avails us of medical schools on a tax-supported basis.

It would seem that social science has a wonderful opportunity to develop intelligent controls in a technological age, and if lags between the development of material culture and social controls are to be avoided it must do so. Only through a close study of some of the possible effects of the release of a new machine on human relationships can we allay the dire consequences.

Ogburn, in discussing this problem, raised the question as to who could predict the effect of an invention on a culture, once it were developed. Who could have foreseen the far-reaching effects of the steam engine on almost every phase of Western life? This question is enough to indicate that intelligent social control in relation to technology is not a simple problem, and that social science cannot hope to solve it soon if it can ever completely do so. But it can help to soften the shock of readjustment by the application of intelligence to the problem. Few people could have foreseen what the automobile would do to old patterns of courtship, the stimulus it would give to the romantic impulse, the extent to which it would break down sex taboos and make for sex license. Neither could anyone have foreseen all of the effects of the electric light upon family and recreational patterns. On the other hand, we can predict at least a few results in connection with most inventions, and by the development of intelligent control devices we can reduce to some extent the lag in adjustment between the technological aspect of man's experience and the regulative aspect.

TECHNOLOGY AND THE LIFE PHILOSOPHY OF PROGRESS

Progress as a dominant concept in human thinking is to a large extent a product of the machine age, and is kept alive by mechani-

---

[6] This is according to findings of a U. S. Technical Committee on Medical Care, reported in 1938. For a popular summary of various aspects of the social effects of the present medical system see "Diagnosing the Doctors," *The Reader's Digest*, August, 1938, pp. 1–5; it also appears in *The American Magazine*, June, 1938.

cal invention. Most early civilizations conceived of the great life as having already been lived. Utopia was in the past; the golden age had already been. Man had fallen from a previous high state and could never hope to return to it as far as his present life was concerned, although he did hope to attain it in the hereafter. Today quite the opposite philosophy has permeated Western society. Man has become habituated to accepting the new, and conditioned to expecting that the new will be better than the old. The modern advertiser using modern means for diffusion has demonstrated to the public that the device of yesterday is outmoded. And wherever machine civilization exists, the same dynamic lesson is borne home. One who has seen the automobile of 1900 and compared it with the machine of today can no longer speak of the past as being the glorious age. Such object lessons face the average man in his daily experience again and again, and bear home to him the emphatic truth that in the realm of technological devices the past is bad, the present is good, and the future must be far better.

In a technological age men live in the midst of numerous technological devices. Experience becomes colored with the desire for the new, and a certain confidence that the new will be better. Such thinking becomes a habit of mind, and is applied not only to machine techniques but to all of life. In past ages civilization had not yet flowered; men were groping in ignorance and superstition; science had not become the hand maiden of humanity.

Of course the past was drab. Sixty years ago we had no electric light; forty years ago we had no automobile or airplane; twenty years ago we had no radio. The present is glorious. Today television is appearing on the scene, along with air conditioning and traveling in the stratosphere at unheard of speeds. Certainly tomorrow holds promise, so men in a scientific age are inclined to reflect.

Even a great financial depression can only temporarily dull the Western man's faith in progress as a universal law of civilization, in fact, as a universal law of man. It may be true that man's faith in progress as demonstrated by the machine is not applicable to other realms of his experience, but, be that as it may, the machine has taught progress. It has taught the value of change. It has made the mysterious come to be commonplace. It has given man a grip of what was once supposed to be supernatural, and brought it into the control of a purely natural realm.

The implications of this philosophy to potential social control are almost incomprehensible. Today in a world where technology has demonstrated the advantages of foresight and planning, where each year various important spheres of man's life are completely revolutionized, where man has faith in the tools he works with, there has opened a way for the regulation of the affairs of man with reference to preconceived ends such as the world has never seen. It is true we are not yet trying to control by these devices toward certain ends, except in limited spheres, because we have not decided upon ends to be sought in larger spheres. If we were to conceive larger ends, the tools are at hand for the making of a new type of progress.

The Place of Social Science in an Age of Technology

Natural science applied to the world of raw materials is rapidly transforming the life of modern man through technology, the product of invention. This creative force remakes man's material world, and because man's nature is changed by the world he lives in, technology becomes a part of him, and of his relationships. Whether one considers the machine of today a Frankenstein monster or one hundred million horsepower at man's service is a matter of viewpoint, but regardless of the stand taken all must acknowledge that machines make man a different creature than he would be without them. Even the most optimistic are compelled to recognize that machines are primarily responsible for many of the problems that plague our social order. Whether one interprets these problems in terms of lag between mechanical change and change in social adaptation or by some other terminology matters little. The fact remains that man has not fully adapted his life to the machine and is constantly being shocked out of old ways of living and thinking by new inventions.

It would seem that in a world of this character social science should come to play a larger part in speeding up the adjustment of behavior patterns and control devices to technical change. Greater skill in predicting the probable effects of new inventions would hasten the invention of new control devices. Social science has been building on a broad foundation and it is not too much to hope that it will be able to realize such aims. After all, natural science had many years start on social science, and a technological age was upon us when the social sciences were still in their swaddling clothes.

CONCLUSION

The major difficulty with modern technology which bears on the problem of social control is that it disturbs social relations to the extent that values lose their meaning, established habits become out of place, old definitions for behavior rapidly become obsolete. Personality is less elastic than the mechanical structure in which it is molded. The machine revolution has not only created widespread unemployment by the machine displacement of men, but it has destroyed integrated life patterns of whole communities and of whole generations, has made old moral codes so obsolete that many old definitions and human values no longer apply. Charity no longer means what it once did in simple society. The very practice of the old form of neighborly charity is now condemned as immoral, since the government has found it necessary to administer as a part of its social responsibility a professionally directed relief program. The moral standard in family relationships no longer seems to be to multiply and replenish the earth, but rather to control reproduction in the light of one's economic self-sufficiency. We are coming to define unlimited propagation in the family, without any possibility of supporting the offspring, as an unmoral exercise.

So technology may even interfere seriously with deep-seated customs. With regard to the use of tobacco by women, under our present system of machine production of cigarettes, and machine production of advertising, and machine made means of diffusion, the nonsmoker is almost a social misfit in some circles. Smoking becomes a mark of sex equality, an index of a new freedom, one which has been brought about by carefully planned advertising designed to reward with net profits the great corporations which control the technology. Even the Orient is brought under the influence of the advertising of these corporations, and a new market among both sexes is created abroad, regardless of what it may cost the oriental nations in the way of disruption of established patterns.

Thus inventions and technology have become the chief agencies of social change in our modern dynamic society, not only changing habits on the mechanical side, but making an impact on morals, religion, values, in fact, on the entire system of social control. Age-old mores and folkways give place to "technicways." The disintegration of the old controls brings in the new.

Social science is rapidly developing a foundation, first, for understanding the problem of control in a technological age, and second, for predicting the effects of techniques on behavior, and is thereby hastening the invention of new regulative devices to suit the conditions which the new age of technology creates.

SELECTED REFERENCES

Bossard, Joseph H. S., *Social Change and Social Problems*, revised edition, chap. 7. Harper and Brothers, New York, 1938.

Chapin, F. S., *Cultural Change*, parts 3 and 4. D. Appleton-Century Company, New York, 1928.

Chase, Stuart, "Gasless America," *The Nation*, vol. 123, pp. 586–587. 1926.

Chase, Stuart, *Men and Machines*, pp. 118–122. The Macmillan Company, New York, 1929.

Chase, Stuart, "My Great-Great-Grandfather and I," *The Nation*, vol. 123, pp. 190–192. 1926.

Cornelius, J. J., "An Oriental Looks at Christian Missions," *Harper's Magazine*, vol. 154, pp. 598–606. 1927.

Coyle, David C., and Others, *The American Way*, pp. 18–44. Harper and Brothers, New York, 1938.

Folsom, J. K., *The Family*, pp. 183–211. John Wiley and Sons, Inc., New York, 1934.

Gillette, John M., and Reinhardt, James M., *Current Social Problems*, pp. 778–780. American Book Company, New York, 1933.

Merz, Charles, "A New Turkey Challenges Islam," *Our World*, vol. 4, pp. 71–76. 1923–1924.

The National Resources Committee, *Technological Trends and National Policy*. United States Government Printing Office, Washington, D. C., June, 1937.

Odum, Howard W., "Notes on Technicways in Contemporary Society," *American Sociological Review*, vol. 2, pp. 336–346. June, 1937.

Ogburn, William F., editor, *Recent Social Changes for years 1927–*

1931 (published annually). University of Chicago Press, Chicago, 1927–1931.

Ogburn, William F., *Social Change*, part 4. The Viking Press, Inc., New York, 1923.

Pitt-Rivers, G., "The Effect on Native Races of Contact with European Civilisation," *Man*, vol. 27, pp. 2–7. 1927.

Rivers, W. H. R., *Essays on the Depopulation of Melanesia*, pp. xviii–116. Cambridge University Press, Cambridge, 1927.

Stamp, Josiah, "The Impact of Science Upon Society," *Science*, pp. 237 ff. September 11, 1936.

Wallis, Wilson D., and Willey, Malcolm M., *Readings in Sociology* (selection by L. S. Gannett, "Americanization and Social Change in China"), pp. 104–108. F. S. Crofts and Company, New York, 1932.

PART V

MEANS OF SOCIAL CONTROL

PART V

MEANS OF SOCIAL CONTROL

CHAPTER 19

MEANS OF SOCIAL CONTROL

GENERAL CLASSIFICATION OF MEANS OF SOCIAL CONTROL

Because of the great diversity of methods by which human beings are capable of influencing members of their kind, any adequate discussion of means of social control must necessarily take into account a wide range of specific devices. Some authors, however, have attempted to simplify the problem by defining two or three principal categories under which all means of control can be subsumed.

Each of the classifications which follow throw some light on the problem and help to clarify our understanding of the processes of social control. Since this is true, all points of view are worth consideration. It should be kept in mind, however, that probably a number of other equally imposing classifications might be developed. No doubt there are many ways of approaching the problem of social control, and this field, like any field in science, is a happy hunting ground in which anyone has the right to develop his theories in the hope that ultimately they will find a place in the general body of knowledge which will accumulate over a period of years.

PHYSICAL FORCE AND HUMAN SYMBOL METHODS [1]

Viewing the matter very broadly, we may say that there are two outstanding methods of procedure in this work of control, (1) the physical force method and (2) the human symbol method. For our purposes it is important to distinguish these two types clearly. Let us see what the methods would be in each case.

(1) When a workman wishes to impose his will upon a stone, he has to make applications of physical energy in some form. He cannot stand back and wish it away as is done in fairyland; he can-

---

[1] From Frederick E. Lumley, *Means of Social Control*, pp. 14-17. Used by permission of D. Appleton-Century Company, Publishers, New York, N. Y.

not command it to get up and move off. When the mother wishes to have a very young child take a bath, she is in the same situation as the man with the stone; she has to lift it up, carry it to the bath room, and do the scrubbing. When the policeman desires to have the arrested culprit go to jail, he has to reckon, not only with the dead weight of the man, often, but also with any resistance exerted, unless the prisoner volunteers to go along peaceably. In some cases, one policeman could not take a man to jail at all. There are many instances in our human relationships when order is maintained, will-transference is effected, by applications of physical force. Nothing else seems to succeed.

But, with physical control as the *only* means for the management of human beings, the maintenance of a *social* order would be impossible. . . .

(2) . . . man has developed a quicker, a more economical, a more personality-respecting, a more order-preserving way of procedure— the symbol way. This method is so old and so familiar that we never reflect upon its marvels; we never try to guess what would happen to human affairs if it were eliminated. But, we must never forget that the use of this method, not only in control but in many other relationships of life, lifts man to a new level and distinguishes him from other creatures. If man lost this art, he would rapidly degener- ate into some unimaginable form; his civilization would dissolve over night. The physical method is absurd because there is an infinitely better method. But what do we mean by the symbol method of control?

The gesture of pointing towards the door, for the purpose of conveying the idea, "Shut the door," is a symbol. We can write the word "apple" on the blackboard and immediately an image of an apple will come to mind; writing is all symbolism. We can wave the flag of our country and that activity arouses feeling and senti- ments of loyalty. Now the flag is, intrinsically, nothing but a piece of cloth with certain colors and marks on it. Of itself it is very little; but it *stands for* or *points toward* something else which is very differ- ent; it *represents* the country. The olive branch has come to stand for peace. H_2O stands for water. A figure of a portly old gentleman with a high hat, "John Bull," stands for England.

Man has gradually built up extensive systems composed of these symbols. A pantomime by some aesthetic dancers would be such a system. Language is such a system. The ritual in a church, a grand parade, the account books of a business firm, large libraries, are familiar examples of these symbol-systems. They are often very complex and stand for or call forth very complicated responses. They have been devised primarily for the purpose of moving people about in desired ways. The teacher says to the pupil: "Jimmie, go to the board and write out the lesson." This is a symbol-complex of sounds. If he extracts her meaning, if he gathers from these sounds the intention which she has for him and goes to work accordingly, we say that she has controlled him. Yet she did not *touch* him in the narrow sense; she did not *force* him in the physical sense; she *communicated* with him by symbols—sound symbols in this instance—and had her way with him by this means. This is the human way.

One of the best discussions of control through symbolic behavior is that by La Piere and Farnsworth.[2] Symbols, they hold, consist in those actions of human beings which have significance because they have socially designated meaning. They conceive of society as being primarily a system of symbols, and of social life as consisting to a considerable extent in the manipulation of these symbols. They also consider that behavior is controlled primarily in terms of symbols. Because we have these symbols, force is seldom required to keep the social order running. Most of our symbols take some form of speech—talking, writing, reading, thinking; or some form of gesture—looking, acting, or facial expression.

Thurman Arnold, in his *Symbols of Government*,[3] shows a deep appreciation of symbols which regulate governmental and economic affairs. He shows that these symbols represent for us the ideals of our system of government, and stresses the fact that social institutions generally require "faith and dreams to give them morale." They must appear beautiful and symmetrical and logical in order to command the respect of men and the adherence of followers. If man loses faith in these symbols we call him radical. "When belief in current symbols wavers, social unrest grows."

[2] Richard T. La Piere and Paul R. Farnsworth, *Social Psychology*, chaps. 4 and 5, McGraw-Hill Book Company, New York, 1936.
[3] T. W. Arnold, *The Symbols of Government*, Preface, chaps. 1, 10. See also his *Folklore of Capitalism*, Yale University Press, New Haven, 1937.

FORMAL AND INFORMAL CONTROLS

At least two authors have classified controls into formal and informal types.[4] Clark, in discussing social control in the field of business relations,[5] defines formal controls as those exercised primarily through the official "machinery of government and backed by compulsory mandates." Behind these formal controls are custom, tradition, religion, education, public opinion, and the like, which he designates informal controls. These informal controls operate much more directly, and are likely to be even more effective.

Kimball Young uses the same terms with quite the same meaning.[6] He thinks of formal controls as being those operated by the state through law and the various administrative devices consciously developed by the ruling body, whereas the informal controls consist of such traits as mores, public opinion, codes, ideals, religious convictions, and other traits which may have developed more or less unconsciously through trial and error. It is assumed that the informal controls precede the development of formal controls, and that formal controls come to play a dominant role in those complex societies in which personal, intimate, face-to-face relationships are minimized.

CONSCIOUS AND UNCONSCIOUS CONTROL

Cooley talked in terms of conscious control and unconscious control, and concluded that the aim of intelligence is to achieve a more rational conscious control of society.[7] He believed that while we should continue to allow most of the details of life and society to be run on a habit and instinctive level, we should also give attention to the larger phases of social organization, trying to understand somewhat how the society ought to work, and exerting the necessary authority at the proper time and place to improve its working.

It will be remembered that Russell Gordon Smith preferred

---

[4] Other authors employ the classification, though they do not define it. See, for instance, Carl A. Dawson and Warner E. Gettys, *Introduction to Sociology*, revised edition, pp. 612–614, The Ronald Press Company, New York, 1935.

[5] John M. Clark, *Social Control of Business*, pp. 221–223.

[6] Kimball Young, *An Introductory Sociology*, pp. 523–524, American Book Company, New York, 1934.

[7] Charles H. Cooley, *Social Process*, pp. 382–383.

to apply the term social control only to that control rationally
and consciously directed.[8]

REWARDS AND PUNISHMENTS

Giddings finds that the constraint exercised by society can be
reduced to rewards and punishments.[9] Because men faced praise
and blame, avoidance and rebuke, indulgence and license, pen-
ance and fine, suspension and expulsion, corporal punishment
and maiming, imprisonment and execution, they learned to submit and to obey. It is through this educative process that men
are forced into accepting the approved modes of conduct. Toward
the perfection of discipline, and the firm establishment of standards of behavior, and the building of character in line with these
standards, society consciously directs its efforts. First this direction is blundering, but with social experience it becomes more
skillful. Folkways come to incorporate the more effective methods of social discipline, stateways the cruder forms, but always
the society must maintain conformity to a type of standard
which it has established as essential to social efficiency. The
object in view from the outset of social development has been
to diminish the failures and multiply the successes of human beings in their struggle for existence.

EDUCATION AND SOCIALIZATION AND SANCTIONS

Gillette and Reinhardt state that there are two general modes
by which social control operates: (1) education and socialization, and (2) sanctions; i.e., rewards and penalties. They say:

. . . Society exercises social control over its members by means of
two general modes. One of these is education and socialization.
Under this process the minds and characters of individuals are
gradually directed and trained so as to adjust themselves harmoniously to the demands and needs of society. The other is control by
sanctions. Under this system, society sets up rewards and penalties
external to the personalities of the social members and so induces
or coerces individuals to perform the work, the duties, and to make
the adjustments it desires. Modern states resort to both methods
but, since it is so much easier to use force and to set up penalties

---

[8] Refer again to Chapter 1.
[9] Franklin H. Giddings, "Studies in the Theory of Human Society," p. 206.

than to create appealing rewards for conduct, the former is largely in the ascendent. Our laws are the expression of control by sanctions and they are usually accompanied by penalties for violation. Since law is largely the foundation of government, and government is the central legislative and administrative organ of the state, the latter is seen to operate dominantly by means of sanctions.[10]

PATERNAL CONTROL AND SOCIAL CONTROL

Dowd, looking back through centuries of human experience, concludes that paternal control came first, social control having been developed only in more recent times, with the growth of democracies.[11]

He uses the term paternal control to cover that period in the evolution of society in which society was relatively undifferentiated, in which leadership played the prime role in control, leadership such as that exercised by the paternalistic father in the family, the king in the state, the priest in the religious order, and the master in the workshop. In this stage of development, control was largely in the folkways and mores, and was exercised only by authoritative leaders. Not until this paternalistic system of control disappeared did social control develop.

He applies the term social control to complex societies in which leadership has become widely diffused and differentiated, in which special organizations and activities have developed, so that a large number of people, in fact, eventually the majority, or the collective whole, come to exercise control. Thus, he is using the term social control to refer to democratic control. He feels that the transition from paternal control to social control took place gradually down through the years of history so that one cannot mark the exact time of the transition.

DEVICES ESTABLISHING ORDER AND THOSE MAINTAINING IT

No dual system of classification of control devices has been entirely satisfactory, and it seems doubtful that any can be made that will be serviceable, except for specific purposes of analysis. For certain purposes, the classifications discussed have usefulness. In fact, in the early part of this book, we made use of the

---

[10] John M. Gillette and James M. Reinhardt, *Current Social Problems*, p. 759. By permission of American Book Company.
[11] Jerome Dowd, *Control in Human Societies*, pp. 136, 137, 147.

classification of conscious, deliberate, rational means of control as compared to unconscious, spontaneous, unplanned methods. These concepts have meaning and utility. The same is true of the arrangement into formal and informal means, which carry much the same connotation as those just mentioned.

But while simple, dual classificatory schemes are at times useful, they are never adequate. How much less adequate then is any effort to isolate specific control devices from the *milieu* of social processes. Such attempts at best give but a sketchy and unrealistic picture of the process of social control. Yet, there is some value in isolating devices and trying to see how they operate. Many books have been written with just such an end in view.[12]

It has already been observed that this book gives little space to specific means of social control. The writer has felt that a more useful picture of control devices can be given by showing them at work in their natural setting. Thus, rather than discuss such factors as propaganda, advertising, and public opinion as control devices, he has shown them in operation in our secondary group society, with its numerous agencies of mass impression (chap. 12) and in economic (chap. 15) and governmental (chap. 17) institutions. Instead of describing such devices as ridicule, social pressure, and gossip, as such, he has shown how they work in the primary group (chap. 10) and in social institution of a primary group nature (chap. 13).

We have assumed in the development of this book that a fairly useful two-fold classification of social control devices might be made, along the following lines: (1) devices that are essential to the establishment of order and (2) devices that maintain order. Obviously, there are many devices that lie in both fields, in fact, most of them do to some extent, but even so, the classification has some meaning if the viewpoint of this work is accepted.

Under the heading of devices that establish order are included all devices and social processes employed in the building of personality for the social system. As should be clear by now, this work conceives control fundamentally to consist of the socializa-

---

[12] One of the most interesting is Lumley's *Means of Social Control*. Numbers of books dealing with public opinion or some phase of it as a control device have appeared, and books written on such subjects as advertising and propaganda as control devices are numerous.

tion of the individual, so that he embodies in his personality the patterns of his social group and conforms generally in his likes and dislikes, values and habits, to the patterns of the cultural structure in which he is to function. Or to state it in slightly different words, control is established by building human nature from raw, original nature, through the educative process, which, broadly conceived, covers the entire process of socialization.

The process of maintaining order, that is, of enforcing social rules, is a part of the process by which personality is built. One learns by being reproved in a thousand ways, some subtle, some overt, some mild, some brutal. But after socialization is complete, after society has done its best to build human nature, the job frequently is found to be not well done. Many individuals reach maturity, when the organism loses its plasticity and becomes relatively rigid, without having acquired the social patterns that are essential to a self-control, adequate for purposes of social control. Hence, society must maintain devices for enforcing order. Even very socialized individuals never entirely lose their original nature. Beneath the superstructure of social habits and social values lies hidden the raw nature of natural man. Social threats are needed to help enforce social habit. Even the church has had to hold over the convert the threat of damnation, in case he succumbs to temptation and backslides. There is, then, a kit of tools which the social order uses to hold the machinery together and to "tighten the screws" on offenders. As has been stated, these devices do not always stand out clearly from those that are employed to establish order, but there is enough difference so that the classification has utility.

The sketchy descriptions of isolated control devices which follow, arranged according to the dual classification mentioned above, are not complete or exhaustive.

Special Control Devices Employed in Building Social Order

The most important means of building social order is to train the individual to conform with the dominant ideals of the given society. This is done through the process of conditioning the individual to habitual patterns of life. Society has many means by which group-accepted habits and attitudes are formed.

William James, in a classic discussion of habit formation,

showed the steps in the development of successful and effective habits. These included repetition without permitting an exception to occur, and opportunity to keep the habit established by exercising it frequently.[13]

The following paragraphs illustrate ways in which society conducts a part of this process of establishing social habits and attitudes. It will be seen that culture patterns have provided elaborate devices whereby the individual is thoroughly grounded in what the group considers social habits and attitudes.

Ceremony, the original form of regulation. Herbert Spencer, in his work, *Principles of Sociology*, places considerable emphasis on ceremonial, ecclesiastical, and political institutions as devices for social control. He conceives of these institutions as regulating human conduct, because they, more than other institutions, are concerned with restraining and directing behavior. He holds that ceremonial institutions were the *most* fundamental, appearing first in societies as an outgrowth of fear of the supernatural, but giving way to political and ecclesiastical institutions as the society advanced.

If, disregarding conduct that is entirely private, we consider only that species of conduct which involves direct relations with other persons; and if under the name government we include all control of such conduct, however arising; then we must say that the earliest kind of government, the most general kind of government, and the government which is ever spontaneously recommencing, is the government of ceremonial observance. More may be said. This kind of government, besides preceding other kinds, and besides having in all places and times approached nearer to universality of influence, has ever had, and continues to have, the largest share in regulating men's lives.

. . . daily intercourse among the lowest savages, whose small loose groups, scarcely to be called social, are without political or religious regulation, is under a considerable amount of ceremonial regulation. No ruling agency, beyond that arising from personal superiority, characterizes a horde of Australians; but every such horde has imperative observance. Strangers meeting must remain some time silent; a mile from an encampment, approach has to be heralded by loud

---

[13] William James, *Principles of Psychology*, chap. 4, Henry Holt and Company, New York, 1890.

cooeys; a green bough is used as an emblem of peace; and brotherly feeling is indicated by exchange of names. Similarly, the Tasmanians, equally devoid of government save that implied by predominance of a leader during war, had settled ways of indicating peace and defiance. The Esquimaux, too, though without social ranks or anything like chieftainship, have understood usages for the treatment of guests. Kindred evidence may be joined with this. Ceremonial control is highly developed in many places where other forms of control are but rudimentary. The wild Comanche "exacts the observance of his rules of etiquette from strangers," and "is greatly offended" by any breach of them. When Araucanians meet, the inquiries, felicitations, and condolences which custom demands, are so elaborate that "the formality occupies ten or fifteen minutes." Of the ungoverned Bedouins we read that "their manners are sometimes dashed with a strange ceremoniousness;" and the salutations of Arabs are such that the "compliments in a well-bred man never last less than ten minutes." "We were particularly struck," says Livingstone, "with the punctiliousness of manners shown by the Balonda." "The Malagasy have many different forms of salutation, of which they make liberal use . . . Hence in their general intercourse there is much that is stiff, formal, and precise." A Samoan orator, when speaking in Parliament, "is not contented with a mere word of salutation, such as 'gentlemen,' but he must, with great minuteness, go over the names and titles, and a host of ancestral references, of which they are proud."

That ceremonial restraint, preceding other forms of restraint, continues ever to be the most widely-diffused form of restraint, we are shown by such facts as that in all intercourse between members of each society, the decisively governmental actions are usually prefaced by this government of observances. The embassy may fail, negotiation may be brought to a close by war, coercion of one society by another may set up wider political rule with its peremptory commands; but there is habitually this more general and vague regulation of conduct preceding the more special and definite. So within a community, acts of relatively stringent control coming from ruling agencies, civil and religious, begin with and are qualified by, this ceremonial control; which not only initiates but, in a sense, envelops all other. Functionaries, ecclesiastical and political, coercive as their proceedings may be, conform them in large measure to the requirements of courtesy. The priest, however arrogant his assumption, makes a civil salute; and the officer of the law performs his duty subject to certain propitiatory words and movements.

Yet another indication of primordialism may be named. This species of control establishes itself anew with every fresh relation among individuals. Even between intimates, greetings signifying continuance of respect begin each renewal of intercourse. And in presence of a stranger, say in a railway-carriage, a certain self-restraint, joined with some small act like the offer of a newspaper, shows the spontaneous rise of propitiatory behaviour such as even the rudest of mankind are not without.

So that the modified forms of action caused in men by the presence of their fellows, constitute that comparatively vague control out of which other more definite controls are evolved—the primitive undifferentiated kind of government from which the political and religious governments are differentiated, and in which they ever continue immersed.[14]

Ritual as a means of habituating the individual to group practices and attitudes.

. . . Ritual is the perfect form of drill and of the regulated habit which comes from drill. Acts which are ordained by authority and are repeated mechanically without intelligence run into ritual. If infants and children are subjected to ritual they never escape from its effects through life. Galton says that he was, in early youth, in contact with the Mohammedan ritual idea that the left hand is less worthy than the right, and that he never overcame it. We see the effect of ritual in breeding, courtesy, politeness, and all forms of prescribed behavior. Etiquette is social ritual. Ritual is not easy compliance with usage; it is strict compliance with detailed and punctilious rule. It admits of no exception or deviation. The stricter the discipline, the greater the power of ritual over action and character. In the training of animals and the education of children it is the perfection, inevitableness, invariableness, and relentlessness of routine which tells. They should never experience any exception or irregularity. Ritual is connected with words, gestures, symbols, and signs. Associations result, and, upon a repetition of the signal, the act is repeated, whether the will assents or not. Association and habit account for the phenomena. Ritual gains further strength when it is

---

[14] From Herbert Spencer, *The Principles of Sociology*, ¶ 343, vol. 2. Used by permission of D. Appleton-Century Company, Publishers, New York, N. Y.

rhythmical, and is connected with music, verse, or other rhythmical arts. Acts are ritually repeated at the recurrence of the rhythmical points. The alternation of night and day produces rhythms of waking and sleeping, of labor and rest, for great numbers at the same time, in their struggle for existence. The seasons also produce rhythms in work. Ritual may embody an idea of utility, expediency, or welfare, but it always tends to become perfunctory, and the idea is only subconscious. There is ritual in primitive therapeutics, and it was not eliminated until very recent times. The patient was directed, not only to apply remedies, but also to perform rites. The rites introduced mystic elements. This illustrates the connection of ritual with notions of magical effects produced by rites. All ritual is ceremonious and solemn. It tends to become sacred, or to make sacred the subject-matter with which it is connected. Therefore, in primitive society, it is by ritual that sentiments of awe, deference to authority, submission to tradition, and disciplinary cooperation are inculcated. Ritual operates a constant suggestion, and the suggestion is at once put in operation in acts. Ritual, therefore, suggests sentiments, but it never inculcates doctrines. Ritual is strongest when it is most perfunctory and excites no thought. By familiarity with ritual any doctrinal reference which it once had is lost by familiarity, but the habits persist. Primitive religion is ritualistic, not because religion makes ritual, but because ritual makes religion. Ritual is something to be done, not something to be thought or felt. Men can always perform the prescribed act, although they cannot always think or feel prescribed thoughts or emotions. The acts may bring up again, by association, states of the mind and sentiments which have been connected with them, especially in childhood, when the fantasy was easily affected by rites, music, singing, dramas, etc. No creed, no moral code, and no scientific demonstration can ever win the same hold upon men and women as habits of action, with associated sentiments and states of mind, drilled in from childhood. Mohammedanism shows the power of ritual. Any occupation is interrupted for the prayers and prescribed genuflections. The Brahmins also observe an elaborate daily ritual. They devote to it two hours in the morning, two in the evening, and one at midday. Monks and nuns have won the extreme satisfaction of religious sentiment from the unbroken habit of repeated ritual. . . .[15]

---

[15] From William Graham Sumner, *Folkways*, pp. 60–62. By permission of Ginn and Company.

Codes as a means of standardizing group practices.

So far as people agree in matters of ethics or conduct they establish codes, and such codes, whether or not they embody ultimate ideals or absolute right, are powerful forces for the control of those who come under their influence. Those who accept the code fully are coerced through their own consciences as well as through the pressure brought to bear by their fellows. Those who reject the code utterly may feel no pricks of conscience in violating it, but they still feel the social pressure, except as they can form a morally independent community with its own moral code, such as that of professional criminals or revolutionists.[16]

Tradition as a blue print.

. . . The role of tradition in social life, like that of heredity in physiological life, is to hand down a portion of the past, to wit, the stream of impelling tendencies which carry over from one generation to another. As heredity establishes continuity between successive generations in a given biological species, so tradition perpetuates within the respective social groups the characteristic ideas and standards. Like heredity, tradition does not hand down all the traits of predecessors. Each is a selective influence, in the main perpetuating only fundamental characteristics. No social group which is also a culture group is, therefore, without tradition; indeed it is frequently said that savages have no other guide. If one asks them why they do a certain thing they reply, "this is what our fathers told us," or, "so it was in the long ago." But this aspect of savage life has been exaggerated. Everywhere savages are guided by tradition, but also everywhere they show an ability to escape certain portions of the past. All tribes have accounts of the past representing phases which they neither embody nor seek to embody in actual regime. In short, savages are perhaps no more bound to the past than are civilized peoples. We tend to rationalize present action and to give logical reasons for our behavior, whereas repeatedly the real reason is not the one we proffer, but is merely our disposition to adhere to the past. Savages, on the other hand, admit that they do things because their ancestors did them; indeed they proclaim the fact.

Tradition plays a dominant role in all important civilizations; in

---

[16] From John M. Clark, *Social Control of Business*, p. 223. By permission of the University of Chicago Press.

fact the extent to which a civilization has advanced is correlated with the degree to which its traditions have advanced. Greece and Rome attained their highest achievements at a time when tradition had a strong hold. The low ebb of civilization from the third century A.D. to the twelfth, or thereabouts, was synchronous with the low ebb of tradition. Only when the tradition of Western Europe attached itself to Greek and Roman civilization was there a renaissance. Tradition gave stability to the Church, making it the great power of the Middle Ages. French civilization did not develop characteristic traits until the peoples of France shared a common tradition.

In England tradition has had a firm hold upon the national culture. The continuity of English culture and English national development is insured less by institutions and government as such than by traditions. The deeper the roots of tradition, the greater its permanence, and the greater the possibilities of orderly continuous development. France, less obedient to tradition, passes from revolution to revolution while effecting important social and political changes, whereas England, a country in which tradition holds sway, follows its leading strings from evolution to evolution. No country of Western Europe has shown such stability as has England, none has shown such logical and continuous development, none has been such a stronghold of tradition. When revolutionary changes are brought into line with tradition they become evolutionary; social stability is not theatened, but accommodation to tradition facilitates transition to a new order. In large part this is due to the fact that tradition makes possible the utilization of the past. In doing so it plays in social life a part analogous to that played in individual life by memory, which is the function whereby a mental state is influenced by a past act or experience.

Though we speak of tradition as a force of the past influencing the present, in reality the present has hold of the past, controlling group activity in the light of that portion of the past which we call tradition. For the past as such has no influence, and only when the present preserves phases of it do the latter persist as influences. Portions of the past which the group forgets or disregards form no part of its traditions.

The selection implied by tradition is one of its outstanding characteristics. If it handed down all of the past it would not be a guide; and its wisdom is shown by the nature of the selection. Without tradition the group could not profit from its past, but would drift from circumstance to circumstance, from program to program, and without profiting from experience.

Tradition, therefore, is a steadying influence in group action, and thanks to it group life has continuity and aim. It holds the group to a consistent course of action, giving it purpose and direction. The tradition of the Monroe Doctrine, for example, whether wise or not, imparts consistency to American international policy, as does the tradition established in Washington's *Farewell Address*. So long as a group follows traditions it has a definite aim. This, of course, does not mean that every tradition is a good one, or that any tradition is so good that it could not be better. From time to time, therefore, a progressive society realizes the inadequacy of its traditions and remakes them.

Nothing is more serviceable than good traditions. England's greatness is not due to a merit inherent in tradition as such, but rather to the value of her particular traditions. Other peoples, too, have traditions—China, Japan, Russia—but these have not yielded so large a measure of social and political profit. Also, with few exceptions, no nation has shown so much ability as has England in refashioning national traditions and in making them conform with the needs of a new day. Good traditions are as necessary to social life as is good inheritance to physiological life, and in social life we can remake the influences of the past which are to be effective in the present. We can not choose our physiological ancestors, but we can choose our social traditions; for we can select the influences of the past whose social descendants we wish to be. Tradition is Janus-faced: we can open the doors of the temple at will, and can orient it as we wish.

When we appeal to the words of George Washington (or those attributed to him) as guides for action in political affairs, we show our disposition to follow tradition, for our selection of him as a guide is a means of creating a national tradition. Similarly the references to Lincoln show that we wish to establish him and his counsels as part of the national tradition.

Tradition is indispensable to intelligent group life. Without it the group could not profit from the past, there would be no continuity of policies from one decade to another, and individuals would not know what to expect from the group in which they live. Tradition is the handing on of the past to the present. To hand on the less valuable elements of the past is to weaken the group; to hand on the nobler elements, the fitter guides to action, is to elevate the group, or at least to give it levers by means of which it can elevate itself. In perpetuating certain traditions rather than others the group in effect decides that those specific ones shall be the incentives to group action. Yet, though each group should decide its own affairs, not infrequently these are decided for it by preceding generations whose dictates on certain things the group does not question. If it did question them these same traditions would lose the control which the venerable past bestows upon them; for only that past is venerable which the group chooses to venerate, and only that portion of the past holds sway as tradition which the present recognizes as potent.

The motives which govern the group in making the selection from the past which we call tradition vary from time to time and from group to group. A powerful impulse at work in the group brings traditions into line. Thus if religion is a leading stimulus, there is a bulwark of religious tradition; if a form of government has strong grip—an "unlimited" monarchy, for example—the monarchical tradition is strongly entrenched. There is a tendency for a culture to bring tradition into line with its drives. . . .[17]

Control through building superstitious fears.

Mrs. Elsie Clews Parsons has assembled some interesting material showing how belief in the supernatural is a very potent means of preserving the primitive social order. The "bogy-man" who carries off naughty children, who eats and kills unmanageable juniors, is appealed to by primitive parents to keep the children where they belong and out of the way of adults. The owl will come and take away noisy children of the Thompson River, Kootenay, and Sioux Indians. Caffre children are threatened with the Nomgogwana monster. The Gineet-Gineet of the Euahlayi tribe of New South Wales is alert to catch bad children in his net.[18]

The dictates of fashion.

Conventionalization also comes into play to cover the dress of the ballet or burlesque opera and the bathing dress. Conventionalization

---

[17] From Wilson D. Wallis, *An Introduction to Sociology*, pp. 186, 187, 189, 190. By permission of F. S. Crofts and Company.

[18] From F. Stuart Chapin, "Primitive Social Ascendancy Viewed as an Agent of Selection in Society," *Proceedings of the Twelfth Annual Meeting of the American Sociological Society*, 1918, vol. 12, p. 62. By permission of the American Sociological Society.

always includes strict specification and limits of time, place, and occasion, beyond which the same dress would become vicious. Amongst Moslems and Orientals this conventionalization as to dress has never been introduced. We are familiar with the fact that when a fashion has been introduced and has become common our eye is formed to it, and no one looks "right" or stylish who does not conform to it. We also know that after the fashion has changed things in the discarded fashion look dowdy and rustic. No one can resist these impressions, try as he may. This fact, in the experience of everybody, gives us an example of the power of current custom over the individual. While a fashion reigns its tendency is to greater and greater extravagance in order to produce the desired and admired effect. Then the toleration for any questionable element in the fashion is extended and the extension is unnoticed. If a woman of 1860, in the dress of her time, were to meet a woman of 1906, in the dress of her time, each would be amazed at the indecency of the dress of the other. No dress ever was more justly denounced for ugliness, inconvenience, and indecency than the crinoline, but all the women from 1855 to 1865, including some of the sweetest who ever lived, wore it. No inference whatever as to their taste or character would be justified. There never is any rational judgment in the fashion of dress. No criticism can reach it. In a few cases we know what actress or princess started a certain fashion but in the great majority of cases we do not know whence it came or who was responsible for it. We all have to obey it. We hardly ever have any chance to answer back. Its all-sufficient sanction is that "everybody wears it," or wears it so. Evidently this is only a special application to dress of a general usage—conventionalization.[19]

One of the most interesting aspects of fashion in our time is its rapidity of change. Modern means of diffusion have immensely hastened the spread of fashion in clothes, sports, words, and tools. Some fashions reach the level of fads or even crazes —pee-wee golf, yo-yo tops, send-a-dime letters, and the big apple.

SPECIAL CONTROL DEVICES EMPLOYED IN MAINTAINING SOCIAL ORDER

It requires more than codes, convictions, mores, conventions, and the like, to keep members of society in line. Ever and anon

---

[19] From William Graham Sumner, *Folkways*, p. 185. By permission of Ginn and Company.

the tendency toward individualism leads to divergent behavior, and occasionally a person, because his organic drives are too strong, because he has not been completely socialized, or because for some reason he does not agree with the principles propagated by the social group, jumps the fences of regulation that have been established.

Society has developed numerous means for disciplining such individuals. Some devices are mild; some are extremely severe. They range from friendly correction expressed in gestures of disapproval, to the heart-rending device of ridicule; from the loss of privileges or from fines to the death penalty. The instances presented are suggestive of the many and various techniques which society has at its disposal to see that order prevails.

A comparison of non-resistance and force as means of social control. Brute force, which regulates by domination of a physical nature, is one extreme of social coercion. This form may find expression in any type of social institution or social group; the family, the gang, or the state may have authoritative patterns enforced by an iron hand. This is control on the most elementary level. It brings obedience by compulsion. Historically, control by force has been a very important influence in social regulation. In the environment of the child, force still rules when one child clashes with another, because the child's world is a world without law. Likewise, in frontier situations, where the ordinary control devices of more refined society are absent, the rule of strength takes their place and the big man again has his day.[20]

In the field of international relations, force has always been resorted to when words failed, and frequently even before the vocabulary was exhausted.

It is usually considered evidence of social progress when a family, a social institution, or a nation reaches the point where control can be exercised on more refined levels.

At the opposite extreme from force is a technique which in world cultures seems to have characterized Oriental societies more than others; that is, the technique of non-resistance, a most subtle and indirect method of coercion, and one which is very prominent in Christ's Sermon on the Mount, in which he advo-

---

[20] Paul H. Landis, *Three Iron Mining Towns: a Study in Cultural Change,* chap. 14.

cated turning the other cheek, going the second mile, and giving the extra garment.[21]

In our day of world struggle through force of arms, Mahatma Gandhi has been the most striking character in the field of passive resistance.[22] In his struggle on behalf of the Indians in South Africa, and later for recognition of the peoples of India, he staged an exhibition of self-abnegation and torture which has no parallel in modern times. Not only did he preach the doctrine of non-resistance to his followers, but he sacrificed himself, providing the world with an outstanding example of what non-resistance can accomplish. Going even beyond the doctrine of *ahimsa* (non-killing), he condemned the exercise of resentment against people who considered themselves his enemies. The warfare he staged was non-coöperative, and centered in a war of wills and ideals rather than of arms. It was a quest for freedom on the spiritual frontier, in which spiritual ideals were matched against the cold steel of British rule.

In 1924 when he felt that the Hindu and Mohammedan factions needed to be brought closer together, in order to realize the success of his cause, Gandhi drew aside to fast and pray, pledging his followers that he would not eat food and would not return until a unified program was adopted. On the nineteenth day this was accomplished, and Gandhi's fast ended. Thus was demonstrated the power of non-resistance to solidify a group from within as well as to fight a spiritual battle with an enemy power from without.

Between these two poles of control, there is a tremendous range of possibilities. An ideal of the modern world is to approach nearer the point of control through spiritual and idealistic forces, and to get away from the more brutal types of control which force represents.

The penalties for violating taboos.

In initiation ceremonies the social hold upon the novice is strengthened by taboo. Boys and girls of the Lower Murry tribes in Australia are told that to eat emu, wild duck, swans, geese, black duck, or the eggs of any of these birds will cause their hair to become

---

[21] Matthew 5:39, 40, 41.

[22] For a good discussion of Gandhi's activities see C. F. Andrews, *Mahatma Gandhi's Ideas*, and Frederick B. Fisher. *That Strange Little Brown Man Gandhi.*

prematurely gray and their muscles to shrink. If a Urabunna initiate should allow a woman to see one of the secret sticks, he and his mother and sisters would drop dead.

Those who commit incest among the Omeo tribe of Victoria are beaten by the "jidjigongs" or snakes. Anyone who married into prohibited subclasses of the Queensland savages would die because his behavior was offensive to Kohin, an earth-roaming spirit of the Milky Way. The islanders of the Malay Archipelago believe that sickness will follow the eating of stolen food from tabooed fields. Batak thieves are cursed by the magic of the great priest of Baglige. Iconoclasts among the Dakota, Ainu, and in the Malay Archipelago will be punished by supernatural powers.

Australian blackfellows are educated from their infancy to believe that departure from the customs of the tribe will inevitably be followed by such evils as becoming prematurely gray, being afflicted with ophthalmia, skin eruptions, or sickness, and death from evil magic. African Bakalai believe that if a man should eat his totem the women of his clan would miscarry and give birth to animals of the totem kind, or die of some awful disease. If a man of the Elk clan of the Omahas ate of any part of the male elk, he would break out in boils and white spots on different parts of his body. Among the Samoans the man who ate a turtle would grow very ill, and the turtle within him would say, "He ate me; I am killing him." Members of the secret society of the Hohewachi, fixing their minds on an offender against Omaha tribal custom, thrust him from all helpful relations with man and animals, so that he suffers misfortune or death. And so it goes, belief in the supernatural being invoked to terrify children into obedience to parents, adults into conformity to custom, and all offenders into submission to society. In this way a selected and approved conduct is obtained and the social order preserved without violence.[23]

Superstition as a means of maintaining group patterns.

. . . Backward communities are even now trying to keep the individual down, often by means of superstition, and they use the modern means of the printed page for this purpose. As an illustration I may refer to my own case.

At the age of seven I had mastered the art of reading in German

---

[23] From F. Stuart Chapin, op. cit., pp. 62–63. By permission of the American Sociological Society.

sufficiently well to try my hands at short connected narratives. An almanac which was sold in thousands of copies was about the only means to satisfy my desire. One of the stories was intended to convey a warning against atheism and infidelity. It contained only ten or twelve lines, but made a deep impression on me which I have not been able to overcome to this day.

The gist of the story may be summed up in one sentence. "A hog-dealer who had grown rich, became an atheist, threatened to shoot God, and was turned into a pig; he was a Serbian." Two pictures were added to make the text impressive—one showing the Serbian in the midst of a large gathering aiming his shotgun toward the sky; the other showing him still in that attitude, but turned into a pig. The expression of the bystanders was correspondingly one of horror in one case, and of joy in the other. Text and pictures supplemented each other neatly.

There are five points in that short story, each exercising some control. The man was a hog-dealer, therefore an inferior individual of whom one must beware. He had grown rich, and naturally became an infidel, thus illustrating the biblical saying that it is easier for a camel to pass through the eye of a needle than for a rich man to enter into the Kingdom of God. Class hatred taught with a vengeance. The man was a Serbian—the implication being that in a well-regulated German community such dreadful blasphemy could not take place, although it might happen in far-away Serbia with its inferior, if not barbarous, people. He was turned into a pig—the lowest and most unclean domestic animal. This act of God was a complete vindication of His own existence and of religion.

I read the story several times in order to get its full meaning. It effectively cured my budding disbelief for a number of years, and implanted an ineradicable race prejudice in me. One of my colleagues at the university suffers from it. Although he is a fine fellow and excellent scholar, and notwithstanding the fact that we are good friends, an emotional chasm opens up between me and him when I speak to him. The prejudice of race implanted many years ago still survives emotionally, although intellectually it is dead.[24]

After reading such discussions as the one by Chapin on taboos in primitive society, the student will be inclined to assume that

---

[24] From Rudolph M. Binder, *Proceedings of the Twelfth Annual Meeting of the American Sociological Society*, 1918, vol. 12, p. 110. By permission of the American Sociological Society.

the phenomenon has meaning only in primitive society, or at best in backward communities, such as described in Binder's article on superstition, but this is not the case.

A. M. Tozzer in his *Social Origins and Continuities* [25] has indicated that superstitious fears are prominent as forces in behavior at the present time in our society, using college student reports as evidence.

The writer also, in several college sociology classes, has collected accounts by students of superstitions and the use of various good luck charms, fetishes, and ritualistic formulae. The extent to which students profess to believe in and to practice certain superstitions is amazing. They usually appear, as Tozzer's case histories also show, in connection with examinations, games of chance, and athletic events—the crisis-experiences in the life of the student that are thought to have a chance outcome.

The wide belief in luck, and the common use of luck charms among criminals and professional athletes is common knowledge. In the case of both groups, life centers around a series of chance outcomes. If modern man has become less superstitious than primitive man it is due to the fact that he has reduced the chance element in life by science.

Laughter as a means of maintaining group standards.

. . . We find no human societies in which laughter does not figure as part of the social life, as, in fact, a part of the group language. If scorn is the lash, laughter is the jolly policeman who keeps the social traffic going after the approved manner, whose power inheres not in itself, but lies in the tribal standard which it bodies forth. Ethnologists have not found a group of human beings who are devoid of laughter of this sort.

A few examples of the expression and repression of laughter in primitive society will make clear its social utility. In their perverted pedagogy, the Australians teach the youths what to do by showing them the things they should not do. As part of the ordeal of training through which the young men pass when being initiated into tribal life, the old men perform ridiculous pranks which the youth must watch, always restraining the laughter which they tend to give way to at sight of these exhibitions. A large part of these initiation

---

[25] Pp. 225–230 of his work summarize his findings; pp. 242–266 reproduce a number of the student accounts.

ceremonies is designed to give the young men a respect for their elders, this being one way of inculcating such respect. Laughter at a person is, in a sense, an assertion of superiority to him, and the youths may not risibly make such assertion. The performance would be ridiculous if done by any other than the aged. Performance by the aged takes it out of the realm of the laughable, for the elders set the standards for the group. An Eskimo has little of the sensitiveness which we associate with the intimacies of domestic life, but he cannot stand the derision and laughter of a rival. He will sometimes break over the tribal rules and kill the man who laughs at him. He laughs best who laughs last—that is his argument, and it is a convincing last word in the dispute. The tribesmen in the Plains area of North America are among the most tireless and daring warriors in all primitive society, yet they cannot stand the laughter, directed against them, of their fellow-men. Laughter is one of the principal means of holding in line the members of the various warlike organizations which flourish in these tribes. A man of one of these societies who resents the abduction of his wife by a fellow-member, this being no violation of the rules of his order, is laughed at by the other members of the organization until his resentment passes.

Let these examples suffice. They show that laughter is a means of expressing and maintaining the group standard. It reminds people of their place in the social group and is an efficient, if gentle, reminder that they had better keep where they belong. It is an expression of the proprieties of the occasion to which the individual must attend. When a person laughs at himself, he is, in the main, assuming the group standard, applying to himself the standards which the group applies to him. He assumes in his own person the duties of policing his conduct.[26]

Ridicule as a device for abolishing war, crime, and misdoings.

Even the animals know the power of derision. I have owned smarter dogs than my Larry, and I have learned to train them well without violence. But though Larry dislikes scolding and hates to be confined in our laundry, he never really is upset until we laugh at him. He is almost ill when we treat him as if he and his actions are silly.

I have held some public positions, one where some pomp and

[26] From Wilson D. Wallis, "Why Do We Laugh," *Scientific Monthly*, 1922, vol. 15, pp. 343–347. By permission of the Science Press.

puffery might have been put on parade by me, but when I wanted to bring a stubborn personality around to the hitching post of world equity or home-made horse sense, I always tried to remember the method I used in extremity with my two children when they were very young. They have been, even from the crib days, astute enough to play the game of life; they rarely presented any problems. The exception was the rare moment when they became audacious, stubborn little "repeaters," as the criminologists say. Then the something-had-to-be-done moment arrived. Loathe to engage in severe measures involving haste and suggesting parental anger, I suddenly became inspired. I demanded that the bottle of iodine and the tiny brush be employed. In the end the punishment, though seldom needed, was self-inflicted. The iodine was used to paint indelible mustaches and goatees upon faces otherwise dignified. The result was sure-fire. The children, unable to face the ridicule of playmates, music teachers, or our guests, retired to some meditative retreat and always came out, after I had removed the stains by my secret process, good-naturedly asking to call the whole thing off.

"Suppose we took Al Capone and made him sweep street crossings, or go down Michigan Boulevard every day carrying a sign or a transparency saying, 'I'm the Great Capone—the biggest racketeer of History—the Cupid of 'Em All.'"

"That is what I mean," I said to the editor. "Exactly what I mean. We are leaving our weapon of ridicule, of derision, up on the shelf of society's unused assets. We don't laugh at crime and war; we don't make them ridiculous. . . ."

Even my blue-nosed Puritan ancestors had more imagination! They advocated a policy of putting offenders into stocks or tieing placards around their necks or ducking them in the horsepond—all of which may not be up to the improved form of joshing the criminal . . .

Probably the best place to use ridicule is in the cases of the juvenile offender. I commend my iodine mustachios to the juvenile courts of these United States. A few daisy chains around the neck of the "tough boy" of the neighborhood would prevent the hatching of a gangster with a machine gun. The placard to be worn on pain of ending the suspension of a more serious sentence could be offered as alternative to the penalties prescribed.[27]

---

[27] From Richard Washburn Child, "We Can Kill War," *Good Housekeeping*, February, 1932, vol. 94, pp. 26, 27, 184. Reprinted by permission.

One of the most interesting examples of the use of the derisive technique in handling offenders was practiced by a judge in the Spokane, Washington, traffic court in 1937. Those convicted on charges of drunken driving were given an ample dose of castor oil in the court.

Public opinion as a pervading force.

The behavior of groups shows that public opinion is not a mere metaphor but is a pervading force, often more efficient in securing results than are physical forces. It determines the attitude and the behavior of individuals functioning in group life, brings conformity out of confusion, and imparts purpose where previously there was none, focusing divergent opinions upon a posited accomplishment. This and that individual may have divergent views about the advisability of the group's resenting an affront and declaring war, but once a given opinion gains assent war is inevitable, or, as the case may be, peace is assured. Sometimes an opinion becomes a driving force before which other opinions bend. The opinion that the Holy Sepulchre had to be rescued from the infidels swept through medieval Europe and initiated the Crusades. "War fever" is well named, for opinions on war issues induce fever heat which spreads like contagion. There is some truth in John Adams' statement that "the Revolution was effected before the people." And later, Freneau, "the poet of the Revolution," wrote: "public opinion sets the bounds to every government, and is the real sovereign of every free one."

Civilization differs from savagery in the extensiveness of public opinion, the group in which it acts in savagery being small. In civilization the sphere of public opinion is constantly enlarging because of books, magazines, newspapers, telephone, telegraph, and radio. Larger groups than ever before are subject to the play of an idea and are susceptible to a given opinion.[28]

Law. In our society, law, probably more than any other single device, is a supposedly rational system by which we aim to maintain order. It is essentially a system of prohibitions and penalties, although it includes many other phases. Most of what we think of as law, however, is negative. Law sets up a system of standards and provides the penalties for their violation.

---

[28] From Wilson D. Wallis, *An Introduction to Sociology*, pp. 193, 194. By permission of F. S. Crofts and Company.

Its greatest weakness on the psychological side is that it makes no provision for socializing the individual along the line of its aims, except as the government has attempted to do so through the public school system. The law and its enforcement agents usually assume that the law is an end in itself, that its very existence is sufficient to command public respect, that education of the public in the intricacies of law, if such must be done, will be accomplished through the enforcement of penalties.

If we spent half as much time educating the individual concerning the necessity of specific laws and their meaning in terms of human welfare as we spend in trying to enforce them, law, like some more effective means of social control, could come to have an inner meaning to the individual, instead of remaining an eternal force. Such an approach would supply a dual advantage. We would soon learn that a good many laws, much of law enforcement technique, and much of court ritual actually have no social meaning, and would better be discarded in favor of socially justifiable procedures.

Law has come to be, and must in the future remain, one of the most important control devices in a secondary group world. Its responsibilities are great, but more than any institution of our society its practices are a carry-over of the past. Even the church, which has borne the brunt of much criticism as a medieval institution, is generations ahead of the law in social vision and in social practice.

CONCLUSION

The means of social control may be grouped in various ways, most classifications so far developed being two-fold. Some of those used are physical force and human symbols methods; formal and informal means; conscious and unconscious means; rewards and punishments; education and socialization as contrasted with sanctions; paternal (centralized) control as contrasted with social (democratic) control. The writer, working on the assumption that classifications are useful according to one's approach to the problem, and that no scheme can be devised with universal utility, classifies devices into two rough groupings, those employed in building order and those employed in maintaining order, neither category being mutually exclusive.

According to the view of this book, order is established largely by means of the educative or socializing devices that society employs in the building of personality from original nature. Very influential in this field are the devices whereby are established habits and attitudes designed to prepare the individual to participate in the normal life of the group, sharing its notions of morality, propriety, values, and goals. Such devices as ritual, ceremony, codes, conventions, traditions, superstitions, taboos, ideals, and hero worship are among those utilized in the developing of social nature.

But education is never sufficient in itself. For any of a number of reasons the educative process often is poorly accomplished from the standpoint of group welfare, and sometimes is unable to hold original nature in check. Therefore, punishments of diverse sorts must be brought into play as occasion demands. All societies have a ready store of means of enforcement from which to draw when such are needed. At the one extreme is brute force used for coercion, at the other, the more subtle device of passive resistance, which in capable hands seems to be equally powerful and perhaps less expensive than physical force. Between these extremes are numerous penalties which may be resorted to, pricks and prods for keeping the individual in the middle path. In primitive society the number and kind of penalties for violating taboos, superstitions, and established practices are limited only by man's inventive genius. The red lights of danger glare at many a crossroad. So also in modern society superstitions, widely held, call for practice or avoidance under the threat of imagined dire consequences. The ring of scornful derisive laughter, the sting of unfavorable public opinion, is like a lash to the man who has learned to seek group approval.

In our secondary group society, law, with its prohibitions and penalties, has become an important technique for control. That it is a necessary device cannot be questioned, but that it is overused in our society, and very often wrongly used is equally true. The most deeply embedded in tradition of any tool of our culture, it still tries to control by external and archaic means, and still features penalties rather than education.

SELECTED REFERENCES

Addams, J., "A Modern Devil Baby," *American Journal of Sociology*, vol. 20, pp. 117–118. 1914.

Andrews, C. F., *Mahatma Gandhi's Ideas*. The Macmillan Company, New York, 1930.

Arnett, C. E., and Others, "Prestige as a Factor in Attitude Changes," *Sociology and Social Research*, vol. 16, pp. 49–55. September, 1931.

Arnold, T. W., *The Symbols of Government*. Yale University Press, New Haven, 1935.

Austen, Nancy Virginia, "Suicide A La Mode in Japan," *Current History*, vol. 15, pp. 83 ff. October, 1921.

Benedict, Ruth, "The Science of Custom," *The Century Magazine*, vol. 117, pp. 641–649. April, 1929.

Bent, S., "Propaganda Rules the Waves," *Review of Reviews*, vol. 95, pp. 38–40. February, 1937.

Black, H. L., "Inside a Senate Investigation," *Harper's Magazine*, pp. 275–286. February, 1936.

Blanshard, P., "Manufacturing Public Opinion," *New Republic*, vol. 69, p. 102. December 9, 1931.

Blumer, H., and Hauser, P., *Movies, Delinquency and Crime*. The Macmillan Company, New York, 1933.

Bogardus, E. S., *Leaders and Leadership*. D. Appleton-Century Company, New York, 1934.

Bowden, A. O., and Others, "Study in Prestige," *American Journal of Sociology*, vol. 40, pp. 193–203. September, 1934.

Broome, Edwin C., *Report of the Committee on Propaganda*. National Education Association of the United States, Washington, D. C., 1929.

Brown, George Rothwell, *The Leadership of Congress*. Bobbs-Merrill Company, Indianapolis, 1922.

Burr, Walter, *Community Leadership*. Prentice-Hall, Inc., New York, 1929.

Busch, Henry Miller, *Leadership in Group Work*. Association Press, New York, 1934.

Chapin, F. Stuart, "Primitive Social Ascendancy Viewed as an Agent of Selection in Society," *Proceedings of the Twelfth Annual Meeting of the American Sociological Society*, vol. 12, pp. 62–63. 1918.

Child, Richard Washburn, "We Can Kill War," *Good Housekeeping*, vol. 94, pp. 26 ff. February, 1932.

Clark, John M., *Social Control of Business*, pp. 221–223. University of Chicago Press, Chicago, 1926.

Cooley, Charles H., *Human Nature and the Social Order*, chap. 9. Charles Scribner's Sons, New York, 1922.

Cooley, Charles H., *Social Process*, chaps. 11, 31, and 32. Charles Scribner's Sons, New York, 1918.

Crowell, E. M., "Congress, and the Power of the Press," *New Republic*, vol. 89, pp. 321–322. January 13, 1937.

Davis, Barnes, and Others, *An Introduction to Sociology* (selection by L. L. Bernard), pp. 484–488. D. C. Heath and Company, New York, 1931.

Davis, Barnes, and Others, *Readings in Sociology*, pp. 575–603. D. C. Heath and Company, New York, 1927.

Dicey, Albert Venn, *Lectures on the Relation Between Law and Public Opinion in England, during the Nineteenth Century*. The Macmillan Company, New York, 1905.

Doob, Leonard W., *Propaganda*. Henry Holt and Company, New York, 1935.

Dowd, Jerome, *Control in Human Societies*. D. Appleton-Century, Company, New York, 1936.

Eldridge, Selba, *Public Intelligence; A Study of the Attitudes and Opinions of Voters*. University of Kansas, Department of Journalism Press, Lawrence, Kansas, 1935.

Falk, Alfred T., *Short Talks on Advertising*, third series. Bureau of Research and Education, Advertising Federation of America, New York, 1935.

Fisher, Frederick B., *That Strange Little Brown Man Gandhi*. Ray Long and Richard R. Smith, Inc., 1932.

Giddings, Franklin H., *Studies in the Theory of Human Society*, pp. 206 ff. The Macmillan Company, New York, 1922.

Gillette, John M., and Reinhardt, James M., *Current Social Problems*, pp. 759 ff. American Book Company, New York, 1933.

Gosling, Thomas Warrington, *Science and Opinion*, pp. 471–472. National Education Association of the United States, Washington, D. C., 1934.

Gruening, Ernest Henry, *The Public Pays; A Story of Power Propaganda*. The Vanguard Press, New York, 1931.

Harris, H. K., "Newspaper as the Nation's Greatest Educator," *Education*, vol. 56, pp. 498–500. April, 1936.

Hiller, E. T., *Principles of Sociology*, chap. 39. Harper and Brothers, New York, 1933.

Hopwood, Eric Clark, *Fortification by Public Opinion*, pp. 759–768. National Education Association of the United States, Washington, D. C., 1925.

House, F. N., *The Range of Social Theory*, chap. 24. Henry Holt and Company, New York, 1929.

Huxley, A., "Notes on Propaganda," *Harper's Magazine*, pp. 32–41. December, 1936.

Jackson, G., "Miracles at Malden," *The Nation*, vol. 129, p. 662. December 4, 1929.

Jordan, Arthur M., *The Harmful Effects of Propaganda and Their Avoidance*. National Education Association of the United States, Washington, D. C., 1935.

Keller, A. G., *Man's Rough Road*. Frederick A. Stokes Company, New York, and Yale University Press, New Haven, 1932.

Kenyon, T., "Witches Still Live," *North American Review*, vol. 228, pp. 620 ff. November, 1929.

Kolodin, Irving, "Propaganda on the Air," *American Mercury*, pp. 293–300. July, 1935.

Landis, Paul H., *Three Iron Mining Towns: A Study in Cultural Change*, chap. 14. Edwards Brothers, Ann Arbor, 1938.

Lasswell, Harold D., *Propaganda Technique in the World War*. F. S. Crofts and Company, New York, 1927.

Le Bon, Gustave, *The Crowd*. T. Fisher Unwin, Ltd., London, 1803.

Lipsky, A., *Man the Puppet*, pp. 33–34, 52–53. Frank-Maurice, Inc., New York, 1925.

Lumley, Frederick Elmore, *Means of Social Control*. D. Appleton-Century Company, New York, 1925.

Lumley, Frederick Elmore, *The Propaganda Menace*. D. Appleton-Century Company, New York, 1933.

Malinowski, B., *Myth in Primitive Society*. W. W. Norton and Company, New York, 1926.

Mead, Margaret, *Sex and Temperament in Three Primitive Societies*. William Morrow and Company, New York, 1935.

Merriam, Charles Edward, *Four American Party Leaders*. The Macmillan Company, New York, 1926.

Park, R. E., and Burgess, E. W., *Introduction to the Science of Sociology*, chap. 12. University of Chicago Press, Chicago, 1924.

Pigors, Paul, *Leadership or Domination*. Houghton Mifflin Company, Boston, and The Riverside Press, Cambridge, 1935.

Ross, Edward Alsworth, *Principles of Sociology*, first revision, chap. 51. D. Appleton-Century Company, New York, 1930.

Sidis, B., *The Psychology of Suggestion*. D. Appleton-Century Company, New York, 1898.

Special Section, "The Press and the Public," *New Republic*, vol. 90, pp. 177–191. March 17, 1937.

Spencer, Herbert, *The Principles of Sociology*, pp. 3 ff. D. Appleton-Century Company, New York, 1910.

Strong, A. L., "American Propaganda in Russia," *The American Mercury*, vol. 32, pp. 48–55. May, 1934.

Strout, Richard Lee, "The Radio Nostrum Racket," *The Nation*, pp. 65–66. July 17, 1935.

Sumner, William Graham, *Folkways*. Ginn and Company, Boston, 1906.

Thomas, N., "What About the Use of Violence?", *The World To-morrow*, vol. 15, pp. 105 ff. April, 1932.

Thomas, W. I., "The Behavior Pattern and the Situation," *Publications of the American Sociological Society*, vol. 22, pp. 12–13. University of Chicago Press, Chicago, 1928.

Tozzer, A. M., *Social Origins and Continuities*, pp. 223–230, 242–266. The Macmillan Company, New York, 1925.

Tralle, Henry Edward, *Psychology of Leadership*. D. Appleton-Century Company, New York, 1925.

Veblen, Thorstein, *Theory of the Leisure Class*. The Macmillan Company, New York, 1905.

Walsh, W. T., "Rise Up and Walk," *North American Review*, vol. 227, p. 399. April, 1929.

Wang, Betty, "Folk Songs as a Means of Social Control," *Sociology and Social Research*, vol. 19, pp. 64–69. September, 1934.

Werner, M. R., *Barnum*. Harcourt, Brace and Company, New York, 1923.

White, William Allen, and Meyer, Walter E., *Conflicts in American Public Opinion*. American Library Association, Chicago, 1925.

Williams, M., "Grave at Malden," *Commonweal*, vol. 11, p. 160. December 11, 1929.

Winston, Sanford, *Culture and Human Behavior*, pp. 198 ff. The Ronald Press Company, New York, 1933.

CHAPTER 20

SOCIAL CONTROL AND BEHAVIOR PROBLEMS AMONG CONTEMPORARY YOUTH

THE CONTROLS IN THE CHILD'S WORLD

Childhood is a time of extensive conditioning for social life, rather than of full participation. It is a preface to social activity in the life of the group. The child is excluded from the adult world because he lacks sufficient equipment in the way of language, habits, attitudes, and values to compete with adults. He lacks them because they have to be acquired, and he has not had the necessary time in which to acquire them. Also, part of the equipment for participation, such as that for establishing family life, can come only with physical maturation. Childhood is a period of obtaining the experience that will enable the individual to participate when he reaches the adult stage. In this sense, all of childhood is lived with adulthood in view.

Control over the child's world rests in the hands of the adult generation, except for that which children exercise over each other through such primitive and spontaneous devices as superior force or cunning. The child as a natural consequence of living in human society, and of participating in phases of its culture, and as a result of deliberate teaching by adults, becomes socialized along the lines of the particular society into which he is born.

THE TRANSITION FROM CHILDHOOD CONTROLS TO ADOLESCENCE

As the child reaches physical maturity, he is expected to abandon the rough and tumble methods of authority which ruled his child's world, and to realize that he is no longer an apprentice being prepared for a disciplined adult world, but that he is actually nearing that world, and must come to regard himself as an adult and therefore responsible for his own conduct. This period of transition has been labeled adolescence. The individual is expected to emerge from adolescence a self-controlled member of society, and if he has not become such, the penalties that society has established for disobedience will then be exacted of him. The fullest realization of self-responsibility, however, probably does not come until the person himself becomes a teacher of the traditions by having children of his own toward whom he feels a responsibility for socializing.

Let us focus attention briefly on this stage called adolescence which has come to be considered a very critical period in the life cycle of every individual.

ADOLESCENCE AS A SOCIOLOGICAL FACT

The famous works of G. Stanley Hall [1] in the field of adolescent psychology at the beginning of the century, and those of others since, firmly establish the fact of a physiological adolescence. These same works also developed a social psychology of adolescence.

The fact of a physiological change during which the individual gradually emerges from a sexually immature creature to a sexually mature creature is demonstrable in experience as well as in science. But the thesis that emotional turmoil, intellectual rebirth, moral awakening, and social expansion are an inevitable social psychological accompaniment of adolescence is highly questionable, even though it was the foundation stone of Hall's adolescent psychology.

Discoveries in cultural anthropology [2] are convincing to the effect that the psychological and social manifestations of adolescence depend not upon physical fact, but upon what the society makes of this period of physical development. In some societies the social transition to adulthood is so smoothly made that none of the supposed psychological and social manifestations which Hall considered an inevitable counterpart of physical adolescence appear, while in others they seem to appear in an even more violent form than in our own.

The point which these discoveries make is that what Hall described as a part of adolescent psychology and its social mani-

---

[1] G. Stanley Hall, *Adolescence*; also, *Youth, Its Education, Regimen, and Hygiene.*

[2] See Margaret Mead's *Coming of Age in Samoa*; also her *Growing Up in New Guinea.*

festations is really a product of our peculiar culture, and not of physical adolescence. We in our culture expect certain changes in youth when they reach a certain age, changes that make of them new social and psychological creatures. The same changes might come earlier or later, if the social order demanded it, and actually are entirely independent of physical maturation. We are delaying social adolescence by prolonging the period of infancy, so that we no longer expect many things of the sixteen year old that were once taken for granted. We are easing the shock of adolescence by spreading the period over a longer length of time.

Generally in our culture the youth first comes face to face with the system of social control on his own responsibility during the so-called period of adolescence. Some youths face it early, others later, but in our society they usually meet it first when they transfer from the primary group to the secondary group. As long as the individual remains in the primary group, even if far beyond the adolescent stage, he remains subject to controls designed especially for juvenile members. Ordering and forbidding, respect for elders, and regard for wishes of loved ones reign in his consciousness. He reaches manhood in a true sense only as he leaves the primary group and faces a cold world on his own. In our society he usually reaches this stage during physical adolescence. In some societies he does not reach it in his youth, but assumes manhood responsibilities only as the elders die and he has to take their place as patriarch of the family or tribe.

THE TRANSFER OF YOUTH TO THE WORLD OF ADULT CONTROLS

In our society the individual who does not enter college faces the transition from primary group to secondary group somewhere during the years from fifteen to twenty-four, when he first goes out beyond the confines of the intimate group to earn a living. For almost two hundred thousand farm youth each year this means migrating to town or city. But those from town and urban environments also must leave neighborhood and family groups, to stand on their own feet in a secondary group world. To express this transition in terms of social control, they become self-regulated or, failing to do so, carry the responsibility for breaking the codes. Those who go to college ordinarily face the transition upon arrival on the college campus. Their worst strug-gles occur during the first semester, but the entire college period is one of adjustment to the values of an adult world and an adult system of social control.

The adolescent period in our society has become one of crisis for both college and non-college groups. Studies of urban room-ing house districts hint at the crises that some persons must go through in making their adjustments. Student autobiographies often reveal the stresses which college youth experience in adjust-ing themselves. This process of adjustment to the controls of an adult world has not been adequately studied, but the evidence strongly suggests that the turmoil is caused by the social system, and not by the maturing of instincts or of sex functions.

As a problem in control it merits serious study, for we generally recognize that if the youth fails in making the transition normally, he will in all probability become a problem case from the stand-point of social regulation for the rest of his life. Criminals are made before they reach the age of twenty-five; socialized adults, also. Though our intentions be of the best, we often fail in helping the child to make the transition to the world of adult con-trols. If the child makes it successfully, he becomes the good citizen, the faithful churchman, the respected adult.

Controls Among Contemporary College Youth: A Collection of Case Studies [3]

The following papers are from accounts of college youth who as freshmen are making the transition from childhood to ma-

---

[3] A Note on Method: These materials from life are an afterthought, having been added after the first draft of the manuscript for the book had been com-pleted. The writer was teaching a class of 38 students in introductory sociology, most of the group being second semester freshmen, the remainder being sopho-mores. The last two days of the course were spent on social control and as a part of the assignment for these two days, students were asked to write a short paper telling why they behaved as they did, naming the specific reasons why they do things which may be distasteful to them and what kept them from doing things they would like to do but did not do. The writer had no intention of using the papers in this book, the assignment being given as one of several similar devices, such as an autobiography which was required as a term paper, for getting the student to apply what he had learned in the course to his experience-world. But much to his surprise, the papers seemed to give for the most part an honest, revealing, and fairly unsophisticated statement of motives, or supposed motives, for conduct. It seemed that this group of state-ments, in addition to adding life and vitality to Part Five of this book, might

turity. Their analysis of the process as it operates on a college campus is both interesting, and as a start toward comprehension, revealing, though certainly not adequate for complete understanding.

THE DOMINANCE OF FAMILY PATTERNS

More important than any other single influence mentioned is the family and its teachings, regard for parents' wishes or feelings, regard for family status. One or more of these points is stressed in most of the accounts submitted by the class. The papers below are typical in illustrating this consciousness of family controls.

"It's not religion but family responsibility that keeps me right." (Female)

Why do I behave as I do? I've often wondered myself! Before, though, I have never really taken time out to analyze the forces that have influenced my actions.

To begin with, I can almost eliminate religion as having an influence upon me because, even though I have gone to Sunday school and church, I've never believed there was a heaven and hell as such. Ever since I can remember, I have not thought that by living religiously and absolutely right one went to heaven, and that by doing wrong one went to hell when death came. I think we get our

---

give the student of social control some insight into the system of social control under which a college group lived from birth until they reached their present age of about eighteen years. The author has found them most suggestive.

Not all of the papers are presented. A few students dealt with the problem from an impersonal, theoretical standpoint. There was some duplication, and there were a few papers which indicated that the student had no understanding of the problem. These papers were omitted. Except for these omissions, all papers are included without modification, except for a few grammatical and word changes made in some of the more poorly written papers. A few of the titles are used by the student, but most of them were written by the author. They are meant to indicate what the student seemed to consider the major influences in his behavior.

The classifications employed are for convenience only. It will be obvious to the reader that there is much overlapping of topics.

In each case the words *male* and *female* indicate whether the paper was written by a man or woman. The predominance of women's papers in the selections quoted is probably explained chiefly by two factors: first, there were twenty-one women and seventeen men in the class; second, there were nine A and B students among the women and only one among the men; hence, one would expect the women's papers in this class to be of better quality.

heaven and hell on earth. I am not sure whether I think there is any kind of an after life. I think the dead live on in spirit in the minds of their living friends and relatives more than in a definite place in the hereafter.

My parents and family standards and ideals have played a very large part in molding my actions. Daddy used to reprimand me, but he never said definitely not to smoke or drink or lie or steal. Neither did Mother ever give me any rules to follow. Like all mothers she gave me advice about the world. Both Daddy and Mother set good examples of manhood and womanhood for us children to follow, and as we thought a great deal of our parents, it was the natural thing for us to copy them.

They used to tell us about the virtues and vices of our relatives, and gave us the impression that we were from a very good family, and strongly implied that we should uphold the standards.

After Daddy died was when I really needed discipline and guidance. Mother never liked to discipline us children. She told me I could judge for myself what was right and wrong in the situations I encountered more wisely than if she would give me rules to follow. She said that living in a different age from the one in which I lived, she did not feel capable of telling me exactly what to do, and she relied a great deal upon my own judgment.

Being next to the oldest in a family of five children, I felt, also, that my actions and the reputation I had would reflect on my brothers when they began to grow up. Always this is in the back of my mind—in the things I did in high school and in the things I am doing in college. It has made me develop a conscience which I doubt I would have had if I had not felt this way.

When I was a freshman and sophomore in high school, I thought it was smart to "tear around," and smoke, and have a good time that way. My conscience always bothered me, but the group I ran around with never did anything very drastic or anything much different from what every high school group does. However, about that time I started going with a boy whom I thought a great deal of. He believed in girls behaving themselves, and took a lot of the wild ideas out of my head. Because I did think so much of him, he influenced my actions considerably.

I think the factors I have discussed, and also the fact that I have a sense of curiosity and a very definite mind of my own, make me behave as I do.

"*Mother rules me.*"   (Female)

The chief influencing factor in my life, the factor that has had the most effect in determining whether I shall act a certain way or not, has been my mother. My mother's wish has been the unwritten but inescapable law which I have more or less adhered to throughout my brief life. If mother did not want me to stay all night with a friend, I definitely did not stay all night with a friend. If she wanted me to stay at home for a few days and rest, I stayed at home and went through the motions of resting, at least.

My mother has been my guide and rule for as long as I can remember. My father enters into the picture but seldom. I respect and admire him, but he does not concern himself with shaping my life as mother does. I do not mean by this that I am weak-minded, or a "yes" girl. I am very independent and self-assured. However, my mother is one of the few persons who is also independent and sufficiently self-assured to put me in my place without great difficulty.

Mother is not the only factor that determines what I shall do or shall not do. I have no doubt that I inherited certain restrictive attitudes from both parents. The only thing that stops me from attempting many projects is my subconscious self. I instinctively know that certain things, as far as I am concerned, should not be done, and other things must be. Some acts are just naturally repulsive to me, and I don't need anyone to tell me that they are not proper.

My environment also played its part in my life. By living in the country while I was young, I learned that people, children at the time, will tolerate some acts and will not tolerate others. This environmental attitude taught me how to judge what was right and what was wrong. Also, after I had lived in the city for a while I learned more about doing the accepted thing. I learned that if I failed to do a required act or indulged in a forbidden act, I was punished or restricted in my behavior in some way.

None of us like to admit that we are governed to any extent by public opinion. We are, however, and I am no exception. I do not care to be discussed in an undesirable way, and therefore I base my actions accordingly. I do not think that I adhere as much to this censor as many people do, but there is no doubt that it plays a fairly important part in determining how I shall act.

The planned life. (Female)

All of us have had definite training and experiences that cause us to act the way we do. My parents have always been religious and have instilled in me through their teachings the necessity for being honest, dependable, trustworthy, and conscientious.

I am afraid to go against convention or to do anything that would make myself conspicuous. So through this fear I have tried to do not the new things, but the things that I have seen other people do. I would not have my hair cut the way I do if I had not seen someone else do her hair that way.

I have led a sheltered life and have not paid much attention to the affairs of world interest. I have had most of my decisions made for me, and therefore I act as the people with whom I associate act.

This analysis of myself points out to me that I show no originality and perhaps am not getting as much as I could out of life. I must learn to decide things for myself and show some interest in others.

Family standards. (Female)

This problem of why I behave as I do, and why other people behave, is an interesting subject. From the very beginning, since I have been old enough to realize anything, my parents have had certain principles that they have stamped into my life. My parents have talked over with me the problems in one's life, those which a person has to face. I have learned the ways in which a young girl must act in public in order to keep up her reputation. Nowadays most people think it is alright for a girl to smoke, but my parents are some of the very few who believe it is not exactly right for a girl to smoke. I have had pounded into me the evils of smoking for such a long time that I have never cared to do it. I know that if I ever did begin to smoke it would hurt my mother very deeply. I can remember the first time I ever saw a woman smoking, and my reaction toward it. I was only about five years old, and we were eating in a restaurant. I stood up in my chair and pointed my finger at the woman and yelled at the top of my voice, "Mother, see that woman smoking, isn't that awful!" Of course, my folks were mortified over the way I acted, but I had heard so much about the evil of women smoking that I could not help the way I responded to it.

The religion problem is another factor which affects the way a person will behave. I have noticed that usually the persons attending church and Sunday school have higher morals than those people who never attend church, or who never realize that there is a church. I know I began to go to Sunday school when I was very young, and the little stories I read in the classes showed me what was right and wrong to do in society.

The associations that one's parents keep and also the friends that one makes in school and in public will govern one's behavior. Usually though, one's environment will determine the kind of people you will make for friends.

Projection. (Male)

My parents have projected upon me various thoughts and philosophies. Perhaps these theories may not be exactly right, yet they have been good enough for them, and I feel that they should know. It is what I have always been accustomed to, and until I find something better, I shall stick to this. My parents have taught me some manners, and although I may not be Emily Post, I feel that I know a little about etiquette. I try to be as mannerly and as polite as I can because I truly like to have someone be polite to me. "Do unto others as you would have them do unto you" seems very appropriate and I try to follow this to the best of my ability.

"A sense of obligation to my family." (Male)

When I was a small boy still going to grade school, I used to want to do things such as smoking and drinking, but then upon thinking what would happen if I were caught I would refrain from doing them. My father was very strict on these things which has led me to keep away from both of the habits.

When I grew older I thought how I would like to take out girls and go to dances, but in the small community in which I lived one could not do these things because the people all knew about it and would spread a lot of gossip.

When the time came for me to go to college I was to pick my course for my life work. I chose foreign trade as my major. I did not want to go to college at first but my folks wanted me to and were willing to send me. I was going to tell them that I did not want to go to school, but, then they were the ones who told me what to do, and as they had told everyone that I was to go to college, I went because I did not want people to talk about me as a boy who did things against his parents' wishes.

After two years of college, I want to go more than ever, because I see that one has to have an education to get any place in the business world. I take things here at college because I think they will help me in obtaining the goal that I have set for myself, and not because I want to take them. I have taken many courses that I would not take if they were not required in order to graduate. I don't care about getting good grades except to please my parents and to make my record look good. I get what I can out of all the courses and then worry about the grade.

Since I go to college on my father's money mostly, I think it is nothing but fair to do my part. I do not like to have him send me, however, and I try to earn what I can. Therefore, I have a job washing dishes to help pay my room and board. I don't like to have the other fellows say that my father is putting me through school. This is just another reason why I save all the money I make when I work in the summer, though I would much rather spend most of it and have a good time.

On this campus it has long been the custom of the upper classmen only to wear cords. I would like to wear them also, but the fact that the other fellows would take them off of me any place, even in the streets, makes me forget about wearing them. It is not only embarrassing to be in the street without pants, but it is against the law. I wear the traditional sophomore pants because of the custom.

I go to class most of the time to get what I can out of the lectures, but I also go because my profs insist upon good attendance. There are times that I would like to go out and get good and drunk and forget things, but I don't because it is against the rules and principles of my fraternity and the community.

I would like to forget about making a living and having responsibilities of a family in the future, and go to the South Sea Islands and live a life of leisure and rest, ignoring the outside world. I don't do these things because of public opinion, not that I would care what they would say about me after I was gone; what they would say about my family, and how they would feel would trouble me.

At times I would like to tell the present government administration what I think of them, but because of the fact that it is against the law and public opinion, I don't. The same thing applies to the college at times.

My goal to become a good business man in foreign trade has made me act according to the customs and ways of the society in which

I live, because the people are the ones with whom I have to get along in order to be a good business man. If I did not do as the rest did, I would not be accepted by the whole group, and thus could not be a success.

I have heard a lot about war and have seen pictures of it. I hate it and don't mind telling anyone so because I do believe in my opinion. On that one point I don't care what other people say about me or my parents. I would never go to war unless forced and, therefore, I don't believe that I would go, because I would probably be put in jail or shot for treason. However, at the present time there is no control against talking against war so I do it whenever I feel like it.

Like any other man I have had certain biological urges, but I have always kept my respect for the other sex because of social control. Anything that I do that has anything to do with the rest of the people with whom I live or am in contact, I do as they do. I do this because I have to live with people and would not like to live alone. I try to keep in step with the rest. The other things that I do, I do because I want to.

THE REALIZATION OF GROUP EXPECTANCY

Several individuals make it clear that they are always conscious either of the effect their behavior will have on others, or of the way others will treat them if they do not behave thus and so. Therefore, they follow conventional patterns to avoid censure or to find approval, being guided by a conscience instilled by a group important in their past experience.

"I respect others' opinions of me." (Female)

Why do we act as we do? There are as many different answers to that question as there are people, for I believe that everyone has personal explanations for his behavior in different situations. At the same time, it is rather difficult for a person to analyze his actions and arrive at a definite conclusion concerning them.

It is true that none of us act just as we desire or as our natural impulses prompt us, for there are many inhibitions and taboos surrounding human behavior. The way a person reacts to these restrictions is greatly influenced by his family background and the manner in which he has been taught. I can only cite myself as an example. My parents are people who are usually known as "good, law-abiding

American citizens." Naturally they taught their children that they should not steal what didn't belong to them, that they should tell the truth and be obedient, that they should be courteous, and that in general they should "do unto others as they would be done by."

I don't know how these standards of behavior came to be, in the first place, but that is how they were given to me. Merely having parents who instilled standards of good conduct into one does not make these standards the basis for living, but it does help to establish this basis. I believe thoughts of breaking moral laws do not occur so readily to those who have had such a family training in childhood, but when temptation to overstep the boundaries does arise it takes more than family training to control the temptation.

For instance, if I were sadly unprepared when a surprise test were given, and saw a way to cheat and make a grade of 100%—I wouldn't refrain from cheating merely because my parents would disapprove. In the first place, I would be afraid of getting caught in the act of cheating. Being caught would mean both punishment of some sort, and the ostracism of the other members of the class. As far as I am concerned personally, it is not so much fear of punishment as it is fear of public opinion which would restrain me. It would not bother me greatly to know that I would be punished for breaking a law if I also knew that no one would find out about it.

Of course if the punishment were severe—such as a lashing or life imprisonment—then I would probably pause and consider the punishment, but for such a thing as cheating it would be the dread of public opinion which would restrain me.

I would fear losing the respect of my classmates and would dislike having them look upon me as a cheat. I would fear having them criticize me and hate to be mistrusted by them. Then too, even if I were not caught outright, I would be constantly worrying for fear someone had seen me. Perhaps this is called one's conscience, but at any rate it would keep the act foremost in my mind for a time at least, and prevent my being at ease—and after all peace of mind is something.

One reason that people wish to be well-liked and respected by their fellows is that most of us have an aim which we are trying to fulfill and that aim necessitates the help of others. Our acquaintances will give us aid and boost us only when they like us and feel friendly toward us. Whether we realize it or not, we seem to behave as we do because we want something which we can get only through this type of behavior. Most of the time I am never conscious of acting to produce a desired result, but directly or indirectly, I believe that I do pattern my behavior to obtain some aim and goal I have set up.

My religion would not occur to me as a restraining factor in mere everyday matters. In more serious and weighty offenses I would probably refer to my religion, but for such matters as cheating, stealing, or lying, I believe that religious codes would not occur to me. The reasons that I would restrain myself from breaking most moral laws are purely personal ones.

I'm afraid that I would not consider other people so much as I would worry about how the breach of conduct would affect myself. I would fear my conscience, the chances of severe punishment, the chances of discomfort and harm to my person, and the disapproval of public opinion. I would pattern my actions to promote some aim of my own and to benefit myself in some way which I desired. Of all the restraining influences on my behavior, I believe that, for myself, public opinion is most important.

These reasons I have offered for my behavior are not noble ones and sound very selfish, but I believe that they approach the truth, to a certain extent at least.

" 'Be conventional' is my motto." (Female)

Why did I do that——that is perhaps the most common question we ask ourselves after doing a fool-hardy stunt or making an impulsive decision. And yet this just shows that we bow down to our irresistible urges at times and turn our backs on convention. Why don't we always behave as we would like to?

Perhaps it would be a good thing if we would try to analyze our actions now and then toward people in general, sex, religion, work, play, and so forth. Yes, it would be a very good idea; so I shall start in with people in general.

People have always been a source of interest to me. To the general run, so to speak, I am usually very friendly because I like people and prefer to be that way. However, there are times when some particular person or even a group of persons "hits me the wrong way." And what do I do? Usually nothing. If some blustering bully stamps into the office, where I am receptionist, and raises a rumpus about seeing the boss do I tell him where to head in? No, I treat him just as sweetly as I do the other callers and handle him with my smoothest pair of kid gloves. Why don't I tell him exactly what I think. Because business conventions dictate otherwise, and it would cost me my job.

As to a group that goes against my standards and ideas, I do nothing about it except perhaps to pour my bitter comments into the ears of my best friends, but as to standing up and defying the group all by myself—I wouldn't have the gumption to do it. I don't know why, either, unless it is that I was always brought up with the idea that "little girls should be seen and not heard," and it still affects me. Then too, I'm not very "quick on the comeback" and oftentimes lack the courage of my convictions because of this.

My attitude toward sex is one that is entirely dictated by convention and public opinion. I value my reputation more in this respect than in anything else. I will admit that there are times when I may feel like letting myself go, but I've never been sufficiently stirred for my emotions to sanction it, and I dislike thinking that I would ever be weak enough to do so—under illicit conditions anyway. I know that if our culture didn't put such a taboo on intimate sex relations (except between man and wife) I would think nothing of it. Sex is one conventional trait I would not care to rebel against.

Religion in my mind is a jig-saw puzzle. I really don't know what I believe. I have never gone to church a great deal, but from what I have attended, I've come to the conclusion that I will get just as much out of it as the next fellow by doing what I consider right and just. I truly think churches today are commercialized too much. It seems to me that very few Protestants are sincere about their religion, and that most of them go to church for the benefit of their business and the society column write-up that they get out of it—maybe I think so strongly on this point because I know quite a few people who go to church for just these reasons. Nevertheless, I still haven't any use for Protestant churches and their teachings—and by the way I am a Protestant—so I just don't go to church. Don't think me an atheist though, because I do believe in a Supreme Being.

Work and play I couldn't get along without. Of course, I prefer certain types of both, such as secretarial work, and dancing, swimming, and so forth, but if I had to earn money by doing work distasteful to me I would do that work anyway—this act would be prompted no doubt by my parents' influences (and probably by my appetite).

In the line of recreation we many times get "roped in" on something we don't especially care about, and nine out of ten of us will adhere to the code of being a good sport. I always do, unless the crowd is doing something very much against my principles. And it has to be something very, very much against them before I will make myself heard; I dislike being a "wet blanket" intensely. This isn't the teachings of my parents; it is the law of the younger set which I learned very early in life. I think in this respect more than anything else most of us will let public opinion govern our better judgment.

This all boils down to the fact that, not being of a radical nature, I let the conventional thing govern my actions in almost everything I say and do, and keep my resentful feelings to myself. But after all, if you want to get along in this world you can't be a radical. And you might just as well obey convention, because convention is a lot older and a lot more experienced than you are, and if you treat her right you will at least be happy while you are in the world.

"It's expected of me." (Male)

I act the way I do because I think it is expected of me. I restrain from doing many things which I would like to do because of my group. It is in the mores of the group and although it may seem right to many people, it would be looked on with disapproval in the group. Secondly, I restrain myself because I wouldn't want to do anything which would displease mother or reflect on my parents in a bad way. They were brought up in their environment and they tend to project their ways and actions onto their children. Third, I act in the manner I do to save myself from discomfort. I try to act the way others do to avoid being noticed and pointed out, because I know it is the only way to save myself from being ridiculed.

Public opinion. (Male)

I figure that all of my actions in public are based on the desire to be what people expect me to be. Very often I have a sudden impulse to do some silly thing, and I have to repress the feeling because I would be embarrassed if I did it. I'm grown up now, and people expect me to act grown up. There isn't much that can be said about it because there is really only one reason for my actions. Of course, I do some things because there are certain pleasures that I crave, but I do those things in the way that is conventional. If there weren't any other people on the earth beside myself, it is hard telling what I would do, or how I would act.

(See reference list at end of Chapter 21.)

SOCIAL CONTROL AND BEHAVIOR PROBLEMS AMONG CONTEMPORARY YOUTH (Continued)

INSTITUTIONALIZED PATTERNS

In addition to those papers which stress the family primarily are those which stress the effect of concepts developed by other social institutions with which they have associated, such as the church, the school, or the state.

"The day of judgment and regard for my present status." (Female)

Why do I behave as I do? My first impulse was to say that I did it because that is the way I want to behave. But you ask, "Why, then, do you want to behave the way you do?" After being cornered with both of these questions, I realize that I do not always behave as I please, but that when I do, there is something behind my wanting to behave in that particular way.

Religion has played a fairly important part in the culture in which I was raised. Although I have not always thought of it in exactly these words, that is one thing which has been a firm guide in many of my actions. I have always, to a certain extent, wanted to be able to make a decent accounting of myself if such a thing as a Day of Judgment ever comes. This idea has never obsessed me, but when I have had tendencies to get a little off the "right path," that thought has usually come to my mind. The fact that I lived with my grandparents, and that my grandfather was a minister, had considerable effect on my behavior until I was ten or eleven years old. After all, I was a representative of the church, and I must fashion my actions to suit such a role.

The thing that stands out in my mind during those years was the fact that I could not say "gee, gosh, darn, and heck," as the children of my age did. The ideals of our family had no place for such language and the result was that, for several years, I had two variations of our language—one which I used with my contemporaries and one which I used in the family group. After I was in high school, I realized the foolishness of this and accepted the family's standards.

As a child, I was allowed a great deal of self-expression—too much for my own good, I can see now. The point I wish to make is that perhaps I really was allowed to do more as I pleased than many children. However, I will have to admit that my expressions, whether in words or actions, were influenced by the culture around me. Ever since I can remember I have had to think before I did something out of the ordinary, and decide whether it would bring shame to the family. That has been so firmly impressed upon me that the very words "family honor" arouse a strong impulse in me to express myself in a manner which certainly would not make the family proud of me.

After I went to live with my father and step-mother, I met new barriers. Mother is a school teacher and our town is one of only 20,000 people. Whatever you do and say is the subject of much conversation, especially if someone in your family is an employee of the public. It seemed to me, during my junior and senior high school days, that I was constantly having to remember that Mother was a school teacher, and that whatever I did reflected upon her. After I graduated from high school, instead of being simplified, the situation became more complicated. I obtained the position of secretary to the registrar and principal of the high school. Now I was in a similar position to Mother. Everything I did and everywhere I went must be right in the eyes of the taxpayers, the people for whom I worked. Do not misunderstand me—the things I wanted to do were not so terrible, but it was the fact that there are always a few people in a small town who do a lot of talking, about very unimportant things that controlled many of my actions.

There was a period in my life when commands and threats played the strongest part in controlling my actions. When I was between twelve and fifteen years of age, I had an intense desire to break some of the rules of society to which I had always had to conform and many of the rules which my parents had always enforced. Threats or commands evidently were the only solution to control this impulse. It was not until after I began working that this urge left me. As I look back on those three or four years, I see that up to that time I had always been firmly controlled, but my grandparents had not made these various controls so obvious or unpleasant. When I was put into the new environment with my father and step-mother, these controls were not hidden. In fact, they were stressed so strongly that I do not wonder that I wanted to bolt out and practically ruin everything that stood in my way.

Praise from my parents or friends has always been effective in controlling my behavior. I enjoy knowing that what I have done has pleased someone, and that someone has wanted to encourage me by giving me a certain amount of praise. Then, too, persuasion has been influential. Many times I am too easily persuaded, but nevertheless, that factor has been used to lead me to better things. Until the last year or two, I had a horror of being laughed at. I have not been able to trace that fear back to its origin, but it has been a tremendous battle to overcome that feeling. I believe that, now, I have practically conquered it, at least to the point where I seldom worry about whether my actions will make people laugh at me.

As for my behavior here at college, I have little to say. I have become accustomed to observing rules and saying nothing about them. Here on the campus, practically everything we do is under very strict rules. You can do little or nothing about them, so why not be a "sport" and have a good time, even though some of the rules seem ridiculous?

Why do I behave as I do? I have not answered the question completely to my satisfaction—perhaps I never will. It seems to me that you can tell only to a certain point why you do these things, and after that, who knows?

"I have been taught what is 'proper'."   (Female)

In answering the question of why I behave as I do, I must first take into consideration the fact that most all of my years of training were given to me in a Catholic school by the Sisters of Charity. This helps to account for the fact that I believe myself to act more cultured and to have a better fixed position, in the role I play in society. By this I mean that I have been trained to know how to act, and how to control myself.

I behave as I do because I have also had a wonderful training at home from parents who disciplined me, and taught me right from wrong. I would, in no way that may injure the pride and interests of both my mother and father, do wrong just to give me more pleasure in life. The fear of hurting them guides my conscience in telling me that my actions reflect back on my parents and my home life. That is the main reason for my trying to lead a good, clean, natural life.

Another reason I behave and act as I do is that I am guided by the mores by which everyone abides. Of course it is much easier to do wrong just because we know we should not do it. That is the reason mores affect us. They are laws by which every human being must live.

As I am a Catholic, there are a lot of so-called "laws" that we as Christians must not break. These are called the Ten Commandments. In these we are taught that we are to follow the rules of God, and these rules, like the mores, guide our lives to a goal that we will in time attain if we do not break them. I feel that this is the main reason I behave as I do. I would not go out and steal from my neighbor, nor would I kill my neighbor's child. I would not commit adultery, nor would I curse or use blasphemous words in public. I know all this would be wrong. If we were allowed to commit these offenses against society we would be like beasts, not humans.

Although I act according to all the rules of society, I have not figured out yet why at times I find myself acting extremely queer. I guess though one can't always figure out why he does certain things.

I have tried to account for my behavior, but find when one stops to analyze himself as to "why" he does this and "why" he does that, it is not an easy job. However, in applying this to sociology, I guess it is just the environment in which I was taught that makes me act the way I do.

"My habits have been formed by social institutions." (Female)

It is often difficult for one person to understand just why another fails to see things in the same light as he. Some people fail to realize that there are many factors which influence a person's behavior in a given situation, or influence his attitudes toward a certain idea.

My behavior is largely a result of the habits formed during the early part of my life. These habits were influenced mainly by my cultural background. The principle factors determining this cultural background were the home, the school, the church, the community, and the nation. It was these different social institutions which formed my basic habits, developed my philosophy of life, and oriented me toward a definite goal. My organic nature also played an important role, and the attitude of other people toward my actions determined to a great extent what I would do.

In order to explain these influencing factors more clearly, I should first of all like to consider the importance of my cultural background on my behavior. It was in the home that I spent the first six years of my life, the most plastic period. Of course, my brother and I had our squabbles, but there was not any hair pulling or breaking of furniture, and I was always taught to try to get along with others. As I grew older, this had a definite economic result on our family. Since we were in a business which served the public, we could not afford to have many people disapprove of our actions. Consequently, I naturally developed a friendly spirit toward all people. In the home, also, I was taught to respect my parents, my teachers, and my elders. Of my parents, I believe my mother projected her ideas on me more than my father. She has very definite ideas against women smoking, drinking, and dancing in public. These ideas have been so very deeply instilled into me that to this day I have no desire whatsoever to drink, smoke, or attend the "public rat races."

The school also has aided in the formation of my habits. Probably the most outstanding of these early acquired habits is punctuality. From the first grade throughout my secondary education I was taught to be on time. One thing I have learned since I came to college is that most social affairs start at least fifteen minutes after they are scheduled. During my freshman days I was usually the first person to arrive "on the scene of action." The school (also the home) taught me the value of reliability. If I was given a task to perform, it was up to me to see it through.

In addition to the influences of the school, the church infused in me the basic virtues of life—humility, beauty, unselfishness, and helpfulness. This social institution has played a dominant part in the fixing of many of my religious habits, attending church and prayer.

The community in which I was reared also influenced my behavior. Since it is a small rural community a very friendly atmosphere prevails. Families exist as a unit and are very much interested in the people who live around them. I believe this rural environment has made me much more conscious of my fellow associates at college than the city-bred child.

To a small extent the nation also has had an effect on my behavior. The school and the home have taught the principles of democracy until I have developed an ethnocentric point of view: that democracy is the best type of government under which anyone can live. A feeling of pity for people who live in dictator-ruled countries pervades our country's mores.

There is still another factor which plays an important role in determining how I behave, and that is my organic nature. The environment has been much the same for us three children, but still none of us are alike in our behavior. This can be explained by our organic make up. First of all, I am a girl, and, naturally, I am not as forceful as my brothers. One organic characteristic is that I am more highly emotional. When they do anything, they like to have the group's sanction for it, but if not, it does not bother them a great deal. As far as I am concerned, if I do not have the support of the group I do not tackle a problem. What other people think has too much influence on my life. There are things I do not do at home because "people will talk."

Law and custom. (Male)

Sometimes, even I wonder why I do certain things. This subject is not nearly as pertinent to the sociologist as it is to myself, and this is not my first attempt to analyze myself and my actions.

To begin at the beginning: I imagine the basis of most of my actions and habits can be traced to my early life, although I find new things cropping up every day of my life, and some of them puzzle me to a great extent. Many actions and customs can be traced to both written and unwritten laws upheld by our civilization. These are all impressed so firmly in the mind of a youngster that soon they become habits which he will not break. The most important of these written laws, in my estimation, deals with stealing or robbery. I, as all other children, had the habit for a short time of, should I say, picking up things which did not belong to me, but this habit did not last long because of the punishment that was dealt me on each occasion that I was caught. The difference between right and wrong is learned by the child through a series of lessons. The child is taught right from wrong by punishment when he does the wrong thing. I believe that at times I had three or four lessons at once, but it was evidently for the best, as I feel now that as far as my morals and standard of living are concerned, I am slightly above average.

Human nature is another big factor in the way we behave. I have often wondered if other people take life with the same attitude as

I do, and, strange as it seems, there are many in the same boat with me.

Our social habits are more or less of the unwritten law type. A man is generally a gentleman if the men surrounding him are gentlemen. The greatest share of these customs are learned from observation. True, my mother taught me many things about etiquette, but it was not impressed on my mind until I saw a man tip his hat to a lady or give up his seat in a street car. These things and many others are carried on through force of habit created by years of practice. Many of these customs are beginning to fade now, but I believe that the greater part of them will hold as long as men are the aggressors in matrimonial affairs.

In summing up this subject, I can simply say that the real cause for all of our actions is one of two things: namely, law, and custom; these two govern all peoples in our civilization.

"What keeps me from doing what I wish." (Female. This is one of only two papers that even mention law. Only the part referring to law is reproduced.)

Laws keep me from doing a few things such as speeding in cars, jaywalking, and so forth. I am kept from doing other things I wish to do by fear—fear of justice or fear of injury. An example of the latter is: Fear keeps me from walking out in the street in front of a car.

EMOTIONAL-TEMPERAMENTAL QUALITIES

A few individuals stress the importance of emotional-temperamental traits in their actions. One individual says the most important point of interest is ". . . my unusual temper. When I get angry at something, I have a great deal of trouble keeping myself in hand. When mad, I want to smash everything I come in contact with." This individual did not go on, however, to explain just how he controls this temper, if he does so.

Others indicate the presence of fear, meekness, or the tendency to so direct behavior as to adjust smoothly to difficult situations. One young man gives his views on the importance of personality, which he apparently considers biological. He states a sound principle, even though he uses the term personality in a different sense than it has been used in this book. He says:

In spite of this attempt of the fraternities and sororities to regulate each member and cast them into a mold, there is always an exception, just as there is to any other rule or regulation of behavior. This is caused by personality, which is never the same in any two people. It doesn't seem to make any difference how much training a person has had along a certain line, for if it is contrary to his own mind and personality, he will rebel, and very often he will act in opposite form than he should.

Personality is one thing that cannot be governed by any set rule, or by the books of any author. In many respects, I believe that this is the real governing influence of a person's life. The background of mores and customs, which has been trained into a person all his life, acts as a factor in developing his personality.

"True to form usually but at times I am a rebel." (Female)

You ask me what controls what I do. I must say in answer that many different things have controlled my doings at various times. At the earliest period of my life I could probably have replied that it was because Mother or Daddy said it was wrong or right that I did or did not do such and such a thing. But now, as I have grown older, I find that a great many factors play important parts in what I do. Curiosity makes me do many things. I tried smoking for sheer curiosity. I decided that since so many people were smoking there must be some attraction, and I was determined to try to find that attraction. Other things I have tried just to see if I would be punished or get caught.

As to what keeps me from doing things, I don't always know. Sometimes it is religion, but my religion is rather spasmodic. At times I feel it strongly, while at other times I ignore it almost entirely. People, too, sometimes influence what I do. I see someone who has attained an exceptional degree of success and has also kept very high moral standards. I study them and admire them and wish to keep myself good and wholesome as this person, my example, has. Once in a while, I get totally discouraged and think that people can do most anything and get by with it, and then I think of my mother and father and the wonderfully high standards they have set and know that I must never hurt them. Sometimes I feel I must do right because they are still paying the bills and as long as this goes on, I should always aim to please them.

The primary group of my home community has much influenced

what I have done, too. The people of this group have looked up to me and admired me so much that I feel somehow that I owe them something. They watch me almost as closely as do my parents, and have trusted me so far that I feel I must do as they wish me to do.

These are the main reasons I have acted as I have, and, of course, my own standards which I have set up play an important part, too. These reasons may be good or poor, but they are actualities.

"I fear the consequences of behavior." (Male)

That seems a very interesting question to me because I must admit that I have never paused to consider why I have done certain things, although I realize there is a definite reason for every action.

My cultural heritage has been perhaps the greatest influence in forming my pattern of behavior. Since the time I have been able to understand, I have been drilled in the manner of acting acceptable by society. Great care was taken that I should present myself favorably to the public. The status of our family group is judged by the products of the home, and the role we play is definitely affected by public opinion. Of course, my parents lived in an age preceding our time, and their modes of thinking and acting had to be modified as civilization progressed and the society of which they were members recognized new and acceptable ways of acting. They taught me what they thought was right, and because I respect them and their knowledge, I adhere as closely as possible to their teachings. Through my desire for a pleasing personality I have borrowed as many desirable traits as my contacts with people have permitted.

Religion is another controlling factor in my behavior pattern. Although not a religious man, I attended church when I was younger and I believe that the impression the teachings of Christ made upon me have helped form my behavior pattern. The people who abide by the commandments are less sinful than the rest, and that is the way that I want to be.

Personal appearance became very important to me as I met more people. First impressions are hard to displace and because I want to make friends with and be accepted by those I meet, I think that personality and personal cleanliness are highly important. I strive to keep up with the "times," and no one is more jubilant than I when I can produce a joke that is falling for the first time upon the ears of the audience. Being clothes-conscious is a feeling that arises from contact with men and women who are fashionably dressed. I am ever contrasting my garb with those around me. Clothes of a few years past would be considered terribly out-of-date, and the wearer would be considered with reserve and laughed at.

A summary of this discussion, I feel, condenses into one main element. I act as I do because I am afraid of what people might think of me, and afraid of the reflection on my family of actions not acceptable to this society.

"The meek inherit the earth." (Female)

It's now after nine P.M. and this paper is not completed yet. I realized before that it would take a number of hours, and that I should have started sooner. Why do I behave as I do?

Perhaps one of the fundamental reasons for my behavior in most circumstances is that I value other people's opinions too highly. As a result, I'm usually hasty in finishing my required work, and very likely don't do as well as I am capable of doing. When someone asks a favor of me, I dislike to refuse them; and if it is at all possible, I try to fit the task into my day's schedule. Although I don't consider myself the Casper Milquetoast type of personality, yet I do let people impose upon me at times. I don't mean to sound conceited, but I'm merely trying to be frank and honest.

I think it is interesting to do little tasks for people if you have the time, because so many of them turn out to be novel experiences and different from what one expected. For example—ushering. One evening I was asked to substitute for a girl friend at one of the college plays. After a moment's hesitation and the thought that I did want to see the play, I agreed. The job was fun. Now I'm on as a "steady," and get as much enjoyment from it as I did at first.

Why have I let people impose on me? Because all through school I always thought I had an inferiority complex, and now at college that feeling has at times almost disappeared. The friendly contacts with a hundred girls here in the dormitory, and close friendships with a few, have given me a greater sense of balance—of what the group as a whole expects of one, and not the individualistic viewpoint. After all, it is through group influence—primary and secondary— that our mores and folkways have been developed and changed from time to time.

Another point is that I like peace. Petty squabbling and bickering with that undercurrent of distrust and bitterness disturb me terribly, so that at times I am willing to sacrifice my point rather than prolong the antagonism.

The second reason lies in the strictness of my upbringing, and, more important, in my natural timidity. In my home, common courtesy has always been stressed, and now I find it difficult to relax and join in the banter usually exchanged in a group of young people; and because I want them to like me, I want to say things that are pleasing or flattering to them. I am sincere, but this isn't the way one gets along with others, as formality and shyness are not accepted. College has really helped me, I believe, but there is always room for improvement.

The third factor represents my goal in life. I have set one although it is rather indefinite. At the present time, it is to graduate from college, get a good stenographic position with opportunities for advancement, and to repay my parents for their generous sacrifices. Some time later on, I want to get married.

I don't believe that small personal goals should be stressed so much in one's mind, such as the desire to be asked to join a certain "honorary." You should do your best at all times, and forget about the rewards. If you are worthy, you will not be left out. Also the most pleasant happenings come as complete surprises, and as a result, are even more appreciated.

In general, I behave as I do because I consider it the expected procedure in the various groups in which I participate. At times, I admit, I value too highly the good opinion of those few who, because of their status, I admire and wish to imitate. Yet, many times, what I consider the expected procedure isn't so any longer; consequently, all I can do is what I myself consider right. Yet, my creed of personal behavior is interwoven with the opinions of others, so that the whole consideration revolves in a vicious circle, leaving one doubtful and upset as to what exactly represents the true you.

"I am the retiring type." (Female)

I don't believe many people realize the reason they do things. They just do them. They don't seem to stop and think that what they do is different from what other people do, and that there must be something that makes each person in his own way act as he does.

Ever since I have been little, I never have been able to quite figure out why I am afraid of imposing on people. My mother or father have never licked me, although I have been scolded many times. I can't ever remember anyone making me feel shy, but I have had that tendency all along. I am afraid to go into a crowd and talk to them for fear of not being welcome. I have never wanted to seem too forward. Here on the campus I will walk around and not look at people in passing cars for fear that they may think I am trying to flirt with them. I pass up many of my friends on the street for this very same reason. We have lived in an out-of-the-way place for many years. This might account for my actions. My nature, however, tends to be friendly, and I will treat people fairly decently. I may tend to put on a superior accent, because I have such an inferiority complex.

In my case, my actions seem to be all bound up, from childhood, with fear of public opinion, and my own sense of what I feel is right; I believe in most cases my conscience guides me.

"I protect my emotional complexes."   (Female)

I find it extremely difficult to begin telling precisely why I behave as I do, because until I came to college and took a course in sociology, I had never so much as wondered about the question.

Primarily, I presume, the main cause for my general behavior is the particular cultural environment in which I lived from the time I was born to the present date. When I was very young—and here I might add that I am the youngest of three girls in our family—I was constantly "babied," petted, and given my own way. Had it not been for one certain incident in our family life, I might still be in the same so-called "spoiled" position. While the incident I speak of was in itself a tragedy, as it completely broke up our family life, I still believe that it did me good in one way. The above-mentioned happening was the separation of my parents when I was about fourteen years old, and, finally, their divorce about three years later. This experience had one advantage for me in that it knocked me out of a terrible state of selfishness and conceit. Another factor entering into the picture is that soon after the divorce my two sisters were married, thus leaving my mother, with whom I have lived ever since, and me entirely on our own.

For these reasons I have since been more independent, better able to take care of myself, and have had more ability to stand on my own two feet. One fact that strikes me as peculiar is that more than one person has told me that I act at times over-independent. I trace this particular characteristic of mine back to my environment since the time I was fourteen and started living alone with my mother. Another trait that I must admit having is that of being snobbish at times. I'm afraid that I must confess being one of numerous persons who try to cover up an inferiority complex by a superior manner. Again that sudden change of environment, brought about by my parents' separation, comes into effect; for if our home life had continued as it normally should have, I don't believe I would have developed an inferiority complex. The fact that this change came when I was in the act of changing my environment from one secondary group to another: namely, that important step from grade school to high school, is also extremely important, as I was at the time beginning to mature rapidly. I remember very well listening longingly to other children tell of their happy home life, of how they did this and that with their "Daddy," whom I can but faintly recall living with, and of how their whole family went on a certain trip together, and so forth. This gave me the feeling that they all had something important that I didn't have, all of which resulted in an inferior feeling.

There are a few traits that I have carried over from my primary group environment before the divorce. One of these seemingly trivial traits is a certain daring, an "always take a chance" characteristic, that I seem to have developed. I have found this more noticeable since I have been living in the secondary group life environment in college. While some small incidents that have happened to me in college seem immaterial and trivial now, I realize that I have meanwhile been developing certain characteristics that will be more evident later in life, and at the present date, I don't know if they will be for better or for worse. While I seem to progress perfectly well in group life, I constantly find myself taking some silly chance, such as climbing out a window, sneaking out on a 7:30 school night, or smoking in my room. I trace these patterns of behavior back to my very early childhood when I was extremely spoiled and had absolutely no respect for authority.

I personally believe that most of my behavior patterns can be traced back to cultural environments in both my primary and secondary groups. While heredity may enter into the question of why we behave as we do, I don't believe that it is of much importance. Heredity did, however, give me one outstanding trait, that of a rather fiery temper. Of course, much of my temperament has been developed through my background in the family. The only significance of my having inherited this temper is that it in turn has developed other traits, all of which lead back to environment.

MODELS

Two individuals stress the importance of example, apparently tending on the one hand to pattern their behavior to a considerable extent after another or others whom they respect, or on the other hand, to avoid certain behavior because they reacted negatively to a bad example.

The influence of example. (Female)

I have analyzed my actions for the past few days in an effort to discover why I behave as I do. Control of behavior comes from several sources: the family, the friends, the culture and laws of the country, and oneself.

When the child is very young, his behavior depends entirely on the rules set down by his parents. He has, at first, no conception of any other rules of conduct. Some of the ideals given to him by his family will remain with him always.

As he grows, he finds other things he would like to do; at the same time, he finds new "do's and don'ts" that are set up to combat these new desires. Perhaps he attends church, wherein he discovers that only certain conduct will entitle him to peace hereafter. He learns the attitudes of playmates and finds that they approve some actions and ridicule others. He learns, through education in schools, the reason that certain types of behavior are sanctioned while other conduct is considered socially improper; he learns about laws and why they should be obeyed. By the time he has reached the " 'teen age," he has, through all of these contacts with the outside world, formed quite definite ideas of right and wrong. He has accepted certain standards to be his own, and has rejected others because he felt they were unworthy. This may be termed the "honorable" age.

Later, these standards will change. I will illustrate this change by my own experiences and ideas. I found that my own behavior pattern had developed along these same general lines until the late 'teens. Since then, personal desires have influenced my actions to a marked degree. I know this sounds strange at first. Yet, thinking over my life so far, I find that many of the things I considered most important during the earlier years have been broken down when the desire for certain actions have become sufficiently strong. Prejudice against certain practices, such as smoking, were broken down when I saw people whom I regarded highly indulging.

Culture of the country has a great deal to do with behavior. People in Europe and America wear clothes, and because they do, I do. Because it is customary to eat three meals a day, I do, although I am often not hungry. Because most young people of certain means attend college, I am here.

Laws, made for the good of all, are commonly obeyed. Yet, when personal desires, coupled with intense emotions, become strong enough, the most ethical and revered of these laws are broken. Emotions are a great stimulant for certain kinds of behavior. One may be actuated by love, hatred, fear, until he is not far removed from the wild beast. Murder, violent rages, and hysteria are the product of ungoverned emotions. I have seen people become almost insanely angry, and the sight so disgusted me that I keep a close rein on my own emotions insofar as good taste is concerned.

I believe that those born in rural areas are less open to change in their basic standards than are their city friends. Churches, family ties, may be the cause of it, but it is nevertheless true. In this instance, environment is a factor in the growth of the behavior pattern. When the young person is placed in a different environment, his standards do change. He behaves differently in college than he does at home. This is proof, I believe, of this fact.

Complexes, common to children of twelve to fifteen years, are overcome by education. Learning about personality problems in the school has completely erased any complex that I might have had. Education, in this way, influences the conduct of the young person.

Goals may be considered as criteria for conduct by some, but I feel that there are no important goals in the lives of most young people of this section. Plans are so often upset, and death has interceded in so many friend's lives that the ultimate plans are subordinated so that they do not constitute an important behavior control. It is the code of most people whom I know to live only for today, for no one knows what tomorrow may bring, and there is no use worrying about it.

In conclusion, it is my theory that behavior is influenced by all the contacts and experiences that one is subject to. These standards, however, are always subject to change by personal desire.

Example and precept. (Female)

All my life I have been absolutely frank in all I say. If I don't like a thing or person I make no bones about saying so. This has been the result of my very early childhood. Our neighbor lady, who visited with my mother very frequently, used to say many sweet things that she never meant, and I knew she didn't; so my mother told me to always say what I meant, and not to say things that weren't true just to please people. This has gotten me into many arguments, but then, I think nobody respects me the less for saying so.

One of my best characteristics is that I never talk about people behind their backs; this has resulted from going to Sunday school. One of my first Sunday school teachers lectured to us on the sin of talking about people, and told us to overlook their bad points and just notice their good ones. This is one of the compliments that people always give me, and I am very proud of it.

The Code of Youth

Only two papers stressed to any extent the tendency of modern youth to have a code which differs from the family pattern and perhaps from that of the adult world. These, however, to the author, are the most meaningful papers of the lot. It seems that even sociologists have not given sufficient attention to the fact that many modern youth, in addition to living within the pattern of the family, tend to develop a code which applies primarily to youth—a code which the adult world does not understand, and frequently does not even know.

As large groups of young people come to attend high school and college, these codes probably become increasingly important in shaping their behavior. It is quite obvious that, in the case of the group which is discussed in this chapter, family patterns are still the predominant influence, and yet these two individuals, and some others to a lesser degree, indicate that they are actually conscious of pressure of a young people's group, and feel that frequently this young group has codes that are not exactly in harmony with those of the family, the neighborhood, or even of the adult community. A comparable situation probably never existed among primitive peoples,[1] and still does not

---

[1] Usually the youth societies among primitives are recognized institutions of the adult community. Our youth groups are to a considerable extent the product of spontaneous organizations, and unrecognized by the adult society.

exist to a very great extent in isolated rural communities, even in our nation, where rural youth are much more under the supervision of the family than are urban youth. Yet I suppose most high school youth feel the pressure of the youth group increasingly.

"Once my family, but now my friends and my purse control me." (Female)

What controls me? I have always been independent-minded; however, I have quite definite ideas of right and wrong. These are traditional in my family circle and I naturally adhere to them. I have no particular fear of the disapproval of either of my parents, but I am happier if I please them. This is only natural, because it is extremely unpleasant to have friction in the home. This family control was very strong when I was a small child. In fact, I can well say it was my only control. I recall an occurrence in which this respect and awe of my parents' advice was almost destructive. We lived on a farm about fifteen miles from town. When my mother and father left me alone with my two brothers one day while they went into town, we children spent the day playing hide-and-go-seek. My elder brother hid in a trunk which was full of old clothes, and as he pulled the lid shut, it automatically locked. When he couldn't get out, he yelled for my brother or me to unlock it. Although the key was in the lock, we could not open it. We considered running to the home of our nearest neighbor for assistance, but were afraid to do this, because my mother had told us specifically not to leave the house. It was raining and we didn't want her to find mud on our shoes, and so, after vainly hacking the lid of the trunk with a butcher knife, we decided to wait for my mother's return. It was so stuffy in my brother's hiding place that he fainted and was still unconscious when my parents returned home. My mother couldn't understand our lack of practical sense, but she had told us to stay in, and nothing but her consent could have induced us to leave the house.

As I have grown older, however, this family control has become weaker every year. I no longer fear or respect my parents' wishes very much—I tolerantly humor them. Unless it is something I definitely do not want to do, I obey their wishes just to keep peace in the family. While I am living away from home, the control of my friends is substituted for my family control. I want my actions to meet with the approval of my friends. I find that most of the girls with whom I live act and talk similarly from constant association.

Beside being controlled by family traditions, there are mores and folkways of our culture that determine what we shall consider good and bad—right and wrong. If the majority of people ignored these rules, our civilization would no longer be a civilization, but a world of chaos. I do things, without reasoning why, in the way I am expected to do them.

Although I have no religious control whatsoever, the golden rule is written on my mind. Very often when I consider doing something that concerns another person I realize that I would resent someone doing the same to me, and I decide not to do it. Most people are considerate of others, and refrain from doing things to which they will object.

Economic control is, in my opinion, the strongest, most persistent control of all. Everyone's actions are determined and restricted by his financial status, no matter how rich or how poor he may be. For instance, the drinking of liquor would be more prevalent on the campus if students had more money to spend. There would be more cars and probably all students would belong to fraternities and sororities. Money is king in our world.

Being an easy going person, I never have the urge to do anything particularly drastic. Many people think with their hearts instead of their brains, and I must admit that I am one of these. When I want to do a thing I do it, even if my practical sense tells me I should not. My desires, however, are limited to trivial matters, and I am never condemned for satisfying them.

Summarizing, I am slightly controlled by family customs, traditions of our culture, consideration of others, and my financial condition. Generally speaking, however, I follow my heart.

"My ideas of conduct." (Female)

Sometimes I wonder if it pays to behave oneself. There are naturally times when I do behave myself, and then again there are times when I don't.

I have my own code of morals, somewhat affected by my parents' views, but on the whole established by myself.

For instance, I don't smoke. I have been both complimented and embarrassed for that. Since most every girl I run around with smokes, and that excessively, it is somewhat of a novelty for them to kid me, though for some reason, I feel that some of them at least admire me for refraining from it.   Why do I?   Well, first of all, it is too expensive, and it doesn't help one's health whatsoever; in fact, I hear it is most detrimental.   Then too, most every girl who so indulges is only doing it to show off and be smart.   In my opinion, it lowers them to a great extent.   And I feel well rewarded for my abstinence when the boys who are worthwhile appreciate the fact that I don't smoke.   It is not only the boys, but middle-aged people, people who know and who have been around, who congratulate me for being so wise.

Once in a while when I'm out with a crowd of kids who are in the mood for drinking, I am rather puzzled as to what to do.   If I refuse, they think I'm a prig and a wet blanket; if I do it, it hurts me because I hate the stuff and I know it isn't doing me any good. When I'm tired and the evening is dull, a glass of wine does wonders, but to go to a cafe and spend a whole evening in such a wasteful manner is not my idea of a good time.

There is also the boys' side of it.   They like to take out a girl who will be sociable and full of fun.   If he wants some liquor, then she should be agreeable.   But I try to accept dates where I won't be expected to be quite so agreeable.

That also goes for this business of necking and petting.   I hate those words, so I'll use one commonly heard in my home town; namely, "checking."

A fellow will see just how far he can go with a girl, and the harder she is to get the more he likes her.   He'll take out the one that is loose and will check with anyone and everyone where no one will see them.   But the girl that he is proud to show to his friends and the general public is the other girl, his real girl.

In other respects, I usually act too impulsively; I don't stop to think first whether or not it is just the thing to do.   Several times when there's been nothing doing in the evening, a group of us would get together and try to think of something to do.   I'd suggest something; once we stacked a girl's room and we really had fun, only afterward we regretted doing it, because the girl was so nice and really didn't deserve it.

I dislike very much people who talk about others behind their backs.   If I don't care for someone, I ignore her and try to keep my distance.   It makes me ill to see someone so nice to a person and then talk so terribly about that person a few minutes later behind her back.

I love to have a good time, just as everyone else does, but I hate loud, conspicuous people. When I'm out in the public eye, I like to be seen and to make a favorable impression, but people that show off and make themselves obvious just don't appeal to me. A boy that is loud and noisy when he has a date just isn't on my accepted list. I have found out through experience and observation that what a girl believes and tries to live up to means little or nothing when she has "fallen for a guy." All his faults and failings are blissfully ignored by the girl, or else she is so in love with the fellow that his good points far outnumber his bad ones and she doesn't care about them.

My parents have always judged the fellows that come to see me by their appearance and manners, and so I have come to see them and pass on them through my folks' eyes too.

I can always have all the dates I want, and therefore I think sometimes I'm not quite as careful and particular about my clothes and personal appearance as I could be, for I don't have to try especially hard to catch their eyes; in fact, I try to discourage many of them.

I have been told by one of my teachers that I have been too free and friendly with the boys in my folk dancing class, where everyone is a P. E. major and knows everyone else. We are all in rather jovial moods because that type of dancing does help everyone to break down any of that ill-at-ease feeling. Some of the boys are rather rough and crude, but one can't be too stiff and stuck up to them, because I tried it and it certainly doesn't go over. Then I was nice and laughed with them and let them hold my hand, and I had them all joking with me and also Miss ——— on my neck. Anyway, I think of boys as friends, almost in the same manner as I do girls. I like to have a good time with them, not on the basis of sweethearts but just as pals.

I'm afraid I have been a tomboy and roughneck too long to change now to the sweet, demure type of girl; and personally I like it better anyway, because I am having a very good time and still am considered, to my knowledge, a well-behaved girl.

Conclusion

The following points are of interest in this summary of student reactions to the question of why they behave as they do: First and most important of all, the influence of the family seems very dominant in the consciousness of this group of freshmen college youth. Apparently even in our time, when the family is supposed to be disintegrating, and when youth are supposed to have revolted from the family, the college freshmen in this group still regard their parents' wishes very highly, and are governed to a great extent by the desires of their parents.

These youth are conscious that they are living constantly before spectators. They are aware of the response their action will bring from others, and govern themselves accordingly. Whether this consciousness of group surveillance is higher among the college group than among other youth would be hard to say. It is possible that this group is more analytical of such phenomenon than the non-college person because they were just completing a first course in sociology.

Of other institutionalized patterns aside from the family, those of the religious institutions loom most large. There is little mention of law, even though in our culture every individual is surrounded by this control device.

Emotional and temperamental qualities are mentioned as affecting the behavior patterns of youth, tending either to make them submissive to social controls, or aggressive and militant.

Models and examples are mentioned as being effective in certain cases. If one should consider the parents also as models this influence is highly important. Models act as both positive and negative influences. There are types to be patterned after, and types to be scrupulously avoided.

The code of youth, while not stressed much in these papers, is suggested. It seems obvious that some youth, when they leave the family circle, fall into a youth group which has a code of its own, and which tends to become very influential in their experience, even tending to replace the family as the chief agency of control.

From discussing this problem somewhat with college students, and from reading a great number of college students' autobiographies over a period of seven years, the author is inclined to believe that the code of youth is a very important influence in the life of contemporary high school and college students. The fact that the group consisted largely of freshmen probably explains why the youth pattern is not stressed as much as the family pattern. Also, the school where these papers were written is located in a rural area, and draws heavily from the small town and the farm for its student enrollment. Most of these individuals have not yet been "weaned" away from home. Undoubtedly if one were to take a similar group of papers from college seniors he would find that the standards of the college group have come to dominate much more largely than they appear to do among this group of freshmen. It is very likely that many younger persons living in metropolitan communities have come to be controlled mainly by youth codes.

SELECTED REFERENCES

Dimock, H. S., Rediscovering the Adolescent. Association Press, New York, 1937.

Elliott, Mabel A., and Merrill, Francis E., Social Disorganization. Harper and Brothers, New York, 1934.

Flügel, J. C., The Psycho-Analytic Study of the Family. Hogarth Press, London, 1931.

Garrison, Carl C., The Psychology of Adolescence. Prentice-Hall, Inc., New York, 1934.

Hall, G. Stanley, Adolescence. D. Appleton-Century Company, New York, 1905.

Hall, G. Stanley, Youth; Its Education, Regimen, and Hygiene. D. Appleton-Century Company, New York, 1906.

Loeb, E. M., Tribal Initiations and Secret Societies. University of California Press, Berkeley, 1929.

Lowie, R. H., Primitive Society. Boni and Liveright, New York, 1925.

Mead, Margaret, Coming of Age in Samoa. William Morrow and Company, New York, 1928.

Mead, Margaret, Growing Up in New Guinea. William Morrow and Company, New York, 1930.

Mead, Margaret, Sex and Temperament in Three Primitive Societies. William Morrow and Company, New York, 1935.

Sadler, William S., Piloting Modern Youth. Funk and Wagnalls, New York, 1931.

Seabury, David, Growing into Life: A Magna Charta of Youth. Boni and Liveright, New York, 1928.

Thom, Douglas A., Normal Youth and Its Everyday Problems. D. Appleton-Century Company, New York, 1932.

Thomas, W. I., *The Unadjusted Girl*. Little, Brown and Company, Boston, 1924.

Tozzer, A. M., *Social Origins and Social Continuities*. The Macmillan Company, New York, 1925.

Turfey, Paul H., *The Growing Boy: Case Studies of Developmental Age*. The Macmillan Company, New York, 1930.

Weber, E. A., *The Duk-Duks*. University of Chicago Press, Chicago, 1929.

PART VI

THE BREAKDOWN OF SOCIAL CONTROL AS A FACTOR IN SOCIAL PROBLEMS

PART VII

CHAPTER 22

THE RELATION OF SOCIAL CONTROL TO PERSONALITY DISORGANIZATION

The processes of social control as exercised by groups with different standards invariably cause personality conflict, in any person belonging to more than one group. This fact can best be understood by examining a concrete case of an individual subjected to two culture patterns. The following account of the experience of a college student, whose parents grew up in the culture of the deep South, but who, before she was born, moved to a community in the Northwest, where the philosophy of life, especially with respect to the role of woman, was quite different, shows the conflict experienced from absorbing one set of values, codes, and standards in the home, and another in the school and community.

PERSONALITY DEVELOPMENT UNDER DUAL SYSTEMS OF CONTROL: A CASE STUDY [1]

I was born on a large western wheat ranch, the second child and eldest daughter in a family of seven. My parents, middle-aged at the time of my birth, had recently moved from a tobacco plantation in Virginia. They had grown up there, and the morals and customs of society in the old South were well-integrated in their personalities. In the South the pioneering stage has long passed; in the far West many attitudes of the frontier persist.

My family had come from ancestors of high social status in their former community. Their ideas of perfection in behavior were positive, well-defined, and very definitely influenced by religious experience. One did not judge people by such superficial standards as beauty, wealth, or education. Judgment was based on those more lasting and spiritual qualities which characterized "quality folks." These qualities included manners, respect for authority, unselfish-

---

[1] From a student autobiography in the author's collection.

ness, honor, hospitality, morality, and family background. No reason in the world was sufficient to excuse one from even as much as a display of unwillingness to obey someone in authority. If one did disobey, it was a source of much humiliation to the family. This family disapproval was the most efficient method, and practically the only means of control used with the children.

Another important trait was that one should never hurt someone else's feelings except for a legitimate reason. In the case that there was good reason, then one felt justified in completely "burning the person alive." But even in such instances one was supposed to maintain a certain dignity—a reserve that was never broken down. One mark of a fine person was his perception of the feelings of those about him. This sense was developed to as high a degree as possible.

I myself always addressed my elders by their title. It was a violation of an important point of behavior not to do so, and a source of shame. All my elder cousins were addressed as "Cousin Mary," "Cousin John," and so forth. The children in the western neighborhood thought this queer.

One never displayed an emotion unless it was a desirable one. Crying in public, laughing loudly, showing one's disappointment in not receiving an honor, or one's pleasure at someone's misfortune— these were serious misdemeanors. One was ashamed of those who violated this standard, and the guilty one was looked upon with so much disapproval that seldom did he repeat the offense.

Smoking was not taboo for men, but for women to smoke was terrible. They would no more think of smoking than of doing farm work or going somewhere at night unescorted by either an older woman or a man. The men in the family considered it their duty to protect women, who were supposed to be clinging vines. It was a source of much shame for a man to allow a woman's name to be slandered in his presence. It made little difference if the remark made were true or not. Much the same feeling existed in regard to one's friend.

Women were not supposed to be burdened with knowledge of finances, although the wife often by indirect methods had a great deal to say in business matters. Her place was supposedly in the home, acting as hostess, training the children, and guarding her health. Above all things, she was not supposed to dominate her husband; but if anyone displeased her it was her husband or brother or father who settled the matter, especially in the case of her being slighted or insulted by another man. The matter of family and personal honor was regarded with great seriousness.

A promise was as sacred as anything could be. For instance, if one lost a thousand dollars because of an unimportant promise, one kept that promise without flinching. Furthermore, the loss was never openly regretted.

Excessive drinking was looked upon with disgust, although drinks with dinners and so forth were thought to be quite in order. Drinking parties were considered to be completely below the dignity of folks of quality; only common people had them.

If one had little money, he would sacrifice practically all the material things of life before his pride would allow him to accept a loan under certain conditions. One could borrow with a clear conscience from a person of high moral standing and of equal social status with himself. But to borrow from some common person, or someone who had little social standing, was seldom done. A person did nothing to increase his financial standing or reputation that did not conform to the highest ethics of the code of honor. If one starved to death, one did so willingly, rather than accept something from a person who had stained one's honor.

The family background of any person was taken seriously into consideration in judging that person. It was a profound belief in the family that swans do not come from a crow's nest. However, if one's behavior were excellent and one were accepted in every other respect, a poor family background was more or less disregarded. It was not the family name that counted, but they firmly believed that only with a good background could one have the other desirable traits.

As to their feeling of the relation of the white to the Negro, there was no doubt in their minds as to what they believed. Negroes were regarded as very desirable in their place. But that place was not on an equal plane with whites. The respectable Negro was not despised, except when he overstepped his privileges, and every person of good social standing knew the Negro's place. A Negro cannot feel equal to a white—as soon as the white gives him equal privileges, the Negro feels superior, because the white, in doing so, has violated the code of conduct expected of him both by his own race and also by the inferior Negro. Those who made an attempt to convince them of the injustice of the fixed system of accommodation under which the races live in the south were looked upon with disgust and a slight feeling of contempt. Those who merely believed in race equality, but did not project their beliefs, were looked upon with both pity and ridicule because of their utter ignorance of the situation.

In the West my family was proud of their different culture. They avoided primary group contacts in the new community, and guarded against any assimilation of its culture into their own life patterns. It was an out-group, and was therefore inferior and undesirable.

During the first five years of my life my experience was almost entirely within the family group. I had intimate and harmonious contacts with everyone whom I knew or with whom I had any social contact. There was little conflict. I accepted without question the standards of my family. The mores, respect for authority, generosity, and manners of the southern culture were transmitted to me, both formally and informally, and I readily assimilated them. My range of participation was limited. My play group consisted of my older brother. There was no neighborhood group, as we were geographically isolated.

My first secondary group experience of any consequence came when I entered school. This marked the beginning of the conflict in my personality, due to the cultural differences of my primary and secondary groups. The other children talked with a different accent, and never said "ma'm" or "sir" when speaking to someone in authority. They swore, and contradicted the teacher. They had never been to church and ridiculed those who did go. My brother and I wondered why we were different. We had no standard by which to judge our new friends except our own. The integrity of our own standards was fast becoming a matter of doubt to us, under the criticism of the strong out-group. We developed a feeling of inferiority, but compensated for it to some extent by changing our accent to conform to that of the group into which we desired acceptance. We consciously tried to adopt the folkways peculiar to those of the new group. In time I became known as a bright pupil, and excelled in games and running. Perhaps this was a form of compensation for my feeling of inferiority caused by my peculiarity in the eyes of the new group but, if so, it was quite unconscious as far as I was concerned. With this role established my sense of competition grew to be very keen, and in fact, my whole personality developed on the basis of competition. When other children were not present, there was always my brother to overcome. Although I was often successful in this competition, no superiority complex developed. The praise of my high grades, speed in running, adeptness at games, and spirited disposition served only as compensation for my feeling of inferiority resulting from the knowledge that I was not like the other children. Again and again the question arose in my mind as to whether they or I were peculiar.

A difficult period of adjustment due to the breaking away from primary group control began when I entered high school. I encountered such a bewildering mass of new situations and experiences that my inferiority complex, carried over from early childhood, steadily became worse. Because of the cultural background of my family I could associate with only a very select group in the school. Morality was the chief standard for selection. Invitations had to be refused because someone's father drank excessively or because his sister was "wild." I would not rebel directly. My respect for authority was much too well integrated for that. But nevertheless, I resented the fact that my parents wanted to control my activities. I was beginning to accept more and more the patterns of the culture of my companions, who represented the out-group, and cast aside those of my family group.

After high school I entered college in a town some distance from home. Each time I returned home for a visit, things and people there seemed more changed. People who once seemed very polished and broadminded appeared much more narrow, and everything seemed to move more leisurely than before. It was not that the things had changed. It was that my standard of judging them was different. It was that I had adopted the standards of my new society.

PERSONALITY DISORGANIZATION AND THE SYSTEM OF SOCIAL CONTROL

We have long since ceased looking for the source of personality conflict and disorganization within the individual alone. Instead, we recognize that in most cases the environment is at the root of his personal problems; he is unable to adjust his inner life to the system of control imposed by the external surroundings. He is disorganized because (1) he lives in a disorganized culture where controls are ill defined, or (2) he is a marginal man, unable to select between conflicting cultures those traits which would make for an integrated personality, or (3) he embodies within his own personality the control devices of two or more groups with very diverse standards, or finally, (4) he is unable to regulate organic impulses and bring them in line with systems of control accepted by his group.

Personality problems of any sort may very possibly be a direct reflection of the effectiveness or lack of effectiveness of the system of control. Perhaps more often these problems reflect the effectiveness with which the individual has been able to harmonize his own life patterns with the regulative system.

Our society has been noted for personality disorganization as reflected in crime, insanity, neuroticism, and general maladjustments. In addition to those who have completely broken are thousands of other poorly adjusted people who flock to psychiatrists, hypnotists, faith healers, and quacks of various sorts. The increasing popularity of astrology, phrenology, palmistry, faith cures and psychological and pseudo-psychological literature suggests the mental stress and personality strain of our time. Only if one understands the extent to which our life is a conglomeration of many culture patterns and a motley of many groups with diverse standards, can he begin to appreciate the reasons for personality disorganization in America, which during the last century, has become famous as a melting pot of many nations. It is not simply a melting pot of people of diverse races and nations, it is a melting pot of people with different standards, different philosophies of life, different systems of social regulation. In such a world, personality problems are inevitable. Moreover, our modern machine technology has created a society of pervasive social change which in itself tends to undermine the established systems of control, to destroy life philosophies, in fact, to tear down systems of control more rapidly than society can rebuild them. In addition, we have been a mobile people, shifting to and fro in migratory currents, most of these currents tending to move cityward, although some also move toward the country each year. This constant shifting back and forth breaks people from their moorings. Old controls which operated effectively in one environment may be entirely inadequate in another. The individual, contacting new stimuli, encountering new worlds of thought and regulation, frequently finds himself without a rudder to steer his course. Only through an understanding of these factors can the personality problems found in contemporary culture be grasped in their entirety.

Most studies of the urban community have shown that divorce, suicide, insanity, delinquency, and crime are closely identified with areas of disintegrated cultures. The personality problems so common in any urban-industrial culture rarely appear in well-integrated societies, such as the stable, familistic society of old China. In fact, it is unlikely that any such problems have ever been prominent in the primary group societies of the ancient world, or in primitive societies of past or present, for in such societies the individual throughout life is surrounded by well-integrated and uniform culture patterns which he absorbs, and once having done so, is fully prepared to live. In the complex cultures of the Western world no individual is adjusted for life when he has absorbed the patterns of his particular group, whether it be his primary group or some other. He must, as he moves from place to place, become reacculturated and readapted to new systems of regulation.[2] Even our rural population is highly mobile and susceptible to the influence of change.

One of the chief aims of modern education, according to the educational theorists, is to prepare the individual to live in a world of social change, to teach him to be adaptable, and to readjust himself quickly to new circumstances.

These facts of experience in American life not only make personality integration difficult, but also make the problem of control a formidable one. Any maladjusted person who accepts the codes of no one group, who constantly shifts from this line of thought to that, soon loses all power of self-regulation. He is carried along with the tide of opinion of whatever group he happens to represent at that particular time. There is some evidence that such a state of affairs is not only unfortunate for personality, but for the entire social system.

A very penetrating analysis of this whole problem has been made by L. K. Frank, who says in brief:

This cultural conception reveals human conduct, not as whimsical or volitionally controlled, but as the way the individual takes over the ideas, beliefs, and practices of the traditional group life and, under their guidance, carries out his life-processes. In a secluded group where, over a long period of time, men have worked out a unified culture with appropriate sanctions and beliefs, the individ-

---

[2] The effects of mobility on personality are considered from an interesting angle in Norman S. Hayner's "Hotel Life and Personality," *American Journal of Sociology*, March, 1928, vol. 33, pp. 784–795.

ual ordinarily finds the pattern of his life prepared for him and, within the permissions and restrictions it offers, he can achieve his life and fulfil his social responsibility. His culture dictates what he will be aware of, how he will respond to it and explain it, and what he can and must do with his organic needs and functions. In homogeneous cultures, individuals of aberrant temperaments are less likely to find it difficult to conform to the patterns laid down by their culture; when forced to do so, they can adapt themselves with a minimum of strain because their culture does not offer conflicting choices. In some cultures it is the practice even to give specific exemptions to an individual whose temperament makes it difficult for him to conform to the patterns that are recognized as socially normal; such exemption saves the individual deviant from anxiety or guilt.

When we regard Western European culture that has emerged from an almost incredible background of conflict and confusion and mixture of peoples, and see that for centuries it has not been unified either in ideas and beliefs or in socially approved practices, we can begin to understand the etiology of the sickness of our society. Our culture has no unanimity of individual or social aims, no generally accepted sanctions, and no common patterns of ideas or conduct. All our basic ideas, conceptions, and beliefs have been in process of revision for the last three hundred years or more, beginning with the displacement of the older notions of the universe and man's place therein and going on now to the supersedure of the traditional animistic, voluntaristic conceptions of human nature and conduct and man's relation to his society. The American scene, moreover, has been successively invaded by representatives of widely different nationalities, who have accelerated the decay of the early American tradition that our changing industry has made inevitable. The picture is sufficiently familiar and has been adequately described so that no prolonged description is needed here.

If we bear in mind this culture disintegration, then our so-called social problems and the seeming perversity of individuals become intelligible. They are to be viewed as arising from the frantic efforts of individuals, lacking any sure direction and sanctions or guiding conception of life, to find some way of protecting themselves or of merely existing on any terms they can manage in a society being remade by technology. Having no strong loyalties and no consistent values or realizable ideals to cherish, the individual's conduct is naturally conflicting, confused, neurotic, and antisocial, if that term has any meaning in the absence of an established community purpose and ideal. The more skilful contrive to profit from the social confusion and their own lack of scruples, while others evade or break laws, become mentally disordered or diseased, or otherwise violate the older codes of conduct, damaging themselves and those whose lives they touch. No one is happy, it is apparent; the successful are driven as relentlessly as the failures by their sense of guilt, their compulsions, and their frustrations.[3]

SOCIAL CONTROL AND SPECIAL PERSONALITY PROBLEMS

The following selections are composed of concise statements by various authors, on the relationship between social control and selected personality problems. Each relates the pathology of the individual to the system of social control under which he lives.

Suicide and the breakdown of social control.

. . . The Renaissance, having established the fact that every journeyman tinker was a creature of marvelous potential sensibility, proceeded to put a value on his reactions to life. The Reformation turned the same journeyman into a hearth-stone theologian and urged him to formulate private judgments on such hitherto injudicable matters as God's ways to man. An accessible press inspired him to write pamphlets, and what's more, sign his own name to them. Political idealists lifted him to electoral heights, and thus set individual theory adrift on chartless seas of political action. The Industrial Revolution showed him the way to possible wealth as the reward of private enterprise. It was all very exciting and wonderful —that is, until quite recently, when the alarming climb of the suicide and insanity rates began to indicate that the individualist tinker and his progeny were breaking down beneath their burden, and that a poisonous fever was churning in the modern bloodstream.

As a factual footnote to the familiar theory that suicide thrives where individualism prospers, the following figures may be of significance: Males, traditionally possessed of greater and more numerous individual outlets, are four times more apt to commit suicide than

---

[3] L. K. Frank, "Society as the Patient," *The American Journal of Sociology,* November, 1936, vol. 42, pp. 338–340. By permission of the University of Chicago Press.

females. Suicides among Protestants are more frequent than among dogmatically circumscribed Catholics. Italy, with an oppressive non-latitudinarian dictator, has a suicide rate of only ninety-two per million, while Germany, whirled in the dusty chaos of three dozen parties (1930) has a rate of 243. Literate persons in all countries, even though enjoying marked economic advantages, kill themselves in greater numbers proportionally, than their illiterate brethren. It is notoriously apparent that when education, leisure, and the other concomitants of a rich individualism are present, the suicide rate rises rapidly. That rate has been climbing steadily for the past fifty years; since 1870 the average number of suicides per million has trebled in Europe and America. In 1931 the United States had a suicide rate of 200 per million, which means that over twenty-five thousand persons committed suicide in our country last year.

It was not always so. There have been whole centuries, the Thirteenth for example, when the world was organized on a warmly maternal basis. When Mother Church and Mother Earth, those twin bountiful breasts of refuge, soothed and supplied the emotional needs of men; when unquestioning obedience to authority—the king, the priest, the guild—was the easy lot of man, then there were no suicides. There were no suicides because there were no stranded individuals squirming on the sharp sands of a defeated world. Men swam comfortably in the amniotic fluid of prenatal security and anonymity; as independent entities, they were not yet born; the warm peace of the womb lay upon them and all their psychic hungers were filled. They built cathedrals and composed prayers, and painted murals of the Mother and Son—the best cathedrals, prayers and murals that we know of, though their names or their troubles are not known to us. They were, happily, not individuals—and still more happily, had no desire to be.

If it were possible to return to that golden age of anonymity and infantile peace, of child-like faith and ready acquiescence to authority, I am certain that the suicide rate would drop to zero overnight. But time runs not back, and despite the exhortations of well-intentioned shepherds, it is as impossible to return to that security as to return to the comfort of a good cry at mother's knee. No, that is not the therapy, nor is it even the direction that the therapy must take. There can be no recession from the individual stand, however costly it is to hold. Such victory as men may win in the struggle for stability and happiness must be won on the difficult terrain where life meets the adult individual in unending conflict.[4]

In this selection Robinson has made suicide, like many problems of personality disorganization in the West, an issue growing out of individualization. Not all suicide is of this character, however.[5] In some nations, notably in Japan, it has been required by custom under certain conditions, and has had no relationship to individualization. One committed suicide to save his face, to win honor, or in protest against some wrong, as in the case of the Japanese who killed himself on the steps of the American Embassy in protest against the enactment of the Japanese exclusion act. "Hara-kiri," literally "belly cutting," as a method of suicide has been a part of Japanese custom since antiquity.[6] But American suicide is different. It is not a thing of custom but an individual matter, and motivated by personal not institutional factors.

Personal degeneration and the breakdown of tradition. William McDougall, discussing problems of abnormal psychology,[7] has described the intellectual uncertainty and lack of decisive judgment which characterizes many individuals of our time. Being without ideals and a supreme personal goal, they are without character and motive power. He suggests that in the modern world few attain complete integration of character because "we no longer grow up under the influence of some one well-defined moral system supported by the authority of unquestioned religion." The child in America finds himself surrounded by the "odds and ends" of religious and moral systems.

In such a world, McDougall concludes, birth rates fall, crime and divorce increase to alarming proportions and young men ask, "Is life worth living?". In addition many adults find their work uninteresting, and consequently face conflict. In the absence of dominant ideals and strong purposes many in our time are

[4] From Henry Morton Robinson, "The Case of Suicide," *North American Review*, October, 1932, pp. 304–307. Reprinted by permission.

[5] For a comprehensive discussion of suicide see Ruth S. Cavan's *Suicide*.

[6] A good popular discussion of "Hara-kiri" is found in Nancy V. Austen's "Suicide A La Mode in Japan," *Current History*, October, 1921, vol. 15, pp. 83–85.

[7] William McDougall, *Outline of Abnormal Psychology*, Charles Scribner's Sons, New York, 1926, pp. 215–217.

unable to resolve conflicts, and as a consequence suffer neurotic disorders and mental breakdown.

Personality disintegration and the cultural structure.

The harmony or disharmony between the demands placed upon a person by his own and adjacent categories or by the social norms is a problem of cultural and structural integration and, correlatively, of personality organization. The demands placed upon a person and the behavior pattern presented to him may be consistent or inconsistent in their meaning, as viewed from within the given culture. As long as one conducts his living in conformity with what others—usually categories of other people—expect from him, and, obversely, when others reciprocate according to norms, tensions are infrequent. However, if there are contradictions between the norms or between these and personal preferments, the logical or meaningful contradictions involve the person, and may be mistakenly interpreted as his own aberrance. The absence of such subjective conflicts under the same conditions constitutes quite different social phenomena.

Cultures differ in the degree of integration. Especially is the culture that has many new inserts or accretions by borrowing or invention likely to have discordant elements that lack congruity. Such dissonance has unlike significance, depending on whether the inconsistencies pertain to the categories or to other culture data which do not involve norms of social relations. Furthermore, while it is generally supposed that a dominant idea of the culture tends, if given enough time, to permeate those phases which have a logico-meaningful relation, variations in the details will, nevertheless, occur in complex versus simple, and dynamic versus relatively static societies.

Our own culture contains incompatible streams of ideas that have coexisted without fusing. These at times produce personality tensions and subjective conflicts, proving that the person is exposed to these illogical norms. However, some categories isolate themselves from one or the other of these incompatible ideas. Such considerations afford specific instances of the concurrence of the social organization and personality patterning.[8]

The hobo, a man with freedom but without purpose. Park has shown how the hobo has developed a certain frame of mind

---

[8] E. T. Hiller, "The Social Structure in Relation to the Person," *Social Forces*, October, 1937, pp. 43, 44. Reprinted by permission.

characterized by a great variety of experience but a lack of a definite vocation.[9] He is a man without a goal, except that of moving. He therefore develops a romantic temperament, a wanderlust. He is a man with freedom, but one who has lost direction. He is an extreme individualist, sacrificing everything for freedom. He becomes not only a homeless man, but a man without a cause.

PERSONALITY IN AN UNCERTAIN WORLD

Walter Lippmann has discussed at length in *A Preface to Morals* the unusual extent to which modern man has achieved freedom, but in achieving it has lost his faith in tradition, regulation, and standards, until he is truly a man with freedom but without purpose. His defiance of the Methodist code, and his atheistic tendencies have brought him no peace of mind. Lacking moral authority, he is easily coerced by opinions, fads, and fashions. He has forsaken the old order, where compulsion was painful but acceptable because it was inflicted by an all-knowing God, for a new order where compulsions of necessity exist and are extremely painful. No landmarks guide his conscience; he must make his own way.

A college student in his autobiography writes:

I feel as though I were groping in the dark—not knowing just what is right and how right it is. I see in the cinema some "he-man" seducing various innocent girls and wonder if that isn't the thing to do. Evidently it is, if one is looking for some excitement in life. I have always been taught that sex is a mysterious and fascinating forbidden land whose adventures are completely taboo. I have observed a tendency to avoid the subject at certain times and in certain places; namely, in the church, classroom, and home. Elsewhere it is flaunted before me in every form—on billboards, in magazines, plays, and movies. These conflicts have caused considerable mental turmoil in the last five years, but perhaps due to maturity I am overcoming them.[10]

CHANGE AND PERSONAL DEMORALIZATION

Thomas and Thomas have shown how modern methods of communication, the development of rapid transportation, the

---

[9] Robert E. Park, "The Mind of the Hobo: Reflections upon the Relation Between Mentality and Locomotion," *The City* (Park and Burgess).

[10] From the author's collection.

concentration of people in cities, the growth of the industrial order, the decline of community and family life, the weakening of religion, the commercialization of pleasure, and similar far-reaching problems in our culture tend to break down the "moral norms and behavior practices of all classes of society."

Activities have evolved more rapidly than social structures, personalities more rapidly than social norms. This unstabilization of society and of behavior is probably no more than a stage of disorganization preceding a modified type of reorganization. When old habits break down, when they are no longer adequate, there is always a period of confusion until new habits are established; and this is true of both the individual and society. At present, however, it is widely felt that the demoralization of young persons, the prevalence of delinquency, crime, and profound mental disturbances are very serious problems, and that the situation is growing worse instead of better.[11]

Cooley has contrasted the problem of social control in a stable society with that in a dynamic society,[12] saying that the rigid morality of savages reflects the sameness of their social life. He also suggests that the rigid moral system of China is a product of a stable social system. In a rapidly changing society, control by mere habit is impossible. Conflicting tendencies abound, so that a person must be either "intelligently moral" or degenerate. He must either build a synthesis of experience or have no synthesis.

MOBILITY AND PERSONAL DISORGANIZATION

America has been made by an alien people, a people who have constantly climbed upward in their struggle for status and recognition, who have rapidly shifted from the old to the new, from one social class to another. Many problems in control grow out of this situation,[13] in which the continuity of life never remains for long unbroken, and the persons involved have paid heavily in

[11] William I. Thomas and Dorothy Swaine Thomas, The Child in America, p. xiii. By permission of Alfred A. Knopf, Inc.

[12] Charles H. Cooley, Human Nature and the Social Order, p. 369.

[13] Even in 1930, 40 million of the 122 million people in the United States were foreign born, or children of foreign born. For an interesting discussion of some of the social implications of this fact see Pauline V. Young's "Social Problems in the Education of the Immigrant Child," American Sociological Review, 1936, vol. 1, pp. 419–429. See also David C. Coyle, et al., The American Way, Harper and Brothers, New York, 1938.

nervous and mental breakdown, delinquency and crime, despair
and suicide. Movement, whether upward or sidewise, unsettles
man, psychologically and often morally. By movement he escapes restrictions only to face new ones which he may not understand.

The following paragraph is a summary of a quotation from the
autobiography of a girl whose home was broken by death, and
who throughout childhood and youth up to the time of coming to
college, had shifted from one relative's home to another in various western states, the different homes each having different
life patterns. At the age of 19, while a college freshman she
writes:

"I am still wandering around in this maze of conflicting training; wondering what I will be like if I become molded to an acceptable pattern. My life has become without aim, without a
goal to work forward to, a little without meaning. At present I
have decided to step back into my shell, and out of the conflict
of codes and desires and personalities that seem to make up society."

One of the most striking pictures of personal disorganization
growing out of a situation in which people are so mobile they
have escaped almost all control is that drawn by Zorbaugh, of
the area of furnished rooms [14] in which the whole population
turns over every four months, and where at least half the keepers
have been in charge of their places only six months or less. Here
71 per cent of all houses take roomers, of whom 52 per cent are
single men, 10 per cent single women, and 38 per cent couples;
but 60 per cent of these couples are unmarried. Most of the
roomers are white-collar workers of from 20 to 35 years of age.
In addition to the pathological marital situation there are many
evidences of other abnormalities such as attempts at suicide,
escapes into dreams, as a refuge from an unbearable existence,
substitution of an object or pet for human beings as a point of
emotional attachment. This world of furnished rooms is an
anonymous world largely without control and one into which
personality cannot fit without considerable difficulty.

Norman S. Hayner has described personality problems and

---

[14] See his article, "The Dwellers in Furnished Rooms, An Urban Type," in
E. W. Burgess' *The Urban Community;* also his *The Gold Coast and the Slum,*
chap. 4.

delinquencies of hotel dwellers, who are highly mobile and achieve an unusual degree of anonymity.[15] They have broken all attachments to things, places, and people, and as a result are often restless and unhappy, even though they can do very much as they please.

MENTAL DISEASE AND THE SYSTEM OF SOCIAL CONTROL

Robert E. L. Faris has advanced the thesis that there is a close relationship between social control and the schizophrenic (dementia praecox) personality.[16] The substance of his argument follows:

The schizophrenic is characterized by eccentric behavior and seclusiveness. "Typically, the isolated person makes a struggle to establish intimate social relations, and feels lonely when he fails. In the beginning of the process the 'seclusiveness' or 'shut-in' trait is not the cause, but the result, of the isolation. The other eccentricities follow from this seclusiveness."

To normal people conformity "is so much a part of their habits that they do not sense the social control that has molded them. When there is no longer any necessity or desire to communicate with others, or to appear reasonable to them, there is nothing to preserve the order in the mental life of the person." Thus his eccentric behavior is a result of freedom from social control.

"Illogical thought" is also a condition of isolation. The person is indifferent to logic because he has no need for it. "When there is no desire to be understood or no hope of being understood, there is no need for the use of logic."

The schizophrenic's delusions and false beliefs are not abnormal because they are false but because they are unconventional. "If three hundred people at a camp meeting see and hear the devil, they are not called schizophrenic." The person must be alone in his delusion.

In the larger cities in rooming houses, and so forth, it may be so difficult for a sensitive person, or one uncertain of his status,

---

[15] Norman S. Hayner, "Hotel Life and Personality," *American Journal of Sociology*, March, 1928, vol. 33, pp. 784–795.

[16] Robert E. L. Faris, "Cultural Isolation and the Schizophrenic Personality," *American Journal of Sociology*, September 1934, vol. 40, pp. 155–164. For a summary of evidence bearing on this problem as found in the city of Chicago see H. Warren Dunham, "The Ecology of the Functional Psychoses in Chicago," *American Sociological Review*, vol. 2, pp. 467–479, August, 1937.

to establish contacts that he may become as isolated as a prisoner in solitary confinement, and with a similar result. In Chicago, the high rates for schizophrenia "are sharply concentrated in the hobo, rooming-house, and most deteriorated slum areas."

"Ellsworth Faris observed that among some of the Bantu peoples in central Africa there is no disobedience, no violation of the folkways and mores, no punishment, and the children do not even make mistakes in grammar. The informal social control is so strong that a withered old woman can give orders to the strong young men of the village." Faris failed to find a single case of "shut-in" personality among these people. However, schizoid types do exist among primitives whose social situation favors isolation.

Re-establishment of intimate contacts seems to improve many schizoid patients.

The interesting point of this analysis is that schizophrenia seems to be related to an ineffective system of control under which the individual, although he has a kind of liberty, is unable to use it to his advantage because he lacks social contact and direction. Those primitives who live under a rigid, authoritative system of regulation avoid the type of mental stress which in our culture drives the sensitive person into a dream world to escape reality.

The Marginal Man and Social Control

The man who lives between two cultures, participating to some extent in both is always a problem in social control. Contact of cultures tends to "emancipate the individual man" but such a person is facing a constant threat to personality disorganization, because he is living under dual systems of control. It is among marginal individuals that some of our worst problems of personality disorganization have originated. Insanity rates have been highest among our immigrant groups who have tried desperately to bridge two social worlds with their personality. Oriented to the system of social control of their fatherland, they face the almost impossible task of mastering the minimum essentials of the new culture, and of learning enough of its social regulations to be accepted as members. Delinquency and crime rates have been highest among immigrant children, a condition undoubtedly representing the first stages of breaking away from the system of control of the parental culture.[17] The newcomer adopts American culture without fully understanding the meaning of freedom, and often develops into a misfit in both the old and the new cultures.

The half-caste races have faced perhaps even a greater problem of social adjustment than the immigrant, being accepted by neither pure race and therefore not living fully under their systems of social control. As Reuter has shown,[18] the person of mixed blood usually is not willing to live as one of the inferior group and cannot attain status in the superior group. He is a part of neither world of social regulation.

Personality Disorganization Growing out of the Inability to Adjust Organic Drives to Social Restrictions

Social control is necessarily restrictive, more so for some individuals than their organic drives will permit. A society which insists upon continence before marriage, and then delays marriage far beyond puberty, must inevitably expect some sex delinquency. A social order that insists upon monogamy must expect some unsanctioned polygamy. A society that denies a man the means for satisfying basic organic needs—food, clothing, and shelter—must expect theft. There will probably always be some individuals who cannot conform to the social definitions established by the group. The more restrictive the codes, the more numerous violations are likely to be.

Striking and conclusive evidence of this fact is presented in Ruth Benedict's *Patterns of Culture*.[19] She shows that although the human being, because of his "enormous malleability" by native endowment, is ordinarily capable of being fitted into any culture pattern into which he is born, not all individuals find the system of regulation imposed by their culture equally con-

---

[17] This is an established fact with regard to immigrant children in the city. See E. H. Sutherland, *Principles of Criminology*, pp. 115–116, J. B. Lippincott Company, Chicago, 1934. Donald R. Taft has indicated that it is not true of the child of the rural immigrant who continues to live in an intimate, well-knit primary group world with its more effective system of social regulation. See his "Nationality and Crime," *American Sociological Review*, October, 1936, p. 725.

[18] E. B. Reuter, "The Personality of Mixed Bloods," *Personality and the Social Group*, E. W. Burgess, editor, chap. 5, University of Chicago Press, Chicago, 1929. See also E. V. Stonequist, *The Marginal Man*, chap. 2, Charles Scribner's Sons, New York, 1937.

[19] See especially chap. 8.

genial. Fortunate is the individual whose potentialities coincide
with the behavior patterns accepted by society. If they do not,
he is likely to be seriously frustrated, or if he chooses to express
himself regardless, he is certain to be considered at least eccentric
by his social group. From this point she goes on to show that
pathological types are a matter of social definition. Many cultures make a place for what we call the neurotic; in them he is
normal. The simpleton and fool has often had a respected place
in society's affairs. A trance, in our society, is an abnormal phenomenon, but in the history of Western Europe, as in other
societies, it has been thought a mark of sainthood, a sure evidence
of close contact with the divine. Homosexuality is apparently in
line with the natural potentialities of some members of the human race, and many cultures in their system of social control
have recognized it as such, though in societies which exclude it
from their set of definitions, it is abnormal. Our culture, in demanding conformity in almost every phase of behavior, necessarily subjects many persons to tremendous stress. We make
little room for nonconformity, and ridicule eccentricity; we pay
the penalty in personality disorganization.

Miss Benedict's analysis takes us one important step further,
showing that those personality types considered most normal
under one system of social control may be thought most abnormal
under a different system. She cites the Puritan divines, who in
their day as the leaders of the people, enjoyed unparalleled prestige. It was they who caused the witches of New England to be
put to death. Perhaps many ego-centered business men in our
culture would be considered extremely abnormal from the standpoint of another set of social definitions.

One can over-emphasize the point that organic drives are necessarily responsible for those violations of social codes involving
natural appetites such as sex, hunger, or ego display. The cause
may lie in the fact that the individual was never adequately
trained in the restraints of his social group. However, it is difficult to harness successfully the more violent organic drives.

LIMITED GROUP PARTICIPATION IN A COMPLEX SYSTEM OF CONTROL

Probably few individuals in our society have reached the place
in their own mind where they have decided which values are

worth seeking wholeheartedly.   Only by a process of limited participation in social life can personality function fully and maintain its integration.   In a complex social order this fact is especially important, because in such an order many values are presented to every individual, and selection in terms of definite life
goals becomes essential.

It is as important to know what to neglect as it is to know
what to possess.   Probably half the trouble many face in personality adjustment grows out of the fact that they are too ready
to accept the suggestions and to be subject to the pressures of
numerous groups which may have purposes entirely different
from their own; whereas, if they would decide once and for all
which values they mean to seek as goals of life, they could very
easily cast aside suggestions that are out of harmony, and avoid
the distraction and nervous tension inherent in diffusing activity over too much territory.

Selection is the secret of directed effort in any complex society.   In fact, modern living requires one to decide what little
bit in life he will experience.   In a rich cultural heritage one must
needs cast aside a great deal.   The person who has made up his
mind concerning the values he will seek is already well on the
way to personal adjustment and to successful living.   No individual in a complex society can experience more than a small
part of that society, and the sooner he comes to a realization of
this fact, the sooner will he begin to live intelligently and to
choose wisely, thus becoming immune to the numerous conflicting controls that various groups would impose upon him.

Conclusion

This chapter has drawn attention to the relationship between
personality demoralization and the system of social control.   The
point of view was developed that personality disorganization does
not originate primarily within the individual, but rather in the
individual's experience with different systems of control.   It was
shown that mobile peoples tend to have high rates of personality
disorganization, because they shift from one system of social
regulation to another; that a country like our own with its diverse
nationality and cultural backgrounds necessarily contains a large
number of people who have not made up their minds as to
which system of control to obey.   The highest proportion of

social inadequates are found in those areas where culture patterns, and consequently systems of regulation, are most diverse and least effective.

Personality disorganization is closely correlated with the system of social control in force. It may be so lax as to give the individual too much freedom, in which case he may use it unwisely. If he embodies different systems of control within his personality, constant mental turmoil may be the consequence. In moving to and fro, he may acquire some of the freedom from control that the hobo achieves, but in so doing, lose his direction on an uncharted sea of unknown social experience. The trouble may possibly lie in part within the nature of the individual; he may have organic drives so strong that they cannot be curbed. We have learned, however, to seek first of all within the system of social control under which the individual lives, the reason for his failure to obey social codes, and we have found the new approach most helpful to the understanding of his behavior problems.

SELECTED REFERENCES

Beach, W. G., *Social Aims in a Changing World*, introduction and chap. 1. Stanford University Press, Stanford University, 1932.

Blumer, H., and Hauser, P., *Movies, Delinquency and Crime*. The Macmillan Company, New York, 1933.

Bossard, Joseph H. S., *Social Change and Social Problems*, revised edition, chap. 7. Harper and Brothers, New York, 1938.

Burgess, E. W., *The Urban Community* (selection by H. W. Zorbaugh, "The Dweller in Furnished Rooms: An Urban Type"), pp. 98–105. University of Chicago Press, Chicago, 1926.

Carpenter, Niles, *The Sociology of City Life*, pp. 217–218. Longmans, Green and Company, New York, 1931.

Cavan, Ruth Shonle, *Suicide*. University of Chicago Press, Chicago, 1928.

Cooley, Charles H., *Human Nature and the Social Order*, chap. 11. Charles Scribner's Sons, 1922.

Dunham, H. Warren, "The Ecology of the Functional Psychoses in Chicago," *American Sociological Review*, vol. 2, pp. 467–479. August, 1937.

Editorial, "New Reasons for Suicide," *Our Opinion*, vol. 74, pp. 728 ff. June, 1923.

Editorial, "Suicide and Irreligion," *Christian Century*, vol. 44, pp. 358–359. March 24, 1927.

Elliott, Mabel A., and Merrill, Francis E., *Social Disorganization*. Harper and Brothers, New York, 1934.

Evans, W., "She Has Never Grown Up; Martyr Complex," *Better Homes and Gardens*, vol. 9, pp. 16 ff. July, 1931.

Faris, Robert E. L., "Cultural Isolation and the Schizophrenic Personality," *American Journal of Sociology*, vol. 40, pp. 155–164. September, 1934.

Hayner, Norman S., "Hotel Life and Personality," *American Journal of Sociology*, vol. 33, pp. 784–795. March, 1928.

Hiller, E. T., *Principles of Sociology*, chap. 37. Harper and Brothers, New York, 1933.

Hiller, E. T., "The Social Structure in Relation to the Person," *Social Forces*, pp. 43 ff. October, 1937.

House, F. N., *The Range of Social Theory*, chap. 23. Henry Holt and Company, New York, 1929.

La Piere, Richard, and Farnsworth, Paul, *Social Psychology*, chaps. 14 and 15. McGraw-Hill Book Company, New York, 1936.

Lee, B. Y., "Study of the Growing Suicide Problem in China," *China Weekly Review*, vol. 72, pp. 256 ff. April 20, 1935.

Lippmann, Walter, *A Preface to Morals*. The Macmillan Company, New York, 1929.

Lippmann, Walter, *Public Opinion*. The Macmillan Company, New York, 1932.

Lynd, R., "Suicide," *New Statesman*, vol. 32, pp. 659–661. March 2, 1929.

McDougall, William, *Outline of Abnormal Psychology*, pp. 215 ff. Charles Scribner's Sons, New York, 1926.

Moley, R., "Crime as a Profession," *Current History*, vol. 30, pp. 999 ff. September, 1929.

Park, Robert E., and Burgess, Ernest W., *The City*, pp. 158 ff. University of Chicago Press, Chicago, 1925.

Robinson, Henry Morton, "The Case of Suicide," *The North American Review*, pp. 304 ff. October, 1932.

Schmid, C. F., "Suicide in Minneapolis, Minnesota, 1928–32," *American Journal of Sociology*, vol. 39, pp. 30–48. July, 1933.

Schmid, C. F., *Suicides in Seattle, 1914–1925: An Ecological and Behavioristic Study*. University of Washington Press, Seattle, Washington, 1928.

Tannenbaum, Frank, *Crime and the Community*, part 1. Ginn and Company, Boston, 1938.

Thomas, William I., and Thomas, Dorothy Swaine, *The Child in America*. F. S. Crofts and Company, New York, 1928.

Thomas, William I., *The Unadjusted Girl*. Little, Brown and Company, Boston, 1923.

Thomas, W. I., and Znaniecki, Florian, *The Polish Peasant in Europe and America*, vol. 4, pt. 1; vol. 5, pt. 2. Chapman and Grimes, Boston, 1920.

Young, Kimball, *An Introductory Sociology*, chap. 28. American Book Company, New York, 1934.

Young, Kimball, *Source Book for Social Psychology*, chap. 24. F. S. Crofts and Company, New York, 1933.

Young, Kimball, *Source Book for Sociology*, chap. 28. American Book Company, New York, 1935.

Young, Pauline V., "Social Problems in the Education of the Immigrant Child," *American Sociological Review*, vol. 1, pp. 419–429. June, 1936.

Zorbaugh, H. W., *The Gold Coast and the Slum*. University of Chicago Press, Chicago, 1929.

CHAPTER 23

THE BREAKDOWN OF CONTROL AS A FACTOR IN SOCIAL PATHOLOGY

The problems of personality disorganization and social pathology are at a good many points inseparable, and no chapter division can make it otherwise. So in this chapter the emphasis will be more especially upon those pathologies tending to be group wide in given areas, and somewhat less upon the specific pathologies of the individual, though there must necessarily be some overlapping.

In the background of this approach is the Thomas and Znaniecki concept of *social disorganization* as a *"decrease of the influence of existing social rules of behavior upon individual members of the group."* [1] They show that social disorganization is not necessarily reflected in personal disorganization; one may reject some group rules as a means to better personal organization. Neither is effective group organization necessarily wholesome. Wholesomeness depends on breadth of organization. Social disorganization does not, therefore, correspond identically to individual demoralization. On the other hand the breakdown of social definitions is often related to pathological conditions both in the group and in the individual. In fact, considerable evidence that has accumulated in various sociological studies during the last few years indicates the very close connection between community controls, and in fact, the entire regulative system of a society, and pathological conditions developing within that society.

More and more the sociologist is looking to the control system of the group for an explanation of social pathology, and less and less is he seeking it in factors inherent in human nature.

"A little reflection," says Lumley, "will show that all social problems are ultimately problems of social control—capital and

---

[1] W. I. Thomas and Florian Znaniecki, *The Polish Peasant in Europe and America*, vol. 4, part 1, p. 2.

labor, prostitution, taxes, crime, international relations. When these are sifted to the bottom and their ultimate meaning is discerned, they are simply social situations requiring control." [2]

From the broadest viewpoint Lumley is correct. Certainly it has been proven beyond a doubt that a relationship exists between a great number of pathological conditions and the breakdown of the system of social control. Especially noteworthy are the findings in the fields of juvenile delinquency and criminology.

Similarly, suicide has been correlated with disintegrating community patterns by a number of authorities. Cultural shock, experienced by migrants to the urban community, which is usually lacking in effective controls, leads to pathological conditions. Immigrants to America, and especially their children, frequently become demoralized because adequate controls do not exist in the cosmopolitan environment of the cities in which they settle.

Equally extreme, and perhaps even more so, has been the demoralization of many of the primitives who have come in contact with the white man and his civilization. Anthropologists have given us excellent descriptions of how these peoples assimilate Western culture and in so doing overthrow the regulations of their old society, with the result that they find themselves in a world over which they have lost their grip, and in which they have no interest.

In this chapter, selected instances of social pathologies are discussed simply to show the important part that the presence or absence of an effective system of social control plays in the development of pathological patterns.

Delinquency and Crime in Relation to Social Control

First, let us take the field of delinquency and crime. Shaw,[3] Thrasher,[4] and others [5] have shown that school truancy, juvenile delinquency, and adult crime tend to be centered in communities surrounding the business district of the city, communities in which controls have broken down. Usually these communities

---

[2] Frederick E. Lumley, *Means of Social Control*, p. 14. Used by permission of D. Appleton-Century Company, Publishers, New York, N. Y.

[3] Clifford R. Shaw, *et al.*, *Delinquency Areas*.

[4] F. M. Thrasher, *The Gang*.

[5] H. Blumer and P. Hauser, *Movies, Delinquency, and Crime*, The Payne Fund Studies, The Macmillan Company, New York, 1933.

are cosmopolitan in population composition, heterogeneous in standards of life, and transitional in existence, shifting from an older residential section to a newer community of business and industry. In these "interstices of the formal and established order" [6] resistance to crime and delinquency is very low. In fact, sanctions for non-conventional behavior of community-wide scope tend to develop. Also, in these areas there is a whole constellation of pathological conditions, each of which supplements the other. The larger and more normal social groups outside the slum do not maintain sufficient grip over slum institutions, agencies, mores, and codes to enforce the generally accepted standards.

Because conduct is learned, children growing up in these areas are subject to the principles of an environment which makes delinquency easier than normal behavior. Here group approval is forthcoming for conduct which conflicts with law and other less formal regulations of normal society. The child thus tends to develop a criminal pattern of life which consists essentially in having learned to respond to the stimuli of a small, specialized group with criminal standards, rather than learning to live in harmony with the codes of men in the larger world.

Heterogeneity of patterns of life, heterogeneity of population, and diversity of standards probably explain many phases of American crime. The average American's philosophy of law and law observance is akin to that of the criminal. Actually, about the only difference between the average citizen and the criminal, according to Tannenbaum,[7] is that the citizen evades the law, whereas the criminal deliberately breaks it, gaining the admiration of a group which considers law breaking in harmony with its codes. In a closely-knit underworld gang, controls and standards are well developed and very rigid. The criminal code, though, is vicious because it accepts and encourages conflict with society. A professional criminal understands very well that his liberty, in fact, his very life, depends upon his loyalty to his own group and his observance of its codes.[8] Crime, to a criminal, is a business proposition, a way of making money and of acquiring status and distinction. It is not the easiest way, but it is a way.

[6] F. N. House, *Range of Social Theory*, p. 144.
[7] Frank Tannenbaum, *Crime and the Community*, p. 22.
[8] *Ibid.*, chap. 3.

If one happens to live in a community where criminal patterns are predominant, if one chances to become identified with crime, or if one is ostracized by the normal social group, then crime offers practically the only way of achieving distinction, social status, wealth, recognition, publicity, and the other things that make life sweet and worth living.

Education for crime must be looked upon as habituation to a way of life. As such it partakes of the nature of all education. It is a gradual adaptation to, and a gradual absorption of, certain elements in the environment. As an educational process it depends upon instruction, stimulus, approval, companionship, conversation, idealization. It has its elements of curiosity, wonder, knowledge, adventure. Like all true education it has its beginnings in play, it starts in more or less random movements, and builds up toward techniques, insights, judgments, attitudes. It gradually takes on constructive skills. It depends upon companionship and approving judgment. Like all education it utilizes the material and ideal elements in the environment; it could not come to pass otherwise. It uses what there is to be found in the neighborhood. These may be such humble things as junk heaps, alley ways, abandoned houses, pushcarts, railroad tracks, coal cars. It begins with the easy things that can be picked up, pilfered, carried off, eaten, disposed of. It requires companionship and encouragement. It is a social process, like all education for life. Friends, companions, brothers, gangs, participate, encourage, amuse, tease, praise, blame, compensate. It is a part of the adventure of living in a certain way in a certain environment. But both the environment and the way of using it must already be there. Both the material and the social environment are prerequisite. For the career of the criminal to develop there must not only be the friends in the gang, the habits of the older companions already prepared to make certain adjustments through previous instruction, but there must also be the support of the older generation. . . .[9]

SUICIDE AND SOCIAL CONTROL

Suicide is also related to the breakdown of community controls. Durkheim, in his work, *Le Suicide*, points out that in primitive societies, where collective consciousness was strong, suicide was at a minimum. Cavan, in her study, *Suicide*, has

---

[9] *Ibid.*, p. 51. By permission of Ginn and Company.

shown that in the early days of Greece and Rome, and during the Renaissance, both being periods of marked change, old customs and old ideas were destroyed, personal problems increased, and suicide came to be accepted as a means of settling personal difficulties. Cavan stresses the "coincidence of outbreaks of suicide with periods of social disorganization." Where community organization breaks down there is a good opportunity for personal disorganization to develop, for normally inhibited impulses are permitted free range. Cavan found that in certain disorganized areas of Chicago suicide rates were extremely high. Areas of disorganization do not necessarily cause suicide, but suicide and mental derangement are both symptoms of personal and social disorganization.

Poverty and Social Control

Poverty at one time was thought to be due mainly to moral decadence. Those individuals failing to maintain their economic self-respect were charged with depravity of character. Of course, there were some worthy poor, but the "devil's poor" far outnumbered them.

As early as 1909 Edward T. Devine advanced the idea that poverty is primarily economic—the outgrowth of maladjustments which result directly from conditions for which society is responsible.[10] Challenging the idea that poverty is ordinarily due to shiftlessness, drink, over-reproduction, or other personal faults and stating that such an explanation was in the same class with notions of witchcraft and demoniacal possession, he suggested that the true causes of poverty should be sought in the social system —not in the personality of the individual.

The assumption made here by Devine during the first decade of this century, that poverty is not so much an individual matter as one of social disorganization, has come to be the accepted philosophy of our day. Moreover, our poor-relief practices now conform with this point of view. We recognize that in our economic order, where uncertainty, unpredictability, and considerable chaos prevails, many will inevitably be caught in the maelstrom and find themselves in want through no essential weakness of their own.

---

[10] E. T. Devine, *Misery and Its Causes*, chap. 1, The Macmillan Company, New York, 1910.

PROBLEMS OF REACCULTURATION

Migration is a frequent cause of serious pathological problems. For instance, murder rates tend to be highest among groups facing extreme problems of reacculturation. Warden Lewis E. Lawes has shown that during the years 1850 to 1870, after the great Irish migration, the Irish led in the number committed to Sing Sing for murder.[11] Between 1890 and 1919, the period of the Italian migration, foreign born Italians took the lead, with the Irish second. Since 1920 the foreign born Italians have maintained their top ranking, but the Negroes, who migrated to the North in large numbers just after the World War, have come into second place. If murder may be accepted as an index of cultural maladjustment, the above data seem to indicate that the period of reacculturation, during which the immigrant group is not susceptible to control devices of the new society in which it has settled, is likely to give rise to many serious pathological problems.

The high delinquency rate among children of immigrants in urban communities, already discussed, may be attributed to the fact that they are living under no definite system of social control. They are growing away from the old-world system of the parents and are gradually absorbing a new system of control, but are under the authority of neither.[12]

Thomas and Znaniecki in their discussion in *The Polish Peasant in Europe and America*,[13] have shown how the peasant, in his shift from the great family, with its intimate primary group organization and system of restraints, to the urban-industrialized American community, tends to break down in the adjustment process and frequently loses his orientation to his former system of life. He may cast off all the old rules or only a few of them. He may eventually succeed in making a new adjustment to life and in orienting his personality to a new system of organization, but often he fails in the process of readjustment, and demoralization results.

---

[11] "The Death Penalty at Sing Sing: What the Figures Show," *Survey*, 1927, vol. 59, pp. 69–70.

[12] See Pauline V. Young's "Social Problems in the Education of the Immigrant Child," *American Sociological Review*, June, 1936, vol. 1, pp. 419–429, for an interesting discussion of other phases of this problem.

[13] Vol. 4, chap. 2.

Scarcely less intense is the adjustment which many rural youth must make who leave a simple farm environment, with its effective control devices, for the liberalized freedom of an urban society, where few controls exist except those which can be avoided easily. Comparatively little study has been made of this problem, but undoubtedly many of the problems of maladjustment and ineffective regulation in the modern city can be traced to mobile groups living in environments where old controls are no longer operative, but where no new substitutes have been found.

In discussing the problem of city migration, Carpenter has introduced the term "culture shock," which describes the condition which an individual coming into an entirely different environment in the urban community may experience in becoming reoriented to a new system of regulation. He says,

. . . The migrant from the country to the city encounters such a new and unfamiliar universe of experience that the change is almost bound to visit upon him a distinct shock. This shock-effect of migration into the city is discussed at length elsewhere. Here it may merely be pointed out that, in the author's opinion, many of the disorganizing effects of the city upon the individual (crime, mental breakdown, etc.) are to be interpreted not so much as effects of city life as such, but rather as the effects of the sudden impact of the characteristically urban set of conditioning influences upon a personality that has been accommodated to a characteristically non-urban set of influences. In short, certain individuals break down as a consequence of their failure to become adequately reconditioned to the city.

One further point may be noted. The shock-effect of the city may be carried into the second or even the third generation of migrants. Many conditioning influences are imbedded in traditional folkways. Others are passed on from one generation to another, by conscious precept or by imitation, particularly when the migrating group is also an immigrant group, as is often the case in the cities of the United States. That is to say, there may be reverberations for two or more generations of the shock-effect attendant upon country-to-city migration.[14]

---

[14] Niles Carpenter, *The Sociology of City Life*, New York, 1931, pp. 217–218. By permission of Longmans, Green and Company.

The Breakdown of Control and Social Decay
among Primitive Peoples

The conquest of the white man among primitive peoples everywhere has offered numerous opportunities for observing the decay of simple cultures in the face of Western imperialism. Many anthropologists testify to the tendency of the white man's civilization to debase the natives. Frequently their religion dis-integrates, their moral system decays, and their family system breaks down in the face of the overpowering influence of the white man's world, parts of which the native may absorb but most of which he does not understand. He becomes a man who no longer believes in his old practices and so is no longer under their control, and yet one who has not acquired the restraints of the white man's world. Personal and social disintegration often result.

In our own nation we have seen the effect of the white man's subjugation of the Indian. The white man's liquor and the white man's sex codes have demoralized him, because he lacked the white man's restraints. At one time it looked as though the Indian would disappear, but in recent years he has absorbed more and more of the white man's culture, and at the present time seems well on the way to fairly successful accommodation.

Franklyn states the native problem pointedly:

Native people in general have a very low opinion of whites, and no wonder; for they have learned to their costs that the stranger in their midst, who in many cases was welcomed to the land as an incarnate god, not only acts as a devil, but an extraordinarily petty and con-temptible devil into the bargain, one who teaches truth is sacred and lives by transparent lies; one who preaches that war is wicked, yet slays his fellows. Syphilis is called the white man's disease, alcohol the white man's medicine. We claim to be a superior people, yet contact with us is the touch that kills; tribal organization shatters before the frown of our justice; native arts and crafts expire in the fetid breath of our industry; and the civilizing force of tabu and mana sinks to death beneath the icy pall of our religion. As theologians, as administrators, as traders, we have brought disease and despair, dis-integration and death, upon a people whose right to live was no less than our own, and whose title to the land they lived in was far greater. Now, as anthropologists, we must face the problem we have created and, before the remnants of the subject races have expired, do something to restore joy in life and pride of race to the people.

We have made the vast blunder of believing that culture could be cast off like a worn-out garment, and we have learned that it must be flayed off like a skin, causing the victims of our folly to suffer in the shedding. Just as the Church was powerless to prevent venereal disease in Europe, so it is powerless to preserve South Sea Islanders; just as the doctors came to the rescue of sick humanity at home, so must the anthropologists go to the rescue of the decaying races abroad. For anthropology consists not only in recording outlandish speech, collecting crude carvings and listening to savage obscenities, but it does this in a manner enabling us to look on native life through native eyes and see, not filthy and revolting exhibitions of degradation in savage customs, but part of a vast culture complex which represents the life of man.

It is obviously our Christian duty to repair the vast damage, restore power to the chiefs, dethrone the cheap policeman and, instead of attempting to proselytize, spend our zeal in protecting; for the frenzied prayers of the South Sea savage fell upon the ears of the God who created him, whether that God was represented or revealed. Life to the savage meant service to his fellows, and service to his God. He had discovered that the teleological end of human existence is "to be good, great and joyous, beautiful and free," and he lived up to his ideal, before we brought ruin upon him. The savage was, and in some cases still is, spiritually superior to the man in the streets of London, Paris and Berlin.

Humanity demands that the missionary, the administrator, and the trader shall lend an ear to the anthropologist and, if he will not admit defeat and retire in good order, at least mend his ways, and hold the fort with a more sympathetic outlook upon savage customs, and with greater respect for the human rights of the unfortunate subject races so rapidly moving along the rough road to total extinction.[15]

Pitt-Rivers, in a similar analysis of the degeneration of the primitive who faces Western civilization,[16] offers the suggestion

---

[15] Julian Franklyn, "Racial Decay Among Savages," The Contemporary Review, December, 1934, vol. 146, No. 828, pp. 730–731, 736. Reprinted by permission.

[16] G. Pitt-Rivers, "The Effect on Native Races of Contact with European Civilization," Man, 1927, vol. 27, pp. 2–7.

that a primitive civilization is so disrupted by contact with the white that the native loses all confidence in his culture, and as a consequence loses his purpose in living.

Examples of the Temporary Breakdown of Social Control

Situations may arise, within a social group, where social controls are temporarily disrupted. In such cases one gets a glimpse of the significance of social control, and also of the significance of the disintegration of social control to pathological developments.

Breakdown of control in a crisis. In times of crisis such as induced by tornado, fire, flood, explosion, or destruction by war, the old habits of life are suddenly destroyed, and all existing systems of control, even including those of the state, are temporarily thrown out of gear. The entire social mechanism is thrown out of line. General chaos reigns. In the midst of the ruins after an earthquake or explosion, human greed manifests itself, as human scavengers cover the area picking the pockets of the dead, stripping rings from their fingers or cutting off fingers to get at their rings more easily. Such plunder occurs on every hand, since many individuals when freed from the compulsive elements of social control have no motives for right behavior.[17] Orderly rescue work and reconstruction are impossible until some authority takes charge. Often a military force arrives on the scene, and strict orders may be issued to shoot all looters. Fences are built to protect property. Force is necessary in order that the recovery of the dead and the reconstruction of property may get under way.

One of the most extensive sociological studies of a crisis situation is that of Samuel Prince dealing with the Halifax disaster during the World War.[18] Halifax was a naval base where shiploads of ammunition were stored, and out from which vessels sailed carrying cargoes of high explosives. People lived in constant fear of an enemy attack from the air or a submarine attack from the sea, realizing that if a bomb should explode in the harbor the town would be destroyed and many lives blotted out. Hence, every precaution was taken, the lights being turned out at

---

[17] Read accounts of the San Francisco earthquake (April 18, 1906) in newspapers or magazines.
[18] Samuel H. Prince, *The Halifax Disaster.*

night so that the city would be hidden. On a December morning in 1917 a Belgian ship pulled into the harbor and accidentally jammed against a ship loaded with powerful explosives, lying at anchor. Without a moment's warning the entire harbor blew up, and much of the town was destroyed. Thousands of people were killed; the ones yet living fled for refuge to a hilltop where they sat trembling like frightened beasts.

Firemen and policemen, men habituated to acting in crises, were the first to regain their composure and begin the work of restoring order. Rescue work was organized. Military rule, force, and violence were used when necessary in the absence of the established social restraints.

What happens in such catastrophes is illustrative of what would happen throughout our entire social system if social control were suddenly removed and man were left without regulations to hold him in check.

Breakdown of control on the frontier. The frontier town, illustrated by the cow town or the mining town,[19] has been noted for the absence of legal codes, sex creeds, and general social refinements. Usually such towns are predominantly male, the first women being of the prostitute class. The struggle to make ends meet, to conquer nature before nature conquers man, to get the most in bare satisfactions from living, lest one perish in living, occupies so much of man's time and consumes so much of his energy that he quite naturally neglects the so-called finer things of life. In a frontier situation the strong man usurps the power of regulation, and brute force comes to dominate. Primitive justice is instated; the revolver substitutes for law. The man who is quick on the trigger and who has no scruples attains status and prestige, and comes to be respected and feared by all members of the community.

Women, uninhibited by refined usages, gain a certain respect and admiration by defying all the patterns that are ordinarily considered feminine in more established societies, because values are different than in the normal community. Saloon keepers, because they perform a service which is considered necessary in a frontier town, are frequently held in high esteem. In many a

---

[19] For a more extensive discussion of the problem of control in the mining town see Paul H. Landis' *Three Iron Mining Towns, A Study in Cultural Change,* chaps. 7 and 8.

settlement of this type they have been influential enough to control elections and also to control the politicians. The system of social control is adapted to the necessarily crude, rough-and-ready conditions of existence. The entire community becomes pathological from the viewpoint of one living outside, although the members of the group may perceive no abnormalities.

Culture Lag as a Defect in Social Control

To W. F. Ogburn belongs the credit for the concept "culture lag." [20] He invented the term to describe the tendency of technological culture to outrun nonmaterial culture, and also the tendency for related phases of material culture to get out of adjustment because of differential rates of change. In contemporary culture one of the important "lags" lies in the failure of our society to develop a system of social control that will effectively regulate a world transformed by technology.[21] As Coyle has expressed it, a part of the difficulties in American life are due to the "failure to install new controls as fast as new machines." [22] Social and legal adjustments cannot keep pace with technological advances.

Obviously a "lag" of this character is frought with potentialities for producing pathological conditions in every institution touched by a technological age—and few institutions, if any, escape.

Insecurity and Individualization as Related to Pathology

The extreme emphasis on individualism in our culture, accompanied by, and in part caused by, a lack of established, consistent patterns of behavior, reflects in the insecurity of many groups and helps explain the development of pathological classes. In the economic sphere few traditions protect the weak from the strong, or the strong from each other. Social classes are too ill-defined to form effective policies in relation to competing groups. Few group definitions are well enough established to provide a basis for security and certainty in competitive relationships.

Under such a way of life, large groups at the margin of the

---

[20] W. F. Ogburn, *Social Change*, Part 4.
[21] This problem has been discussed at greater length in chapter 18.
[22] David C. Coyle, et al., *The American Way*, pp. 18–27.

economic system must inevitably face poverty, unemployment, and consequent personal disorganization. Such ills are as much a part of the system of life as is individualism. In fact, for the sake of individualism we have sacrificed security.

LOCATING RESPONSIBILITY FOR SOCIAL PATHOLOGY

The combined effect of a culture which provides an uncertain world for the individual, and of a new knowledge of human nature which blames man's misconduct on experience rather than on instinct, has been to make society responsible for pathological conditions. We no longer consider the slums a product of perverted human nature, but rather perverted human nature the product of the slums. We no longer have God's poor and the Devil's poor, but New York City's poor, the United States Steel Corporation's poor, the Depression's poor. We are still strong for individual initiative and enterprise in all fields of human endeavor, but at the same time we frankly recognize that such endeavor is bound to be thwarted in many cases by impersonal forces in the system of social control. We still say to every man, "Make a name for yourself, be a millionnaire, be a president; but if you end up an anonymous hobo, poor, unwanted, and unknown, we will shoulder part of the blame."

Because we have come to accept pathology as an inevitable phase of our system of life, measures for improvement are aimed primarily at improving the cultural structure, rather than at reforming the victim. It is recognized that the individual can be reformed only by reshaping his experience-world. Increasingly, the failure of certain classes and individuals is being regarded as a phase of impersonal social forces within the social system, and not as the fault of the individual or class that becomes the victim.

CONCLUSION

Many of the most pressing pathological conditions in our society are in part a product of an inadequate system of control. Crime and delinquency, suicide, poverty—all thrive in areas where the system of social organization is weak, where regulative forces are impotent. Another group of pathological conditions center about those groups, who, because of contact with two or more systems of control, live under neither. Problems of primitives who unfortunately have encountered the white man, problems of Americanization, and problems of "culture shock" of migrants to urban communities are some of the results. Finally, numerous pathological conditions arise throughout our culture because of the failure of the system of social regulation to keep pace with technological changes.

SELECTED REFERENCES

Addams, J., "A Modern Devil Baby," *American Journal of Sociology,* vol. 20, pp. 117–118. 1914.

Atkinson, H. A., "Can Religion Stop War?" *Missionary Review,* vol. 54, p. 37. January, 1931.

Bisch, Louis E., "Inside of the Criminal Mind," *Saturday Evening Post,* pp. 14–15. June 12, 1926.

Black, J., "Burglar Looks at Laws and Codes," *Harper's Magazine,* vol. 160, pp. 306 ff. February, 1930.

Black, J., "What's Wrong with the Right People?" *Harper's Magazine,* pp. 75–82. June, 1929.

Bossard, Joseph H. S., *Social Change and Social Problems,* revised edition, chap. 7. Harper and Brothers, New York, 1938.

Burgess, E. W., editor, *Personality and the Social Group* (selection by Robert E. Park, "Human Migration and the Marginal Man"), chap. 6. University of Chicago Press, Chicago, 1929.

Burgess, E. W., editor, *Personality and the Social Group* (selection by E. B. Reuter, "The Personality of Mixed Bloods"), chap. 5. University of Chicago Press, Chicago, 1929.

Chafee, Z. Jr., "Complexities of Crime," *Outlook,* vol. 152, p. 341. June 26, 1929.

Coyle, David C., and Others, *The American Way,* pp. 18–24. Harper and Brothers, New York, 1938.

Devine, Edward T., *Misery and Its Causes,* chap. 1. The Macmillan Company, New York, 1910.

Elliott, Mabel A., and Merrill, Francis E., *Social Disorganization.* Harper and Brothers, New York, 1934.

Folsom, J. K., *The Family,* chap. 28. John Wiley and Sons, Inc., New York, 1934.

Fosdick, H. E., "What Can the Minister Do?" *Review of Reviews,* pp. 44–46. December, 1932.

Frank, Lawrence K., "Society as the Patient," *American Journal of Sociology,* vol. 42, pp. 338–340. November, 1936.

Franklyn, J., "Racial Decay among Savages," *The Contemporary Review*, vol. 146, pp. 730–736. December, 1934.

Gauss, C., "Decline of Religion," *Scribner's Magazine*, vol. 95, pp. 241–246. April, 1934.

Jastrow, J., "How Misery Breeds Crime," *North American Review*, vol. 229, pp. 305 ff. March, 1930.

Kenyon, T., "Witches Still Live," *North American Review*, vol. 228, pp. 620 ff. November, 1929.

Landis, Paul H., *Three Iron Mining Towns, A Study in Cultural Change*, parts 2 and 3. Edwards Brothers, Ann Arbor, 1938.

Lawes, Lewis E., "The Death Penalty at Sing Sing: What the Figures Show," *Survey*, vol. 59, pp. 69–70. 1927.

Lippmann, Walter, *A Preface to Morals*. The Macmillan Company, New York, 1929.

Michael, Jerome, and Adler, Mortimer J., *Crime, Law, and Social Science*. Harcourt, Brace and Company, New York, 1933.

Mowrer, Ernest R., *Family Disorganization*, pp. 110 ff. University of Chicago Press, Chicago, 1927.

Ogburn, W. F., *Social Change*, part 4. The Viking Press, Inc., New York, 1923.

Pitt-Rivers, G., "The Effect on Native Races of Contact with European Civilization," *Man*, vol. 27, pp. 2–7. 1927.

Prince, Samuel Henry, *Catastrophe and Social Change, Based upon a Sociological Study of the Halifax Disaster*. Columbia University Press, New York, 1920.

Rivers, W. H. R., *Essays on the Depopulation of Melanesia*, pp. xviii–116. Cambridge University Press, Cambridge, 1927.

Shaw, Clifford R., and Others, *Delinquency Areas*. University of Chicago Press, Chicago, 1929.

Shaw, Clifford R., *The Jack-Roller*. University of Chicago Press, Chicago, 1930.

Slosson, E. E., "Revival of Witchcraft," *Collier's*, vol. 83, pp. 48 ff. May 25, 1929.

Stonequist, E. V., *The Marginal Man; A Study of Personality and Culture Contact*, chaps. 3 and 4. Charles Scribner's Sons, New York, 1937.

Sutherland, Edwin H., *Principles of Criminology*. J. B. Lippincott Company, Chicago, 1934.

Tannenbaum, Frank, *Crime and the Community*, part 1. Ginn and Company, Boston, 1938.

Thomas, W. I., and Znaniecki, Florian, *The Polish Peasant in Europe and America*, vol. 4, pt. 1; vol. 5, pt. 2. Chapman and Grimes, Boston, 1920.

Thrasher, Frederic M., *The Gang*. University of Chicago Press, Chicago, 1927.

Wallas, Graham, *The Great Society*. The Macmillan Company, New York, 1920.

Young, Pauline V., "Social Problems in the Education of the Immigrant Child," *American Sociological Review*, vol. 1, pp. 419–429. June, 1936.

Zorbaugh, Harvey W., *The Gold Coast and the Slum*. University of Chicago Press, Chicago, 1929.

CHAPTER 24

SOCIAL REVOLT

Revolt as a Normal Social Process

Social control can be too rigid, and smother individual expression. If individuals have tasted freedom, suppression brings revolt and the disruption of the social order. On the other hand, regulation can be so lax that the individual loses his balance never to regain it, for a personality does not always reconstruct itself when the props fall out from under it, although social orders always do. Societies cannot exist without social control devices, and any disorganization must therefore be temporary, a transitory phase in the life of the group.

The fact that social control is necessary to the existence of society does not do away with the possibility that it may become too inflexible and over-bearing, so much so that members of society find it intolerable. The tendency of all institutional structures, and of the whole social organization, is to drift toward too great restraint. When that extreme is reached, there usually arises a nucleus of people who, finding life in the group unendurable, make articulate their galling under the yoke of suppression, or rally the complaining forces and engineer revolt. This is more especially so in societies which have permitted the growth of individualism. In a static society it is conceivable that a people may be so completely dominated by authority that not only the power to revolt is gone but also the desire to rebel.

History holds many instances of individuals who rebelled against the restraints of the social order and tried to seek a more satisfactory life by developing patterns which ran more or less counter to the social definitions. Radicals and reformers are always active, but more especially so in eras when freedom of expression is permitted. Those who would usher in the new regime and destroy the old never sleep. Such revolt often is a sign of life and progress, for the rebel is often the man who initiates the new

442

and who points the way to a better adjustment. Nonconformity produces change. Any system of social control which does not permit it brings stagnation, and unless authority is well established, prepares the way for more violent revolt, such as that involved in revolution when whole classes rebel.

REVOLT AND INDIVIDUALIZATION

Revolt is no less an index of growing individualism than it is an expression of freedom from authority. It is more to be expected in a heterogeneous culture where the individual has opportunity to choose from a variety of patterns than in a homogeneous culture, where one authoritative pattern is presented, and where the individual therefore sees open only one way of life. Restraint is most galling to those who have tasted the freedom which an individualistic social order permits. People long accustomed to arbitrary controls probably would never revolt, did they not come in contact with a system of life permitting greater individualism. Thus the majority of youth in the Amana Colony [1] remained fairly content with the patriarchal pattern established by their elders until the automobile brought in visitors, among them youths of the outside with short skirts, bobbed hair, and silk stockings, who engaged in romantic courtship relatively free of paternal domination. Contact with the outside group was revealing, in that it suggested a new and alternative pattern. Similarly, in port cities of the Orient arbitrary systems of control sanctioned by centuries of custom have broken down under the influence of Western civilization.[2] Likewise, Turkish women shed their veils and defied the age-long domination of the male, under the stimulus of contact with the West, where new patterns of freedom have been fostered.[3]

---

[1] The Amana Society is a colony in Iowa that for a period of about 200 years has been communistic. It originated in Germany and eventually migrated as a unit to rural Iowa, where social isolation was possible until the coming of the automobile. Then a paved state highway was constructed which cut through one town in the Colony. In 1932 the Colony was abandoned as a communistic unit and organized as a capitalistic corporation, individualism replacing the old authoritative order.

[2] Charles Merz, "A New Turkey Challenges Islam," Our World, 1923–1924, vol. 4, pp. 71–76.

[3] "Social Change in Japan," The Nation, 1926, vol. 123, pp. 235, 652; also, Vera Kelsey, "If a Chinese Leaves His Village," Asia, 1924, vol. 24, pp. 463–469.

Nonconformity as a Phase of Revolt

Society, in order to function perfectly and intact, must maintain a delicate balance between social control and freedom. There are limits of freedom under which human nature runs riot, and under which no society could survive. On the other hand, there are limits of suppression which either kill individuality or provoke the grossest type of rebellion and disintegration of the entire system of social control. Conformity and nonconformity are both essential to a stable social order. Self-assertion must find its place, but so also must submission to social discipline. They are both normal phases of a healthy society. It is desirable not only that man be one of the crowd, but that he be able to stand alone against the crowd and cut out a new path in defiance of the social controls, venturing out as a pioneer in the new realm of social conquest, reform, or reconstruction.

Cooley has presented two aspects of nonconformity: (1) rebellion or "contrary suggestion," leading to an avoidance of accepted standards without the substitution of other standards; (2) an appeal from present standards to new ones, both processes usually working together. He finds two causes for nonconformity, intrinsic contrariness, and fixing the imagination on the "ideas and practices of other people whose mode of life he finds more congenial." [4]

People of natural energy, he believes, take pleasure in the enhanced self-feeling that comes from conscious rebellion, derive joy from self-assertion. Braving disapproval, for courageous men, is a tonic.

Whether or not the nonconformer is accepted depends to a considerable extent upon the reforms he sponsors, and upon the way in which he sponsors them. A nonconformist who dares defy the social order and succeeds becomes the hero of the next generation. A nonconformist who defies the existing system of control and fails is crushed beneath a burden of social condemnation, and soon forgotten.

Social revolt is quite as much to be expected as conformity, in an individualistic social order such as our own, and a wise social system will make provision for it, both on an individual and on a

---

[4] Charles H. Cooley, *Human Nature and the Social Order*, pp. 297–298.

class basis. Political revolt on the group level, as exhibited in the elections of democratic societies, and in the periodic overthrowing of the cabinet in power, provides a regular and fairly orderly method of public expression and of group revolt. Countries with rigid political systems which permit no revolt must foster isolation in a world of social contact, or eventually face revolt of a serious character. Because such revolt comes infrequently, and only after extensive grievances have accumulated, it therefore tends to be violent in character, usually taking the form of a revolution.

Human beings are somewhat like children in their periodic desire to evade authority. I suppose there are few children who did not sometime in early youth revolt against their parents, even to the extent of secretly packing their belongings into a suitcase and heading down the road away from home. Irritated by parental discipline, they set forth to find liberty and elbow room beyond the restrictive boundaries of home.

At times, when prohibitions are rigid, and normal human interests springing from biological drives are completely submerged, life becomes a drab affair for the human animal deprived of all normal means of self-expression. At such a time widespread revolt may develop and lead to license. The case of prohibition is an example in point. Puritanism and the extreme reaction which followed it is another. The pioneer work code has undergone a reversion in the present emphasis on recreation and pleasure.

Youth Revolts More Often Than Age

Nonconformists tend to appear among the young and energetic. Everywhere, it is youth that struggles against the social traditions. The old generation endeavors to uphold the old ways, the old conventions, the old controls. The new generation, seeking new experience and new conquests, challenges the social order, defies the prohibitions, and cuts new trails. Thus the process of disorganization frequently appears among youth, as well as reform and the process of social improvement. Thomas and Znaniecki, studying the adjustments of the Polish peasant, conclude that it is the new generation that revolts against the established regulations. They describe the process of youthful revolt in brief as follows:

. . . it is everywhere the younger generation through which new attitudes mainly penetrate a community, and the struggle between
social tradition and social novelty always becomes, in some measure
at least, identified with the opposition between the old and the young.

In the new generation, on the contrary, the desire for new experience is always stronger originally than the desire for security, and
becomes checked only by a social training which limits the field of
possible novelties.   Even in the most conservative primary-group,
where the methods of social control are particularly efficient in producing an early stabilization, the period when new experiences outside of the social routine still have a strong appeal for the individual
certainly extends beyond the age of twenty.   This means that there
is a period of five to ten years during which almost every individual
is both open to socially prohibited or unforeseen suggestions, and
able to act in accordance with these suggestions.
When, therefore, the community enters in contact with the outside world, the youth are naturally the first to develop new attitudes
and to import new values.   It is evident that under these conditions
the movement, if not directed by educated and mature leaders, is not
likely to be constructive, since only those attitudes tend to develop
and only those values appeal to the individual which he is prepared
to accept.   The undirected attention of the peasant youth is thus
most easily captivated by superficial aesthetic and hedonistic objects—clothes, trinkets, smoking, fancy foods and drinks. . . .

It must be understood, of course, that the process of disorganization which starts with the young generation is a complicated matter.
As a certain group of young people grow older and take the place of
their parents, they have to moderate their new attitudes in adaptation
to traditional problems and to old responsibilities which they are
forced to face; they bring indeed a new and discordant element into
the community, but not as radically new and discordant as might
have been expected judging by their earlier attitudes.   At the same
time, however, a new group of young people has taken their place as
the revolutionary factor; the attitudes of these are different from those
of the old generation, but may be also different from those of the
preceding young group.   And so on, with increasing complexity.[5]

---

[5] William I. Thomas and Florian Znaniecki, *The Polish Peasant in Europe and
America*, vol. 2, pp. 70–72, 80, 81.   By permission of Chapman and Grimes.

The process of youthful revolt here described as characterizing the peasant immigrant from Poland is characteristic of youth generally, especially when they face alternative patterns of life. In our individualistic social system, many youth during the period of adolescence, which bridges the regulated period of childhood and the relatively free period of maturity, when they are experiencing the liberating effects of greater age and new experience, exercise their new freedom to an extreme that may border on revolt. Some, in the quest for freedom of expression, challenge many established values. This period in life has often been referred to as the one in which young people "sow their wild oats," the assumption being that it is a period in life only, that with growing maturity and experience, with the increasing responsibilities of adulthood, regard for social discipline will somehow come, as Thomas and Znaniecki say it comes to the Polish peasant when he passes the critical period of youth and reaches adulthood. He does not return to the restricted limits of childhood as represented in the old parental patterns, but becomes more regulated than in his youth.

HISTORICAL EXAMPLES OF INDIVIDUAL REVOLT

With the dawn of the modern era, when notions of individual freedom and of political democracy were developing in the transition from the old authoritative order based on an all-powerful church and state, certain social thinkers expressed a vigorous protest against authority, and became patrons of individual freedom. A brief review of the mental processes of some individuals who championed revolt is interesting.

Rousseau is famous for his violent protest against social regulation. The gist of his philosophy of revolt may be summarized in his words as follows:

Everything is good as it comes from the hands of the Creator; everything degenerates in the hands of man.

Our wisdom consists of servile prejudices; our customs are nothing but subjection, restriction, constraint. Civilized man is born, lives, dies in slavery: at his birth he is bound in swaddling clothes, at his death nailed in his coffin; and, all the time he has worn the image of man, he has been held no less fast by our institutions.

A man can only do as he pleases when he needs not to use the arms of another for his purpose. Hence it follows that the greatest of all blessings is not authority but liberty. The man who is really free only desires what he can then perform; he can then perform all that he desires. This is my fundamental maxim.

In the state of nature, equality is a real and inviolable fact, the difference between man and man never being great enough to make one dependent on another. In the social state, it is a fictitious and impracticable right; the means intended to maintain it serve only to destroy it. The force of the State joins with the strong to oppress the weak, and destroys the equilibrium which Nature has put between them. From this first contradiction between appearance and reality proceed all the others which are found in society. The many will always be sacrificed to the few, and public to private interests. The specious names of justice and subordination will always be made the instruments of violence and the weapons of wrong. It follows that those distinguished orders of men, which pretend to be useful to the others, are in reality useful only to themselves at the other's expense; we may conclude what consideration they deserve by the laws of reason and justice. It remains to see whether the rank which they have assumed is any more favourable to their own happiness, in order that we may know what judgment we should each form of our own lot. To aid us in this enquiry, we must begin by making ourselves acquainted with the human heart.

If it were a question only of showing our pupil Man in disguise, we might save ourselves the trouble; he will see enough of him without our assistance. But, since the disguise is not the man, and since he ought not to be led astray by appearances, let us paint mankind as they really are, not in order that he may hate them, but rather that he may pity them and not desire to resemble them. . . . With this intent, we must now take a different line from that which we have hitherto followed; we must instruct our pupil rather by the experience of others than by his own. . . . His own companions should be chosen with a view to making him think well of them; but we wish him to know the world well enough to think ill of its doings. He should know that man is naturally good, he should perceive it in his own heart, and should judge of his neighbor by himself; but he should observe how society depraves and corrupts him; he should discover the source of its vices in its prejudices; he should be inclined to esteem individuals, but to despise the mass; he should see that all men wear the same mask, but that some of their faces are much more handsome than the masks which cover them.[6]

Similarly, Thoreau, in our own nation, developed a love for a kind of freedom that only a man existing without society could achieve; so he took himself to the woods, and there attempted to live an ideal life. His experience of living without the ordinary restraints of the social order are described in his *Walden; or Life in the Woods.*

The greater part of what my neighbors call good I believe in my soul to be bad, and if I repent of anything, it is very likely to be my good behavior. What demon possessed me that I behaved so well? You may say the wisest thing you can, old man—you who have lived seventy years, not without honor of a kind—I hear an irresistible voice which invites me away from all that. One generation abandons the enterprises of another like stranded vessels.

I think that we may safely trust a good deal more than we do. We may waive just so much care of ourselves as we honestly bestow elsewhere. Nature is as well adapted to our weakness as to our strength. The incessant anxiety and strain of some is a well-nigh incurable form of disease. We are made to exaggerate the importance of what work we do; and yet how much is not done by us! or, what if we had been taken sick? How vigilant we are! determined not to live by faith if we can avoid it; all the day long on the alert, at night we unwillingly say our prayers and commit ourselves to uncertainties. So thoroughly and sincerely are we compelled to live, regimenting our life, and denying the possibility of change. This is the only way, we say; but there are as many ways as there can be drawn radii from one centre. All change is a miracle to contemplate; but it is a miracle which is taking place every instant. Confucius said, "To know that we know what we know, and that we do not know what we do not know, that is true knowledge." When one man has reduced a fact of the imagination to be a fact to his understanding, I foresee that all men will at length establish their lives on that basis.

I went to the woods because I wished to live deliberately, to front only the essential facts of life, and see if I could not learn what it had to teach, and not, when I came to die, discover that I had not lived. I did not wish to live what was not life, living is so dear; nor did I

---

[6] Selections from Jean Jacques Rousseau's *Emile.*

wish to practise resignation, unless it was quite necessary. I wanted to live deep and suck out all the marrow of life, to live so sturdily and Spartan-like as to put to rout all that was not life, to cut a broad swath and shave close, to drive life into a corner, and reduce it to its lowest terms, and, if it proved to be mean, why then to get the whole and genuine meanness of it, and publish its meanness to the world; or if it were sublime, to know it by experience, and be able to give a true account of it in my next excursion. For most men, it appears to me, are in a strange uncertainty about it, whether it is of the devil or of God, and have *somewhat hastily* concluded that it is the chief end of man here to "glorify God and enjoy him forever."

Still we live meanly, like ants; though the fable tells us that we were long ago changed into men; like pygmies we fight with cranes, it is error upon error, and clout upon clout, and our best virtue has for its occasion a superfluous and evitable wretchedness. Our life is frittered away by detail. And honest man has hardly need to count more than his ten fingers, or in extreme cases he may add his ten toes, and lump the rest. Simplicity, simplicity, simplicity! I say, let your affairs be as two or three, and not a· hundred or a thousand; instead of a million count half a dozen, and keep your accounts on your thumb nail. In the midst of this chopping sea of civilized life, such are the clouds and storms and quicksands and thousand-and-one items to be allowed for, that a man has to live, if he would not founder and go to the bottom and not make his port at all, by dead reckoning, and he must be a great calculator indeed who succeeds. Simplify, simplify. Instead of three meals a day, if it be necessary eat but one, instead of a hundred dishes, five; and reduce other things in proportion. . . .

One afternoon, near the end of the first summer, when I went to the village to get a shoe from the cobbler's, I was seized and put into jail, because, as I have elsewhere related, I did not pay a tax to, or recognize the authority of, the state which buys and sells men, women, and children, like cattle, at the door of its senate-house. I had gone down to the woods for other purposes. But, wherever a man goes, men will pursue and paw him with their dirty institutions, and, if they can, constrain him to belong to their desperate odd-fellow society. It is true, I might have resisted forcibly with more or less effect, might have run "amok" against society; but I preferred that society should run "amok" against me, it being the desperate party.

However, I was released the next day, obtained my mended shoe, and returned to the woods in season to get my dinner of huckleberries on Fair Haven Hill.[7]

The revolt of these two men was for the purpose of developing individualism rather than suppression, a token of an age of individualism, rather than a revolt against powerful restrictive authority.

LITERATURE OF PROTEST

In the literature of any society which allows freedom of expression one can note varied symptoms of revolt. The Hebrew minor prophets, in their literature of protest, envisioned a new social order and decried the social injustice of their time. Today we have many who cry out against the various forces of suppression, and who, in a literature of criticism and deprecation, try to destroy old codes, overthrow old authorities, and make way for a better system of social regulation. Many writers are not content with merely interpreting the world; they want to make the world over.

Much of this literature of revolt is a cry for an enlightened social conscience, for increased social legislation, for greater individual freedom and expression, a cry to overthrow the domination of wealth, privilege, or power. Often these symptoms of revolt may be interpreted as danger signals, and especially when their volume increases to unusual proportions is it a good sign that there is something wrong with the prevailing system of social control. Some expression of protest is in itself, however, advantageous, in that it indicates that people are relieving themselves of their grievances. Moreover, protest may bring reform without violence.

THE PROCESS OF BREAKING SOCIAL CONTROLS AS A PHASE OF MENTAL EXPERIENCE

The individual in the initial steps of breaking established regulations, especially if they have become a part of his system of habits, usually encounters considerable emotional resistance, in theological terms, "the pangs of conscience." With repeated offenses, the emotional sensitivity becomes less and less, until

---

[7] Selections from Henry David Thoreau, Walden; or Life in the Woods.

eventually he may practice exactly the opposite type of behavior with the same facility, and with a sense of security equal to that previously experienced in practicing the established behavior. That is, one's moral sense or one's sense of obligation to social regulation in any sphere is modified by experience. Any experience which leads one to examine patterns critically comes ordinarily from having been introduced to a new group with a conflicting set of standards. If the individual then remains in the new group, the adjustments, as he goes through this transition from old to new type of controls, are relatively easy. But if he returns to the old group where its patterns are again prominent, he faces resistance. The diversity of experience in the modern world arising in the mobility of individuals from group to group, and from social class to social class makes this problem of adaptation to new systems of social control a very important one, and a source of much personality conflict.

On the Organic-Psychological Necessity for Revolt

Most forms of human revolt have called forth an apology from students of human nature. No less an authority than William James assumed that war was an organic and psychological necessity, and that only through war, or some substitute, could the race retain its "manly virtues." In his famous essay "Moral Equivalents for War," [8] he devises substitutes for war which will make it possible for manliness to develop without the carnage of war. A program startling in its similarity to that of the present Civil Conservation Corps, which would provide young men with the opportunity to expend their energies in fighting nature for a year or two, instead of fighting human beings, was his chief substitute.

Cooley in describing the revolt of children, suggests that the child obtains a thrill from his disobedience, a peculiar sense of originality and of achievement that comes from being defiant and wilful.[9] Much human meanness has been justified by the remark, "Oh, that's human nature," inferring that we must expect man to kick over the traces occasionally and give vent to appetites, passions, or desire for self-expression.

Freud's theory offers an amazing apology for man's sex nature,

---

[8] William James, *Memories and Studies*, chap. 11.
[9] Charles H. Cooley, *Human Nature and the Social Order*, p. 298.

and if one accepted it fully he could readily justify, on the grounds of organic and psychological necessity, almost any form of sex behavior that varied from social controls.

An age which permits all sorts of license on the grounds that human nature must be satisfied is followed by reaction in the form of reformations, revivals, crusades, purity campaigns, crime commissions, prohibitions, and other such sanctifying activities. When a certain satiation point in expression is reached the only satisfaction possible comes from reform. Thus, Roman debauchery was followed by medieval celibacy. St. Augustine's riotous youth terminated in conversion, after which he wrote his *Confessions*. The saloon and the drunkard brought prohibition.

INDIVIDUAL DIFFERENCES AND REVOLT

Not all individuals feel equally at ease under any one system of social control. Lombroso's theory of an atavistic type, while incorrect in its specific assumptions of biological fact, nevertheless suggests a profound truth of human experience. Many people are so constituted that they simply cannot fit under the prevailing system of regulation, although under some other system they might be quite at ease. Ruth Benedict in her study, *Patterns of Culture*, has demonstrated conclusively that culture patterns, because they put a premium on selected forms of behavior, are not equally "congenial to all individuals living under them." [10] Fortunate indeed is one whose potentialities coincide with the pattern of his society. He who has different leanings is sure to face frustration, or if he seeks his own way, to run counter to the pattern and be condemned. Because human beings are enormously malleable by original endowment, they can for the most part be molded into the culture into which they are born. But woe to the aggressive man born in a pattern calling for submission; woe to an individualistic feminist in a culture where women are put in the same category with flowers; woe to a neurotic woman in an age of witches. Even insanity is defined by the cultural norms of a time and place.

THE ESTABLISHED CHANNELS FOR REVOLT IN AMERICAN LIFE

Social revolt is considered a safety valve, a way of letting off steam, for people who would otherwise accumulate such a list of

[10] Ruth Benedict, *Patterns of Culture*, chap. 8.

grievances that eventually the point of violent outburst would be reached. Our society has always permitted a comparatively large amount of revolt against social control. The extent to which we permit free expression of public opinion by the press and by the radio is almost unbelievable. One from another culture coming to the United States during the days of the depression, and listening to the Huey Longs, the Father Coughlins, the Townsendites, and the New Dealers, each crying their wares to millions of followers, would have wondered how we could afford to allow such extreme freedom of expression. Even in our regular periodic balloting we set up a staged system for revolt, calling upon the masses to express themselves on whatever reform issues may be presented. In the industrial sphere we permit the strike to operate more or less unrestrained by state authorities as long as it remains within set bounds, and ordinarily it has proved to be a fairly orderly method of making those in authority heed the wishes of the laborers.

We in America have one of the most rapidly changing cultures in the world, and therefore we have learned to adapt ourselves quickly to life under new systems of regulation, and as readily to destroy old systems. We have become habituated to change, to experiments, to quick adjustments, to changes in authority, to the shuffling of social classes up and down, to the rise and fall of particular individuals through the democratic processes of public opinion. All these things safeguard our existing system of control because they modify the controls, making them more adaptable to the human beings who live under them.

Under our democratic institutions, the high tensions which are a part of an inflexible social structure do not develop. Also, we have not been so often engaged in war as have many nations. War brings privation and suppression, calling for the exercise of extreme forms of discipline. Every nation reserves the right to dictate to its subjects in wartime, grinding the masses under the heel of military authority so that not infrequently revolutions are a direct product of the rigid controls of war.

WHERE DOES REVOLT END?

When people revolt there are many who immediately conclude that catastrophe lies ahead for society, but this is not necessarily true. Most people revolt only against some one phase of the system of social control which they feel restrains them unfairly, and are not rebels in other spheres. The fact that they can cry loudly against whatever abuses they may have found permits them to live healthfully and happily under a regulated social system.

There is, however, one danger in revolt. It is always difficult to find a stopping place. In this respect, social restraints are not much different from the restraint of credit or the restraint of inflation. Once social revolt reaches large proportions it is difficult to check, and the danger looms up that it will pass beyond the bounds of safety and lead to a period of undue freedom, or even social chaos, before people wake up to the fact that they have increased human liberty too much. This is one of the fears that the Church frequently expresses when old moral codes begin to slip and people begin to lose faith in the traditions. The cry immediately is, "Where will it end?"

THE "DEBUNKING PROCESS" AS AN ASPECT OF REVOLT

In a complex social world, in which most individuals grow up in a homogeneous primary group where standards are rigid and invariable, people must, in adjusting to the larger world, go through a period of life during which they cast aside certain of the regulations imposed by their primary groups. The limitations of even the most liberal of primary groups frequently place stumbling blocks in the way of anyone who would adjust to a different vocation or a different social group in a secondary world beyond.

The "debunking" of established social values, especially when these have become deeply ingrained in the habit systems of individuals, is not an easy process, but often involves much struggle between ideals of the old experience-world and realities of the new. Considerable inner turmoil or even strife with people in the environment may ensue. The fact of this "debunking process" being forced upon almost every individual in our complex modern world creates a vital problem in personality adjustment, and is one of the most fruitful causes of personality disorganization.

The process of casting away established controls is frought with danger because "debunking," while difficult to do in its initial stages, becomes easier with practice. As it gathers momentum it becomes increasingly easy to "debunk" anything and everything, and increasingly difficult to stand by one's earlier convictions. In fact, if my observation of college students is correct, almost every college youth is forced to do some "debunking." If his primary group was extremely narrow and rigid in its conceptions, he faces a more formidable problem than does one whose primary group was liberal and progressive. But almost every individual must needs cast away at least some values as he meets the new experience and ideals of the world of the college or university.

The struggle to reconcile Christianity with evolution has been prominent among many generations of college students, and has been a problem not only of personal ideals but also has involved the establishment of a new basis for conduct and for authority. Similarly, in many phases of behavior the patterns of the new group and the old conflict.

Many college youth, having left the primary group for the first time, face in a new way and on their own initiative such questions as whether to smoke or not, whether to drink with the gang or to remain true to primary group patterns, whether or not to fall into the lax sex behavior of certain members of the new group thus taking advantage of the liberty which the secondary group environment affords.

One sees in college students as they pass from the freshman to the senior year a progressive tendency to "debunk" established principles and previously accepted authoritative guides to conduct. This is a normal result of the liberating effect of college on the individual, but on the other hand, this experience often proves disastrous for a portion of them. There is no question but that college should "debunk" certain values acquired in restricted primary group environments, but some students go the whole way, misconceiving entirely the purpose of their new liberty, and failing utterly to perceive the consequences of completely "debunking" the guide of human experience as expressed in the traditions of their primary group. With some of these individuals, the college experience results in demoralization and personal degeneration. Others, who "debunk" only those values which were peculiar to their primary group but hardly consistent with the values of the larger society, find their college experience broadening in the proper sense. They achieve new liberties but at the same time keep their trend of personality development in line with the general patterns of the larger society. Here as in other situations there is a point beyond which individualization becomes antisocial, beyond which freedom brings destruction.

VIOLENT REVOLT AND THE COMPLETE BREAKDOWN OF CONTROL

Although no social order ever loses all power of regulation, in the case of violent revolt, which is best illustrated by revolution, one sees a breakdown of controls that is relatively complete, so complete in fact, that much unrestrained behavior is manifest. Sorokin, as an outgrowth of his study of historic revolutions, and of his experience in the Russian revolution, has shown how the breakdown of restraints gives rein to organic drives (unconditioned reflexes he calls them) until utter chaos results. This condition prevails until men, being no longer able to stand disorder, begin to reestablish control. The following paragraphs from his work give a glimpse of a world relatively free of controls.

A GLIMPSE AT A WORLD WITHOUT SOCIAL CONTROL [11]

. . . The conduct of the masses swayed now [during revolution] only by elemental unconditioned reflexes grows to be anarchic: one unconditioned reflex is opposed and overridden by the other; one individual oppresses and overrides the others. Famine increases, instead of decreasing, consequently, the reflexes of nutrition are still more oppressed. Personal safety grows more insecure; the death rate rises tremendously, thanks to murders, famine and epidemics. Therefore, the reflexes of self-preservation are more and more oppressed. Confiscations of wealth, taken away first from the rich, later on from the whole population under the guise of ever-heavier requisitions and taxes, oppress the proprietorial instincts. The growth of sexual license oppresses sexual reflexes. The arbitrariness of the governing class oppresses the reflexes of liberty, etc. In short, with but few exceptions, whatever group of fundamental reflexes we touch upon in each one of them, the oppression has increased, not diminished; the more so, the more profound the revolution has been. In this "primitive chaos," *bellum omnium contra omnes*, a general oppression of all fundamental reflexes takes place. It is just during such periods that the theory of Hobbes (who, by the way, promulgated it after the experience acquired during the English Revolution) is justified. People grow less adapted to their surroundings and

[11] From Pitirim A. Sorokin, *The Sociology of Revolution*, pp. 408, 409. By permission of J. B. Lippincott Company, Chicago.

mutual relations. Their attitude towards them is summed up in the words: "It is impossible to continue life under such conditions, order is necessary, order at any cost."

THE AFTERMATH OF REVOLUTION IS A NEW SOCIAL ORDER

The preceding materials have described adequately the revolutionary process and the extent to which it tends to completely destroy many phases of social control, not only in the political sphere but in the sphere of such things as family relations, morals, and property rights. But what finally happens? As pointed out in the introduction, revolt must always work its own cure. No society can get along without a fairly rigid and well-established system of social regulations. As Sorokin has said,

. . . And so men are taught by inexorable teachers; hunger, cold, illness, want and death; they stand before a double dilemma: to perish and die, continuing the revolutionary debauch; or to find a new outlet. Bitter and tragic experience forces men to see that much of what they had looked upon as "prejudice," much from which they had gladly "liberated" themselves was in reality the complex of conditions essential to comfortable social life; to the existence and development of society.

Now the demand for unbridled liberty is superseded by a desire of "order;" the longing for "deliverers" from the Ancien Regime is succeeded by a longing for "deliverers" from the revolution; or, in other words, for organizers of order. "Order" and "Long live the creators of order"—such is the universal clamor during the second period of revolution, alike: in Rome during the times of Caesar and Augustus; in Bohemia towards the end of the revolutionary war; in England during Protectorate; in France during Napoleon's elevation; in 1849–51, in 1871, and in Russia in 1922–24.

. . . Social order is never casual, but is the result of centuries of the adjustment of humanity to its environment, and of its individual members to each other; it is the outcome of centuries of efforts, experience and strivings to achieve the best possible forms of social organization and life. Every stable social organization, however imperfect it may seem from the standpoint of immature radicalism, is, nevertheless, the outcome of an immense condensed real (not fictitious) national experience; the result of innumerable strivings, efforts, experiments of many generations to find the best possible forms compatible with existing concrete conditions. Only an ignoramus, or a man immersed in the fantasies of his own brain, can imagine that such an order, built up and existing for centuries, can present nothing but an immense nonsense, a misunderstanding, a complete mistake.[12]

THE PROCESS OF RE-ESTABLISHING CONTROLS AFTER REVOLUTION

Many other authors have made the same observation, that revolutions leave restrictions in their wake. The period of license is followed by one of reform. The period of anarchy is succeeded by a new political regime which may be quite as severe in its way as the old. In this adjustment period, when controlling authorities are being established, countless struggles between groups trying to gain the place of authority take place. A contemporary writer, in discussing the current wholesale execution in the Soviet Union, analyzes this phenomenon as a normal post-revolutionary trend, a part of the task of re-establishing a system of social control that will eventually make life and property secure. He says in part,

. . . It is a law of history that the men who lead an extreme social revolt seldom survive to enjoy its fruits. France furnishes an excellent object lesson. The main actors on the revolutionary stage, Robespierre and Danton, Marat and Hébert, came to violent ends, mostly on the guillotine to which they had sentenced so many others. In the phrase of the great French philosophical historian, Taine, the Revolution proved a crocodile, devouring its own young.

A Trotskyist publicist recently noted with pained surprise the regularity with which reaction follows revolution, and plaintively asked: Why does the Left make the Revolution and the Right the subsequent Constitution? The answer to this question is quite simple. Reasonably or not, most human beings want to live. And the revolutionary atmosphere, with its combination of lofty ideals and atrocious crimes, professions of world brotherhood and universal espionage, tall talk and short rations, is physically and psychologically unbreathable over a long period, even for people with as great capacity for self-torment as the Russians. Just as the stiff-necked reactionary régime carries within itself the seeds of revolution, so the inevitable excesses of revolution are the harbinger of subsequent reaction.

---

[12] P. A. Sorokin, op. cit., pp. 409–411. By permission of J. B. Lippincott Company, Chicago.

No matter how much terror and propaganda may be injected into him, the plain man finally becomes heartily sick of the obvious frauds of a revolutionary period, of the outlandish new rites which he is compelled to practice, of the lies and hypocrisies which he must profess to keep out of jail, of the motley array of scoundrels, thieves, and morons who are always thrown to the top by a revolutionary upheaval. No words were more odious in England and France than *Puritan* and *Jacobin* after the people had a sufficiently long experience of rule by self-styled saints in the one case and by self-styled friends of the people in the other.

There have been many signs of a similar trend in Russia during the last few years. The normal instincts of self-advancement and self-enrichment have been reasserting themselves. New classes, with markedly differing living standards, have been formed. And for a time it seemed that this unavoidable process of stabilization after revolutionary storm, of restoring old inequalities under new names, of quietly burying those features of the revolutionary order which conflicted most obviously with common-sense and popular feeling, would be carried out under Stalin's own leadership.

Maximilien Robespierre, France's revolutionary dictator, went to the guillotine when his mania of suspicion had reached a point where no Jacobin, no matter how many aristocrats he might have butchered, could feel sure that his own name would not appear in the next proscription list. The mad Czar Paul of Russia was strangled by a group of officers who were apprehensive of sharing the fate of the many victims of his capricious ruthlessness. These are historical warnings which Stalin would do well to heed. His system, at least in time of peace, is pretty well insured against mass revolt. But the most absolute ruler, if he becomes too much of a public menace to his immediate entourage, may find himself eliminated by means of a palace coup.

The broad swing away from internationalism and collectivism and toward nationalism and individualism in the Soviet Union is certain to continue, no matter how much terrorism may occur before some kind of stabilization is reached. Stalin's only alternatives, in the long view, are to swim with this tide or to be swept away by it.[13]

---

[13] W. H. Chamberlin, "Stalin: Portrait of a Degenerate," *American Mercury*, February, 1938, pp. 216–218. By permission of the *American Mercury* and of the author.

Conclusion

Revolt is an important aspect of social control from two viewpoints: (1) revolt brings freedom from too rigid control by ushering in change and compelling leaders to recast the regulative system to fit human needs, (2) it stimulates the individual, keeping alive within him the spirit of freedom. Only the rebel knows the zest of defiance and the hope of reform. Social orders making no provision for orderly revolt court on the one hand stagnation, on the other violence. The masses will vegetate passively under a suppressive system, until rebels arise to usher in "liberty, equality, fraternity." The masses rally to these new leaders who promise to replace mere existence with a full life.

Revolt finds its goals in the development of some substitute system of social regulation, or some change in the social order which will make life more satisfactory to those who defy it. The overthrow of established standards of conduct may for a time engender a liberty bordering on license, but more and more human beings will revert to restraint. In fact, probably there is a rather normal cycle through which society goes with regard to morals, rules, and discipline—extreme restraint, then a period of extreme liberty, and back to restraint—like the swinging of a pendulum. In some fields the cycle may cover a long period, while in others fluctuations may be as rapid as the change of fashions in dress. But always revolt is an essential part of any system of social control which recognizes individualism, as important to the existence of the system as discipline or conformity itself, for it is only as social controls become modified through revolt that they become readapted to social needs, and escape being largely exterminated in a violent revolution. Failing to be modified through a normal process of change and nonviolent revolt, revolutionary upheavals occur, old systems pass, and new systems are instituted.

Revolution, because of its violence and because of its relatively complete disruption of social control, illustrates more fully than most revolts what a social order can be without regulation. Violent conflict of any sort tends to overthrow temporarily many of the established regulations of a society, and consequently, such periods are characterized by moral decay, ruthlessness, and always by the application of force to problems of discipline. After the

American Civil War, the Ku Klux Klan flourished because the old system of accommodation between black and whites had been destroyed. In modern revolutions, numerous killings during postrevolutionary days have served to enforce the codes of the group in power.

Revolution, with its disruption of order, is necessarily a transient phenomena. No matter how complete the destruction of social order, a new order will arise with discipline and restraint. Even violent revolt has its benefits. Only through the breakdown of the ruling classes, and the overthrow of their power, do other classes achieve authority. Through revolution, old cultural values are destroyed and a new objectivity toward the old culture is realized. A period for developing new cultural values by which a people may live is ushered in. Many times general cultural revision can be attained only through revolution, though war no doubt has some of the same effects. The new situations created by war may develop an awareness of the fallacy of certain patterns in the culture, and cause revision.[14] Freedom for women, and prohibition both were a product of the World War. Certain values of our culture were exposed and, once conscious of them, we revised them.

SELECTED REFERENCES

Benedict, Ruth, *Patterns of Culture*, chap. 8. Houghton Mifflin Company, Boston, 1934.

Carpenter, Niles, *The Sociology of City Life*, pp. 272 ff. Longmans, Green and Company, New York, 1931.

Cavan, Ruth S., *Suicide*. University of Chicago Press, Chicago, 1928.

Chamberlin, W. H., "Stalin: Portrait of a Degenerate," *American Mercury*, pp. 206–218. February, 1938.

Cooley, Charles H., *Human Nature and the Social Order*, chaps. 7 and 8. Charles Scribner's Sons, New York, 1922.

Cooley, Charles H., *Social Process*, chap. 14. Charles Scribner's Sons, New York, 1918.

Cooper, Courtney Ryley, *Ten Thousand Public Enemies*. Little, Brown and Company, Boston, 1935.

Cournos, J., "Rebel Mood in Literature," *Current History*, vol. 37, pp. 308–313. December, 1932.

---

[14] Ruth Benedict, *Patterns of Culture*, p. 249.

Cowley, M., "Art of Insurrection," New Republic, vol. 74, pp. 248–250. April 12, 1933.

Dowd, Jerome, Control in Human Societies, chaps. 7–17. D. Appleton-Century Company, New York, 1936.

Elliott, Mabel A., and Merrill, Francis E., Social Disorganization. Harper and Brothers, New York, 1934.

Hart, J. K., "New Folkways," Survey, vol. 53, pp. 341–342. December 15, 1924.

Harvard Tercentenary Publications, Authority and the Individual, (selection by John Dewey), pp. 170–190. Harvard University Press, Cambridge, 1937.

Hiller, E. T., The Strike, pp. 83–99. University of Chicago Press, Chicago, 1928.

Hutchinson, P., "Heretics of the Air," Christian Century, vol. 52, pp. 365, 431, 508. March 20, April 3 and 17, 1935.

James, William, "Moral Equivalents for War," Memoirs and Studies. Longmans, Green and Company, New York, 1912.

Johnson, A., "Coming American Revolution," Yale Review, vol. 23, pp. 649–661. June, 1934.

Kelsey, Carl, "War as a Crisis in Social Control," Proceedings of the Twelfth Annual Meeting of the American Sociological Society, vol. 12, p. 27. 1918.

Kuttner, A. B., "The Cycle of Revolution," New Republic, vol. 20, pp. 86–88. August 20, 1919.

Laski, Harold J., "The Dangers of Obedience," Harper's Magazine, pp. 1–10. January, 1929.

Lippmann, Walter, A Preface to Morals. The Macmillan Company, New York, 1929.

MacIver, Robert, Society, pp. 382–388. Farrar and Rinehart, Inc., New York, 1937.

MacLoughlin, J., "Disintegration of Morality," Catholic World, vol. 135, p. 94. April, 1932.

McConnell, Francis J., Public Opinion and the Steel Strike. Harcourt, Brace and Company, New York, 1921.

Moley, R., "Crime as a Profession," Current History, vol. 30, pp. 999 ff. September, 1929.

Mooney, Martin, Crime Incorporated. Whittlesey House, New York, 1935.

Nitti, F., "From War to Revolution," Current History, vol. 37, pp. 281–284. December, 1932.

Peabody, Richard, "Why Prohibition Has Failed," *American Mercury*, pp. 385–390. April, 1931.

Ross, Edward Alsworth, *Principles of Sociology*, first revision, chaps. 45–49. D. Appleton-Century Company, New York, 1930.

Rousseau, Jean Jacques, *Emile; or Concerning Education*, translated by Eleanor Worthington. D. C. Heath and Company, New York, 1883.

Shaw, R., "Revolutions," *Review of Reviews*, vol. 89, p. 21. February, 1934.

Sorokin, Pitirim A., *The Sociology of Revolution*. J. B. Lippincott Company, Chicago, 1925.

Stonequist, E. V., *The Marginal Man, A Study of Personality and Culture Contact*. Charles Scribner's Sons, New York, 1937.

Thomas, W. I., and Znaniecki, Florian, *The Polish Peasant in Europe and America*, vol. 4, pt. 1; vol. 5, pt. 2. Chapman and Grimes, Boston, 1920.

Thoreau, Henry David, *Walden; or Life in the Woods*. E. P. Dutton and Company, New York, 1908.

Wallas, Graham, *The Great Society*. The Macmillan Company, New York, 1920.

CHAPTER 25

SOCIAL CONTROL IN OUR DYNAMIC SOCIETY:
A CONCLUDING SUMMARY

PERSONALITY BUILDING IN A DYNAMIC SOCIETY

Social control is achieved by patterning human nature to fit the society in which it is to function. It is relatively easily accomplished in static societies which have well established ideas of what the social system is and what it will be in the future. Such a culture can shape its youth through its educational training program in such a way that they conform quite harmoniously.

In a dynamic society, on the other hand, it is never fully known what tomorrow's order may demand. The very trait that has been most firmly established in youth may become a handicap in later adjustment. This problem is not peculiar to formal education only, for it typifies the informal and other institutional aspects of the entire cultural structure as well.[1] What shall the church teach in order to prepare the child for the religion of tomorrow? What shall the college teach its patrons in order to aid them to live the life of the college-bred of tomorrow? What vocational training is essential to youth in order that they may fit tomorrow's industries? Who can say? And in the realm of morality who knows what code may come to predominate in regard to such questions as war, sex, monogamy, or capitalism? Who knows but that some of the sacred symbols of today may soon be discarded?

It is true that there may be values, even in a dynamic society, that are perpetuated age after age, but we do not possess a clear understanding of the values which are permanent and those which are transitory and fleeting. We may even ask whether there is any value that can withstand the impact of an inventive urban-industrial society.

---

[1] James S. Plant, *Personality and the Cultural Pattern*, chap. 18, presents a discussion of educating children for change.

465

The problem of social control in America today is to a great extent a matter of establishing aims and goals for life, or of agreeing to maintain certain goals already established. We know more about educational technique, the conditioning of personality, and the formation of habits, than do most other peoples, but we are undecided concerning the end product to be realized. We are beginning to understand that all human values are relative to time, place and experience, that they are of man's making, and that he can undo them if he will. But with all of this knowledge, we have not yet attempted to establish a rational set of values, even though we have challenged many old ones on the ground that they are the product of chance experience.

We have multiplied experience by numerous contacts made possible by modern means for movement and communication, but have not yet been able to coordinate that experience and give it meaning. We have extended contacts spatially, intellectually, morally, and spiritually, but as yet have not woven from this experience any definite concept of what a larger life might be and how human beings might be prepared for participation in it. In our nation of relative abundance we have multiplied human wants by catering to them increasingly, but in so doing have also increased human needs, because as yet we have developed no concept of satisfaction by which a man may know when he has had enough. Many have even removed from their thought the grand finale in which most human beings have believed, that of heavenly rewards or torture in hell, and in its place have substituted no certain goal of life, either here or hereafter, which will inspire man to keep a steady course. In the struggle to improve man's lot, we have groped for a social motive which would inspire energy and command social action, but we have often failed to define social action for the secondary group.

W. G. Beach gave a very suggestive title to one of his books, "Social Aims in a Changing World," which title in itself states a major social problem. To what social aims can we adapt our program of personality formation? How can we formulate means to achieving ends that in themselves are changing? How can one educate a child and shape his personality for a world that the adult generation which is doing the teaching cannot envision? If we challenge values which have been considered more or less permanent where shall we look for guidance?

If we maintain that certain values are fundamental to social order even in a dynamic age, these values might be defined for a changing world. If these values include social welfare, preparation for a life hereafter, the achievement of human happiness, the realization of the aims of democracy in their highest forms of expression, steps can be taken to form personality for realizing these aims, or such of them or other aims as may seem valid.

The matter of maintaining order in society is largely a matter of conditioning the individual so that his personality will be in harmony with the basic virtues of his age. We know enough today of the means by which personality is formed to be able to make the large majority of individuals jibe with these aims, provided we first decide upon the aims.

Heterogeneity vs. Homogeneity of Patterns as Related to Individualism and Authority

The modern world is one of heterogeneous patterns, a state of affairs which is essential both to individualism and to rapid change. Stability, order, and system are endangered in the presence of a diversity of patterns. Homogeneity in itself has authority. Men who have known only one culture accept its way of life as the only and therefore the right way. Those who have viewed two or more orders of life, or who have seen the old pass and the new ushered in, are much less sure that either is right. "Perhaps there may be many other ways that would work," they say to themselves, "and this being the case, it may be worthwhile to experiment with the untried." It is at this point that diversity of experience challenges the established system by luring the mind with the fascinating possibilities of experimentation in the new and untried.

The extensive mobility of people in our nation, and the abundance of indirect contacts made possible through modern means of communication, creates a heterogeneity of experience, even though individuals may have grown up in a close-knit, unified primary group. We have become so mobile as a people that conditioning for a homogeneous culture such as still takes place in isolated rural areas is a severe disadvantage to the individual when he later is thrown into the heterogeneous mass of secondary group patterns. The old authority is no longer effective, and the search for a new one by such individuals is often fruitless.

INDIVIDUALISM: ITS PRICE AND BENEFITS

We have stressed the breakdown of the personality, the chaos and uncertainty of the social order in an individualistic age that challenges authority, but we should also mention the thrill of personal expression which this same order affords its members. One who has experienced individualism as a system of life is slow to sacrifice freedom for security. Undoubtedly slavery offered more security to the individual than does modern urban industry, but few would exchange the hazards of economic freedom for the security of the slave. People who have tasted freedom will make great sacrifices to retain it, that is, unless it is carried to such an extreme that it breeds intolerable conditions. In that case they give it up willingly in exchange for authority, if modern European conditions are any index. "The certainties of a firm government, however crude, are preferable to the wobbling of the most aspiring idealism." [2] But in our nation we are not yet ready to recognize that only two alternatives exist—absolute authority or chaos.

POSSIBILITIES OF A FUNCTIONAL INDIVIDUALISM IN A CHANGING WORLD

It is not too much to hope that in a world of varied experience we may develop an effective and social type of individualism that will function in a complex and changing social situation. In fact, we seem already to have been developing personality in this direction in American culture. Functional individualism,[3] an individualism of choice, has reached its highest level among sophisticated urban classes who, having chosen certain lines of conformity, disregard conventions in other realms. Greater tolerance for this kind of personality is exhibited in our urban culture than in our rural culture, for the latter still remains relatively homogeneous, simple, and intolerant of divergent types. In that environment an individualism of isolation still survives. Special types have no value in an unspecialized simple society.

The urban stage is well set for the development of a functional

---

[2] A. G. Keller, *Brass Tacks*, p. 88, Alfred A. Knopf, Inc., New York, 1938.
[3] This term was employed by C. H. Cooley to refer to a socially useful individualism as compared to the eccentric individualism that grows from isolation. See his *Social Organization*, chap. 9.

individualism in the interests of more effective social control in our urbanized and ineffectively controlled secondary group world. Here is a setting that offers an unparalleled chance to experiment. Urbane peoples are of a type of mind that will not respond to the old voice of experience—custom, but could be induced to listen to a new voice of experience—science. Urbanity as a habit of mind is somewhat objective, and highly critical of tradition. If it were combined with a curious and sincere interest in a better order, possibilities for improvement would be unlimited.

One thing is certain, as Bernard has pointed out,[4] and as has been suggested at many points throughout this work, primitive social control devices of the old primary group society are inadequate to fortify the individual in an anonymous society against his own vices. And yet urban-industrial civilization is here to stay. In fact, the social order is likely to become even more complex, and human nature must adapt itself even further to urban situations. We must, therefore, learn to think in terms of control devices that motivate people from within, rather than in terms of external compulsives.

A society with our background and present cultural trends can reasonably grant the individual a breadth of choices within established limits. Of course, risks to social order and to personality integration are involved. We have already found it necessary to compensate for individual freedom on the regulative plane by legal restraint, on the personal plane by psychiatry and social work, and on the moral plane by extensive apologizing for those who fail. Barring some great national cataclysm that changes the trend of our cultural development, we will probably develop further along individualistic lines, for we hold that a man should be free, even though that freedom may cost him security, and even though at times he misuses his freedom and thereby threatens the safety of the group.

Personal Objectives vs. Realizations in Our Time

Our nation has not been without a major and unifying philosophy in the past. Theoretically, it was a nation of universal opportunity. In such a society where every individual was given a chance to show his power, great human ideals were developed,

---

[4] Refer again to pp. 172–183.

unparalleled concepts of democracy, and unheard of differences of individual personality and individual initiative were achieved, but all in line with this major cultural goal. With this philosophy, in a land where great resources lay at hand for exploitation, it was inevitable that powerful individuals would, given time, come to dominate the entire social order.

We have seen this state of affairs develop, but only recently have we made any efforts toward curbing it. We have become increasingly conscious of the fact that we sold our resources for a song, that we, the people, today have only the left-overs from a continent of resources that made many millionnaires. We have become aware that legislation has been devised in the interests of powerful individuals and corporations who, having gained control of most of the country's wealth, then proceeded to seize power in the domain of political regulation in order to protect that wealth. A counteraction has been the development of class interests and class struggles, which now are felt in the political realm to the extent that great humanitarian movements are appearing. We are in a period when we are beginning to revaluate the aims, ends, and destiny of our nation. We are beginning to challenge established values in our social order, to ask many questions, and to try many experiments, but as yet there has been formulated no clear-cut definition as to where we want to go.

Do we want to make America a land where every man seeks to be a king, as he did under frontier conditions, and if we do, are we willing to take such steps as may be necessary to realize this goal in a measure, under new conditions which restrict economic opportunity? Or do we, as most established societies have done, want to increase the social stratification, draw lines more carefully between classes, separate men off increasingly into grades and qualities, delimit more and more the spheres of activity in which people born with privileges may operate, and other lesser spheres where the masses must operate, until we eventually approach something of a caste system?

This second alternative is based on the assumption that most men are born to be slaves. Aristotle preached this philosophy, and most societies have practiced it. By fencing men off into classes, and by maintaining the fences by standards of birth, they established caste lines which set the limits to those things for which the person might hope. Those of the lower caste may not have been satisfied, but neither were they often frustrated as they are likely to be in a society like ours, which promises to make every man a king, but which makes many beggars.

The caste alternative is not as undesirable as many might think. It does away with a considerable part of the struggle for power, status, and recognition that now exists in our society. It keeps high aspirations from arising in the mind of the average man, and forces the masses to accept a realistic social world. It gives them a secure world, even though it is rigidly circumscribed.

The two contrasting alternatives are as ancient as mankind. Caste systems operate on the principle that since all men cannot have what they want, it is safer from the standpoint of social order to make them want what they can reasonably be expected to have. A free open class system operates on the principle that every man should want the "world with a fence around it." If he does not get it, he at least will have had the fun of trying, and perhaps through his efforts will have acquired at least a quarter section of land, which is much more than he might have hoped for under a caste system.

The danger to social control is that he may feel that he should have acquired much more than the quarter section and therefore rebel and misuse his freedom, but this is an inherent part of the social risk involved in a free competitive society that erects no bars to privilege.

Perhaps there are many more alternatives for American civilization than the two just mentioned. These two are presented because they make an interesting contrast, and because they suggest two quite opposite ways in which personality may be developed and a system of social regulation established. One need have no axe to grind for either, for both have worked in a measure. But this is certain: either we should seriously try to realize more fully the American ideal, or stop preaching to every man that there is a pot of gold under the near end of the rainbow. Social regulation becomes increasingly difficult when masses of people are unable to realize or to come anywhere near realizing, the hope to which they have aspired.

It becomes a serious matter from the standpoint of control, when thousands of the youth who graduate from high school and college each year cannot even find an honest way of earning their living. We are deluding the individual with the false hope that he may yet regain the freedom that yesterday was his as a matter of course. But in reality that day has passed, and a great deal of frustration is inevitable in the lives of those who realize that they can never attain in our present day that for which they had hoped. We are accustomed to change, and there is no reason why we could not, by diligent effort and clear thinking, establish realistic goals for personality in our social order, and work out the means with the resources at hand for realizing these goals. It cannot be done in a day; it cannot be done in a year. The main thing, if a stable social order is to be realized, is to agree as to what is to be done, and to start definitely on the way toward doing it.

It seems likely that the great mass of people in America still prefer every man to be a king—not in the financial sense necessarily, but in the sense of having freedom of choice to enter what vocation he will; freedom such as will assure him a means of livelihood; freedom such as will give him a voice in court, in government, in industry, in the press, and in the pulpit; freedom to enjoy both work and leisure as an independent soul; freedom to express some of the more intimate, personal ambitions which are nourished in the American schoolroom where the ideals of a citizenship that is constructive, forward-looking, and active in public affairs is emulated.

Ancient peoples accumulated surpluses, created leisure, and developed luxuries by the toil of slaves who lived on less than they produced so that the privileged few might build wealth, who worked long hours that their masters might play, or if so disposed, think, write, and create. It may be that there was no better alternative then, that progress would otherwise have been impossible, but a machine age is not forced to this horn of the dilemma.

We create profits, leisure, and luxury by the toil of machines, but there remains the strange anomaly of our age, and the one which is the greatest threat to our politico-economic order—the materialistic nature of our culture which makes money the open road to almost every human value, but which at the same time creates a system of life under which a manly way to obtain money is permanently denied a multitude. We tell every man that he is born to privilege and high society, that wealth and honor are within his reach, but that he may face situations in which he can obtain neither. It is this discrepancy between values and realizations, between goals and achievements, between promises and rewards, that creates frustration and disillusionment, and brings threats of violence and rebellion. It probably would be a difficult task to change our values and goals. This being the case, the sensible way out would seem to be to modify the system sufficiently so that our resources could be used to make possible at least partial fulfillment of the people's hopes.

There is no freedom in a life which lacks the means to function, nor is there bondage in a rigid system of discipline, if men living in it are given what the culture promises them, be it much or little. Personality demands much or little of life, according to the way it is shaped, but if taught to expect much, it cannot be satisfied with little. It is surprising how happy, contented, and well-regulated people have been without freedom, in societies where there have been no prophets to point a better way. But one cannot practice bondage among peoples who have learned new definitions of freedom. Time was in America when *laissez faire* as applied to business and industry was accepted by every man, because it spelled opportunity for him. He expected to profit under it, and even if he failed, many others of his class and kin succeeded, but today large classes are awakening to the fact that this philosophy now works chiefly to the advantage of the powerful.

There is a growing realization that many of our symbols of liberty are cloaks for hidden power, shields for exploitation, tools of greed, that formal control is in the hands of the big industrialists and is for them, not for society. But on the other hand, there is also a growing recognition on the part of the state and the public generally of the importance of human personality in the social and economic scheme. There is an increasing appreciation of the relation between economic security and personal confidence, between the dignity of labor and the dignity of man, between the useful expenditure of energy and the sense of "belonging" to the human enterprise, a feeling that makes life seem worthwhile, and makes man willing to sacrifice personal interests for social aims.

We probably need to begin to talk less of capitalism, communism, socialism, and fascism, and to face human problems as they are, if personality is to be saved from shock and disillusionment, if the social order is to be prevented from breaking down under the weight of human symbols that forget human acts.

Whether new gestures for a redefined and realistic freedom, and for building the accompanying regulative systems, can proceed fast enough to keep certain of our institutions from crashing yet remains to be seen.

THE QUEST FOR GOALS IN A WORLD WITHOUT AUTHORITY

The world has lost faith to a considerable extent in metaphysical forces as factors in controlling social affairs. Our culture is no longer God-centered. The medieval concept of a Deity who defied natural law, and who projected miracles on the human scene at will in response to the prayer of the devout, has about passed from the contemporary scene. Sophisticated man in a sophisticated culture now challenges an orthodox God, and conceives of a scientific God ruling over an ordered universe, letting nature take its course.

It is becoming increasingly difficult for great masses of people to find meaning in the regulative machinery, and to locate the voice of authority. The same individuals who defy the God of orthodoxy, and who disbelieve in miracles, flock to the astrologers by the thousands in the hope that they may obtain some authoritative word as to what tomorrow holds. Too many of these sophisticated souls who boldly challenge tradition, declaring vigorously that they are able to stand on their own feet, end up in a hospital for the insane,[5] in a psychopathic clinic, or in a prison. Others develop an exaggerated concept of freedom, so that the least social discipline spells frustration. Even in our age, where personality is probably as free as or more so than at any previous age, many feel thwarted. And ironically enough, many nations which have previously experienced at least a part of this freedom which we cherish, have turned their back on it, choosing instead to follow blind authority, because that authority has identified itself with ideals big enough to grip the human spirit and to give the personality a point of orientation which weakened religious creeds, family codes, and economic goals have failed to bring. Even the American political scene has not remained entirely free from messiahs who, by shrouding their authority with high ideals,

---

[5] It has been estimated that on the average one out of every sixteen males and one in nineteen females fifteen years of age and over in the State of Massachusetts will spend time in a hospital for the insane: W. F. Ogburn, and S. R. Winston, "The Frequency and Probability of Insanity," *American Journal of Sociology*, 1928, vol. 34, pp. 822–831.

rally great followings. Characteristically enough, in our country most of the ideals which the messiahs have advocated have been materialistic. It is perhaps only for this reason that they have failed to long retain their followers.

CULTURE CONSCIOUSNESS AND THE PROBLEM OF AUTHORITY

As a nation we have become culture conscious. The average man now places the blame for his troubles where the sociologist places it—in the cultural environment. No longer does he charge Satan with such human ills as poverty, disease, crime, and social chaos. Rather, he puts the blame on the social organization, the capitalist, industry, the President, the government, the Supreme Court, society—always in the cultural structure and man's system of social relations.

Our leaders have to rationalize a great deal in order to satisfy the curious mind of today, and will have to rationalize more to satisfy even the average mind of tomorrow that certain of the customs and sacred symbols which bolster our institutions have social utility. Not long ago institutional values were never questioned, but now, under the impetus of a growing culture consciousness, every institution is being critically evaluated, as is its every control device. Many values cannot stand the test, because they have no rational utility beyond the fact that they are a part of the culture, and for this reason seem to have usefulness. Many of our control devices are but a poor sampling of the numerous possible alternatives; due to chance success in trial and error adjustments, we have come to accept many principles as irrefutable laws of social and institutional life, which originally were but accidental episodes in our cultural history.

The more one people contacts another, as they do in our time of world-wide association, the more they will come to realize the great diversity of human cultures and of human controls. This must inevitably break down feelings of cultural ethnocentrism, of blind loyalty to accepted codes, and will breed a skepticism leading to further inquiry. The masses may also come to realize that experience is man's guide, that social progress can come only by improving upon chance trial-and-error experience, by substituting in its place the tested experience of science.

No longer are we willing to accept mythology and signs to explain rain, although such explanations were universally accepted in the past, and still are by many peoples. Our present knowledge has made it possible to trace the rain drop, from the time it rises off the earth as vapor, to its precipitation back to the earth.

Those who understand human nature no longer accept the notion that the fear of darkness or of snakes is a sort of mythical curse with which man as a creature of instinct is born. Rather we find sufficient explanation in experience, and so train our children to fear neither.

One who understands how superstitions originated can scarcely fear a black cat crossing the road, the number thirteen, or Friday. But here we approach a dangerous point. Can one who understands how the family institution of a given people, or their government, or their religion came into being through trial-and-error adjustments, through the selection of experience, rational and otherwise, any longer respect them?

As absolute and final system, no. As human achievements, yes. But does not the difference in point of view challenge the very foundations of the social order? It does. But this seems to be the stage which our society is rapidly approaching.

How can the new view be reconciled with the social need for an orderly manner of life, which presupposes some concept of authority leading the individual to submit to institutions and their controls? The hope seems to lie in developing within the individual a greater social consciousness, in implanting deeply the notion that though human institutions do not represent the last word in experience, they do, in their better aspects, embody the essence of some of the values man must hold in order to live with his fellows.

Such an awakening is challenging already many institutional values, and finding them wanting. In time perhaps they will give way to values that are social, human, essential to orderly group welfare.

We have the tools of an age of change at hand, with which to build new values. As in the sphere of mechanical invention we build new models from the old, so can we also in the realm of subjective values build new ones, as we come to understand the true nature of these values. Russia, in one generation, destroyed many of the ideals of an old order of life, and established a new order based on a far different philosophy, held together by an entirely new system of controls. She did this with religious, economic, and family institutions as well as with government and technology. How? By understanding that youth becomes the kind of creature he is taught to be, and by keeping always the end product in mind. Thus she has demonstrated more than has any other modern nation the extent to which a country with established, definite aims can achieve them.

It is not suggested that we emulate the end result, nor is it recommended that we adopt the means (neither are suited for us in America, for we do not have Russia's past) but that when once we realize how ideals are made, the problem of motivating the individual by ideals of social welfare does not appear hopeless. Such ideals may well become as effective in social control as the ideals of absolute and final authoritative institutions of the other-worldly-centered Middle Ages once were. A system of control by social welfare motives will need to leave much room for individualization, however, because social welfare in a rapidly changing social order is a matter of changing interpretation, and the person must be sufficiently alert to sense the social act. Under an authoritative order, which is of necessity relatively static, definitions of the social are already known.

Herein lies a stumbling block to control through social motivation, as contrasted to motivation by unchanging absolute principles. Can the social values be known in a dynamic order?

CHANGE AND DEFINITIONS

We are assuming that there is in our society a group of individuals who have broken with authoritative patterns, and that as we become more culture conscious, masses of others will follow suit. We also assume that the trend of the times is toward the establishment of a social basis for proper conduct, that regard for the welfare of others must come to motivate the individual to an orderly life as defined by his time. How can the individual in a dynamic society know the nature of the social act?

In the field of primary group relations as they prevail in the family, neighborhood, and isolated community there is little change from age to age. Love, kindness, concern for the weak, helpfulness—these elemental social traits that must develop wherever man is found, if the helpless infant is to survive and if the social group is to have continuity, appear in much the same form everywhere. Patterns differ, but one can be fairly sure of their universal expression, and that time will not change this fact. It is in the realm of impersonal, secondary group relationships such as urban culture develops that the patterns of conduct are open to question. Here the proper or orderly thing is difficult to define, and past experience is hardly a sufficient guide. Man has lived so little in such groups, and has studied human nature in them such a short time, that often he is at a loss to know the proper course to pursue in such relationships. We have as yet given little attention to understanding the human nature product in urban groups and to understanding ways for more fully socializing the individual in such groups.

Perhaps in our secondary groups we have divorced the individual from all sense of social obligation by making relationships so impersonal. It may be that our society can establish certain universal obligations to be imposed on every man for the good of all, state these simply, and enforce them effectively, and in other spheres permit fairly complete individualism. I have no answer and I believe our time has none to offer as yet.

Sins of Omission of Sociologists

Among sociologists there have been a great number of varying notions as to just how social control is achieved, but a fairly uniform agreement as to why it is necessary. The writer has a feeling that generally the problem of social control has been given too little consideration in contemporary sociology. Sociologists have been too much influenced by the compulsives of their time; having become enamoured with the problem of change, they have almost forgotten that the social order must have ballast. Like the masses, they have been so inclined to challenge authority and to respect change as a tool of progress that they have largely neglected a subject which is probably just as important as change, and perhaps even more so—the problem of order, stability, and permanence.

We do need a picture of change. We need to understand the processes by which it operates, and its implications to man. But can we understand its meaning to man or society if we do not balance this picture of change with the picture of authority, if we do not consider our obligation as scientists of human life to weigh change in terms of its disturbing effects on social organization?

Has not the major problem of our time become that of directing change in such a way that it will not destroy the established order, of harnessing the dynamic forces of our age and making them conform to the need for stability? Has not the major problem of personality in our day when insanity, nervous breakdowns, neurasthenia, and numerous psychopathic afflictions are on the increase, and when chaos threatens the social orders of the West, become that of considering methods of so stabilizing the social order that Western culture will survive, and that human beings living in it can build personalities that will remain intact throughout a lifetime?

Symptoms of social disorganization are one index of the price we are paying for having cast authority aside. The multiplication of laws as a weak substitute for the more permanent device of social regulation, the chaos and disorder that characterize certain aspects of our society—these and many other problems challenge us to give attention to the foundations of the social order.

It is time that we give our attention to a science of social stability, that we study human nature in relation to the system of social control, that we revaluate freedom in terms of what the human organism can tolerate. It may be that we are allowing the individual so much liberty that he breaks down under the strain.

More comparative studies between our culture and those of other people—primitive and modern—are needed in order to better understand the types of social regulation under which a personality can thrive and yet not have so much freedom as to weaken the organism. A stable, authoritative, controlled social order places little stress on personality. Personal insecurity, like social disequilibrium, comes with change, individualism, and freedom. Where is the happy mean between the two extremes?

SOCIAL SCIENCE AS A GUIDE TO ORDER IN A DYNAMIC AGE

If we have reached the point in America where we cannot give men what they want, it may be that we should make them want what we can give them. While one can carry this argument too far, it has a point. Even in an individualistic social order where we do not care to standardize personal wants, probably, as we have suggested, we need to center attention on a few major values desirable to our civilization, and to see that each individual is

taught to seek these core values. We need to train him to conform to these core social ideals, and in other things permit individualism to develop.

If such an approach has merit for social control in a dynamic
age, the part of the sociologist is to try to determine in the light
of societies, past and present, and in the light of our own cultural history what these major social aims should be, and to outline for the school, the state, the church, the family, and the
economic order, means of attaining them.

Of course, this puts the social scientist into the field of practical
affairs, involving him in problems of what the ideal or the "good"
life is. It compels him to consider problems of what *ought to be*
as well as of what *is*, to study not only social organizations and
trends, but means of bringing about better forms of social organization, and of shaping trends to achieve preconceived results. To such suggestions many advocates of pure science,
science for science's sake, will raise a cry of protest, but in the
end, social science, like natural science, will have to justify itself
in a practical world. It will have to deal with problems and in-
vent cures. In large measure these will lie in the immediate future in the field of social control.

Not that pure science needs to be cast aside. The social engineer must know well the laws and processes of social life as revealed by pure science, before he begins tinkering with the social machinery, even though those who now do the most tinkering
abide by no such principle. As an outgrowth of pure science will
come applied science, to be used as a tool in helping define the
core values of our nation's culture, and in helping develop procedures for the attainment of these values. No science is justified
in robbing an age of the values that have held it together, without reconstructing in their place sounder values and methods of
realizing them. I do not wish to imply that social science has
been chiefly responsible for destroying the old authority on which
order was based. It has only lent its influence. An age of change
does not respect tradition. Change itself destroys old landmarks.
The appeal to the authority of tradition as such becomes ineffective. Even though sociology was not primarily responsible
for bringing about the destruction of old values, it will have in the
future a greater part not only in destroying values that have lost
meaning, but in giving meaning to new ones.

Natural science destroyed myths of long standing concerning the nature of the universe, but has justified itself by winning for man control over the same universe that it helped man understand. Social science is helping to shatter the myths and symbols that have served as cornerstones for society and personality. But seeing through old myths is not enough. Control is necessary if a better social order is to be realized, for both an orderly society and an integrated personality can be built only on unquestioned values.

CONCLUSION

The main points of the book and of this chapter may be briefly summarized. At the outset it was assumed that social control is a study of the processes by which society regulates the individual, making him an orderly creature who pays respect to such authority as his group recognizes. It has been assumed that social control serves a dual purpose, (1) that of maintaining society against the ravages of individual expression and (2) that of making the individual a human being, and having made him so, helping him to defend himself against his own vices and appetites which tend to reduce him to the level of his original nature, an animal rather than a human level.

The view has been developed that social control is achieved primarily through the socializing processes by which human nature is developed, although it is recognized that enforcement techniques must at times supplement the educative, personality building processes in order to make society secure against dangerous innovations. Social groups, the cultural structure, institutions, and numerous devices of control contribute to the socializing process and also to the enforcement process. Under the heavy weight of all of this machinery, cultural structures often crash. The balance of social order is a delicate moving equilibrium that is easily upset. If disturbed it is at great cost, both to society and the individual, as our study of personal and social disorganization indicated.

In this chapter we have attempted to understand the problem of control as we now face it in our dynamic society. We have tried to understand (1) why socialization is poorly accomplished in our society, (2) why the process of socialization is often ineffective under the conditions of modern life in the secondary group, with the personal and social consequences of this failure exhibited in numerous pathological conditions, and (3) what to do to improve the system of control.

The principal reasons that socialization is poorly accomplished under conditions of modern life are: (1) Mobility from group to group provides experience under a heterogeneity of patterns, so that no one system of life becomes habitual and no one system of attitudes and values effective. (2) Agencies of diffusion and of mass impression provide a similar heterogeneity of experience, even in the absence of mobility, and with the same consequences. (3) Rapid change weakens experience as a guide to conduct, because the experience that proved effective in the world of yesterday does not prove so today, and present experience does not always show the way to act tomorrow. Before we today finish teaching the child to live, a new world may arise, about which we ourselves know little.

Social control fails under modern conditions primarily (1) because socialization is poorly accomplished, (2) because even where well accomplished on a primary group basis it often makes the individual a misfit in the secondary group where he is destined to live, and (3) because organic nature is too strong to be controlled by the socialization process applied, or by the restraints imposed. This may be because the controls make too little apology for original nature, or in individual cases it may be because animal nature is too strong for regulation by any of the techniques that a society might reasonably be expected to use.

The price of failure to maintain an effective, secure, and stable system of control takes its toll in mental and moral lack in the individual, in disorganization, chaos, and revolt in the society. Most social problems are traceable to the system of social control in operation. In it one finds the clue for many pathological conditions.

Finally we took up the question of what to do in a dynamic society to improve the system of social regulation: (1) We can multiply enforcement techniques, prohibitions and penalties, curbing individualism by increasing coercive authority. Many nations are choosing this as the way out, for they conceive it to be the least disastrous of alternatives. (2) Perhaps we can slow down the rate of change, at the same time working for a type of authority that comes through stability, but I doubt if much is to be hoped for here. (3) We can give greater attention to adapting the process of socialization to the kind of a world in which we live, in an attempt to develop a *functional individualism*. A useful individualism would seem to be one which maintains rigid uniformities in realms of conduct known to be essential to social welfare, but which in other things allows for great diversity. As a part of this process we would strive for a situation in which the average man could realize our social aims. Such a development is in line with the cultural trend of American life, and offers a desirable way in which individualism might flower and society progress. However, it is a dangerous alternative from the standpoint of social control and requires that a great deal of intelligence be applied to the problem of social equilibrium. (4) Social science might be able to guide the way if as much attention were given to a study of the essentials on which a stable moving equilibrium might be built, as is now given to the study of change.

SELECTED REFERENCES

Beach, W. G., *Social Aims in a Changing World*. Stanford University Press, Stanford University, 1932.

Bernard, L. L., "Conflict Between Primary Group Attitudes and Derivative Group Ideals in Modern Society," *American Journal of Sociology*, vol. 41, pp. 611–623. March, 1936.

Bossard, Joseph H. S., *Social Change and Social Problems*, revised edition, chaps. 5, 6, and 7. Harper and Brothers, New York, 1938.

Chapin, F. Stuart, *Cultural Change*, part 2. D. Appleton-Century Company, New York, 1928.

Cooley, Charles H., *Social Organization*, parts 2 and 4. Charles Scribner's Sons, New York, 1909.

Cooley, Charles H., *Social Process*, chap. 32–35. Charles Scribner's Sons, New York, 1918.

Ellwood, Charles Abram, *The Psychology of Human Society*, pp. 255–256. D. Appleton-Century Company, New York, 1931.

Folsom, J. K., *The Family*, chap. 28. John Wiley and Sons, Inc., New York, 1934.

Harvard Tercentenary Publications, *Authority and the Individual* (selection by John Dewey), pp. 170–190. Harvard University Press, Cambridge, 1937.

Keller, A. G., *Man's Rough Road*, chap. 1. Frederick A. Stokes Company, New York, and Yale University Press, New Haven, 1932.

Landis, Paul H., "The Life Cycle of the Iron Mining Town," *Social Forces*, pp. 245–256. December, 1934.

Landis, Paul H., *Three Iron Mining Towns, A Study in Cultural Change*, chap. 15. Edwards Brothers, Ann Arbor, 1938.

Lippmann, Walter, *A Preface to Morals*. The Macmillan Company, New York, 1929.

Lippmann, Walter, *The Good Society*. Little, Brown and Company, Boston, 1937.

Lippmann, Walter, *The Phantom Public*. The Macmillan Company, New York, 1925.

MacIver, Robert M., "Social Philosophy," *American Journal of Sociology*, vol. 39, pp. 835–841. May, 1934.

Ogburn, W. F., *Social Change*, part 5. The Viking Press, Inc., New York, 1923.

Plant, James S., *Personality and the Cultural Pattern*, part 3. The Commonwealth Fund, New York, 1937.

Sorokin, Pitirim A., *Social and Cultural Dynamics*, vol. 3, chap. 16. American Book Company, New York, 1937.

Sorokin, Pitirim A., *Social Mobility*, parts 2–6. Harper and Brothers, New York, 1927.

Soule, George Henry, *A Planned Society*. The Macmillan Company, New York, 1932.

Spengler, Oswald, *The Decline of the West*. Alfred A. Knopf, Inc., New York, 1926.

Stamp, Josiah, "The Impact of Science upon Society," *Science*, pp. 237 ff. September, 1936.

Thomas, W. I., and Znaniecki, Florian, *The Polish Peasant in Europe and America*, vol. 4, pt. 2. Chapman and Grimes, Boston, 1920.

Wallas, Graham, *The Great Society*. The Macmillan Company, New York, 1920.

Young, Kimball, *An Introductory Sociology*, chap. 29. American Book Company, New York, 1934.

Young, Kimball, *Source Book for Sociology*, chap. 29. American Book Company, New York, 1935.

Young, Pauline V., "Social Problems in the Education of the Immigrant Child," *American Sociological Review*, vol. 1, pp. 419–429. June, 1936.

INDEX OF NAMES

Abel, Theodore, 205
Abraham, Father, 56, 119, 258
Adams, John, 355
Addams, J., 131, 357, 439
Adler, Mortimer J., 98, 125, 307, 440
Allport, Floyd H., 41, 44, 48, 63
Allport, Gordon, 115
Anderson, John E., 48
André, Albert E., 91, 92
Andrews, C. F., 349, 358
Aristotle, 26, 27, 288, 470
Arnett, C. E., 205, 305, 358
Arnold, T. W., 283, 284, 285, 286, 295, 305, 333, 358
Aswell, E. C., 305
Atkinson, H. A., 439
Austen, Nancy Virginia, 358, 413

Bakke, E. Wight, 276, 286
Barnes, Harry E., 19, 22, 54, 64, 93, 359
Barnum, P. T., 185, 186
Bartlett, F. C., 116, 131, 139
Barton, Bruce, 114
Beach, Walter G., 184, 253, 423, 466, 483
Beard, Charles A., 305
Bell, B. I., 253
Bellamy, Edward, 63
Benedict, Ruth, 69, 77, 88, 89, 93, 116, 118, 121, 127, 132, 137, 147, 358, 420, 421, 453, 462
Benjamin, Harold, 270
Bent, S., 205, 358
Bernard, L. L., 19, 37, 48, 54, 63, 169, 172, 177, 179, 180, 184, 291, 305, 469, 483
Bernays, E. L., 205
Binder, Rudolph M., 351, 352
Bisch, Louis E., 439
Black, Hugo L., 195, 205, 358
Black, Jack, 439
Blanshard, P., 358
Blumenthal, Albert, 156, 166
Blumer, H., 358, 423, 427
Bogardus, E. S., 63, 136, 358

Bossard, Joseph H. S., 132, 184, 205, 270, 327, 423, 439, 483
Bowden, A. O., 358
Breed, F. S., 270
Broome, Edwin C., 358
Brown, George Rothwell, 358
Brown, Lawrence Guy, 48, 63, 77
Bryce, James, 305
Buell, K. L., 287
Budd, Josephine E., 89, 93
Burgess, E. W., 11, 22, 35, 233, 360, 417, 420, 423, 424, 439
Burnham, William H., 48
Burr, Walter, 358
Busch, Henry Miller, 358
Byrd, Richard E., 126

Calverton, V. F., 117, 132
Capone, Alphonse, 110, 193, 354
Carpenter, Niles, 183, 423, 432, 462
Carter, H., 305
Castle, M. J., 147
Cavan, Ruth S., 147, 233, 413, 423, 429, 430, 462
Cavanaugh, F., 253
Chafee, Z., Jr., 439
Chaffee, Grace E., 152, 166, 217
Chamberlin, W. H., 460, 462
Chambers, M. M., 270
Chapin, F. Stuart, 54, 93, 233, 253, 294, 295, 321, 327, 346, 350, 351, 358, 483
Chase, Stuart, 286, 327
Child, Richard Washburn, 354, 358
Churchill, Winston, 205
Clark, John Maurice, 253, 257, 270, 286, 334, 343, 358
Clay, Curtis H., 195, 196
Cochran, M. L., 205
Comte, August, 30
Cooley, Charles H., 35, 48, 53, 54, 55, 60, 63, 64, 77, 132, 136, 142, 144, 147, 152, 154, 166, 169, 177, 178, 184, 253, 277, 278, 279, 280, 286, 300, 306, 334, 358, 359, 416, 423, 444, 452, 462, 468, 483

Cooper, Courtney Ryley, 462
Corbett, Elizabeth, 286
Cornelius, J. J., 327
Coughlin, Father Charles E., 201, 202, 203
Cournos, J., 462
Cowley, M., 463
Coyle, David C., 130, 132, 147, 288, 306, 327, 416, 437, 439
Crile, George W., 48
Cross, F. C., 147
Crowell, E. M., 359
Curry, B., 253

Dane, C., 233
Danton, Georges-Jacques, 459
Davenport, Frederick Morgan, 244, 253
David, King, 241
Davis, Jerome, 19, 22, 54, 64, 93, 359
Dawson, Carl A., 18, 334
Denison, J. H., 60, 64
Devine, Edward T., 430, 439
Dewey, E. A., 194
Dewey, John, 110, 270, 463, 483
Dicey, Albert V., 306, 359
Dieffenbach, A. C., 253
Dimock, H. S., 398
Divine (See Father Divine)
Doob, Leonard W., 359
Douglas, W. A. S., 306
Dowd, Jerome, 12, 22, 35, 184, 233, 254, 270, 286, 306, 336, 359, 463
Downey, June Etta, 98, 115
Dublin, L. I., 147
Duffus, R. L., 244
Dugdale, E. T. S., 306
Dunham, H. Warren, 418, 423
Durkheim, Emile, 28, 29, 30, 429

Earhart, Amelia, 126
Eaton, Hubert, 113, 114
Eddy, Sherwood, 271
Edwards, Jonathan, 120
Eldridge, Selba, 359
Elliott, Mabel A., 398, 424, 439, 463
Ellison, Jerome E., 293
Ellwood, Charles A., 142, 143, 147, 254, 257, 306, 483
Evans, W., 424

Falk, Alfred T., 286, 359
Father Divine, 111
Faris, Ellsworth, 48, 64, 419
Faris, Robert E. L., 418, 424

Farnsworth, Paul, 43, 48, 53, 54, 64, 78, 148, 333, 424
Finney, Ross L., 22, 64, 77
Fisher, Frederick B., 349, 359
Fiske, C., 254
Fleming, P., 286
Flügel, J. C., 398
Flynn, John T., 196, 198
Folsom, Joseph K., 224, 233, 327, 439, 483
Forbes, Rosita, 70, 77
Fosdick, H. E., 439
Foskett, John M., 27, 28, 29
Frank, G., 271
Frank, Lawrence K., 409, 411, 439
Franklyn, Julian, 433, 434, 440
Freneau, Philip, 355
Freud, Sigmund, 38, 48, 95, 452

Galton, Sir Francis, 341
Gandhi, M. K., 132, 349
Gantt, W. H., 43
Garrison, Carl C., 398
Garvie, A. E., 248
Gauss, C., 440
Gerold, Katherine, 306
Gerould, K. F., 105
Gettys, Warren E., 18, 334
Giddings, Franklin H., 9, 22, 335, 359
Gilfillan, S. C., 313
Gillette, John M., 22, 257, 271, 306, 327, 335, 336, 359
Ginzburg, Benjamin, 64, 77
Glueck, E. T., 271
Gosling, Thomas Warrington, 359
Grant, U. S., 111
Graves, W. Brooke, 205, 254, 271, 286, 306
Groves, Ernest R., 115
Gruening, Ernest Henry, 359

Hall, G. Stanley, 38, 363, 398
Hankins, Frank H., 254
Harper, Manley H., 271
Harris, H. K., 359
Hart, H., 132
Hart, J. K., 463
Hartmann, George W., 41, 48, 147
Hauser, P., 358, 423, 427
Hayner, Norman S., 409, 417, 418, 424
Hearst, William Randolph, 302
Hébert, Jacques, 459
Heer, C., 306

Heill, Clark L., 64
Heinz, A. Heinz, 306
Herrick, Judson C., 147
Herskovits, M. J., 94, 116, 133
Hiller, E. T., 20, 22, 35, 137, 147, 166, 359, 414, 424, 463
Hilmer, Hermann, 69, 77
Hitler, Adolph, 109, 199, 302, 306
Hobbes, Thomas, 27, 28, 30, 33, 457
Hobhouse, Leonard Trelawney, 93
Hoffman, W., 69
Holland, Gerold, 115
Holmes, Joseph L., 205
Holt, Arthur E., 168, 169, 184
Hoover, Herbert, 303
Hopwood, Eric Clark, 359
Horton, Henry P., 49
House, F. N., 35, 48, 77, 93, 167, 254, 360, 424, 428
Howard, George Elliott, 19, 22
Howe, Q., 254
Howerth, I. W., 271
Hutchinson, P., 254, 463
Huxley, A., 360

Ilin, M., 264
Insull, Samuel, 169
Isaac, 56, 258

Jackson, G., 360
Jacob, 56
James, William, 74, 78, 271, 338, 339, 452, 463
Jastrow, J., 440
Jefferson, Thomas, 303
Job, 101
Johnson, A., 463
Johnson, B., 205
Johnson, Cladius O., 306
Johnson, Hugh S., 201, 203
Jones, Buck, 110
Jordan, Arthur M., 360
Jowett, Benjamin, 35, 288, 306

Kandel, I. L., 266, 271
Kavanaugh, Marcus A., 306
Keller, A. G., 93, 147, 233, 234, 254, 286, 306, 360, 468, 484
Kelsey, Carl, 463
Kelsey, Vera, 443
Kempf, E. J., 147
Kenyon, T., 132, 360, 440
Kittredge, George Lyman, 132
Knight, Frank K., 22, 118, 286

Köhler, Wolfgang, 41, 43, 48, 62, 64, 147
Kolodin, Irving, 201, 203, 360
Kroeber, A. L., 82, 93, 132
Krupskaya, 267
Kuttner, A. B., 463

Laird, D. A., 286
Landis, Judson T., 171, 234
Landis, Paul H., 48, 76, 78, 93, 101, 102, 115, 171, 234, 260, 304, 306, 348, 360, 436, 440, 484
Landon, Alfred M., 302
La Piere, Richard, 43, 48, 53, 54, 64, 78, 148, 206, 292, 307, 333, 424
Laski, Harold J., 463
Lasswell, Harold D., 198, 206, 360
Lawes, Lewis E., 431, 440
Layman, Geoffrey, 148, 307
Lazaron, M. S., 254
Le Bon, Gustave, 360
Lee, B. Y., 424
Lengyel, Emil, 307
Lenin, Nikolay, 267
Leslie, Kennethe, 157, 158, 167
Lewis, Sinclair, 167
Lichtenberger, J. P., 33, 35
Liebling, A. F., 111
Lindbergh, Charles A., 111
Lincoln, Abraham, 303, 345
Link, Henry C., 132, 254
Lippmann, Walter, 64, 68, 78, 101, 115, 206, 251, 254, 415, 424, 440, 463, 484
Lipsky, A., 360
Locke, John, 27, 28, 30, 33, 37, 73, 78, 238, 254
Loeb, E. M., 398
Logan, Edward B., 300, 307
Lombroso, Cesare, 38, 49, 453
Long, Huey, 201
Lowie, Robert H., 93, 398
Luccock, H. E., 254
Lumley, Frederick Elmore, 11, 22, 35, 39, 206, 331, 337, 360, 426, 427
Lunacharsky, 267
Luther, Martin, 120, 124
Lynd, Helen Merrell, 274, 286
Lynd, Robert S., 274, 286, 424

Machiavelli, Nicolo, 307
MacIver, Robert M., 35, 78, 132, 144, 148, 307, 463, 484
MacLoughlin, J., 463

Magner, J. A., 254
Malinowski, B., 61, 80, 81, 94, 116, 132, 288, 360
Marat, Jean Paul, 459
Marx, Fritz Morstein, 291, 307
Mather, Cotton, 120
Mather, William G., Jr., 175, 177, 184
Matthews, M. Taylor, 273, 286
McConnell, Francis J., 463
McDougall, William, 413, 424
McDowell, J., 254
McKelway, St. Clair, 111
Mead, Margaret, 78, 117, 124, 125, 132, 143, 148, 218, 234, 360, 363, 398
Melvin, A. G., 271
Merriam, Charles E., 360
Merrill, Francis E., 398, 424, 439, 463
Merz, Charles, 327, 443
Meyer, Walter E., 148, 361
Michael, Jerome, 307, 440
Miner, J. R., 255
Moley, R., 424, 463
Mooney, Martin, 463
Moses, 56
Mowrer, Edgar A., 307
Mowrer, Ernest R., 175, 184, 234, 255, 440
Mowrer, Mrs. Harriet R., 234
Murchison, Carl, 115
Mussolini, Benito, 109, 199, 264, 265

Napoleon, 16, 262, 458
Nevins, Allan, 206
Niebuhr, R., 255
Nitti, Francesco F., 265, 271, 463
Nock, A. J., 77, 78

Odum, Howard W., 85, 294, 307, 317, 321, 327
Ogburn, William F., 49, 64, 94, 147, 180, 223, 234, 313, 315, 321, 323, 327, 328, 437, 440, 484
Orman, F., 287
Ortega, José, 317
O'Shea, M. V., 218, 271

Park, Robert E., 11, 22, 35, 49, 94, 360, 414, 424, 439
Parsons, Elsie Clews, 64, 346
Parsons, Talcott, 124
Pascal, Blaise, 40

Paul, the Apostle, 38, 56, 57, 108
Paul, Czar of Russia, 460
Pavlov, Ivan P., 43, 49
Peabody, Richard, 464
Pearson, Karl, 110
Pecora, Ferdinand, 197
Pigors, Paul, 360
Pistrak, 267
Pitkin, W. B., 206
Pitt-Rivers, G., 122, 328, 434, 440
Plant, James S., 94, 117, 132, 184, 224, 234, 255, 271, 287, 307, 465
Plato, 26, 27, 35, 307
Platt, C., 132
Plunkitt, George, 296, 297
Ponce de Leon, 119
Pope Innocent VIII, 120
Pound, Roscoe, 307
Prince, Samuel Henry, 435, 440
Prucha, L. C., 271

Read, C. F., 255
Reinhardt, James Melvin, 22, 257, 271, 276, 287, 306, 327, 335, 336, 359
Reisner, Edward H., 263, 271
Reuter, E. B., 234, 420, 439
Rice, Stuart A., 120
Richards, E. L., 148, 234, 271
Richelsen, I., 255
Riordan, W. I., 307
Rivers, W. H. R., 117, 132, 328, 440
Robespierre, Maximilien, 459, 460
Robinson, Henry Morton, 413, 424
Roosevelt, Franklin D., 200, 201, 302, 303
Roosevelt, Theodore, 303
Ross, Edward Alsworth, 9, 10, 14, 22, 23, 31, 35, 39, 64, 78, 142, 148, 257, 277, 307, 309, 360, 464
Rousseau, Jean Jacques, 27, 29, 30, 33, 447, 449, 464
Runner, J. R., 234
Russell, O. D., 148

Sadler, William S., 398
Saint Augustine, 255, 453
Saint Simon, 30
Sapir, Edward, 70, 71, 78, 94, 133
Sarah, 258
Sarvis, Maude Taylor, 234
Schmid, C. F., 424
Schweitzer, A., 255
Seabury, Davis, 398

Seldes, G., 133
Shatsky, 267
Shaw, Clifford R., 167, 427, 440
Shaw, R., 464
Shorey, Paul, 35, 307
Sidis, B., 41, 120, 186, 360
Slosson, E. E., 440
Smith, Russell Gordon, 12, 13, 23, 65, 66, 78, 334
Smith, T. V., 288, 307
Smith, W. B., 271
Smith, William C., 222, 226, 234
Snedden, D., 271
Sockman, R. W., 255
Sombart, Werner, 123, 126, 133
Sorokin, Pitirim A., 32, 39, 40, 49, 94, 457, 458, 459, 464, 484
Soule, George Henry, 484
Spencer, Herbert, 23, 30, 320, 339, 341, 361
Spengler, Oswald, 484
Stalin, Joseph, 199, 460
Stamp, Sir Josiah, 314, 315, 328, 484
Stefansson, Vjalmar, 117, 133
Steffens, Lincoln, 294, 307
Stein, Ludwig, 35
Steiner, J. F., 163, 167
Stelzle, Charles, 255
Stern, Bernhard J., 167, 234
Stocking, Collis A., 287
Stonequist, E. V., 420, 440, 464
Stratton, G. M., 272
Strong, A. L., 361
Strout, Richard Lee, 361
Sullivan, Lawrence, 308
Sullivan, W. L., 255
Sumner, William Graham, 84, 85, 86, 87, 94, 117, 133, 138, 167, 342, 347, 361
Sutherland, Edwin H., 292, 420, 440

Taft, Donald R., 420
Taine, Henri, 459
Tannenbaum, Frank W., 58, 78, 115, 162, 163, 204, 272, 308, 425, 428, 440
Tarde, Gabriel, 64
Tawney, R. H., 255, 287
Teggart, Frederick J., 68, 69, 78, 148
Thom, Douglas A., 398
Thomas, Dorothy Swaine, 416, 425
Thomas, N., 361
Thomas, William I., 18, 66, 67, 78,

95, 96, 97, 99, 115, 125, 136, 148, 163, 167, 184, 216, 229, 232, 234, 235, 361, 399, 416, 425, 426, 431, 441, 446, 447, 464, 484
Thompson, Warren S., 102
Thoreau, Henry David, 449, 451, 464
Thrasher, Frederic M., 167, 427, 441
Tolson, C. A., 148, 272
Towney, B. W., 124
Tozzer, A. M., 352, 361, 399
Tralle, Henry Edward, 361
Turfey, Paul W., 399

Van Loon, H. W., 115
Van Sweringen, O. P., 196, 197
Veblen, Thorstein, 277, 287, 320, 361
Volborth, G., 43

Wallas, Graham, 94, 184, 206, 287, 308, 328, 441, 464, 484
Wallis, Wilson D., 18, 23, 61, 133, 158, 346, 353, 355
Walsh, W. T., 361
Wang, Betty, 361
Ward, Lester F., 12
Washburne, C., 272
Washington, George, 111, 303, 345
Watson, John B., 37
Weber, Max, 124, 255, 287
Weber, E. A., 399
Werner, M. R., 185, 361
Westermarck, Edward Alexander, 94
Wheeler, Burton K., 196, 197
Whelpton, P. K., 102
White, William Allen, 148, 361
Wilder, Robert Holman, 287
Willey, M. M., 94, 116, 120, 133, 328
William II of Prussia, 263
Williams, James M., 49, 64, 78, 115
Williams, M., 361
Williams, Whiting, 61, 64
Winston, Sanford, 49, 79, 94, 140, 141, 148, 184, 361, 474
Wissler, Clark, 42, 49, 64, 94
Wolfe, W. B., 235
Woody, Thomas, 268, 272
Wordsworth, William, 232
Worthington, Eleanor, 464
Wycliff, John, 104

Young, J. W., 287
Young, Kimball, 10, 11, 23, 49, 64, 94, 123, 133, 220, 221, 235, 287, 334, 425, 484

Young, Pauline V., 167, 416, 425, 431, 441, 484

Zeleny, Leslie D., 22
Znaniecki, Florian, 18, 96, 115, 167, 184, 229, 234, 425, 426, 431, 441, 446, 447, 464, 484

Zorbaugh, H. W., 76, 94, 417, 423, 425, 441

INDEX OF SUBJECTS

Abnormal psychology, 413–414
Accommodation
  between groups, 103, 462
  of the Indian, 433
  in the primary group, 153–154
Adjustment (See Personal adjustment;
    Social adjustment)
  of college youth, 364–365, 455–457
  of half-caste races, 420
  of immigrants, 221–222, 225–232,
    419–420, 431, 445–447
  lag in, 321–323, 325, 437
  problems of, 99
  through revolt, 442–443, 455–457
  after revolution, 459–460, 461
  to systems of control, 451–452
  techniques of, 82–83, 93, 161
  to technology, 318, 325
  trial and error, 84–85
  of youth, 221–222, 431–432, 455–
    457
Adolescence (See Youth)
  in primitive society, 76
  as a sociological fact, 363–364
  as a transition period, 362–363, 365
Adolescent psychology, 363–364
Advertising, 185, 186
  control by, 282–283, 326
Age composition (See Social composi-
    tion)
Agencies of control (See Control de-
    vices; Mass impression; Institu-
    tions)
  government and law as, 288–305
  science and technology as, 309–327
Amana Colony
  control in, 151–152, 443
America (See Ethos; Society)
  channels for revolt in, 453–454
  Christian church in, 238–253
  cities in, 168–169
  crime in, 428
  education in, 269–270
  individualism in, 135–136

America—(Continued)
  personality disorganization in, 407–
    411, 416, 427
  provincialism of, 89
  social control in, 465–483
  values in, 123–131, 180–182, 466
  work mores in, 275
American family
  as an agency of control, 209–233
  failure of, 223–225
American Indians
  demoralization of, 433
  disintegration of culture of, 122
  goal of life of, 120–121
  status among, 119
American Medical Association, 323
Anarchy
  social, 30
Ancestor worship, 56, 101, 153
Antisocial instincts, 38–39
Applied sociology
  aim of, 7
Atavistic man, 38
Attitudes
  definition of, 97
Authority (See Leadership; Social con-
    trol)
  in caste societies, 127
  culture consciousness and, 475–477
  desire to evade, 445
  in the family, 216, 218–219
  of government and law, 288–290, 305
  of homogeneity, 467
  ideals and, 289–290
  lack of, 415
  and order, 24–35, 478–479
  of religion, 236, 240–241, 246
  science as, 309–311
  search for, 468, 474–475
  source of, 12, 14–18, 33, 285
  of stateways compared to that of
    folkways, 293–294
Authority pattern
  in family life, 216, 218–219

Behavior
  orderly, (See Social control)
  problems of, 362–398, 423, 456
Behavior patterns (See Patterns of life)
  in the city, 171–172, 183
  influence of technicways on, 317–321
Biological composition of groups, 75–76
Biological plasticity, 257
Breakdown of controls, 224, 401–462
  (See Personality disorganization; Social pathology; Social revolt)
  in the immigrant family, 225–233
Bribes
  to legislators, 297
Builder's Creed, 113–114
Business
  control by, 281–285

Capitalism
  folklore of, 283–285
  philosophy of, 124, 129
Carnal man, 38
Case method, 145
Caste system, 103
  as an alternative, 470–471
  as a device for limiting access to values, 104–105, 114
  wealth under, 127
Catastrophe (See Crisis)
Cemeteries (See Death)
Censorship
  as an instrument of selective mass impression, 199–200
Ceremony
  control by, 339–341
Change (See Social change)
  belief in, 129
  as a tool of progress, 478–479
Character
  definition of, 97–98
Charity in modern society, 326
Child psychology, 215–216, 218
Childhood
  controls of, 362
  goals of, 99–100
  in New Guinea, 143, 218
Children
  conditioning of, 216, 362
  revolt of, 452

China
  absence of personality problems in, 409, 416
  ancestor worship in, 101
  effect of diffusion of mechanical inventions in, 311–312
  kinship group in, 153
  marriage in, 258
  social control in, 84, 89–92
  status in, 119
Choice of values, 129–130, 187–188
  (See Social values; Freedom)
Christian Church (See Church)
  in America, 238–253
  as a cultural compulsive, 251–252
  decline in influence of, 249, 250–251
  emphasis of, 128–129
  eternity-centered, 239–245
  as an influence in control, 236–253
  morality-centered, 239, 240, 245–249
Christian ideals, 248
Christian model
  as a pattern for behavior, 245, 246, 253
Christianity, 108 (See Christian Church)
  and the evolution theory, 456
Church (See Christian Church)
  change in approach of, 145
City (See Secondary groups; Urban society)
  breakdown of the neighborhood in, 153, 168–169
  delinquency and crime in, 427–428
  difficulties of control in, 171–172
City dude, 275
Civic ideals
  need for, 177–180
Civic virtues
  corruption of, 173–174
Civilization (See Culture; Western civilization)
  progress as a law of, 324
  public opinion in, 355
  role of tradition in, 343–344
Classes (See Social classes)
Clergy (See Priestly group)
"Club opinion," 74–75
Codes
  of criminals, 428–429
  as forces for control, 343
  of youth, 392–398

College youth
adjustment of, 364–365
control among, 182, 365–398
mental conflict of, 415
superstitions of, 352
tendency to "debunk" among, 456–457
Communication
modern devices for, 186–187
Communistic group
control in, 151–152, 252
Communities (See Rural communities)
"Compensation," 98
Competition
and the open class system, 127–128
Competition-success pattern, 124–128
Concepts (See Mental concepts)
Conditioned response principle, 34, 43–44, 53
Conditioning process, 42, 338 (See Learning process)
in the family, 215–217, 362
Conduct (See Social control)
cultural conception of, 409–411
Confessions, 453
Conflict (See Mental conflict)
of family patterns, 226–229
of models, 112
between racial groups, 102–103
of values, 106, 115
Conflicting mass stimuli, 187–189
Conformity (See Socialization)
habit of, 62–63
and individual differences, 140–142
in the primary group, 162
Conscience, 451
religious, 242–243
as the voice of the group, 56–59, 63
Conservation of natural resources, 321
Conspicuous consumption, 180, 277, 285
Contact
as a factor in revolt, 443
technology as a factor in, 311–313
Control devices, 4, 20–22, 46–47, 241, 331–357 (See Social control; Mass impression; Controls; Law; Agencies of control)
of advertisers, 282–283
establishing of, 174–180
need for new, 322
of the political party, 300–304

Control devices—(Continued)
in the primary and in the secondary group, 160, 170, 171
Controls
breaking of, 451–452
conscious and unconscious, 334–335
formal and informal, 334
paternal and social, 336
re-establishing of, after revolution, 459–462
used in establishing order, 336–347
used in maintaining order, 336–338, 347–357
among youth, 362–398
Convention
control by, 374–376
Conventionalization, 346–347
Conversion
religious, 244–246
Corporations
control by, 283–285
Corruption of civic virtues, 173–174
Court procedure, 292–293
Courtship (See Marriage)
Crazes, 55, 110, 347
Crime (See Criminals)
and the breakdown of control, 427–429
patterns of, 58–59
responsibility for, 144–146
ridicule as a weapon against, 353–355
waves of, 188–189, 194
Crime news (See Crime wave)
as an aid to control, 194–196, 205
Crime waves
as an aid to control, 194
part of the newspaper in, 188–189
Criminal prosecution, 292–293
Criminals (See Crime)
as atavistic men, 38
goals of life of, 107
patterns of life of, 427–429
publicity given to, 189
use of machine techniques by, 313
Crisis
breakdown of control in times of, 435–436
Crusades, 123
"Cultural compulsives," 117, 124
Christian influences as, 251–252
Cultural goals
concept of, 116–118

Cultural goals—(Continued)
  and education, 269–270
  integration of, 122–123
  and universal opportunity, 469–470
Cultural heritage, 83, 137, 215, 221
Cultural inertia, 161, 282
Cultural lag, 321–323
  as a defect in social control, 437
Cultural milieu, 14–15, 118, 122, 217
Cultural traits, 116 (See Culture patterns)
Cultural values (See Culture)
  and American education, 269–270
  revision of, 462
Culture
  American, 123–131
  continuity of, 81, 92–93
  disintegration of, 410–411
  as a factor in socialization, 79–93
  goals within, 116–118, 469–470
  hierarchies of values in, 138–139
  maladjustments in, 321–323
  as a mold for personality, 81–82
  other-worldly-centered, 3
  and personality disorganization, 414, 420–421
  as a phase of group experience, 79–80
  projection of, 209–215
  revision of, 462
  as a technique of adjustment, 82–83
  unity of the individual with, 136–139
  urban-industrial, 13–14
Culture consciousness, 475–477
Culture patterns 116–131 (See Culture)
  conformity to, 409–411, 420–421
  diversity of, 467
  goals of life defined by, 120–122
  revision of, 462
"Culture shock," 183, 427, 432
Custom, 84 (See Tradition; Mores)
  authority of, 87–92, 293–294, 304
  control by, 382–383
  suicide as a, 413
  and technology, 326

Daredevil
  role of, 122
Darwinian theory, 30–31
Daydreaming, 218

Day of judgment
  fear of, 377
Death
  attitudes toward, 113–114, 119
Death-bed promises, 56
"Debunking," 251
  as an aspect of revolt, 455–457
Definition of the situation, 67
Definitions (See Social definitions)
  and caste lines, 103
  and change, 477–478
  development of, 312, 326
  diversity of, 73–74
  of morality, 71–73, 248
Degeneration, 166 (See Personality disorganization; Demoralization)
  personal, 413–414
  of primitives, 433–435
Delinquency (See Crime)
  and the breakdown of control, 427–429
  patterns of, 58–59, 156
  in the primary group, 161, 217
  responsibility for, 144–146
Dementia praecox, 418–419
Democratic philosophy, 99, 129
Demoralization (See Personality disorganization; Degeneration)
  and change, 415–416
  of college youth, 456
  of Polish immigrants, 231
  in the secondary group, 182
Depression
  frustration during, 276
  and man's faith in progress, 324
Derision
  control by, 353–355
"Derivative group," 169, 172
Desire (See Drive)
  for immortality, 242
  for the new, 324
Devices of control (See Control devices; Controls; Agencies of control)
Dictators, 111, 115, 201 (See Totalitarian states)
Dictatorships
  ideals of, 290
Diffusion
  technology as a factor in, 311–313
Discipline
  in the family pattern, 218–219

Discipline—(Continued)
and personal freedom, 143–144, 146
of work, 273–275
Disillusionment
religious, 250–251, 253
Disorder
economic forces promoting, 273–285
Divine law, 24–25, 33, 238
Divorce rate
increase in, 181, 217, 258–259
Drive (See Organic drives)
concepts of, 95–96
desire for recognition as a, 125
Drunken driving
cure for, 355
Dual personality, 112
Dual values, 106
Duty
sense of, 242–243, 246

Earthquakes
breakdown of control after, 435
Eccentricity, 135, 421
Economic control, 394
Economic forces promoting order and
disorder, 273–285
Economic valuation (See Pecuniary
values)
Education
aims of, 256–257, 409
control of biological factors by, 258–260
for crime, 429
religious, 246–247
as selective participation in social experience, 268–269
as a socializing agency, 256–270,
335–336
and the state, 261–268
universal, 269–270
Educational philosophy
and the problem child, 145–146
Educative process, 3, 261 (See Learning process)
Emotional-temperamental qualities
control by, 383–390, 397
End of the world
fear of, 243
Epicureanism, 130
in the family, 224
Epidemics (See Mental epidemics)
Equality of the sexes, 102, 226, 326

Eskimo
authority among the, 17
Essay on human understanding, 238
Eternal life, 246 (See Life everlasting)
Ethnocentrism, 290, 475
Ethos
American, 123–130
meaning of, 14–15, 117, 131
Evangelism
as a factor in control, 244–245, 247
Evolution
and Christianity, 456
theory of, 30–31, 128
Example
control by, 390–392, 397
Experience
as a guide, 45–47, 144–146
Exploitation
of the child, 219
under the factory system, 321–322
and leadership, 185–186
of natural resources, 321, 470
by selfish interests, 186–187, 473
Explosion (See Halifax disaster)

Factory system, 321–322
Fads, 55–56, 347
Faith (See Religion)
loss of, 250–251
Family (See Primary groups)
as an agency of control in America,
209–233
authority pattern in, 218–219
in China, 153
control by latent patterns in, 219–222
dominance of patterns of, 366–372,
397
failure of control in, 223–232, 393–394
as a goal of life, 108–109, 114, 119–120, 180–181
as a social institution, 260, 315–316
Family patterns
conflict of, 226–229
dominance of, 366–372, 397
Farm household
work activities in, 275
Farm workers
religion of, 244
Farm youth (See Rural youth)
Fascist education, 264–265

Fashions, 55
control by, 346–347
Feminine values, 102
Flagellants movement, 123
Folkways
authority of, as compared to that of stateways, 293–294
as control devices, 12, 79, 84–85, 88–89, 335
development of, 317–320
Force
control by, 331–332, 348–349, 436–437
Forest Lawn Memorial-Park, 113–114
Freedom
of expression, 453–454, 468, 472
of the hobo, 414–415, 423
for the individual, 134–146, 447–451, 461–462, 469, 472
limits of, 444, 457, 479
of modern man, 415, 423
and the search for authority, 468, 474, 475
Friends
influence of, 393–394
Frontier areas
goal of life in, 101
individualism in, 134–135
lack of community controls in, 75–76, 436–437
Frustration
as a result of unemployment, 276
Fugitive Papers, 12
Functional individualism
possibilities of, 468–469, 483
Functionalism, 116
Furnished rooms (See Rooming houses)
world of, 417

Gangster society, 69 (See Criminals)
German education, 265–266
Goals of an age (See Social values)
as factors in social guidance, 116–131
Goals of life
of childhood and youth, 99–100
concept of, 95–98
of criminals, 107
defined by culture patterns, 120–122
of the different sexes, 102
as a factor in control, 95–115
and the family, 108–109

Goals of life—(Continued)
importance of, 107–108, 422, 466
of middle age, 100–101
models as a source of, 110–112
of old age, 101–102
the quest for, 474–475
and race, 102–103
and religion, 108, 237–238
in rural and urban society, 180–182
social aspect of, 98–99
of social classes, 103–105
in totalitarian states, 109–110
utilitarian and materialistic, 109
within vocations, 106–107
Gossip
in the newspaper, 176–177
in the rural community, 156–158, 175
Government (See State)
authoritative aspects of, 288–289
effect of inventions on, 315–316
extra-legal invisible, 294–300, 304–305
origin of, 28
as a regulative agency, 288–305
in the United States, 284–285
Graft (See Political corruption)
Greek thinkers, 26–27
Group control, 8, 151–152 (See Social control; Groups)
Group expectancy (See Social expectancy)
"Group mind," 8
Group patterns (See Patterns of life)
deterministic nature of, 70–71
diversity of, 73–74
homogeneity of, in the primary group, 160–162
laughter as a means of maintaining, 352–353
superstition as a means of maintaining, 350–352
Group payment plans
for medical aid, 323
Groups (See Races; Primary group; Secondary group; Primitive society)
definitions of, 65–68, 71–74, 82
effect of, in limiting experience, 68–69
identification with, 55, 63
influence of, on man, 56–63
interaction of, 4

Groups—(Continued)
  participation in, 421–422
  priority of patterns of, 65–66, 409–410
  role of, in socialization, 65–77
  social composition of, 75–76
  tradition as a guide to, 343–346
Growing Up in New Guinea, 143
Guilds
  as control devices, 89–92

Habits
  change in, 314, 326–327
  formation of, 338–339, 380–382
Halifax disaster, 435–436
"Hara-Kiri," 413
Health insurance, 323
Hobo
  lack of purpose of, 414–415
Hobohemia
  control devices in, 76
Home
  broken by death, 417
"Honest graft," 296
Honor
  as affected by pecuniary values, 280
  notions of, 75
Hotel dwellers
  personality problems of, 417–418
Household budget, 278
Human experience
  continuity of, 81
Human interest story
  as a form of gossip, 176–177
Human motivation, 95–115
Human nature (See Original nature;
    Man)
  as containing a vicious streak, 39–40
  development of, 63
  as instinctive, 9–10, 30–31, 37
  plasticity of, 257
  potentialities of, 24–25
  as the product of control, 31
  and revolt, 452–453
  as the source of authority, 27
  views of, 53–54
Human symbol method of control,
    331–333

Ideals, 110, 129, 238 (See Cultural
    goals; Civic ideals; Christian
    ideals)

Ideals—(Continued)
  and authority, 289–290, 474–475
  of messiahs, 474–475
  of social welfare, 477, 480
  symbols as, 333
Identification
  of parents with their children, 220
  of self with the group, 55, 63
Idols (See Models)
Immigrants
  problems of adjustment of, 221–222,
    225–232, 419–420, 427, 431, 445–447
Immortality
  desire for, 242
Improvement
  belief in, 128–129
Inborn reflexes
  importance of, 40
Indian (See American Indian)
Individual (See Social control)
  control of, 3
  responsibility of, 144–146
  uniqueness of, 134–135
Individual differences
  and conformity, 140–141
  emphasis on, 99, 134
  and revolt, 453
Individual freedom
  notions of, 447–451, 469
  the problem of, 134–146
Individual initiative, 33, 124, 136
Individual interference with the social
    process, 11
Individual unity with the social group,
    136–139, 144–146
Individualism, 129–130, 142, 146, 348,
    478, 480 (See Individual free-
    dom)
  of the hobo, 415
  price and benefits of, 468
  as related to heterogeneous patterns,
    467
  and social pathology, 437–438
  and social revolt, 442–443, 451, 457,
    461
  and suicide, 411–413
  types of, 468–469, 483
Indoctrination, 262–268, 270, 290
Industrial revolution
  effect of, on the family, 163
Industrialization
  and the problem of control, 170, 172

"Inferiority complex," 98
Inhibition
  the power of, 67
Initiation rites (See Primitive society)
  in primitive society, 76–143
Insecurity
  as related to pathology, 437–438
Instinct psychology, 3 (See Human nature)
Instincts (See Human nature)
  in animals, 36–37
  antisocial, 38–39
Institutional values, 278
  authority of, 475–477
Institutionalized patterns
  control by, 377–383, 397
Institutions (See Family)
  as agencies of control, 209–327, 339–341
  effects of inventions on, 315–316
  social, 4
Intellectual sophistication
  and religion, 251
Interaction
  of groups, 4
Interference
  with the social process, 11
Inventions (See Technology)
  effects of, on institutional controls, 315–316
  effects of, on social views and political philosophies, 316
  effects of, on society, 313–315, 321–323, 326–327
Investigation
  public, 194–198, 204
Isolation
  as a cause of schizophrenia, 418–419
  individualism of, 468

Japanese
  in America, 226
  in Hawaii, 221–222
  suicide among, 413
Jew
  role of, 105, 252
Job
  as the center of personality, 276
  discipline of, 273–274
Judicial system
  weakness of, 292–293

Juvenile delinquency (See Delinquency)

Kinship group
  in China, 153
Ku Klux Klan, 462

Laissez faire
  philosophy of, 473
Land
  as a goal of life, 180
Laughter
  control by, 159, 352–353
Law
  absolute and final, 24
  attitudes toward, 428
  authoritative aspects of, 288–289
  and custom, 293–294, 304
  as a regulative agency, 288–305, 355–356, 357, 382–383
  as rules of the game, 10
  in the secondary group, 171, 175, 183
  in the United States, 105
  weakness of, 291–293, 355–356, 357
Law enforcement, 292–293
  effect of machine techniques on, 313
Laws, The, 26
Leaders, 15–18, 300–301, 461 (See Leadership)
Leadership, 110–112 (See Leaders)
  and mass exploitation, 185–186
  and myth making, 300–302
  as paternal control, 336
Learning process, 43–45
Legislation
  social, 289
Legislature
  crooks in, 297–298
Leisure time (See Recreation)
  and epicureanism, 130
  use of, 100
Le Suicide, 429
Libido
  as a drive, 95
Life (See Goals of life)
  goals of, 95–115
Life everlasting, 243–244, 246
Life patterns (See Patterns of life)
Literature of revolt, 451
Lobbyists, 282, 297–300, 305
  as advisers to congressmen, 298–300

"Looking-glass-self," 58, 60–61, 276
Luck
 belief in, 352
Lynching, 293–294
"Lynchings, Fears, and Folkways," 293

Machine technology (See Technology)
 folkways replaced by, 85
 and personality disorganization, 408
Mainsprings of men, 62
Maladjustments
 in culture, 321–323
 in personality, 244–245
 social, 4
Man (See Human nature; Socialization)
 group influence on, 56–63
 levels of control of, 46–48
 native equipment of, 40–43, 47, 82
 progress as a law of, 324
Marginal man
 personality disorganization of, 419–420
Market
 as an institution, 278, 280
Marriage
 among American-orientals, 227–229
 as based on romance, 123, 224–225, 258–260
 among Polish immigrants, 229–232
Martyr pattern, 121
Masculine urge, 95, 96, 98
Masculine values, 102
Mass behavior, 123
Mass control
 the dilemma in, 186–187
Mass hysteria, 290
Mass impression
 agencies of, 185–205
 censorship as an instrument of, 199–200
 publicity as an instrument of, 189–198
 radio as an instrument of, 200–203
Material culture (See Culture)
Materialistic goals, 109
Medicine
 socialized, 323
Memorial Day riots, 198
Mental concepts
 development of, 67–68

Mental conflict, 182, 419 (See Personality conflict)
 in an uncertain world, 415
Mental disease, 418–419
Mental epidemics, 123, 131
Mesabi Iron Range
 lack of community controls in, 75
Messiahs
 and the search for goals, 474–475
Middle age
 goals of, 100–101
Middle Ages
 the Christian Church in, 239, 284
 nature of the universe during, 24–25, 33
 other-worldly-centered culture of, 3, 128, 477
Middletown, 274
Migration
 as a cause of pathological problems, 431–432
Migratory laborers
 religion of, 244
Mississippi bubble, 123
Mobility
 in America, 408
 and authority, 467
 and personal disorganization, 416–418, 422
Models (See Christian model)
 control of behavior by, 390–392
 as a source of goals, 110–112
Monastic seclusion
 motive for, 244
Money valuation
 place of, 281
 purpose of, 279
Monogamy
 as a part of the mores, 85
Morality
 Christian, 239
 definitions of, 71–73, 248
 relative, 238
 in the secondary group, 183, 248
Morals
 as ties holding society together, 30
Mores
 definition of, 85–86, 317
 development of, 319–320
 diffusion of, 113
 and group welfare, 79, 84
 unconscious assimilation of, 86–87
Mosaic Law, 104, 218

Motivation
  of faith, 250–251
  in man, 95–115
  as a means of controlling the child, 219, 223
  social, 477
Mountain people
  experience-worlds of, 273–274, 275
Movies
  censorship of, 200
Murder
  as an index of cultural maladjustment, 431
Myth making, 300–302
Mytown, 157–158

Natural law
  concept of, 25–26, 30
Natural resources
  exploitation of, 321, 470
Natural science (See Natural law; Technology)
  as a cure-all, 3
  in a dynamic society, 480, 481
Nature
  man's regulation of, 8
Neighborhood group, 152
  breakdown of, 153, 168–169
Neurotic disorders (See Personality disorganization)
New Deal campaign, 200
New Guinea, 143, 218 (See Primitive society)
New Russia's Primer, 263–264
News (See Press)
Newspaper (See Mass impression; Press; Publicity)
  human interest story of, 176–177
Nonconformity, 62, 142, 278 (See Rebels)
  and personality disorganization, 421
  as a phase of revolt, 444–445
Nonmaterial culture (See Culture)
Nonresistance
  doctrine of, 348–349

Occupational groups (See Vocations)
Old age
  goals of, 101–102
Old age pensions, 102 (See Townsend plan)
Open class society
  competition in, 127–128

Open class society—(Continued)
  control in, 103, 471
  religion in, 250–251
Opinion (See Public opinion)
  influence of, 158–160
Opportunity
  universal, 469–470
Order (See Social order)
  and authority, problem of, 24–35, 478–479
  devices used in the establishing of, 336–347, 356–357
  devices used in the maintaining of, 336–338, 347–357
  economic forces promoting, 273–285
  social science as a guide to, 479–481
Orderly behavior (See Social control)
Organic drives
  and personality disorganization, 420–421, 423
Oriental cultures
  contact of the Western world with, 311–312, 326
  technique of nonresistance in, 348–349
Orientation, 98, 122
Original nature, 63 (See Man; Human nature)
  and regulation, 36–48
  as it is understood today, 45–46
Other-worldliness
  as a control device, 241
Other-worldly-centered culture, 3

Participation
  in social life, 421–422
Party organization, 300
Passive resistance (See Nonresistance)
Paternal control, 12, 336
Pathological types, 421
Pathology (See Social pathology)
Patronage, 303–304
Patterns of life, 65–66, 69–71, 77 (See Group patterns; Culture; Culture patterns; Family patterns)
Pecuniary values
  as forces in control, 276–281, 285
Pentecostal faith
  among migratory laborers, 244
Personal adjustment
  appeal to, 242

Personal adjustment—(Continued)
and the "debunking process," 455–457
and evangelism, 244–245
and group participation, 421–422
in the morality-centered church, 246
Personal degeneration, 413–414
of college youth, 456
among primitives, 433
Personal freedom (See Individual freedom)
Personal objectives vs. realizations, 469–474
Personality (See Human nature; Man; Socialization)
culture as a mold for, 81–82, 92
development of, in the family, 209–233
disorganization of, 403–423
in a dynamic society, 465–467
and goals of life, 95–115, 472
integration of, 31–32, 97, 122–123
problems of, 182–183
sacredness of, 129–130
shaping of, 3, 14–15, 21
standardization of, 141
uniqueness of, 134–135, 383–384
Personality and the Cultural Pattern, 117
Personality conflict, 112–113, 115, 129, 163–166, 170, 403–423, 452 (See Mental conflict; Personality disorganization)
and evangelism, 244–245
Personality disorganization, 403–423
and the breakdown of tradition, 413–414
and change, 415–416
and the cultural structure, 414, 422–423
and the "debunking process," 455–457
and insecurity, 437–438
and mobility, 416–418, 422
and organic drives, 420–421, 423
and social pathology, 426
and the system of social control, 407–411, 422
in an uncertain world, 415
Personality maladjustments (See Personality disorganization)
and evangelism, 244–245

Philanthropists, 119
Physical force
as a means of control, 331–332, 348–349
Pioneer society (See Frontier areas)
Plasticity
of the human mind, 257
Play group, 152
Pleasure
as a goal of life, 130
Polish immigrants
disorganization of the marriage group among, 229–232
Political corruption, 173–174, 294–298
Political indoctrination, 262–268, 270, 290
Political organization
rise of, 28–29
Political party
control techniques of, 300–304
and the invisible government, 300
Poverty
causes of, 430
Precept
control by, 392
Predestination, 3
Pre-election polls, 303
Preface to Morals, A, 101, 415
Press (See Publicity)
control by, 189–198, 200, 204–205
Press agents, 187–188
Prestige
accumulation of, 277
value of, 110–112
Priestly group, 110–111
Primary group (See Family)
control in, 14, 151–166, 173–174, 186
in a dynamic society, 162–163
gossip in, 156–158
homogeneity of patterns of, 160–162
influence of opinion in, 158–160
nature of, 152–153
permanence of, 153–154
reputation in, 155–156
sentiment in, 153
shift from, 163–166, 364–365, 455–457
social traits in, 477–478
values in, 180–182, 455–457

Primitive society
  absence of personality problems in, 409, 419
  adolescent rites in, 76, 143, 270
  ceremonial control in, 339–341
  childhood in, 218
  control in, 15–18, 153, 346
  decay of, 433–435
  goals of life of, 121
  groups in, 169
  influence of Western civilization on, 117–118, 122, 251, 427, 433–435
  laughter in, 352–353
  mating in, 258
  the play of opinion in, 61
  ritual in, 341–342
  social power in, 14
  sounds used in, 62
  suicide in, 429
  taboos in, 349–350
  tradition as a guide in, 343
  youth societies in, 392
Principles of Sociology, 339
Prison discipline, 145
Privileged classes, 103–104
Problem child, 145–146
Problems (See Social problems)
Professional ethics, 106–107
Progress (See Social progress)
  belief in, 128–129
  in the economic sphere, 280–281
  and technology, 323–325
Projection
  of culture, 209–215
  by parents, 370
  of unfulfilled ambitions, 219–222, 232–233
Propaganda (See Mass impression)
  as an instrument of control, 198–199, 266
  of political parties, 302
  by radio, 200–203
  in the secondary group, 175, 186–189
  and youth, 109–110
Prophecy
  control by, 243, 246
Propriety
  definition of, 70
Prostitution
  in a frontier area, 75

Protestantism
  effect of capitalism and democracy on, 252
  and individualism, 129
  origin of, 124
  and the priestly classes, 104
Psychology
  abnormal, 413–414
  adolescent, 363–364
  child, 215–216, 218
  instinct, 3
  social, 7–9
Public investigation, 194–198, 204
Public opinion (See Opinion)
  control by, 7, 355, 376
  in primitive society, 16–18, 61
  in the rural community, 175
Publicity
  as a negative control device, 189–194, 204–205
  as a positive control device, 194–198, 204–205
  in the secondary group, 175
Punishment
  as a control device, 335, 357
  as a deterrent to lawbreaking, 292

Race prejudice, 351
Races
  adjustment of half-caste, 420
  discriminatory patterns among, 105
  and the goal of life, 102–103
Radio
  as an instrument of mass impression, 189, 200–203
Reacculturation
  problems of, 431–432
Rebels, 39, 62–63, 77, 142, 384, 461
  (See Revolt; Revolution)
Recognition
  as the first law of social behavior, 125
Recreation
  as a goal of life, 181
Reform
  belief in, 128–129
  of criminals, 145
Regulation (See Social control)
  ceremony as the original form of, 339–341
  by conscious agents, 8–15, 20–21
  by government and law, 288–305
  by impersonal forces, 13–21

Regulation—(*Continued*)
  nature of the problem of, 24–35
  need for foresight in, 322
  of organic drives, 420–421
Relief, 326
Religion (*See* Protestantism)
  as a factor in control, 236–253
  as a goal of life, 108, 114
  inadequacy of, 173–174, 366–367
Religious disillusionment, 250–251, 253
Repression
  in small communities, 165
Republic, The, 26
Reputation
  in the primary group, 155–156
Resources (*See* Natural Resources)
Responsibility
  individual vs. social, 144–146, 251
Restrictions (*See* Regulation)
Revivalism (*See* Evangelism)
Revolt, 105, 146 (*See* Rebels; Revolution)
  in American life, 453–454
  cause of, 165, 278
  champions of, 447–451
  danger in, 455
  "debunking" as an aspect of, 455–457
  and individual differences, 453
  and individualism, 443
  literature of, 451
  of the masses, 290, 442–462
  necessity for, 452–453
  nonconformity as a phase of, 444
  as a normal social process, 442–443
  of youth, 445–447
Revolt of the Masses, 317
Revolution, 105, 443
  the aftermath of, 458–462
  in caste societies, 127
  and the complete breakdown of control, 457, 458
Reward
  as a control device, 335
Ridicule
  as a control device, 159, 353–355
Ritual
  control by, 341–342
Role
  of the daredevil, 122
  of the Jew, 105
  maintenance of, 104

Romantic impulse
  and the automobile, 323
  control of, 258–260
Rooming house (*See* Furnished rooms)
  isolation in, 418–419
Rural family, 153, 393
Rural society (*See* Small town)
  delinquency patterns in, 161
  force of public opinion in, 175
  individualism in, 468
  repression in, 163–164
  values in, 180–182
  work mores in, 275
Rural youth
  migration of, 182–183, 364, 431–432
Russian education, 266–268

Sacred books
  authority of, 241, 247
Sanctions
  control by, 335–336
Savages (*See* Primitive society)
Scarlet Letter, The, 156
Schizophrenia
  as a result of isolation, 418–419
School (*See* Education)
  functions of, 217
  and the problem child, 145–146
Science (*See* Natural science; Technology; Social science)
  as an agency of control, 309–327
  as authority, 309–311
  growth of, 30
Seclusion
  monastic, 244
Secondary group (*See* Urban society)
  agencies of mass impression in, 185–205
  control in, 160, 168–184, 478
  definition of, 169
  establishing controls in, 174–180
  impersonal nature of, 171
  personality problems in, 182–183, 455–457
  transition from primary group to, 163–166, 364–365, 455–457
  values in, 180–182
Security
  lack of, 437–438
  of slaves, 468
Self-control
  meaning of, 8

Self-control—(*Continued*)
relation of, to social control, 142–143
Self-preservation
as the first law of life, 95–96, 124–125
Senate investigation, 195–198, 204
Sentiment
in the primary group, 154–155
Sex distinctions, 102
Sex ratio (See Social composition)
Sex taboos, 83
Sex urges
as fundamental drives, 38, 96
Sin
definition of, 71–73
in the modern world, 108
Slums
breakdown of control in, 427–429
Small town (See Rural communities)
transition stage of, 163
Small-Town Stuff, 156
Social action
need for a definition of, 466, 477–478
Social adjustment, 209–215, 219, 289
(See Adjustment)
Social anarchy, 30
Social ascendancy, 9–10
Social change, 170, 187, 409
and definitions, 477–478
and personal demoralization, 415–416
technology as a factor in, 311–313, 326–327, 408
Social classes
goals of, 103–105
Social composition
as a factor in goals of life, 98–107
of groups, 75–76
Social consciousness, 54–55, 63, 475–477
Social contract theory, 28–29, 33
Social Control, 9
Social control (See Regulation; Control devices; Mass impression)
adjustment to systems of, 451–452
the American family as an agency of, 209–233
breakdown of, 401–462
in China, 89–92
the Christian Church as an influence in, 236–253

Social control—(*Continued*)
contemporary views of the problem of, 30–35
definitions of, 7–22
in a dynamic society, 465–483
and economic forces, 273–285
education as an influence in, 256–275
effect of social composition of groups on, 75–76
goal of life as a factor in, 95–115
importance of government and law to, 288–305
and individual freedom, 134–146
means of, 331–357
pecuniary valuations as forces in, 276–281
as practiced by business, 281–285
in the primary group, 151–166
questions concerning the process of, 3–4, 481–482
relation of, to personality disorganization, 403–423
relation of, to social pathology, 426–439
science and technology as agencies of, 309–327
in the secondary group, 168–184
significance of work to, 274–275
of youth, 362–398
Social customs, 86 (See Mores)
Social definitions (See Definitions)
and change, 477–478
mental concepts limited by, 67–68
of pathological types, 421
Social disorganization, 479 (See Social pathology)
Social education, 261
Social expectancy
as a motive in behavior, 59–63, 155, 160, 372–376
Social group (See Groups)
unity of the individual with, 136–139
Social guidance
goals of an age as factors in, 116–131
Social ideals, 129
Social inadequates, 107–108, 422–423
(See Personality disorganization)
treatment of, 144–146
Social insects, 36
Social instincts, 31

Social institution (See Institutions)
control by, 4, 377–383
marriage as a, 229–232
Social legislation, 289, 322
Social life
participation in, 421–422
Social maladjustments, 4
Social motivation
control through, 477
Social norms, 144
Social order (See Order)
as the aftermath of revolution, 458–459, 461–462
Social pathology
breakdown of control as a factor in, 426–439
responsibility for, 438
underlying cause of, 26
Social philosophy
the core of, 30
Social power
source of, 14
Social pressures, 9, 186, 343
Chinese, 89–92
Social problems, 4 (See Personality disorganization; Social pathology; Social revolt)
breakdown of control as a factor in, 401–462, 426–439
in the primary group, 151–166
in the secondary group, 168–184
Social process
interference with, 11
Social progress
and control, 348
education as a tool for, 268
Social psychology, 7–9
Social responsibility, 144–146, 251, 326; of newspapers, 193–194
Social revolt, 442–462 (See Revolt; Revolution)
Social science
in an age of technology, 323, 325–326, 327
as a guide to order, 479–481, 483
"Social self control," 9
Social selves, 74–75
Social service
and religion, 247–249
Social stratification, 470–471
Social values, 96–115 (See Goals of an Age; Values; Pecuniary values)
change in, 113–114

Social values—(Continued)
"debunking" of, 455–457
as determined by advertising, 282–283
divergency of, 112–113
in a dynamic society, 465–467, 477
and universal education, 269–270
Social welfare
as the new social ideal, 178–180, 184, 477
Social work
and social control, 175, 183, 249
Socialization
as control, 337–338, 481–483
culture as a factor in, 79–93
through education, 256–270, 335–336
and the individual, 134–136, 142–143
the role of the group in, 65–77, 214
Socialized medicine, 323
Societal evolution
and the technicways, 317–321
Society (See Social control; Groups; Culture; Primitive society; Social pathology)
control in a dynamic, 465–483
as a game, 9–10
and the individual, 136–139
Sociologists
sins of omission of, 478–479
Sociology
applied, 7
Sophistication and religion, 251
Sovereignty
concept of, 9–11, 21
the problem of, 28
Speed
change in attitude toward, 314–315
State (See Government)
education as a function of, 261–268, 270
importance of, 291, 305
as the prior authority, 26–27
rise of totalitarian, 109–110
Stateways
authority of, 293–294, 335
development of, 319–320
Status
as a goal of life, 103–112, 122
loss of, 157
regard for, 377–379
roads to, 118–120, 181

Stereotypes
as limiting our mental horizon, 68
Stratification, 104–105, 114, 470–471
(See Social stratification)
Straw men
as a focus of mass attention, 189
use of, in political campaigns, 302
Success pattern
in America, 124–127, 169
Suggestion
control through, 189–194, 204
Suicide, 429
Suicide
and the breakdown of social control, 411–413, 427, 429–430
as escape from social humiliation, 95–96
in a frontier area, 75
and loss of faith, 250
after the stock market crash, 61
waves of, 189
Supernatural power, 24–25
superstitious fears concerning, 346, 350
Supernaturalism
as a factor in control, 236–238
"Super-social control," 10
Superstition
control by, 346, 350–352
Symbolism
control by, 331–333
in our economic system, 283–285, 295, 473

Taboos (See Sex taboos)
and conscience, 57
as mores of prohibition, 79, 85, 237
penalties for violation of, 349–350
Tabula rasa theory, 37
Taxation
as a tool of government, 289, 316
Technicways
in contemporary society, 317–321, 327
Technology (See Machine technology)
as an agency of control, 309–327
as a cause of cultural lag, 321–323, 437
as a factor in social change, 311–313
and the philosophy of progress, 323–325

Technology—(Continued)
place of social science in an age of, 325–326
"Telesis," 12
Temperamental qualities
control by, 383–390, 397
Theory of the Leisure Class, 277
"Third House," 297, 298, 305
Three Iron Mining Towns, 75
Totalitarian states
political indoctrination in, 264–268, 270
rise of, 109–110
Totem group, 15–16
Town (See Small town)
Townsend plan
a result of age composition, 76, 102
Tradition
appeal to, 302–313
as a blue print, 343–346
breakdown of, 109, 163, 413–414
control through, 15–18, 20, 21, 34, 56
as precedent, 79
Traits (See Culture patterns)
cultural, 116
Tropisms
in the plant world, 36

Unemployment
increase in, 100, 326
and personal frustration, 276
United States (See America)
government in, 284–285
Universal education, 269–270
Universal opportunity
philosophy of, 469–470
Universality
appeal to, 303
Universe
nature of, 24–26
Urban society (See Secondary group; Urban world)
adjustment problems in, 431–432
functional individualism in, 468–469
patterns of conduct in, 478
values in, 180–182
Urban world (See Secondary group; Urban society)
difficulties of control in, 171–172
Urban-industrial culture (See City; Urban society)
individualization in, 163

Urban-industrial culture—(Continued)
kinship group in, 153
personality problems in, 408–409
values in, 465
weakness in, 13–14
Utilitarian goals, 109
Utopia
visions of, 246

Vagrancy
laws against, 100
Values (See Social values; Institutional
values)
in America, 123–131, 466
conflict of, 106, 112–113
contrast between urban and rural,
180–182
"debunking" of, 455–457
in a dynamic society, 465–467, 470,
479–480
institutional, 278
pecuniary, 276–281
selection of, 421–422
social aspect of, 98–99
Vice and virtue (See Morality)
Village (See Small town)
Virtue and vice (See Morality)
Vocational adjustments, 221–222
Vocations
and goals of life, 106

Walden; or Life in the Woods, 449
War
substitutes for, 452

Wealth
in caste societies, 127
as a goal of life, 103, 109, 112, 114,
119
as social power, 277
West Coast states
age composition of, 76, 102
Western civilization
influence of, on oriental culture,
311–312, 443
influence of, on primitives, 117–118,
122, 251, 427, 433–435
Will transference, 11
"Will-power," 97
Witchcraft, 120
Wonders of the Invisible World, The,
120
Work
discipline of, 273–275, 285
as a goal of life, 180–181
Work codes, 106–107

Youth (See Projection)
behavior problems of, 362–398
code of, 392–398
demoralization of, 182–183, 456
in the depression, 276
goals of, 99–100, 108
revolt of, 445–447, 455–457
value on, 119
without goals, 109–110